The Faber Book of
CHRISTMAS

Also by Simon Rae

Poetry

SOFT TARGETS (Bloodaxe Books, 1991)

Anthologies

THE FABER BOOK OF DRINK, DRINKERS
AND DRINKING (1991)

THE ORANGE OF FIJI:
Poems for the Worldwide Fund for Nature
(Hutchinson, 1989)

THE FABER BOOK OF MURDER (1994)

The Faber Book of

CHRISTMAS

Edited by

SIMON RAE

ff

faber and faber

LONDON · BOSTON

First published in 1996
by Faber and Faber Limited
3 Queen Square London WC1N 3AU
This paperback edition first published in 1997

Designed by Humphrey Stone

Phototypeset by Intype London Ltd
Printed in England by Clays Ltd, St Ives plc

A CIP catalogue record for this book
is available from the British Library

ISBN 0–571–17441–8

2 4 6 8 10 9 7 5 3 1

For my daughter Albertine
who loves Christmas

This is the month, and this the happy morn
Wherein the Son of heaven's eternal King,
Of wedded maid, and virgin mother born,
Our great redemption from above did bring;
For so the holy sages once did sing,
    That he our deadly forefeit should release,
And with his Father work us a perpetual peace.

That glorious form, that light unsufferable,
And that far-beaming blaze of majesty,
Wherewith he wont at heaven's high council-table,
To sit the midst of trinal unity,
He laid aside; and here with us to be,
    Forsook the courts of everlasting day,
And chose with us a darksome house of mortal clay.

John Milton, 'On the Morning of Christ's Nativity'

From the same desert, in the same night, always my weary eyes awaken to the silver star, always, without disturbing the Kings of life, the three magi, the heart, the soul, the mind. When shall we journey, beyond the beaches and the mountains, to hail the birth of the new labour, the new wisdom, the route of tyrants and demons, the end of superstition; to adore – as the first comers! – Christmas on earth!

Arthur Rimbaud, *A Season in Hell*

CONTENTS

✤ CONTENTS ✤

INTRODUCTION

'How are we going to get through Christmas?' Gina Tull asks her husband, Richard, in *The Information*. Of course, being trapped in a Martin Amis novel, the Tulls have it worse than the rest of us, but it's not a remark that signals a descent into a fiendishly particularized circle of the Amis hell. It is a weary truism that the Festival of the Family is likely to generate more family tension than the rest of the year put together. Whatever pressure a relationship is under, it goes without saying Christmas can only make things significantly worse. It is also, perversely, the worst time of the year to be single, separated, recently bereaved, abandoned or homeless. And of course, there is no escape. From an advancingly early and arbitrary date each year, Christmas lays its heavy pall over every aspect of life: the Muzaked carols, shopping malls picketed by Father Christmases, the TV ads conspiring to lift demand to new heights of absurdity. Christmas, we complain, has become an ever-more omnivorous carnival of kitsch and covetousness, yet every year we dutifully subject ourselves to its debt-spiralling rituals. How indeed are we going to get through it?

Clearly the sensible thing would be to book a holiday coinciding with a Test match in the Southern Hemisphere, and leave the English Christmas far behind. But then, of course, we'd miss it, wouldn't we? Because actually when the fridge is finally crammed to the hinges, the shops finally shut and the last propitiatory card popped into the pillar box, a sort of stunned peace descends. Exhaustion mutates into relaxation and the true spirit of Christmas, resistant both to Tom Lehrer gibe ('draaaag out the Dickens') and mass media hype, stealthily reasserts itself once more, and I, for one, find that I do enjoy Christmas after all.

It has a tradition that threads back through the centuries (intertwined with an equally vigorous tradition of bemoaning present-day Christmases compared to the lost glories of the past), and with its promise of generosity,-

conviviality and hope, it offers believers and non-believers alike a true sanctuary at the year's end, the opportunity to recuperate and revitalize the spent soul before re-entering the fray.

I have tried in this anthology to maintain a reasonable balance between the various and, on occasion, extreme views of Christmas. Many writers brilliantly evoke the gloom, impatience or furious despair brought on by the season of regimented good cheer. Christmas wouldn't be Christmas without Scrooge. But then neither would it have survived so long and so universally without its disinterested giving and its headlong pursuit of excess, as pagan energy meets and embraces the Christian message of love and peace to make the world's greatest religious festival the supreme expression of human nature and unworldly aspiration.

There are, of course, a great many Christmas anthologies, several of which I have sampled (and stolen from). There will be many more, and mine can make no claim to be definitive. It is, I hope, fairly representative, though naturally those engaged in the age-old anthology game of spotting glaring omissions will find much missing to delight them. All I can say in my defence is that the pile of rejected material amounted to only a little less than the actual manuscript itself, and many editorial decisions cost me much agonized debate. Should I include a contemporary account of a slave uprising which took place in Jamaica over Christmas in 1831? With great reluctance I took the view that Christmas played too peripheral a part in the drama. Dylan Thomas's 'A Child's Christmas in Wales' – all of it, or just an extract? In the end, nearly all of it, but divided between two different chapters, one extract coming from what was obviously a blueprint or dry-run: 'Conversation About Christmas'. Clement Moore's 'A Visit From St Nicholas' (''Twas the Night Before Christmas') – surely a must? Ultimately I decided I couldn't live with its schmaltzy self-satisfaction, though its seminal status is acknowledged by the inclusion of a modern parody from *Mad* magazine. To those driven mad by this (or that) omission, I offer my apologies, while expressing the hope that even those in least sympathy with my editorial idiosyncracies will find something to please, amuse or interest them in the following pages.

A NOTE ON THE TEXT

The material I have gathered is arranged in what I trust are self-explanatory chapters. Obviously some passages could have found a home in more than one, and sometimes the chapters themselves come close to overlapping. However, I hope some logic, albeit eccentric, may be discerned.

A general anthology is not an academic text, and I believe pages bristling with superfluous information can be distracting. Views differ as to the desirability of notes, dates and the details of publishing history. By and large, I have chosen extracts from longer works that can be read out of their original context without explanatory scaffolding. Though clearly the title of a full-length book should be given at the end of an excerpt, I don't feel the title of a collection of poems or short stories needs to be included in addition to the title of the individual piece. Dates too can be less than helpful. In the case of diaries or collections of letters, the publication date can be years, often more than a hundred years, after the ink has dried. So I have opted to keep the clutter on the page to a minimum. Where a note or a date is required, I have supplied it. Otherwise, the reader is referred to the list of authors where dates are given (where known), and to the acknowledgements, where the publishing details of copyright material will be found.

As with my previous anthologies, I have been greatly helped by a number of people eager to offer suggestions and other assistance. My thanks go to Mark Bland, Anne Bronstein, John Caperon, Oliver Cyriax, Chris Greenwood, Jack Lang, Tony Lurcock, Penelope Rippon, Susan Roberts, Linda Sommer, Julia Stapleton, David Sweetman, Janice Thomson and David Williams.

Jill Grey generously took time off from her own literary labours to help with the research. Her breadth of knowledge and keen insight into the requirements of an anthology were invaluable, and I thank her accordingly. I am also extremely grateful to my editor, Christopher Reid, for his enthusiastic support and encouragement throughout.

Finally, I owe a special debt to Roy Barratt who provided me with the transcript of the Bampton Mummer's Play (published here in its entirety for the first time in its present form), and to Don Rouse and the current mummer's team for permission to use it. For the last three Christmas Eves, I have been privileged to watch the Bampton Mummers perform their play, and have marvelled at the vigour with which this ancient tradition continues, unselfconsciously, and highly entertainingly, into the closing decade of the second millennium. May it survive well into the next.

Simon Rae

❧ I ❧

CHRISTMAS: FOR AND AGAINST

Bah! Humbug!

The door of Scrooge's counting-house was open that he might keep his eye upon his clerk, who in a dismal little cell beyond, a sort of tank, was copying letters. Scrooge had a very small fire, but the clerk's fire was so very much smaller that it looked like one coal. But he couldn't replenish it, for Scrooge kept the coal-box in his own room; and so surely as the clerk came in with the shovel, the master predicted that it would be necessary for them to part. Wherefore the clerk put on his white comforter, and tried to warm himself at the candle; in which effort, not being a man of a strong imagination, he failed.

'A merry Christmas, uncle! God save you!' cried a cheerful voice. It was the voice of Scrooge's nephew, who came upon him so quickly that this was the first intimation he had of his approach.

'Bah!' said Scrooge, 'Humbug!'

He had so heated himself with rapid walking in the fog and frost, this nephew of Scrooge's, that he was all in a glow; his face was ruddy and handsome; his eyes sparkled, and his breath smoked again.

'Christmas a humbug, uncle!' said Scrooge's nephew. 'You don't mean that, I am sure?'

'I do,' said Scrooge. 'Merry Christmas! What right have you to be merry? What reason have you to be merry? You're poor enough.'

'Come, then,' returned the nephew gaily. 'What right have you to be dismal? What reason have you to be morose? You're rich enough.'

Scrooge having no better answer ready on the spur of the moment, said, 'Bah!' again; and followed it up with 'Humbug.'

'Don't be cross, uncle!' said the nephew.

'What else can I be,' returned the uncle, 'when I live in such a world of fools as this? Merry Christmas! Out upon merry Christmas! What's Christmas time to you but a time for paying bills without money; a time for finding yourself a year older, but not an hour richer; a time for balancing your books and having every item in 'em through a round dozen of months presented dead against you? If I could work my will,' said Scrooge indignantly, 'every idiot who goes about with "Merry Christmas" on his lips should be boiled with his own pudding, and buried with a stake of holly through his heart. He should!'

'Uncle!' pleaded the nephew.

'Nephew!' returned the uncle, sternly, 'keep Christmas in your own way, and let me keep it in mine.'

'Keep it!' repeated Scrooge's nephew. 'But you don't keep it.'

'Let me leave it alone, then,' said Scrooge. 'Much good may it do you! Much good it has ever done you!'

'There are many things from which I might have derived good, by which I have not profited, I dare say,' returned the nephew. 'Christmas among the rest. But I am sure I have always thought of Christmas time, when it has come round – apart from the veneration due to its sacred name and origin, if anything belonging to it can be apart from that – as a good time; a kind, forgiving, charitable, pleasant time; the only time I know of, in the long calendar of the year, when men and women seem by one consent to open their shut-up hearts freely, and to think of people below them as if they really were fellow-passengers to the grave, and not another race of creatures bound on other journeys. And therefore, uncle, though it has never put a scrap of gold or silver in my pocket, I believe that it *has* done me good, and *will* do me good; and I say, God bless it!'

The clerk in the tank involuntarily applauded. Becoming immediately sensible of the impropriety, he poked the fire, and extinguished the last frail spark for ever.

'Let me hear another sound from *you*,' said Scrooge, 'and you'll keep your Christmas by losing your situation! You're quite a powerful speaker, sir,' he added, turning to his nephew. 'I wonder you don't go into Parliament.'

'Don't be angry, uncle. Come! Dine with us tomorrow.'

Scrooge said that he would see him – yes, indeed he did. He went the whole length of the expression, and said that he would see him in that extremity first.

'But why?' cried Scrooge's nephew. 'Why?'

'Why did you get married?' said Scrooge.

'Because I fell in love.'

'Because you fell in love!' growled Scrooge, as if that were the only one thing in the world more ridiculous than a merry Christmas. 'Good afternoon!'

'Nay, uncle, but you never came to see me before that happened. Why give it as a reason for not coming now?'

'Good afternoon,' said Scrooge.

'I want nothing from you; I ask nothing of you; why cannot we be friends?'

'Good afternoon,' said Scrooge.

'I am sorry, with all my heart, to find you so resolute. We have never had any quarrel, to which I have been a party. But I have made the trial in homage to Christmas, and I'll keep my Christmas humour to the last. So A Merry Christmas, uncle!'

'Good afternoon!' said Scrooge.

'And A Happy New Year!'

'Good afternoon!' said Scrooge.

His nephew left the room without an angry word, notwithstanding. He stopped at the outer door to bestow the greetings of the season on the clerk, who, cold as he was, was warmer than Scrooge; for he returned them cordially.

'There's another fellow,' muttered Scrooge; who overheard him: 'my clerk, with fifteen shillings a week, and a wife and family, talking about a merry Christmas. I'll retire to Bedlam.'

Charles Dickens, *A Christmas Carol*

Christmas, n. A day set apart and consecrated to gluttony, drunkenness, maudlin sentiment, gift-taking, public dullness and domestic behavior.

Ambrose Bierce, *The Devil's Dictionary*

To Judy Egerton

32 Pearson Park, Hull
17 December 1958

My dear Judy,

What an awful time of year this is! Just as one is feeling that if one can just hold on, if it just won't get any worse, then all this Christmas idiocy bursts upon one like a slavering Niagara of nonsense & *completely wrecks* one's entire *frame*. This means, in terms of *my* life, making a point of buying about six simple inexpensive presents when there are rather more people about than usual, and going home. No doubt in terms of yours it means seeing your house given over to hoards of mannerless middle-class brats and your good food & drink vanishing into the quacking tooth-equipped jaws of their alleged parents. Yours is the harder course, I can see. On the other hand, mine is happening to me . . .

Philip Larkin

Christmas

The bells of waiting Advent ring,
    The Tortoise stove is lit again
And lamp-oil light across the night
    Has caught the streaks of winter rain
In many a stained-glass window sheen
From Crimson Lake to Hooker's Green.

The holly in the windy hedge
    And round the Manor House the yew
Will soon be stripped to deck the ledge,
    The altar, font and arch and pew,
So that the villagers can say
'The church looks nice' on Christmas Day.

Provincial public houses blaze
    And Corporation tramcars clang,
On lighted tenements I gaze
    Where paper decorations hang,
And bunting in the red Town Hall
Says 'Merry Christmas to you all.'

And London shops on Christmas Eve
    Are strung with silver bells and flowers
As hurrying clerks the City leave
    To pigeon-haunted classic towers,
And marbled clouds go scudding by
The many-steepled London sky.

And girls in slacks remember Dad,
    And oafish louts remember Mum,
And sleepless children's hearts are glad,
    And Christmas-morning bells say 'Come!'
Even to shining ones who dwell
Safe in the Dorchester Hotel.

And is it true? And is it true,
    This most tremendous tale of all,
Seen in a stained-glass window's hue,
    A Baby in an ox's stall?
The Maker of the stars and sea
Become a Child on earth for me?

And is it true? For if it is,
    No loving fingers tying strings
Around those tissued fripperies,
    The sweet and silly Christmas things,
Bath salts and inexpensive scent
And hideous tie so kindly meant,

No love that in a family dwells,
    No carolling in frosty air,
Nor all the steeple-shaking bells
    Can with this single Truth compare –
That God was Man in Palestine
And lives to-day in Bread and Wine.

John Betjeman

'An Atrocious Institution'

Like all intelligent people, I greatly dislike Christmas. It revolts me to see a whole nation refrain from music for weeks together in order that every man may rifle his neighbour's pockets under cover of a ghastly general pretence of festivity. It is really an atrocious institution, this Christmas. We must be gluttonous because it is Christmas. We must be drunken because it is Christmas. We must be insincerely generous; we must buy things that nobody wants, and give them to people we don't like; we must go to absurd entertainments that make even our little children satirical; we must writhe under venal officiousness from legions of freebooters, all because it is Christmas – that is, because the mass of the population, including the all-powerful middle-class tradesman, depends on a week of licence and brigandage, waste and intemperance, to clear off its outstanding liabilities at the end of the year. As for me, I shall fly from it all tomorrow or next day to some remote spot miles from a shop, where nothing worse can befall me than a serenade from a few peasants, or some equally harmless survival of medieval mummery, shyly proffered, not advertised, moderate in its expectations, and soon over. In town there is, for the moment, nothing for me or any honest man to do.

George Bernard Shaw, *Music in London 1890–94*

No Counting Pennies Today

Christmas was not like other holidays. It did not want to run in the streets, dance in the public squares, straddle wooden horses, take advantage of the crush to pinch women, throw fireworks in the face of tamarisks. Christmas had agoraphobia. What it wanted was a day of continual bustle and preparation and kitchenwork, a day of cleaning and anxiety

in-case-there's-not-enough,

in-case-we-run-short,

in-case-they-think-it-dull,

then in the evening a small church, not intimidating, allowing itself to be filled benevolently with laughter and whispers, confidences, declarations of love, rumours, and the keen, throaty discords of the choir leader, and hearty men and tarty girls and homes with their entrails stuffed with succulence, no counting pennies today, and the town now nothing but a bouquet of songs, it is good to be inside, to eat well and drink with warmth, blood sausage two fingers thin like a twisty stalk, or blood sausage broad and thick, the mild sort tasting of wild thyme, the hot kind blazing with spice, scalding coffee sweet aniseed cordial milk punch, rums of liquid sun, and good things to eat which brand your mucous membranes or distil them to delight or weave fragrances across them, when somebody laughs, when another sings, and the refrains spread like coconut palms as far as you can see

ALLELUIA

KYRIE ELEISON . . . LEISON . . . LEISON

CHRISTIE ELEISON . . . LEISON . . . LEISON.

Not only the mouths are singing, hands too, feet, buttocks, genitals, the whole fellow creature flowing in sound, voice and rhythm.

Aimé Césaire, *Return to My Native Land* (trans. John Berger and Anna Bostock)

Singing and Dancing

I gesse wel þat ȝonge wymmen may sumtyme daunsen in mesure to haue recreacion and liȝtnesse, so þat þei haue þe more þouȝt on myrþe in heuene & drede more & loue more god þer-by, & synge honeste songis of cristis incarnacion, passion, resurexion & ascencion, & of þe ioies of oure ladi, & to dispise synne & preise vertue in alle here doynge; but nowe he þat kan best pleie a pagyn of þe deuyl, syngynge songis of lecherie, of batailis and of lesyngis, & crie as a wood man & dispise goddis maieste & swere bi herte, bonys & alle membris of crist, is holden most merie mon & schal haue most þank of pore & riche; & þis is clepid worschipe of þe grete solempnyte of cristismasse; & þus forhþe grete kyndenesse & goodnesse þat crist dide to men in his incarnacion we dispisen hym more in outrage of pride, of glotonye, lecherie & alle manere harlotrie.

John Wyclif, 'The Ave Maria'

'O! The Twelfth Day of December'

Enter MARIA

MARIA: What a caterwauling do you keep here! If my lady have not called up her steward Malvolio and bid him turn you out of doors, never trust me.

SIR TOBY: My lady's a Cataian; we are politicians; Malvolio's a Peg-a-Ramsey, and 'Three merry men be we.' Am not I consanguineous? am I not of her blood? Tillyvally, lady!

There dwelt a man in Babylon, lady, lady!

CLOWN: Beshrew me, the knight's in admirable fooling.

SIR ANDREW: Ay, he does well enough if he be disposed, and so do I too: he does it with a better grace, but I do it more natural.

SIR TOBY: *O! the twelfth day of December,* –

MARIA: For the love o' God, peace!

Enter MALVOLIO

MALVOLIO: My masters, are you mad? or what are you? Have you no wit, manners, nor honesty, but to gabble like tinkers at this time of night? Do ye make an alehouse of my lady's house, that ye squeak out your coziers' catches without any mitigation or remorse of voice? Is there no respect of place, persons, nor time, in you?

SIR TOBY: We did keep time, sir, in our catches. Sneck up!

MALVOLIO: Sir Toby, I must be round with you. My lady bade me tell you, that, though she harbours you as her kinsman, she's nothing allied to your disorders. If you can separate yourself and your misdemeanours, you are welcome to the house; if not, an it would please you to take leave of her, she is very willing to bid you farewell.

SIR TOBY: *Farewell, dear heart, since I must needs be gone.*

MARIA: Nay, good Sir Toby.

CLOWN: *His eyes do show his days are almost done.*

MALVOLIO: Is't even so?

SIR TOBY: *But I will never die.*

CLOWN: Sir Toby, there you lie.

MALVOLIO: This is much credit to you.

SIR TOBY: *Shall I bid him go?*

CLOWN: *What an if you do?*

SIR TOBY: *Shall I bid him go, and spare not?*

CLOWN: *O! no, no, no, no, you dare not.*

SIR TOBY: 'Out o' time!' Sir, ye lie. Art any more than a steward? Dost thou think, because thou art virtuous, there shall be no more cakes and ale?

CLOWN: Yes, by Saint Anne; and ginger shall be hot i' the mouth too.

SIR TOBY: Thou'rt i' the right. Go, sir, rub your chain with crumbs. A stoup of wine, Maria!

MALVOLIO: Mistress Mary, if you prized my lady's favour at anything more than contempt, you would not give means for this uncivil rule: she shall know of it, by this hand. *(Exit)*

MARIA: Go shake your ears.

SIR ANDREW: 'Twere as good a deed as to drink when a man's a-hungry, to challenge him the field, and then to break promise with him and make a fool of him.

SIR TOBY: Do't, knight: I'll write thee a challenge; or I'll deliver thy indignation to him by word of mouth.

MARIA: Sweet Sir Toby, be patient for tonight: since the youth of the count's was today with my lady, she is much out of quiet. For Monsieur Malvolio, let me alone with him: if I do not gull him into a nayword, and make him a common recreation, do not think I have wit enough to lie straight in my bed. I know I can do it.

[8]

SIR TOBY: Possess us, possess us; tell us something of him.

MARIA: Marry, sir, sometimes he is a kind of Puritan.

SIR ANDREW: O! if I thought that, I'd beat him like a dog.

SIR TOBY: What, for being a Puritan? thy exquisite reason, dear knight?

SIR ANDREW: I have no exquisite reason for't, but I have reason good enough.

William Shakespeare, *Twelfth Night*

The Voluptuous Month

Christmas Holidays were at first invented and institute in compliance with the Pagan Festivals, of old observed at that very time of the Year. This Stuckius has fully cleared. And *Hospinian* speaketh judiciously, when he saith, that he doth not believe that they who first of all observed the Feast of *Christ's* Nativity in the latter end of *December*, did it as thinking that *Christ* was born in that Month, but because the Heathens *Saturnalia* was at that time kept in *Rome*, and they were willing to have those Pagan Holidays metamorphosed into Christian. Hence *December* was called *Mensis Genialis*, the Voluptuous Month. Whilst the *Saturnalian Days* lasted, the observers of them were wont to send Gifts one to another, which therefore *Tertullian* calls *Saturnalitia*, and *Jerom* giveth them the Name of *Saturnalium Sportulæ*. The like is done by many in *Christmas* time. Again, In the Saturnalian Days, Masters did wait on their Servants, as *Macrobius* and *Athenæus* declare. Hence is that of *Horace*——*Age Libertate Decembri*. The *Gentiles* called *Saturns* time the Golden Age, because in it there was no Servitude, in Commemoration whereof on his Festival, Servants must be Masters. And that amongst *Christmas-keepers* in some parts of the World, there use to be such *Masters of Misrule*, is too well known. From these Considerations not only Protestant writers, but some Papists acknowledge that Christmas Holidays succeed the Old *Saturnalia* of the Heathen.

Now for Christians thus to practise, is against clear Scripture, which commands the Lords People not to learn the way of the Heathen, nor do after their manner, *Jer.* 10. 2. *Lev.* 20. 23. *Ezek.* 11. 12. To observe the Festivals of the Heathen, is one way of partaking with them in their Superstitions. *Tertullian* in his Book against Idolatry, (*cap* 14.) expresseth himself after this manner, *Shall we Christians who have nothing to do with the Festivals of the Jews, which were once of Divine Institution, Embrace the* Saturnalia *and* Januaria *of the Heathen? How do the Gentiles shame us? who are more true to their*

Religion than we are to ours. None of them will observe the Lords-Day for fear lest they should be Christians: And shall not we then by observing their Festivals, fear least we be made Ethnic's?

We might take notice of the *Ethnicism* of this Festival in another respect. It was the manner of the *Gentiles* to celebrate the Birth-days of their Princes and Patrons. And in Imitation of them, Degenerating Christians thought good so far to symbolize with the Customs of the Nations, as to keep the Birth-day of *Christ*, whom they acknowledge to be their Lord and Soveraign.

The generality of Christmas-keepers observe that Festival after such a manner as is highly dishonourable to the name of Christ. How few are there comparatively that spend those *Holidays* (as they are called) after an *Holy manner.* But they are consumed in Compotations, in Interludes, in playing at Cards, in Revellings, in excess of Wine, in mad Mirth; Will *Christ* the holy Son of God be pleased with such Services? Just after this manner were the *Saturnalia* of the Heathen celebrated. *Saturn* was the Gaming God. And (as one saith) the Feast of *Christ*'s Nativity is attended with such Profaneness, as that it deserves the name of *Saturns Mass*, or of *Bacchus his Mass*, or if you will, the *Devils Mass*, rather than to have the Holy name of *Christ* put upon it. Mr. Perkins justly complains that, *The Feast of Christ's Nativity (commonly so called) is not spent in praising God, but in Revelling, Dicing, Carding, Masking, Mumming, and in all Licencious Liberty for the most part, as though it were some Heathen Feast of* Ceres *or* Bacchus. And *Latimer* in one of his Sermons saith, That *Men dishonour Christ more in the 12 Days of Christmas, than in all the 12 Months besides.* Nor is it to be wondred at, if that Festival be accompanied with much Profaneness and Vanity, when the chief Pleaders for them (yea Dr. *Hammond* himself) are not ashamed to justifie the playing at Cards as lawful for a Divertisement on Christmas Holy-days. And is that the way to honour *Christ?* The *Love-Feasts* (though in themselves lawful) which began in the Apostles times, were wholly laid aside amongst Christians, because they had been an occasion of Riotous Abuses. There is much more reason to omit the Observation of Christmas Festivities, which have brought a Deluge of Profaneness upon the World. The Scandal of them calls for their Abolition. The School Doctors affirm rightly, *Etiam Spiritualia non-necessaria sunt fugienda, si ex iis Scandalum oritur.* Things of an indifferent nature, when they become an occasion of Sin, should not at all be used.

Increase Mather, *Against Profane Christ-Mass-Keeping*, 1687

Lord of Misrule

Articles objected by the Commissioners for Causes Ecclesiastical against Francis Saunders, late of Shangton, co. Leicester, and then of Stamford, co. Lincoln. He was charged that there having been in his house, or that of William Stafford, of Blatherwick, at Christmas time, a lord of misrule, he and others had appointed that the lord of misrule must have for a lady or Christmas wife, one Elizabeth Pitto, daughter of the hog-heard of the town; whereupon, defendant putting on a gown, and a shirt or smock for a surplice, read the words set down in the form of marriage in the Book of Common Prayer, putting a ring upon the finger of the woman, and going through the rest of the ceremony, and afterwards, at night, putting the parties into a bed together. Defendant was also charged with being a swearer and a drunkard.

Calendar of State Papers, Domestic Series, Charles I, 1637–1638

A Hue and Cry After Christmas

With a Letter from Mr Woodcock a Fellow in Oxford, to a Malignant Lady in London; And divers pretty passages between her and the Cryer, about old Christmas; and what shift he was fain to make, to save his life; and what a stir there is to fetch him back again.

With many pretty passages, full of Wit and Mirth

A Letter from a scholler in Oxford, to a malignant Lady in London.

Lady,

I Beseech you for the love of Oxford hire a Cryer (I will see him paid for his paines) to cry old Father Christmas, and keep him with you (if you can meet with him and stay him) till we come to London, for we expected to be there shortly and then we will have all things as they were wont. I warrant you, hold up your spirits, and let not your old friends be lost out of your favour, for his sake who is:

Your ever servant Jo. Woodcock.

LADY: Honest Crier. I know thou knewest old Father Christmas; I am sent to thee from an honest scholler of Oxford (that hath given me many a hug and kisse in Christmas time when we have been merry) to cry Christmas, for they hear that he is gone from hence, and that we have lost the poor old man; you know what marks he hath, and how to cry him.

CRYER: Who shall pay me for my paines?

LADY: Your old friend Mr Woodcock of Oxford, wilt thou take his word?

CRYER: I will cry him I warrant you, through the Citie and Countrie, and it shall go hard but I will finde him out. I can partly ghesse who can tell some newes of him, if any people in England can, for I am acquainted with all his familiar friends: Trust me in this businesse. I will bring you word within a few days.

Hooooooo yes, ho-o o-o oo yes, ho oooooo- yes.

Any man or woman, whether Popish or Prelaticall, Superstitious or Judaicall, Ignorant or Jesuiticall, or what person soever, of any Tribe or Trullibub, that can give any knowledge, or tell any tidings of an old, old, old, very old gray bearded Gentleman called Christmas; who was wont to be a verie familiar ghest, and visite all sorts of people both poor and rich, and used to appear in glittering gold silk and silver in the Court, and in all shapes in the Theatre in Whitehall, and had ringing, feasts, and jollitie in all places, both in the Citie and Countrie for his comming: if you went to the Temple, you might have found him there at In and In, till many a Gentleman had outed all the mony from his pocket, and after all, the Butlers found him locked up in their Boxes. And in almost every house, you might have found him at Cards and Dice, the very boyes and children could have traced him, and the Beggers have followed him from place to place, and seen him walking up and downe, and in every house roast Beefe and Mutton, Pies and Plum porrige, and all manner of delicates round about him, and every one saluting merry Christmas; if you had gone to the Queenes Chappel, you might have found him standing against the wall; and the Papists weeping, and beating themselves before him, and kissing his hoary head with superstitious teares, in a theatre exceeding all the playes of the red Bull, the Fortune, or the Cockpit.

For age, this hoarie headed man was of great yeares, and as white as snow, he entred the Romish Kallender time out of mind; as old or very neer, as Father *Mathusalem* was, one that looked fresh in the Bishops time, though their fall made him pine away ever since; he was full, and fat as any dume Doctor, on them all, he looked under the consecrated Laune sleeves as big as Bul-beefe, just like Bacchus upon a tunne of wine, when the grapes hang shaking about his eares; but since the catholike liquor is taken from him, he is much wasted, so that he hath looked very thin, and ill of late; but the wanton women that are so mad after him, do not know how he is metamorphised, so that he is not now like himselfe, but rather like a Iack a lent.

But yet some other markes that you may know him by, is that the wanton

Women dote after him, he helped them to so many new Gownes, Hatts, and Hankerches, and other fine knacks, of which he hath a pack on his back, in which is good store of all sorts, besides the fine knacks that he got out of their husbands pockets for houshold provisions for him: he got Prentises, Servants, and Schollers many play-dayes, and therefore was well beloved by them also and made all merry with Bagpipes, Fiddles, and other musicks, Giggs, Dances, and Mummings, yea the yong people had more merry dayes, and houres before him whilst he stayd, which was in some houses 12 dayes, in some 20, in some more, and in some lesse, then in all the year again: and more Lasses was got with child, when he elevated his sences with his focundity then was in all the time of the lent following.

The Candlemaker, Cardmaker, Cookes, Pimakers, and all sorts of trades seasonable for the time, got well by him, and vended his Commodityes best at his coming, and many a broken poore whore could get up a new baudie house, and a new stock, by the coming of this good fellow . . .

All you therefore that by your diligent inquirie, can tell anie tidings of this ould man called Christmas, and tell me where he may be met withall; whether in any of your streets, or elsewhere, though in never so straitned a place, in an Applewoman staul, or Grocers Current Tub, in a Cookes Oven, or the Maides Porrige pot, or crept in some corner of a shop, where the Cobler was wont so merrily to chant his Carolls, whosoever can tel what is become of him, or where he may be found, let them bring him back againe into England, to the Crier, and they shall have a Benedection from the Pope, an hundred oaths from the Cavaliers, 40 Kisses from the wanton Wenches, and be made Pursevant [t]o the next Arch Bishop; Malignants will send him a peece of Braune, and everie Prentice boy will give him his point next holie Thursday, the good-Wives will keepe him in some corners of their mincepies, and the new Nuntio Ireland will return him to be canonized the next Reformation of the Calender.

CRYER: *Lady I am come to tell you what returne I can make you of the crying of ould Father Christmas, which I have done, and am now here to give you an answer.*

LADY: *Well said honest Cryer, Mr Woodcock will remember you for it.*

CRYER: The poor old man upon St Thomas his day was arraigned, condemned, and after conviction, cast into prison amongst the Kings Souldiers, fearing to be hanged, or some other execution to be done upon him, he broke prison, and got out at so narrow a passage, between two Iron Bars of a Window, that nothing but onely his old gray beard and hoarie hair of his head stuck there, but nothing else to be seen of him; and if you will have that, compound for it, lest it be sold amongst the sequestred goods, or burnt with the next Popish pictures, by the hand of the hangman.

LADY: But is old, old, good old Christmas gone? Nothing but the hair of his good, grave old head and beard left? Well, I will have that, seeing I cannot have more of him, one lock whereof will serve Mr Woodcock for a token. But what is the event of his departure?

CRYER: The poor are sory for it, for they go to every door a begging as they were wont to do (*Good Mrs Somewhat against this good Time*) but Time was transformed, *Away be gone, here is not for you*: and so they instead of going to the Ale-house to be drunk were fain to work all the Holidayes. The Schollers came into the Hall, where their hungry stomacks had thought to have found good Brawn and Christmas Pies, Roast bief and Plum porridge, but no such matter. Away ye prophane, these are superstitious meats, your stomack must be fed with wholesome doctrine. Alas poor tallow-faced Chandlers, I met them mourning through the streets, and complaining that they could get no vent for their Mustard, for want of Brawn.

LADY: Well, if ever the Catholiques or Bishops rule again in England, they will set the Church dores open on Christmas day, and we shall have Masse at the High Altar, as was used when the day was first instituted, and not have the holy Eucharist barred out of School, as School boyes do their Masters against the festival. What shall we have our mouths shut to welcome old Christmas? No, no, bid him come by night over the Thames, and we wil have a back door open to let him in. I will my self give him his diet for one year, to try his fortune, this time twelve month it may prove better.

FINIS.

Anon. (?1646)

Wilful and Strict Observation

Sir Hen. Mildmay to report to Parliament that Council have received informations that there was very wilful and strict observation of the day commonly called Christmas Day, throughout the cities of London and Westminster, by a general keeping of shops shut up; and that there were contemptuous speeches used by some in favour thereof, which Council conceives to be upon the old grounds of superstition and malignancy, and tending to the avowing of the same and contempt of the present laws and Government, and therefore request Parliament to consider further provisions and penalties for abolishing and punishing those old superstitious

[14]

observations, and meeting with such malicious contradiction of offenders in that behalf.

Also that they have received information of frequent resort and exercise of the idolatrous mass to the great dishonour of Almighty God, notorious breach of the laws, and scandal of the Government, wherein they have already taken some course, and desire Parliament to take that matter also into consideration, for further remedies and suppression of that idolatry.

Calendar of State Papers Domestic Series, 1650

1657

25th December   I went to London with my wife, to celebrate Christmas Day, Mr Gunning preaching in Exeter chapel, on Micah vii. 2. Sermon ended, as he was giving us the Holy Sacrament, the chapel was surrounded with soldiers, and all the communicants and assembly surprised and kept prisoners by them, some in the house, others carried away. It fell to my share to be confined to a room in the house, where yet I was permitted to dine with the master of it, the Countess of Dorset, Lady Hatton, and some others of quality who invited me. In the afternoon, came Colonel Whalley, Goffe, and others, from Whitehall, to examine us one by one; some they committed to the Marshal, some to prison. When I came before them, they took my name and abode, examined me why, contrary to the ordinance made, that none should any longer observe the superstitious time of the Nativity (so esteemed by them), I durst offend, and particularly be at Common Prayers, which they told me was but the mass in English, and particularly pray for Charles Stuart; for which we had no Scripture. I told them we did not pray for Charles Stuart, but for all Christian Kings, Princes, and Governors. They replied, in so doing we prayed for the King of Spain, too, who was their enemy and a Papist, with other frivolous and ensnaring questions, and much threatening; and, finding no colour to detain me, they dismissed me with much pity of my ignorance. These were men of high flight and above ordinances, and spake spiteful things of our Lord's Nativity. As we went up to receive the Sacrament, the miscreants held their muskets against us, as if they would have shot us at the altar; but yet suffering us to finish the office of Communion, as perhaps not having instructions what to do, in case they found us in that action. So I got home late the next day; blessed be God!

John Evelyn

Forbidden Fruit

There would have been no church at Gleniffer if it had not been for a Christmas pudding. There would have been no daguerreotype of Oscar Hopkins on the banks of the Bellinger. I would not have been born. There would be no story to tell.

This was not a normal Christmas pudding. It was a very small one, no bigger than a tennis ball. It contained two teaspoons of glacé cherries, three dessertspoons of raisins, the peel of one orange and the juice thereof, half a cup of flour, half a cup of suet, a splash of brandy, and, apart from the size, you would not think it was such an abnormality were it not for the fact that it was cooked in the cottage of my great-great-grandfather, Theophilus Hopkins, in Hennacombe, Devon, England.

Theophilus Hopkins was a moderately famous man. You can look him up in the 1860 *Britannica*. There are three full columns about his corals and his corallines, his anemones and starfish. It does not have anything very useful about the man. It does not tell you what he was like. You can read it three times over and never guess that he had any particular attitude to Christmas pudding.

He was a dark, wiry widower of forty, hard and bristly on the outside, his beard full, his muscles compacted, and yet he was a soft man, too. You could feel this softness quivering. He was a sensualist who believed passionately that he would go to heaven, that heaven outshone any conceivable earthly joy, that it stretched, a silver sheet, across the infinite spaces of eternity. He steeled himself in the face of his temporal feelings as a Royal Guardsman – a carouser and a funny man when at the pub – must remain poker-faced while flies crawl across his eyelids. He was one of the Plymouth Brethren and he thought – there is nothing mad in this particular bit – that the feasts of the Christian Church were not Christian at all. His problem was his temper, although the word is misleading. His problem was his passion. His body was a poor vessel for containing it, and when it came to Christmas each year it was all he could do to keep himself in check. For the most part he used his passion constructively – he was a preacher and it was his great talent to make his listeners share his feelings. He would not call it Christmas. He would call it Yuletide. He had so convinced his small congregation of farm workers, thatchers, warreners, charcoal-burners, fishermen – all those earnest white-laundered folk who, if they could read at all, could only do it slowly, with a finger on each word – so convinced them that Christmas was not only pagan but also popish, that they went out about the fields and lanes on Christmas Day as if it were any other day. Their Baptist neighbours laughed at them. Their Baptist neighbours would burn in hell.

Oscar was fifteen, an age when boys are secretive and sullen. Yet he did not question his father's views. He knew his own soul was vouched safe and when he read the Bible, aloud, by the fire, he placed no different interpretation upon it than the man who poked the little grate and fussed continually with the arrangement of the coal. They both read the Bible as if it were a report compiled by a conscientious naturalist. If the Bible said a beast had four faces, or a man the teeth of a lion, then this is what they believed.

But on this particular Christmas Day in 1856, they had a second servant where previously they had one. The first servant was the large bustling Mrs Williams who brushed her untidy nest of wire-grey hair with a tortoiseshell brush whenever she was agitated. She had been with the family fifteen years, ten years in London, and five years in Devon. In Hennacombe she brushed her hair more often. She fought with the butcher and the fishmonger. She swore the salt air was bad for her catarrh, but it was – as she said – 'too late to be making changes now'. She stayed, and although she was not 'saved', and they sometimes found her hair in their scrambled eggs, she was a part of their lives.

The second servant, however, was not only not 'saved'. She could not even be classified as 'questing'. She was an Anglican who was in the household from charity, having been deserted by her navvy husband and been denied Poor Relief by two parishes, each of whom claimed she was the other's responsibility. And it was she – freckle-faced Fanny Drabble – who was behind this Christmas pudding. She had white bony hands and bright red knuckles and had lived a hard life in sod nuts and shanties beside the railway lines the brawling navvies helped to build. Her baby had died. The only clothes she had was a thin cotton dress. A tooth fell out of her mouth on her first morning. But she was outraged to discover that Oscar had never known the taste of Christmas pudding. Mrs Williams – although she should have known better – found herself swept along on the tea-sweet wave of Fanny Drabble's moral indignation. The young 'un must know the taste of Christmas pudding, and what the master don't know won't hurt him.

Fanny Drabble did not know that this pudding was the 'flesh of which idols eat'.

It was only a small cottage, but it was built from thick blocks of Devon limestone. You could feel the cold limey smell of the stone at the back of your nostrils, even when you were sitting by the fire. If you were in the kitchen, you could not hear a word that was said in the tiny dining room next door. It was a cramped house, with low doorways, and awkward tripping ledges and steps between the rooms, but it was, in spite of this, a good house for secrets. And because Theophilus did not enter the kitchen (perhaps because Mrs Williams also slept there on a bench beside the stove) they could have manufactured graven images there and not been caught.

But Oscar liked the kitchen. He liked the dry floury warmth and he carried the water, and riddled the grate, and sat on the table when Mrs Williams scrubbed the cobblestones. He soon realized what was going on. He saw cherries and raisins. They did not normally have raisins. He had never seen a cherry. On Christmas Day it was expected they would have a meal like any other.

Theophilus had called Mrs Williams up to his study. As this study was also Oscar's schoolroom, he heard the instructions himself. His father was quite specific. It was his character to be specific. He paid attention to the tiniest detail of any venture he was associated with. When he drew an anemone you could be certain that he did not miss a whisker on a tentacle. The potatoes, he said, were to be of 'fair to average size'. There would be half a head of King George cabbage, and so on.

But within the kitchen the treasonous women were kneading suet, measuring raisins and sultanas, peeling a single precious orange. Oscar sat by the bellows and puffed on them until the kettle sang so loud you could hardly hear the hymn that Fanny Drabble hummed. Mrs Williams went running up the stairs like a dervish whose activity is intended to confuse and distract. She made a screen of dust, a flurry of rags. She brushed her hair on the front step looking out through the dripping grey branches, over the rust-brown bracken, to the cold grey sea. She walked around the house, past the well, and put the hair on the compost heap. Oscar knew that Mrs Williams's hair did not rot. He had poked around with a long stick and found it. It had been slimy at first but you could wash it under the tap and it would turn out, with all the slime washed off, to be good as new. This was exactly how Mrs Williams had told him it would be. He was surprised that she was right. His father did not value Mrs Williams's beliefs. She was not scientific. She said there were men who robbed graves just to steal the hair of the dead. They sold it to hair merchants who washed it and sorted it and sold it for wigs, and curls and plaits. This hair still had bulbs at the end of each strand, 'church-yard hair' was what it was called. Mrs Williams lived in a state of constant anxiety about her hair. There were, she insisted, perhaps not in Henna-combe, but in Teignmouth and Newton Abbot, 'springheeled Jacks' with sharp razors ready to steal a living woman's hair right off her head. She brushed her hair on the stairway and the upstairs study. At each place she collected the hair from her brush, made a circle with it, knotted it and put it in her apron pocket. On the day they made the Christmas pudding she did this even more than usual. Theophilus, being a naturalist, may have noticed.

Oscar was not told about the Christmas pudding, but he knew. He did not let himself know that he knew. Yet the knowledge thrust deep into his consciousness. It was a shaft of sunlight in a curtained room. Dust danced in the turbulent air. Nothing would stay still. When Oscar ate his lunch on Christmas Day, his legs ached with excitement. He crossed his ankles and clenched his hands tight around his knife and fork. He strained his ear towards the open kitchen door, but there was nothing to hear except his father breathing through his nose while he ate.

Oscar had a little wooden tray, divided into small compartments. It was intended to house beetles, or shells. Oscar kept buttons in it. They were his mother's buttons, although no one told him it was so. They were not his father's buttons. There were small round ones like ladybirds with single brass loops instead of legs. Others were made of glass. There were metal buttons with four holes and mother-of-pearl with two. He drilled these buttons as other boys might drill soldiers. He lined them up. He ordered them. He numbered them. There were five hundred and sixty. Sometimes in the middle of a new arrangement his head ached.

On this Christmas Day, his father said: 'You have reclassified your buttons, I see.'

The buttons were on the window ledge. It was a deep sill. Mrs Williams had put the buttons there when she set the table.

Oscar said: 'Yes, Father.'

'The taxonomic principle being colour. The spectrum from left to right, with size the second principle of order.'

'Yes, Father.'

'Very good,' said Theophilus.

Oscar scraped his plate of stew clean. He finished his glass of water. He bowed his head with his father and thanked God for what He had provided. And when Mrs Williams came to the door and asked would he please help her add pollard to the pigs' swill, he went quickly, quietly, a light, pale, golden-haired boy. He thought about his buttons, not about what he was doing.

The two women stood side by side like two jugs on a shelf. One was big and floury, the other small and freckled, but their smiles were mirror images of each other and they held their hands in front of them, each clasped identically.

They had 'It' on a plate. They had cut it into quarters and covered it with lovely custard. Mrs Williams pushed her hairbrush deeper into her pinny pocket and thrust the pudding at him. She moved the bowl through the air with such speed that the spoon was left behind and clattered on to the cobble floor.

Mrs Williams stopped, but Fanny Drabble hissed: 'Leave alone.' She kicked the fallen spoon away and gave Oscar a fresh one. She was suddenly nervous of discovery.

Oscar took the spoon and ate, standing up.

He could never have imagined such a lovely taste. He let it break apart, treasuring it inside his mouth.

He looked up and saw the two mirrored smiles increase. Fanny Drabble tucked her chin into her neck. Oscar smiled too, almost sleepily, and he was just raising the spoon to his mouth in anticipation of more, had actually got the second spoonful into his mouth when the door squeaked behind him and Theophilus came striding across the cobbled floor.

He did not see this. He felt it. He felt the blow on the back of his head. His face leapt forward. The spoon hit his tooth. The spoon dropped to the floor. A large horny hand gripped the back of his head and another cupped beneath his mouth. He tried to swallow. There was a second blow. He spat what he could.

Theophilus acted as if his son were poisoned. He brought him to the scullery and made him drink salt water. He forced the glass hard against his mouth so it hurt. Oscar gagged and struggled. His father's eyes were wild. They did not see him. Oscar drank. He drank again. He drank until he vomited into the pigs' swill. When this was done, Theophilus threw what remained of the pudding into the fire.

Oscar had never been hit before. He could not bear it.

His father made a speech. Oscar did not believe it.

His father said the pudding was the fruit of Satan.

But Oscar had tasted the pudding. It did not taste like the fruit of Satan.

His son was long-necked and delicate. He was light, airy, made from the quills of a bird. He was white and frail. He had a triangular face, a thin nose, archer's-bow lips, a fine pointed chin. The eyes were so clean and unprotected, like freshly peeled fruit. It was a face that trusted you completely, made you light in the heart at the very moment it placed on you the full weight of responsibility for its protection. It was such an open face you could thank God for its lack of guile at the very moment you harboured anxieties for its safety in the world. Not even the red hair, that frizzy nest which grew outwards, horizontal like a windblown tree in an Italianate painting, this hair did not suggest anything as self-protective as 'temper'.

He should not have hit him.

He knew this even as he did it, even as he felt himself move like a wind through the cabbage-damp kitchen, which was peopled with stiff and silent mannequins. He saw Mrs Williams reaching for her hairbrush. He saw Fanny Drabble raise her hand to cover her open mouth. He knew, as he heard the remnants of the nasty sweetmeat hiss upon the fire, that he should not have struck his son.

Theophilius saw the two blue marks he had made on his son's neck. They were made by the pincers of his own thumb and forefinger. He regretted the injury, but what else could he have done? The boy had skin like his mother. In a surgery in Pimlico, a Dr Hansen had dropped nitric acid on this skin from a 15ml pipette. Had the boy in the waiting room heard her cry out? She had cancer, and Hansen had removed the growth like this, with drops of acid on her tender skin. What they finally removed was a lump, dark and hard from all this pain. She had died anyway.

He had never struck his son. They had supported each other, silently, not wishing to touch their hurt with words. They were alone in a country where they did not belong. They sat on the red soil of Hennacombe like two London bricks. When the father fell into a brown study, the boy squatted silently, an untidy mess of adolescent limbs, and clasped his father's knee and horny hand. They were united by blood, by the fundamentalist certainties of a dissenting faith, by this dead woman whom they could not talk about directly.

He had thrown her clothes into the sea. He had been half-drunk with anger and grief. He had left the boy in bed and gone running down through the rifle-sight of the combe, carrying her lavender-sweet clothes, not caring to separate them from their wooden hangers. The sea took them like weed, and threw them back along the beach. He dragged them out, searching for a current. The sea rejected them.

It was little Oscar, standing in his flannelette nightgown like a wraith, who finally brought him to his senses.

They had never talked about this with words, but in the silence of their eyes they understood each other and said things that would have been quite unthinkable to say aloud.

Mrs Williams began to brush her hair. She stood, wide and tall, her stomach pushing out against her white starched pinafore, and brushed at that tangled mass of grey frizz which would never right itself. She stooped a little so she might stare out of the seaward window while she did it. Thusk-thusk-

thusk. She brushed as if she were in the privacy of her own room. And such was the conviction with which she brushed that she made herself a room, a little glass cage within the kitchen. It had a door and lock and you might not enter.

'Well,' Theophilus said. He was riddling the grate of the stove. No one dared tell him he was riddling to excess or making coals go through the grate. A long strand of Mrs Williams's hair fell on his own. He did not feel it. Fanny Drabble saw it but did not dare to lift it off.

'Well,' he said, still riddling, back and forth, forth and back, 'Master Hopkins, you will be a good helper and fetch up the buckets.'

'Let me get them, sir,' said Fanny Drabble who was ill, almost to the point of vomiting herself. She knew her tenure to be in danger. She knew it was to do with pudding, but beyond that she really could not fathom. 'Oh, please,' she said. 'Let me go, sir.' And she snatched the grey hair off his head. She could not help herself.

'No,' said Theophilus Hopkins. He did not notice the hair was gone. He kept on at the grate, in-out, out-in. 'That will not be necessary, Mrs Drabble. Master Hopkins and I are going to collect some specimens.'

He looked at her then. She did not understand the look she saw. It seemed weak and watery. It did not match the tenor of the voice.

'But, sir,' said Fanny Drabble, feeling at last that she was free to stoop and pick up the spoon from the floor, 'it be Christmas Day.'

It was then Theophilus turned his head enough to look at his son's eyes. It was then that he saw the damage he had done.

'Christmas Day,' cooed Fanny Drabble, 'and they say the boilers are bursting from all the frost at Exeter.'

When Theophilus looked at her he brought a face whose emotions were related to what he had just seen. The face had nothing to do with Mrs Drabble.

'Christmas Day,' she said gently, not knowing what she did.

'Some call it that,' said Theophilus, standing from the grate. He held out a hand so she must hand him the spoon. She gave it to him. 'Some call it that, but none in my employ.'

'Yes,' thought Fanny Drabble, 'and what a black loveless bastard you are.'

Peter Carey, *Oscar and Lucinda*

The Shop of Ghosts

Nearly all the best and most precious things in the universe you can get for a halfpenny. I make an exception, of course, of the sun, the moon, the earth, people, stars, thunderstorms, and such trifles. You can get them for nothing. But the general principle will be at once apparent. In the street behind me, for instance, you can now get a ride on an electric tram for a halfpenny. To be on an electric tram is to be on a flying castle in a fairy tale. You can get quite a large number of brightly coloured sweets for a halfpenny.

But if you want to see what a vast and bewildering array of valuable things you can get at a halfpenny each, you should do as I was doing last night. I was gluing my nose against the glass of a very small and dimly lit toy shop in one of the greyest and leanest of the streets of Battersea. But dim as was that square of light, it was filled (as a child once said to me) with all the colours God ever made. Those toys of the poor were like the children who buy them; they were all dirty; but they were all bright. For my part, I think brightness more important than cleanliness; since the first is of the soul, and the second of the body. You must excuse me; I am a democrat; I know I am out of fashion in the modern world.

As I looked at that palace of pigmy wonders, at small green omnibuses, at small blue elephants, at small black dolls, and small red Noah's arks, I must have fallen into some sort of unnatural trance. That lit shop window became like the brilliantly lit stage when one is watching some highly coloured comedy. I forgot the grey houses and the grimy people behind me as one forgets the dark galleries and the dim crowds at a theatre. It seemed as if the little objects behind the glass were small, not because they were toys, but because they were objects far away. The green omnibus was really a green omnibus, a green Bayswater omnibus, passing across some huge desert on its ordinary way to Bayswater. The blue elephant was no longer blue with paint; he was blue with distance. The black doll was really a Negro relieved against passionate tropic foliage in the land where every weed is flaming and only man is black. The red Noah's ark was really the enormous ship of earthly salvation riding on the rain-swollen sea, red in the first morning of hope.

Everyone, I suppose, knows such stunning instants of abstraction, such brilliant blanks in the mind. In such moments one can see the face of one's own best friend as an unmeaning pattern of spectacles or moustaches. They are commonly marked by the two signs of the slowness of their growth and the suddenness of their termination. The return to real thinking is often as abrupt as bumping into a man. Very often indeed (in my case) it is bumping into a man. But in any case the awakening is always emphatic and, generally speaking, it is always complete. Now, in this case, I did come back with a shock of sanity to the consciousness that I was, after all, only staring into a dingy little toy shop; but in some strange way the mental cure did not seem to be final. There was still in my mind an unmanageable something that told me that I had strayed into some odd atmosphere, or that I had already done some odd thing. I felt as if I had worked a miracle or committed a sin. It was as if I had (at any rate) stepped across some border in the soul.

To shake off this dangerous and dreamy sense I went into the shop and tried to buy wooden soldiers. The man in the shop was very old and broken, with confused white hair covering his head and half his face, hair so start- lingly white that it looked almost artificial. Yet though he was senile and even sick, there was nothing of suffering in his eyes; he looked rather as if he were gradually falling asleep in a not unkindly decay. He gave me the wooden soldiers, but when I put down the money he did not at first seem to see it; then he blinked at it feebly, and then he pushed it feebly away.

'No, no,' he said vaguely. 'I never have. I never have. We are rather old- fashioned here.'

'Not taking money,' I replied, 'seems to me more like an uncommonly new fashion than an old one.'

'I never have,' said the old man, blinking and blowing his nose; 'I've always given presents. I'm too old to stop.'

'Good heavens!' I said. 'What can you mean? Why, you might be Father Christmas.'

'I am Father Christmas,' he said apologetically, and blew his nose again.

The lamps could not have been lighted yet in the street outside. At any rate, I could see nothing against the darkness but the shining shop window. There were no sounds of steps or voices in the street; I might have strayed into some new and sunless world. But something had cut the cords of common sense, and I could not feel even surprise except sleepily. Something made me say, 'You look ill, Father Christmas.'

'I am dying,' he said.

I did not speak, and it was he who spoke again.

'All the new people have left my shop. I cannot understand it. They seem to object to me on such curious and inconsistent sort of grounds, these scientific men, and these innovators. They say that I give people superstitions and make them too visionary; they say I give people sausages and make them too coarse. They say my heavenly parts are too heavenly; they say my earthly parts are too earthly; I don't know what they want, I'm sure. How can heavenly things be too heavenly, or earthly things too earthly? How can one be too good, or too jolly? I don't understand. But I understand one thing well enough. These modern people are living and I am dead.'

'You may be dead,' I replied. 'You ought to know. But as for what they are doing – do not call it living.'

A silence fell suddenly between us which I somehow expected to be unbroken. But it had not fallen for more than a few seconds when, in the utter stillness, I distinctly heard a very rapid step coming nearer and nearer along the street. The next moment a figure flung itself into the shop and stood framed in the doorway. He wore a large white hat tilted back as if in impatience; he had tight bright old-fashioned pantaloons, a gaudy old-fashioned stock and waistcoat, and an old fantastic coat. He had large wide-open luminous eyes like those of an arresting actor; he had a fiery, nervous face, and a fringe of beard. He took in the shop and the old man in a look that seemed literally a flash and uttered the exclamation of a man utterly staggered.

'Good lord!' he cried out; 'it can't be you! It isn't you! I came to ask where your grave was.'

'I'm not dead yet, Mr Dickens,' said the old gentleman, with a feeble smile; 'but I'm dying,' he hastened to add reassuringly.

'But, dash it all, you were dying in my time,' said Mr Charles Dickens with animation; 'and you don't look a day older.'

'I've felt like this for a long time,' said Father Christmas.

Mr Dickens turned his back and put his head out of the door into the darkness.

'Dick,' he roared at the top of his voice; 'he's still alive.'

Another shadow darkened the doorway, and a much larger and more full-blooded gentleman in an enormous periwig came in, fanning his flushed face with a military hat of the cut of Queen Anne. He carried his head well back like a soldier, and his hot face had even a look of arrogance, which was suddenly contradicted by his eyes, which were literally as humble as a dog's. His sword made a great clatter, as if the shop were too small for it.

'Indeed,' said Sir Richard Steele, ''tis a most prodigious matter, for the man was dying when we wrote about Sir Roger de Coverley and his Christmas Day.'

My senses were growing dimmer and the room darker. It seemed to be filled with newcomers.

'It hath ever been understood,' said a burly man, who carried his head humorously and obstinately a little on one side – I think he was Ben Jonson – 'It hath ever been understood, consule Jacobo, under our King James and her late Majesty, that such good and hearty customs were fallen sick, and like to pass from the world. This greybeard most surely was no lustier when I knew him than now.'

And I also thought I heard a green-clad man, like Robin Hood, say in some mixed Norman French, 'But I saw the man dying'.

'I have felt like this a long time,' said Father Christmas, in his feeble way again.

Mr Charles Dickens suddenly leaned across to him.

'Since when?' he asked. 'Since you were born?'

'Yes,' said the old man, and sank shaking into a chair. 'I have been always dying.'

Mr Dickens took off his hat with a flourish like a man calling a mob to rise.

'I understand it now,' he cried, 'you will never die.'

G. K. Chesterton

If You Haven't Got a Shilling

Christmas came so fast around the corner
We concluded we were lost or perhaps had taken
A misdirection when we'd stopped and spoken
Thankfully to the kindliest-looking stranger.
Perhaps we'd been too thankful to be listening.

Our youngest throat had barely healed from singing,
Our oldest eye from a twinkle. Certain of us
Had said goodbye for good and all to Christmas,
But there nevertheless he was, panting and grinning.
I did hear shouts behind us: 'What's the hold up?'

As we bumped into each other as we pulled up.
Neighbour and neighbour nudged and were crying 'Humbug!'
Or saying 'I'm Dutch if it is!' then 'Eat your homburg!'
When clearly it was. So kids were heaved and held up
To stare comprehendingly at the hinting visage.

We sat down gladly, chuckling back the message,
Greeted with some hysteria, some corpsing,
Indubitably some embarrassment at his timing,
But largely with goodwill. After all, the passage
Is not his fault, his business, or our business.

'Well, if he says so, fine!' was the consensus.
We'll do our bit, we always have, we want to!
We told him we all wondered where he went to
Every year, which brought a tear to Christmas,
Because he really thinks we do all wonder.

Glyn Maxwell

Look on the Merry Faces

Christmas time! That man must be a misanthrope indeed, in whose breast something like a jovial feeling is not roused – in whose mind some pleasant associations are not awakened – by the recurrence of Christmas. There are people who will tell you that Christmas is not to them what it used to be; that each succeeding Christmas has found some cherished hope, or happy prospect, of the year before, dimmed or passed away; that the present only serves to remind them of reduced circumstances and straitened incomes – of the feasts they once bestowed on hollow friends, and of the cold looks that meet them now, in adversity and misfortune. Never heed such dismal reminiscences. There are few men who have lived long enough in the world, who cannot call up such thoughts any day in the year. Then do not select the merriest of the three hundred and sixty-five, for your doleful recollections, but draw your chair nearer the blazing fire – fill the glass and send round the song – and if your room be smaller than it was a dozen years ago, or if your glass be filled with reeking punch, instead of sparkling wine, put a good face on the matter, and empty it off-hand, and fill another, and troll off the old ditty you used to sing, and thank God it's no worse. Look on the merry faces of your children (if you have any) as they sit round the fire. One little seat may be empty; one slight form that gladdened the father's heart, and roused the mother's pride to look upon, may not be there. Dwell not upon the past; think not that one short year ago, the fair child now resolving into dust, sat before you, with the bloom of health upon its cheek, and the gaiety of infancy in its joyous eye. Reflect upon your present blessings – of which every man has many – not on your past misfortunes, of which all men have some. Fill your glass again, with a merry face and contented heart. Our life on it, but your Christmas shall be merry, and your new year a happy one!

Who can be insensible to the outpourings of good feeling, and the honest interchange of affectionate attachment, which abound at this season of the year? A Christmas family-party! We know nothing in nature more delightful! There seems a magic in the very name of Christmas. Petty jealousies and discords are forgotten; social feelings are awakened, in bosoms to which they have long been strangers; father and son, or brother and sister, who have met and passed with averted gaze, or a look of cold recognition, for months before, proffer and return the cordial embrace, and bury their past animosities in their present happiness. Kindly hearts that have yearned towards each other, but have been withheld by false notions of pride and self-dignity, are again reunited, and all is kindness and benevolence! Would that Christmas lasted the whole year through (as it ought), and that the prejudices and passions which deform our better nature, were never called into action among those to whom they should ever be strangers!

Charles Dickens, *Sketches by Boz*

A Christmas Poem

At Christmas little children sing and merry bells jingle,
The cold winter air makes our hands and faces tingle
And happy families go to church and cheerily they mingle
And the whole business is unbelievably dreadful, if you're single.

Wendy Cope

TRADITIONAL CHRISTMAS

From *Marmion*

Heap on more wood! – the wind is chill;
But let it whistle as it will,
We'll keep our Christmas merry still.
Each age has deem'd the new-born year
The fittest time for festal cheer:
Even, heathen yet, the savage Dane
At Iol more deep the mead did drain;
High on the beach his galleys drew,
And feasted all his pirate crew;
Then in his low and pine-built hall,
Where shields and axes deck'd the wall,
They gorged upon the half-dress'd steer;
Caroused in seas of sable beer;
While round, in brutal jest, were thrown
The half-gnaw'd rib, and marrow-bone:
Or listen'd all, in grim delight,
While Scalds yell'd out the joys of fight.
Then forth, in frenzy, would they hie,
While wildly loose their red locks fly,
And dancing round the blazing pile,
They make such barbarous mirth the while,
As best might to the mind recall
The boisterous joys of Odin's hall.

And well our Christian sires of old
Loved when the year its course had roll'd,
And brought blithe Christmas back again,

With all his hospitable train.
Domestic and religious rite
Gave honour to the holy night;
On Christmas Eve the bells were rung;
On Christmas Eve the mass was sung:
That only night in all the year,
Saw the stoled priest the chalice rear.
The damsel donn'd her kirtle sheen;
The hall was dress'd with holly green;
Forth to the wood did merry-men go,
To gather in the mistletoe.
Then open'd wide the Baron's hall
To vassal, tenant, serf, and all;
Power laid his rod of rule aside,
And Ceremony doff 'd his pride.
The heir, with roses in his shoes,
That night might village partner choose;
The Lord, underogating, share
The vulgar game of 'post and pair'.
All hail'd, with uncontroll'd delight,
And general voice, the happy night,
That to the cottage, as the crown,
Brought tidings of salvation down.

The fire, with well-dried logs supplied,
Went roaring up the chimney wide;
The huge hall-table's oaken face,
Scrubb'd till it shone, the day to grace,
Bore then upon its massive board
No mark to part the squire and lord.
Then was brought in the lusty brawn,
By old blue-coated serving-man;
Then the grim boar's head frown'd on high,
Crested with bays and rosemary.
Well can the green-garb'd ranger tell,
How, when, and where, the monster fell;
What dogs before his death he tore,
And all the baiting of the boar.
The wassel round, in good brown bowls,
Garnish'd with ribbons, blithely trowls.

There the huge sirloin reek'd; hard by
Plum-porridge stood, and Christmas pie;
Nor fail'd old Scotland to produce,
At such high tide, her savoury goose.
Then came the merry maskers in,
And carols roar'd with blithesome din;
If unmelodious was the song,
It was a hearty note, and strong.
Who lists may in their mumming see
Traces of ancient mystery;
White shirts supplied the masquerade,
And smutted cheeks the visors made;
But, O! what maskers, richly dight,
Can boast of bosoms half so light!
England was merry England, when
Old Christmas brought his sports again.
'Twas Christmas broach'd the mightiest ale;
'Twas Christmas told the merriest tale;
A Christmas gambol oft could cheer
The poor man's heart through half the year.

Sir Walter Scott

Open House

He afterwards fell into an Account of the Diversions which had passed in his House during the Holidays; for Sir *Roger*, after the laudable Custom of his Ancestors, always keeps open House at Christmas. I learned from him that he had killed eight Fat Hogs for this Season, that he had dealt about his Chines very liberally amongst his Neighbours, and that in particular he had sent a String of Hogs'-puddings with a Pack of Cards to every poor Family in the Parish. I have often thought, says Sir *Roger*, it happens very well that Christmas should fall out in the Middle of Winter. It is the most dead uncomfortable Time of the Year, when the poor People would suffer very much from their Poverty and Cold, if they had not good Chear, warm Fires, and Christmas Gambols to support them. I love to rejoice their poor Hearts at this Season, and to see the whole Village merry in my great Hall. I allow a double Quantity of Malt to my Small Beer, and set it a-running for twelve Days to every one that calls for it. I have always a Piece of Cold Beef and

Mince-pye upon the Table, and am wonderfully pleased to see my Tenants pass away a whole Evening in playing their innocent Tricks, and smutting one another. Our Friend Will *Wimble* is as merry as any of them, and shews a thousand Roguish Tricks upon these Occasions.

I was very much delighted with the Reflexion of my old Friend, which carried so much Goodness with it. He then launched out into the Praise of the late Act of Parliament for securing the Church of *England*, and told me with great Satisfaction, that he believed it already began to take Effect, for that a rigid Dissenter who chanced to dine at his House on Christmas-day, had been observed to eat away very plentifully of his Plumb-porridge.

Joseph Addison, *The Spectator*

Here We Come A-Wassailing

Here we come a-wassailing
    Among the leaves so green,
Here we come a-wandering,
    So fair to be seen:

>   *Love and joy come to you,*
>   *And to you your wassail too,*
>   *And God bless you, and send you*
>   *A happy new year.*

Our wassail cup is made
    Of the rosemary tree,
And so is your beer
    Of the best barley:

We are not daily beggars
    That beg from door to door,
But we are neighbours' children
    Whom you have seen before:

Call up the butler of this house,
    Put on his golden ring;
Let him bring us up a glass of beer,
    And better we shall sing:

We have got a little purse
 Of stretching leather skin;
We want a little of your money
 To line it well within:

Bring us out a table,
 And spread it with a cloth;
Bring us out a mouldy cheese,
 And some of your Christmas loaf:

God bless the master of this house,
 Likewise the mistress too;
And all the little children
 That round the table go:

Good Master and good Mistress,
 While you're sitting by the fire,
Pray think of us poor children
 Who are wandering in the mire:

Traditional

Christmass

Christmass is come and every hearth
Makes room to give him welcome now
Een want will dry its tears in mirth
And crown him wi a holly bough
Tho tramping neath a winters sky
Oer snow track paths and ryhmey stiles
The huswife sets her spining bye
And bids him welcome wi her smiles

Each house is swept the day before
And windows stuck wi evergreens
The snow is beesomd from the door
And comfort crowns the cottage scenes
Gilt holly wi its thorny pricks
And yew and box wi berrys small
These deck the unusd candlesticks
And pictures hanging by the wall

Neighbours resume their anual cheer
Wishing wi smiles and spirits high
Glad christmass and a happy year
To every morning passer bye
Milk maids their christmass journeys go
Accompanyd wi favourd swain
And childern pace the crumping snow
To taste their grannys cake again

Hung wi the ivys veining bough
The ash trees round the cottage farm
Are often stript of branches now
The cotters christmass hearth to warm
He swings and twists his hazel band
And lops them off wi sharpend hook
And oft brings ivy in his hand
To decorate the chimney nook

Old winter whipes his icles bye
And warms his fingers till he smiles
Where cottage hearths are blazing high
And labour resteth from his toils
Wi merry mirth beguiling care
Old customs keeping wi the day
Friends meet their christmass cheer to share
And pass it in a harmless way

Old customs O I love the sound
However simple they may be
What ere wi time has sanction found
Is welcome and is dear to me
Pride grows above simplicity
And spurns it from her haughty mind
And soon the poets song will be
The only refuge they can find

The shepherd now no more afraid
Since custom doth the chance bestow
Starts up to kiss the giggling maid
Beneath the branch of mizzletoe

That neath each cottage beam is seen
Wi pearl-like-berrys shining gay
The shadow still of what hath been
Which fashion yearly fades away

And singers too a merry throng
At early morn wi simple skill
Yet imitate the angels song
And chant their christmass ditty still
And mid the storm that dies and swells
By fits – in humings softly steals
The music of the village bells
Ringing round their merry peals

And when its past a merry crew
Bedeckt in masks and ribbons gay
The 'Morrice danse' their sports renew
And act their winter evening play
The clown-turnd-kings for penny praise
Storm wi the actors strut and swell
And harlequin a laugh to raise
Wears his hump back and tinkling bell

And oft for pence and spicy ale
Wi winter nosgays pind before
The wassail singer tells her tale
And drawls her christmass carrols oer
The prentice boy wi ruddy face
And ryhme-bepowderd dancing locks
From door to door wi happy pace
Runs round to claim his 'christmass box'

The block behind the fire is put
To sanction customs old desires
And many a faggots bands are cut
For the old farmers christmass fires
Where loud tongd gladness joins the throng
And winter meets the warmth of may
Feeling by times the heat too strong
And rubs his shins and draws away

While snows the window panes bedim
The fire curls up a sunny charm
Where creaming oer the pitchers rim
The flowering ale is set to warm
Mirth full of joy as summer bees
Sits there its pleasures to impart
While childern tween their parents knees
Sing scraps of carrols oer by heart

And some to view the winter weathers
Climb up the window seat wi glee
Likening the snow to falling feathers
In fancys infant extacy
Laughing wi superstitious love
Oer visions wild that youth supplyes
Of people pulling geese above
And keeping christmass in the skyes

As tho the homstead trees were drest
In lieu of snow wi dancing leaves
As tho the sundryd martins nest
Instead of icles hung the eaves
The childern hail the happy day
As if the snow was april grass
And pleasd as neath the warmth of may
Sport oer the water froze to glass

Thou day of happy sound and mirth
That long wi childish memory stays
How blest around the cottage hearth
I met thee in my boyish days
Harping wi raptures dreaming joys
On presents that thy coming found
The welcome sight of little toys
The christmass gifts of comers round

The wooden horse wi arching head
Drawn upon wheels around the room
The gilded coach of ginger bread
And many colord sugar plumb

Gilt coverd books for pictures sought
Or storys childhood loves to tell
Wi many a urgent promise bought
To get tomorrows lesson well

And many a thing a minutes sport
Left broken on the sanded floor
When we woud leave our play and court
Our parents promises for more
Tho manhood bids such raptures dye
And throws such toys away as vain
Yet memory loves to turn her eye
And talk such pleasures oer again

Around the glowing hearth at night
The harmless laugh and winter tale
Goes round – while parting friends delight
To toast each other oer their ale
The cotter oft wi quiet zeal
Will musing oer his bible lean
While in the dark the lovers steal
To kiss and toy behind the screen

The yule cake dotted thick wi plumbs
Is on each supper table found
And cats look up for falling crumbs
Which greedy childern litter round
And huswifes sage stuffd seasond chine
Long hung in chimney nook to drye
And boiling eldern berry wine
To drink the christmass eves 'good bye'

John Clare

Absent-Mindedness in a Parish Choir

'It happened on Sunday after Christmas – the last Sunday ever they played in Longpuddle church gallery, as it turned out, though they didn't know it then. As you may know, sir, the players formed a very good band – almost as good as the Mellstock parish players; and that's saying a great deal . . .

'Well, this Christmas they'd been out to one rattling randy after another every night, and had got next to no sleep at all. Then came the Sunday after Christmas, their fatal day. 'Twas so mortal cold that year that they could hardly sit in the gallery; for though the congregation down in the body of the church had a stove to keep off the frost, the players in the gallery had nothing at all. So Nicholas said at morning service, when 'twas freezing an inch an hour, "Please the Lord I won't stand this numbing weather no longer: this afternoon we'll have something in our insides to make us warm, if it cost a king's ransom."

'So he brought a gallon of hot brandy and beer, ready mixed, to church with him in the afternoon, and by keeping the jar well wrapped up in Timothy Thomas's bass-viol bag it kept drinkably warm till they wanted it, which was just a thimbleful in the Absolution, and another after the Creed, and the remainder at the beginning o' the sermon. When they'd had the last pull they felt quite comfortable and warm, and as the sermon went on – most unfortunately for 'em it was a long one that afternoon – they fell asleep, every man jack of 'em; and there they slept on as sound as rocks.

''Twas a very dark afternoon, and by the end of the sermon all you could see of the inside of the church were the pa'son's two candles alongside of him in the pulpit, and his spaking face behind 'em. The sermon being ended at last, the pa'son gie'd out the Evening Hymn. But no choir set about sounding up the tune, and the people began to turn their heads to learn the reason why, and then Levi Limpet, a boy who sat in the gallery, nudged Timothy and Nicholas, and said, "Begin! begin!"

' "Hey? what?" says Nicholas, starting up; and the church being so dark and his head so muddled he thought he was at the party they had played at all the night before, and away he went, bow and fiddle, at "The Devil among the Tailors", the favourite jig of our neighbourhood at that time. The rest of the band, being in the same state of mind and nothing doubting, followed their leader with all their strength, according to custom. They poured out that there tune till the lower bass notes of "The Devil among the Tailors" made the cobwebs in the roof shiver like ghosts; then Nicholas, seeing nobody moved, shouted out as he scraped (in his usual commanding way at dances when the folk didn't know the figures), "Top couples cross hands! And when I make the fiddle squeak at the end, every man kiss his pardner under the mistletoe!"

'The boy Levi was so frightened that he bolted down the gallery stairs and out homeward like lightning. The pa'son's hair fairly stood on end when he heard the evil tune raging through the church, and thinking the choir had gone crazy he held up his hand and said: "Stop, stop, stop! Stop, stop!

[38]

What's this?" But they didn't hear'n for the noise of their own playing, and the more he called the louder they played.

'Then the folks came out of their pews, wondering down to the ground, and saying: "What do they mean by such wickedness! We shall be consumed like Sodom and Gomorrah!"

'Then the squire came out of his pew lined wi' green baize, where lots of lords and ladies visiting at the house were worshipping along with him, and went and stood in front of the gallery, and shook his fist in the musicians' faces, saying, "What! In this reverent edifice! What!"

'And at last they heard'n through their playing, and stopped.

' "Never such an insulting, disgraceful thing – never!" says the squire, who couldn't rule his passion.

' "Never!" says the pa'son, who had come down and stood beside him.

' "Not if the Angels of Heaven," says the squire (he was a wickedish man, the squire was, though now for once he happened to be on the Lord's side) – "not if the Angels of Heaven come down," he says, "shall one of you villanous players ever sound a note in this church again; for the insult to me, and my family, and my visitors, and God Almighty, that you've a-perpetrated this afternoon!"

'Then the unfortunate church band came to their senses, and remembered where they were; and 'twas a sight to see Nicholas Puddingcome and Timothy Thomas and John Biles creep down the gallery stairs with their fiddles under their arms, and poor Dan'l Hornhead with his serpent, and Robert Dowdle with his clarionet, all looking as little as ninepins; and out they went. The pa'son might have forgi'ed 'em when he learned the truth o't, but the squire would not. That very week he sent for a barrel-organ that would play two-and-twenty new psalm-tunes, so exact and particular that, however sinful inclined you was, you could play nothing but psalm-tunes whatsomever. He had a really respectable man to turn the winch, as I said, and the old players played no more.'

Thomas Hardy, Life's Little Ironies

The Ceremonies for Candlemas Day

> Kindle the Christmas brand, and then
> Till sunset let it burn;
> Which quench'd, then lay it up again,
> Till Christmas next return.

Part must be kept, wherewith to teend
The Christmas log next year;
And where 'tis safely kept, the fiend
Can do no mischief there.

Robert Herrick

A Perfect Hunting Day

My first day with the Staghounds was on Christmas Eve and I find the following entry in my diary: '*Coshford; Packman's Green*. Perfect hunting day; came on wet about 2.30. Turned out at Hazelpits Farm and ran well to Wissenden, then on by Chartley Church and Henhurst down the hill and on towards Applestead. Took deer (Miss Masterful) about 2. Nine-mile point. Harkaway in good form. Took a toss over a stile toward the end. Very nice country, especially the first bit.' From this concise account it may seem as if I had already mastered the Coshford topography, but I suspect that my source of information was a paragraph in a local paper.

I cannot remember how I made myself acquainted with the name of the deer which provided the nine-mile point. But in any case, how much is taken for granted and left unrecorded in that shorthand description? And how helpful it would have been now if I had written an accurately observed and detailed narrative of the day. But since the object of these pages is to supply that deficiency I must make my reminiscent deductions as best I can. And those words from my diary do seem worth commenting on – symbolic as they are of the equestrian equilibrium on which my unseasoned character was trying to pattern itself. I wrote myself down that evening as I wanted myself to be – a hard-bitten hunting man, self-possessed in his localized knowingness and stag-hunting jargon. The words might well have been penned by a middle-aged sheep-farmer, or even by Mr 'Gus' Gimling himself. 'Took a toss over a stile' is the only human touch. But taking tosses was incidental to the glory of being a hard rider. What I ought to have written was – that I couldn't make up my mind whether to go at it or not, and the man behind me shouted 'go on if you're going', so I felt flustered and let Harkaway rush at it anyhow and then jerked his mouth just as he was taking off, and he didn't really fall, but only pecked badly and chucked me over his head and then stood quite still waiting for me to scramble up again, and altogether it was rather an inglorious exhibition, and thank goodness Stephen wasn't there to see it. For though Stephen and I always made a joke out of every toss we took, it wouldn't have suited my dignity if he'd told me in cold blood that I was still a jolly rotten rider – the tacit assumption being that my falls were entirely due to my thrusting intrepidity.

It will be noticed that no mention is made of the method by which Miss Masterful was 'taken', although I had witnessed that performance for the first time in my life. As far as I can recollect, Miss M. having decided that the show had lasted long enough, plunged into a small pond and stood there with only her small head appearing above the muddy water. Raucous ratings and loud whip-crackings restrained the baying hounds from splashing in after her, and then genial Mr Gimling, assisted by one of the whiskered wiseacres of the hunt (in a weather-stained black coat which came nearly down to his knees, white cord breeches, black butcher-boots, and very long spurs), began to get busy with a long rope. After Miss M. had eluded their attempts several times they succeeded in lassooing her head and she was persuaded to emerge from the pond. She was then frog-marched away to a farm building, where she awaited the arrival of her conveyance, which was cruising about the country and usually put in an appearance much earlier than might have been expected.

It can also be inferred from my diary that the weather 'came on wet' as soon as I'd started my ten-mile ride back to the railway-station and Harkaway's horse-box, and that the supporters of the Coshford Hunt departed in different directions wishing one another a merry Christmas and a happy New Year. It may also be inferred that poor Miss Masterful sweated and shivered in the barn with heaving sides and frightened eyes. It did not occur to me to sympathize with her as I stood at the entrance to watch them tie her up. I only wondered how far I was from the station and my poached eggs for tea. Any sympathy I had was reserved for Harkaway, who looked as if he'd had more galloping than was good for him. But when I was jogging back by Chartley Church, with my coat collar turned up and the rain soaking my knees, I chuckled to myself as I thought of an amusing incident which had happened earlier in the day.

We were galloping full-tilt along a road just outside a cosy village. An angry faced old parson was leaning over his garden gate, and as we clattered past he shook his fist at us and shouted 'Brutes! Brutes!' in a loud unclerical voice. Excited and elated as I was, I turned in the saddle and waved my whip derisively at him. Silly old buffer! And what a contrast to that jolly sporting parson in a low crowned top-hat who went so well and came up and talked to me so nicely while Miss Masterful was being hauled out of the pond!

I have analysed the orthodox entry in my diary more fully than I had intended. But how lifelessly I recover the breathing reality of which those words are the only relics. The night before hunting: the anxious wonderings about the weather; lying awake for a while with busy thoughts about tomorrow that grow blurred with the beginning of an untroubled sleep. And then Miriam battering on the door with 'it's twenty to seven, sir', and the first look at the quiet morning greyness, and the undefinable feeling produced by the yellow candlelight and the wintry smelling air from the misty garden. Such was the impermanent fabric as it unfolded: memory enchants even the dilatory little train journey which carried my expectant simplicity into the freshness of a country seen for the first time. All the sanguine guesswork of youth is there, and the silliness; all the novelty of being alive and impressed by the urgency of tremendous trivialities.

Siegfried Sassoon, *Memoirs of a Fox-Hunting Man*

Christmas at The Pines

Towards December 25th almost every day brought bulky and interesting packages from friends of either Swinburne or Walter. These would often be opened by me, and sometimes the contents proved both surprising and amusing.

The turkey deserves a special notice and a description of this prepossessing bird may divert the reader, for it stands out in the annals of 'Turkeydom' as a unique specimen differing from any other of its kind in one unusual particular. It was a veritable plutocrat in appearance and half covered with gold! Shorn of feathers and hanging up in a poulterer's shop in the cold staring immodesty of the 'altogether', a turkey is by no means a pleasing or edifying-looking object to the artistic eye, although from a gastronomic point of view it makes quite a different appeal. But the 'gilded fowl' that annually came as a present from Lady Leighton Warren – the sister of the poet Lord de Tabley – was a very superior spectacle. When it came it was paraded round the house as a huge joke, and I christened it 'Midas'. Pinned to its breast were many 'orders' – rosettes of ribbon of divers hues, and the head, feet and scaly shanks, and the whole of its long, hideous, fleshy protuberance of mottled red and blue neck were discreetly covered by a thick layer of gold paint.

Lying in state in a box lined with frilled pink and white paper, and decked out with all the finery of festoons of variegated holly and sprigs of mistletoe, the recumbent scion of a noble house looked almost too gorgeous to be eaten.

For the purpose of buying Swinburne's present, Walter and I decided that a final rampage would prove an interesting wind-up to a busy week. We didn't know what to give the poet, and on Christmas Eve when it was growing quite late, we happened to be passing Buszard's in Oxford Street, and seeing a large printed card in the window bearing the inscription 'Partridge Pies' we entered the shop and Walter asked for one.

The place resembled a bee-hive, so crowded was it with late shoppers. A harassed-looking assistant came forward and conducted us to a counter where wonderful erections, like miniature haystacks, were on view. We chose a medium-sized one for our joint present to Algernon, and while it was being packed up, Walter walked to another part of the shop and came back to where I was sitting, bearing in his hands a box of crackers. 'Who on earth have you bought those for?' I enquired, for I considered crackers quite a ridiculous institution, and never intended buying any. 'Not for *you*,' he retorted with an amused chuckle, and an accent on the pronoun. 'I know you are far too *old* for that sort of thing, so I've bought them for somebody who *will* appreciate them, and you'll see who *that* is – tomorrow!'

Our chief concern now was the safe transit of the pie. As it made a heavy parcel, we carried it in turns, and while I was custodian of the crackers, Walter was responsible for the pie and *vice versa*. In this manner we arrived home, happy and hungry, to find that quite a transformation had been effected during our absence. The house was gay with decorations, and I must say that at The Pines we were not satisfied with half-hearted exhibitions of festivity. There was always a great piece of mistletoe hanging in the hall, and even the staircase and passages were decorated. The 'Christmassy' look of the home at this festive season enhanced by holly and mistletoe reaching nearly to the ceiling and adorning every picture frame, delighted the Bard.

Whilst we were dining, a loud peal at the front door-bell resounded along the hall. It surely could not be the 'Waits' – the two or three wretched urchins who call themselves 'carol singers' would not ring until they had finished afflicting us with 'When Shepherds watch their flocks by night', and similar dirges, for dirges they were as tortured by these dreadful small boys. Our surmise was correct; the boys were still singing through the letter-box in their high treble voices, and the maid came in with the announcement that Mr MacIlvaine's butler had just left a big box with his master's compliments.

This friend, knowing the predilections of the housemates for anything savouring of Christmas had always endeavoured to make his present appropriate to the occasion. He certainly achieved a *coup* this time. When the box was opened, it revealed a Yule log. It was made of some kind of composition or *papier mâché*, and hollowed out so that it could be lighted up inside. I determined to use it as a table decoration on the morrow. This was a happy thought, for Swinburne was charmed with it.

Christmas Day, as is usual in this country of topsy-turvy climatic conditions, was muggy and warmish, instead of the hoped-for cold and frosty morning. This did not please Swinburne at all. He resented any whimsical vagaries on the part of the Clerk of the Weather. He declared at such times he was being cheated out of his rights. What would have pleased him was the scene of the Christmas card of childhood's tradition, a landscape covered with snow, trees clothed in a frosty mantle, icicles hanging from the water-spouts, and all the rest of the paraphernalia of an old-fashioned winter. When it was 'blowing great guns' he was happy, and cold weather so exhilarated him that had there been a snowstorm, and he unable to be out in it, he would have suffered like Tantalus. It did not, however, really matter to the poet what the weather was on Christmas Day. At the best of times, the Sabbath Day was by no means calculated to make *his* heart rejoice, for on that day he was deprived of his usual walk, and on that account alone he heartily detested it. Wimbledon Common, on week-days so restful and unpopulated, was invariably thronged on Sundays and at holiday times. Swinburne never crossed the threshold then, but remained indoors, a very uneasy victim until the crowds had disappeared and left him free to enjoy his walk in peace and quiet.

With Christmas Day and Boxing Day the prospect of 'half a week of Sundays' had to be faced with as much resolution as the poet could muster. So with the characteristic fortitude of a Mark Tapley, he prepared to make the best of it and took credit in being jolly.

The arrival of the postman proved a diversion, and his budget of cards never failed to amuse him. Naturally he got a goodly supply from strangers. What became of these latter, I cannot say. They disappeared – and that is all one knew of them. But cards from relatives and intimate friends adorned his mantelpiece for days. These messages of goodwill always contained some allusion to his two pet subjects – the sea and the children; and Walter responded to Swinburne's gift of a pictured ship by one at the New Year of a pictured baby. It is before me now as I write:

To the Child-lover A. C. S.
From T. Watts-Dunton, New Year's Day, 1906.

On this same occasion a great triumph was secured by the poet's sister, Isabel, who had the happy thought of presenting her brother with a set of reproductions of the ten Bambini by Andrea della Robbia which ornaments the front of the Ospedale degli Innocenti (Foundling Hospital) at Florence.

These quaintly swaddled little boys are not of equal attractiveness, though doubtless all are beautiful examples of skill in modelling. But Swinburne was enthusiastic about them all. He had seen the originals in Italy, and as he showed the little pictures one after another, he could not make up his mind which baby bore off the palm for beauty. How small a thing can gladden the heart of a great man, and for the time being the Bambini made him forget it was a sort of Sunday and that there was no going out for him. As it happened, he managed to fill in his day quite comfortably. There were always his books – his solace and his delight – to browse on. Moreover, there were several chapters from *A Christmas Carol* to be rehearsed for the Dickens reading in the evening, and he devoted some time to getting as near word-perfect as possible. As I have mentioned, I was astonished when I first heard him read *Martin Chuzzlewit* to find he did not so much appear to be reading, as speaking a part learned by rote. Walter told me that Swinburne seldom read anything from Dickens without having previously made a careful study of the chapter or chapters before reading them aloud. Here again was an instance of imitation being the sincerest form of flattery. Dickens must have done the same when reading his own works to crowded audiences.

As in most houses, our Christmas dinner was a family affair – a jolly and homely little gathering. Our only guest, outside the circle of relatives, was Mr Mackenzie Bell, for whom my husband entertained a great regard. For myself, who had only been married a month, it seemed as if some magician's wand had touched me when I found myself presiding at this Dickensian dinner-table. When the table was arranged, looking so pretty with the Yule log in the middle, and little bundles of crackers scattered at intervals over the cloth, Swinburne slipped quietly down from his library, and having got the maid to show him where each member of the party was to sit, he placed an addressed envelope by the side of each cover. These contained the Christmas cards (duly inscribed) which he had been at such pains to select. In the performance of this ritual none of us was ever forgotten by the poet.

A chorus of amusing sallies greeted the entrance of the turkey, 'done and dished', as we recalled the golden glories of the 'noble bird' now guillotined and deprived of most of its splendours.

More fun came at the end when, the repast being over, there was a general pulling of Christmas crackers. Swinburne now appeared to be thoroughly in his element. The fine ceremoniousness with which he bowed across the table to his old friends, Miss Watts and Mrs Mason, as he requested the honour of a 'tug-of-war', was a 'sight for sore eyes', and great was the amusement we all derived from hearing the Bard read the doggerel bits from the mottoes. He kept the table in a roar with his witticisms, and eagerly searched his end of the cracker in the hope that it might contain a specimen of cracker poetry.

Eventually everybody's mottoes were handed to him to read. This was a divine moment for such an elocutionist. He carefully unrolled each little slip of paper, and in as stirring tones as he could command – and the more stupid the lines the more pathos he contrived to put into his voice – he would 'pray silence' for the recital of some absurd morsel. At the conclusion he would cast up the whites of his eyes to the ceiling, and after heaving a tremendous sigh, exclaim, 'A sublime line! – a truly poetic line! What would I not give to have written it!' When it came to the turn of Walter's young niece, Miss Aimée Watts – a charming girl hailing from Australia – or myself, Swinburne's eyes sparkled with mischief. He solicited us both in turn to be his cracker partners, and the motto in each case of course contained some rubbish about love. He endeavoured to make the ridiculous verses more ridiculous still, and loud were the laughs when he read with emphasis and affected emotion such amorous stuff as:

> You are so fair that Cupid's dart
> Can ne'er be pulled from my fond heart.

The motto that resulted from his 'pull' with me was more ambitious. Swinburne rendered the lines as fervently as though they had come straight from Sappho herself. Here they are:

> O valorous knight, whose eyes are as blue
> As the sky which is calm above tempests that grieve,
> My heart is my Christmas present to you,
> So take it and wear it – but not on your sleeve.

'Ah!' he said with the most profound gravity, 'that person, whoever he is, *deserves* to be Poet Laureate.'

When the guests had departed, the poet had quite thrown over the part of Master of the Revels. He was now the serious Dickensian and read the selected passages from *A Christmas Carol*. The peacefulness of the closing hours of the day was in strange contrast to the mirth of the dinner, and I cannot say that I was sorry when the evening came to an end and Swinburne took leave of us with a courteous bow and a cheery 'Good-night.'

Clara Watts-Dunton, *The Home Life of Swinburne*

Under the Mistletoe

From the centre of the ceiling of this kitchen, old Wardle had just suspended, with his own hands, a huge branch of mistletoe, and this same branch of mistletoe instantaneously gave rise to a scene of general and delightful struggling and confusion; in the midst of which, Mr Pickwick, with a gallantry that would have done honour to a descendant of Lady Tollimglower herself, took the old lady by the hand, led her beneath the mystic branch, and saluted her in all courtesy and decorum. The old lady submitted to this piece of practical politeness with all the dignity which befitted so important and serious a solemnity, but the younger ladies, not being so thoroughly imbued with a superstitious veneration for the custom: or imagining that the value of a salute is very much enhanced if it cost a little trouble to obtain it: screamed and struggled, and ran into corners, and threatened and remonstrated, and did everything but leave the room, until some of the less adventurous gentlemen were on the point of desisting, when they all at once found it useless to resist any longer, and submitted to be kissed with a good grace. Mr Winkle kissed the young lady with the black eyes, and Mr Snodgrass kissed Emily, and Mr Weller, not being particular about the form of being under the mistletoe, kissed Emma and the other female servants, just as he caught them. As to the poor relations, they kissed everybody, not even excepting the plainer portions of the young-lady visitors, who, in their excessive confusion, ran right under the mistletoe, as soon as it was hung up, without knowing it! Wardle stood with his back to the fire, surveying the whole scene, with the utmost satisfaction; and the fat boy took the opportunity of appropriating to his own use, and summarily devouring, a particularly fine mince-pie, that had been carefully put by for somebody else.

Now, the screaming had subsided, and faces were in a glow, and curls in a tangle, and Mr Pickwick, after kissing the old lady as before mentioned, was standing under the mistletoe, looking with a very pleased countenance on all that was passing around him, when the young lady with the black eyes, after a little whispering with the other young ladies, made a sudden dart forward, and, putting her arm round Mr Pickwick's neck saluted him affectionately on the left cheek; and before Mr Pickwick distinctly knew what was the matter, he was surrounded by the whole body, and kissed by every one of them.

It was a pleasant thing to see Mr Pickwick in the centre of the group, now pulled this way, and then that, and first kissed on the chin, and then on the nose, and then on the spectacles: and to hear the peals of laughter which were raised on every side; but it was a still more pleasant thing to see Mr Pickwick, blinded shortly afterwards with a silk handkerchief, falling up against the wall, and scrambling into corners, and going through all the mysteries of blind-man's buff, with the utmost relish for the game, until at last he caught one of the poor relations, and then had to evade the blind-man himself, which he did with a nimbleness and agility that elicited the admiration and applause of all beholders. The poor relations caught the people who they thought would like it, and, when the game flagged, got caught themselves. When they were all tired of blind-man's buff, there was a great game at snap-dragon, and when fingers enough were burned with that, and all the raisins were gone, they sat down by the huge fire of blazing logs to a substantial supper, and a mighty bowl of wassail, something smaller than an ordinary wash-house copper, in which the hot apples were hissing and bubbling with a rich look, and a jolly sound, that were perfectly irresistible.

'This,' said Mr Pickwick, looking round him, 'this is, indeed, comfort.'

'Our invariable custom,' replied Mr Wardle. 'Everybody sits down with us on Christmas Eve, as you see them now – servants and all; and here we wait, until the clock strikes twelve, to usher Christmas in, and beguile the time with forfeits and old stories. Trundle, my boy, rake up the fire.'

Up flew the bright sparks in myriads as the logs were stirred. The deep red blaze sent forth a rich glow, that penetrated into the furthest corner of the room, and cast its cheerful tint on every face.

Charles Dickens, *The Pickwick Papers*

You Invite your Nice, but Impecunious Country Cousin for Christmas

(1) In your invitation, make it quite clear that you intend paying her railway ticket and incidental expenses.

(2) On receiving her acceptance, send her the money promptly. Don't wait for Christmas Day, but let her have her presents *at once*. The most useful thing you can possibly send her is a black lace evening frock, and the most useless is a gorgeous feather fan. In smaller ways she would like good gloves, or shoes, and she would probably appreciate the money for a permanent wave.

(3) Don't take too much advantage of her terrible good-nature in doing odd jobs.

(4) Give her a gas fire in her bedroom, and a hot-water bottle in her bed.

(5) Theatres mean a lot to country cousins, and she may prefer two cheap seats to one good one.

(6) If you are going to have her at all, do her handsomely!

Rose Henniker Hutton, *The Perfect Christmas*

Old Christmas

One of the least pleasing effects of modern refinement is the havoc it has made among the hearty old holiday customs. It has completely taken off the sharp touchings and spirited reliefs of these embellishments of life, and has worn down society into a more smooth and polished, but certainly a less characteristic surface. Many of the games and ceremonials of Christmas have entirely disappeared, and like the sherris sack of old Falstaff, are become matters of speculation and dispute among commentators. They flourished in times full of spirit and lustihood, when men enjoyed life roughly, but heartily and vigorously; times wild and picturesque, which have furnished poetry with its richest materials, and the drama with its most attractive variety of characters and manners. The world has become more worldly. There is more of dissipation, and less of enjoyment. Pleasure has expanded into a broader, but a shallower stream, and has forsaken many of those deep and quiet channels where it flowed sweetly through the calm bosom of domestic life. Society has acquired a more enlightened and elegant tone; but it has lost many of its strong local peculiarities, its home-bred feelings, its honest fireside delights. The traditionary customs of golden-hearted antiquity, its feudal hospitalities, and lordly wassailings, have passed away with the baronial castles and stately manor-houses in which they were celebrated. They comported with the shadowy hall, the great oaken gallery, and the tapestried parlour, but are unfitted to the light showy saloons and gay drawing-rooms of the modern villa.

The Sketch Book of Washington Irving

Festive Malice

On Christmas evening we were supposed to be specially festive in the Old English fashion. The hall was horribly draughty, but it seemed to be the proper place to revel in, and it was decorated with Japanese fans and Chinese lanterns, which gave it a very Old English effect. A young lady with a confidential voice favoured us with a long recitation about a little girl who died or did something equally hackneyed, and then the Major gave us a graphic account of a struggle he had with a wounded bear. I privately wished that the bears would win sometimes on these occasions; at least they wouldn't go vapouring about it afterwards. Before we had time to recover our spirits, we were indulged with some thought-reading by a young man whom one knew instinctively had a good mother and an indifferent tailor – the sort of young man who talks unflaggingly through the thickest soup, and smooths his hair dubiously as though he thought it might hit back. The thought-reading was rather a success; he announced that the hostess was thinking about poetry, and she admitted that her mind was dwelling on one of Austin's odes. Which was near enough. I fancy she had been really wondering whether a scrag-end of mutton and some cold plum-pudding would do for the kitchen dinner next day. As a crowning dissipation, they all sat down to play progressive halma, with milk-chocolate for prizes. I've been carefully brought up, and I don't like to play games of skill for milk-chocolate, so I invented a headache and retired from the scene. I had been preceded a few minutes earlier by Miss Langshan-Smith, a rather formidable lady, who always got up at some uncomfortable hour in the morning, and gave you the impression that she had been in communication with most of the European Governments before breakfast. There was a paper pinned on her door with a signed request that she might be called particularly early on the morrow. Such an opportunity does not come twice in a lifetime. I covered up everything except the signature with another notice, to the effect that before these words should meet the eye she would have ended a misspent life, was sorry for the trouble she was giving, and would like a military funeral. A few minutes later I violently exploded an air-filled paper bag on the landing, and gave a stage moan that could have been heard in the cellars. Then I pursued my original intention and went to bed. The noise those people made in forcing open the good lady's door was positively indecorous; she resisted gallantly, but I believe they searched her for bullets for about a quarter of an hour, as if she had been a historic battlefield.

I hate travelling on Boxing Day, but one must occasionally do things that one dislikes.

'Saki', 'Reginald's Christmas Revel'

❦ 3 ❦

CONTEMPORARY CHRISTMAS

The 1981 Night Before Christmas

'Twas the night before Christmas, and one thing was clear –
That old yuletide spirit no longer was here;
Inflation was rising; the crime rate was tripling;
The fuel bills were up, and our mortgage was crippling;

I opened a beer as I watched the TV,
Where Donny sang 'O Holy Night' to Marie;
The kids were in bed, getting sleep like they should;
Or else they were stoned, which was almost as good.

While ma with her ball-point was making a fuss
'Bout folks we'd sent cards to who'd sent none to us;
'Those ingrates,' she thundered, and pounded her fist;
'Next year you can bet they'll be crossed off our list!'

When out in the yard came a deafening blare;
'Twas our burglar alarm, and I hollered, 'Who's there?'
I turned on the searchlight, which lit up the night,
And, armed with my handgun, beheld a strange sight.

Some red-suited clown with a white beard immense
Was caught in our eight-foot electrified fence;
He called out, 'I'm Santa! I bring you no malice!'
Said I, 'If you're Santa, I'm Telly Savalas!'

But, lo, as his presence grew clearer to me,
I saw in the glare that it just might be he!
I called off our Doberman clawing his sleigh
And, frisking him twice, said, 'I think he's okay.'

I led him inside where he slumped in a chair,
And he poured out the following tale of despair;
'On Christmas eves past I was jolly and chuckling,
But now 'neath the pressures, I fear I am buckling.

'You'll note I've arrived with no reindeer this year,
And without them, my sleigh is much harder to steer;
Although I would like to continue to use them,
The wildlife officials believe I abuse them.

'To add to my problem, Ralph Nader dropped by
And told me my sleigh was unsafe in the sky;
I now must wear seatbelts, despite my objections,
And bring in the sleigh twice a year for inspections.

'Last April my workers came forth with demands,
And I soon had a general strike on my hands;
I couldn't afford to pay unionized elves,
So the missus and I did the work by ourselves.

'And then, later on, came additional trouble –
An avalanche left my fine workshop in rubble;
My Allstate insurance was worthless, because
They had shrewdly slipped in a "no avalanche" clause.

'And after that came an IRS audit;
The government claimed I was out to defraud it;
They finally nailed me for 65 grand,
Which I paid through the sale of my house and my land.

'And yet I persist, though it gives me a scare
Flying blind through the blanket of smog in the air;
Not to mention the hunters who fill me with dread,
Taking shots at my sleigh as I pass overhead.

'My torn-up red suit, and these bruises and swellings,
I got fighting muggers in multiple dwellings.
And if you should ask why I'm glowing tonight,
It's from flying too close to a nuclear site.'

He rose from his chair and he heaved a great sigh,
And I couldn't help notice a tear in his eye;
'I've tried,' he declared, 'to reverse each defeat,
But I fear that today I've become obsolete.'

He slumped out the door and returned to his sleigh,
And these last words he spoke as he went on his way;
'No longer can I do the job that's required;
If anyone asks, just say, "Santa's retired!" '

Frank Jacobs

England at Christmas, 1982

O silly little, proud and silly, country
so good at ceremonial, limited wars,
football (occasionally)! Snob Billy Buntery
gives all the rich, rich presents – Santa Claus
has handed out the land. He hates the serfs,
the common people, so uncommonly low;
loves dogs, cats, hunting, cricket, the green turfs
that make a stately-homely postcard show –
quite beautiful, memorials to old greed,
when what there was to take, to steal, to pinch
went to the bastard Baron on his steed
or landowners, enclosing each square inch,

or City men, who raise a joyous anthem
for a fake-lady bossyboots from Grantham.

Gavin Ewart

Carolling

We were terrible lucky to catch
The Ceaucescus' execution, being
By sheer chance that Christmas Day
In the only house for twenty miles
With Satellite TV. We sat,
Cradling brandies, by the fire,
Watching those two small, cranky autocrats
Lying in snow against a blood-spattered wall,
Hardly able to believe our good fortune.
The picture wasn't all that clear,
But the reporter told us how
The cross woman's peasant origins
Came out at the last, shouting
At her executioners 'I have been
A mother to you and this is how
You thank me for it.' We switched over
To join in with the carols
On the blockbuster Christmas special
On the other side, thanking
The stars that had saved us, with no
Effort on our part, from such tyranny.

Bernard O'Donoghue

Awaydays

At breakfast on Christmas Day Stanley was looking chipper in his Playboy Club tie. Bright yellow bunnies gambolled on a black ground. The tie met Stanley's throat in a fat Windsor knot whose points reached halfway around his neck.

'Off to church this morning, Stanley?'

'Only if they got a saloon bar in it. You're talking to the original atheist, you are, chum.' Stanley appeared to inhale his sausage from his fork. I watched it until its blunt tip finally disappeared behind the suction valve of Stanley's lips. 'Catch me in one of those places! Laugh?'

'Stan-lee!' Hilda shook her head at us in a gesture of pantomime despair.

All over the dining room, presents were being unwrapped. At Frances's table, the elderly couple were submerging themselves under a heap of ribbons and tissue paper. Frances ate stolidly on, staring ahead of her into space. It was particularly bad luck on her, because the lady she was sitting beside happened to get the Cliff Court's star present. As she stripped layer after layer of paper from her neat rectangular parcel, her husband put on a studied poker face. As the neighbouring tables began to watch the unsheathing of this marvel, Frances grimly refused to look.

At last it was done. It looked to begin with like a calculator or a transistor radio. The husband leaned over the table and made a noise on it. The wife was baffled by it. She bent her balding white head over it and submitted it to an apprehensive investigation.

It was a Stylophone – a pocket electronic organ. By touching its numbered keys with a metal stylus on the end of a wire, you could produce a Dalek-like musical note. There was a switch to produce a tremolo effect, and instructions for playing 'Silent Night', 'The Camptown Races', 'Annie Laurie' and 'Old Folks At Home'. It was handed round, wondered at, giggled over, gingerly fiddled with. A bold man, rather younger than the average run of Cliff Courters, managed to make it hesitantly burp out the first few bars of 'Silent Night', with tremolo. He got a round of applause. 'You don't have to read music,' he explained, 'you just follow the numbers.' Uncle George, who'd learned to play the tenor horn in 1937, looked as if he wasn't sure whether he held with music by numbers, and went on with his egg, bacon and sausage.

At the end of the room, two ladies who were through with breakfast started off their day with a good laugh. They shook and hooted and clutched on to each other. They looked as if they were emptying themselves out. Still burbling, they passed our table. 'There's nothing like a good laugh to start the day, is there?' said one of them, grabbing her friend and starting up again.

When we went out, there was a queue for the payphone in the vestibule. The line of grannies, all holding their own childish presents, stretched back to the Reception desk. Given toys by their husbands, they'd been reminded of those real children, scattered all over England, from whom they had been divorced this Christmas.

'Hello, Piers!' called one lady into the phone, trying to push her 10p piece into the jaws of the box. 'Hello, Piers, dear! Hello, darling! It's your gran. Did you like your present? Oh. Oh, it's Julia. Hello, Julia, darling . . .'

The children's names rang oddly in the vestibule. Much more than age separated the Elsies and Ediths and Winnies at the phone from the Pierses and Julias at the other end. I imagined Piers at his private school in Surrey, Julia with her pony. Gran, with her package holidays in Majorca and her Mile End laugh, came nowhere in those stakes. Her daughter would be putting out the sherry glasses on the sideboard now, and Steven and Nicola would be looking in for drinks. Much better to think of Gran enjoying herself at the Cliff Court than have her in a messy heap among the stripped pine and Swedish leather.

Stanley the Beetle cornered me on the stairs.

'You sleep alright last night? I didn't. These narrow beds they got. You can't sleep properly in a narrow bed. At home,' said Stanley, making an important announcement, 'I got a King Size bed.' He gave me a mysterious thumbs-up sign and disappeared to his room.

I took a book down to the bar lounge, Edwin Dakin's fat, merciless 1929 biography of Mary Baker Eddy, and tried to read. But it was no good. People circled around me on tiptoe, stared at me, stared at my book, and talked in churchy whispers. I began to feel like a zoo exhibit. The first time I raised my head to light a cigarette, they seized their chance to bring me back to the real world.

'It's obvious you're a big reader,' said a lady in pink called Rene.

'What's that you got there?' asked Cyril her husband, 'the *Decline and Fall*?'

That was a joke with a history. Gibbon was the staple hard tack of the self-improving Victorian working class. When the Boffins came into money in *Our Mutual Friend*, their first act of arrivism is to hire Silas Wegg to read them selected passages from *The Decline and Fall of the Roman Empire*. Gibbon went through hundreds of cheap editions, and in the 1870s it was probably odds-on that anyone seen with a big book was mugging up on his Gibbon. A hundred years later, the name is still a synonym for a long hard read.

'Do you know *The Decline and Fall of the Roman Empire*?'

'The what?' said Cyril.

'I don't either. I don't suppose anyone does much, nowadays.'

'I read a book on holiday last year,' Cyril said. 'Henry Cooper's autobiography. I got to the end of that one. I bought the *Gulag*-whatsit book, too. Never got past the introduction.'

'Cyril's a great reader too,' said Rene. 'I never read books,' she said, in much the same tone of voice that Brenda the Camp Guard had said she didn't touch liquor.

Literary conversation failing us, we got on to more personal topics.

'We've got the dog up in our room,' said Rene.

'Have you told Wilf?'

'Oh, yes. Wilf doesn't mind. Wilf's a dog lover.'

'We've run into a bit of a problem getting rid of the empty tins,' said Cyril. 'If you put them in the waste-bin, he might go after them and cut his tongue. We've put them out of the window, on the sill, for now.'

'You know what he got for Christmas?'

'Who? Cyril?'

'No, the dog. We've given him a Womble. With a little hat and scarf.'

'He's got more toys than a real child, that dog,' said Cyril.

'He loves his Womble. He's got a teddy-bear, too, but we left that in Kettering.'

'What sort of dog is he?'

'Black labrador,' said Cyril. 'He's got a pedigree as long as your arm.'

'Doesn't he mind being cooped up in the room?'

'No,' said Cyril. 'A dog needs seventeen hours of sleep a day. That's a fact. Seventeen hours.'

'And he's got his Womble,' put in Rene.

Linda came in carrying Kafka's *The Trial*.

'Oh, she's a big reader too,' said Rene to her husband.

But Stanley and Hilda had arrived. Stanley was holding the flashest Scrabble set I've ever seen. He stared contemptuously at our books.

'*This*,' he said, tapping his Scrabble board, 'is the one what sorts out the intellects. That's where you really tell the sheep from the goats.'

He set it up on a nearby table, eyeing Linda and me as he did so. The board was built to spin on its axis, and each letter-rest had a cribbage scoring system along its top.

'Nice,' I said.

'£5.75,' said Stanley. 'Want a game, do you?'

We joined them. Linda drew a B and started the game. On the centre of the board, she laid down a G, an R and an E.

'Grease,' said Stanley.

She added another E and a D, and smirked.

Midway through the game, with Linda leading by 120 points, Stanley moved one of his cribbage pegs to credit himself with an extra 200.

'How did you get those, Stanley?' I asked.

'I been getting a lot of triple word scores.'

'Stanley!' said Hilda. 'You haven't. You know you haven't. He always cheats.'

'Perhaps I made a mistake.' Stanley moved his peg back 100 points. 'That about right?'

'A bit more, please, Stanley,' I said.

He moved it back a further ten.

At the end of the game Linda was way ahead, with words like PE-RIM-ETER and STUCCO ('That's not a proper *word*!' moaned Stanley) and FLAG-RANT. Stanley and I went up to the bar.

'Trouble with you is you take it too seriously,' said Stanley. 'It's only a game, you know.'

We were saved from a revenge match by the bell for lunch, a Christmas blow-out with crackers and paper hats. Everyone had brought their cameras into the dining room. We were bathed in the white light of expensive flash equipment. Agfas and Kodaks and Zeiss Ikons and Nikons clicked and whirred. There was hardly a mouthful of turkey during lunch that didn't go on record, to be later screened, or peered at through a plastic viewer, or stuck into an album. Elio and the girl students who were staffing the hotel over Christmas were dragged into the shots. Everybody photographed everybody else. Faces with their eyes tight shut, pulling crackers; posed, dignified faces, held in an immobile photogenic stare; and a few shy, sad faces, caught in the background and on the margins of every picture. I thought of all the strangers who would, in a week or two, be pointing at the blurred, averted face of Frances. 'Who's she?' 'Don't know. Don't remember her. Do you, dear?'

Gorged and flatulent with bird and Christmas pud, we were herded off to guess the weight of the Christmas cake. It looked heavy enough to drag your stomach down into your boots. I can't have been far out with my estimate of eleven stone six pounds. That too was photographed, with Brenda the Camp Guard behind, looking as if she had just given birth to it, her bright smile belied by some monstrous interior agony.

We went up to the television room to watch the Queen's speech. It was filled with rows of women, seated in lines as if they were in a cinema. When the Queen came on, the room became noisily and importantly silent, with lots of *shushes* and coughs and rustlings.

'She looks quite nice, this time, doesn't she?'

'Ssh!'

The Queen was standing in Buckingham Palace Gardens. The colour controls on the set had given her a tinge of frozen, corpselike blue. 'This is a time,' she said, 'when we are all gethered into small groups, and, for those who are lucky enough, into femily groups. This is the season when we are not jest faces in the creowd . . .' From the empty spaces of the royal gardens, the Queen addressed the camera as if it were a corgi that had just done something unpleasant on the lawn. Our own small family group gazed back at her with blank reverence. A knitting needle clicked against its mate. A distant stomach rumbled and was stilled. The Queen picked up a stone from the parapet of an ornamental bridge and dropped it into the wind-scudded water below. 'One small stone,' said the Queen, 'when dropped into a pool creates ripples which spread out.' Her scriptwriter had not allowed for the power of the December winds in SW1. There were waves and drifting scum, but no ripples. The Queen changed her metaphor. 'Grains of sand dropped on to a scale will eventually outweigh a lump of lead.' The heads around me nodded dully, outweighed by turkey and Christmas pudding. Their monarch droned genteelly on.

I tiptoed out and joined the men downstairs. Christmas afternoon is a reflective, melancholy time. The bar lounge was quiet, soft with a ripple of conversation which seemed as if it had spread from a stone dropped into someone's subconscious. They were talking about the war. 'Alex' and 'El Alamein' and 'Anzio' drifted like rags of foam on the surface of the talk.

'Best years of your life. Best years of mine, at any rate.'

'It was the comradeship . . .'

'Your mate in the war . . . he'd share his last fag with you.'

'What were you in, Jock?'

'52nd Argyll and Sutherland.'

'I was in the 50th Tees and Tyne.'

'Remember the Army Manual? Everything done by the book. If it said keep three yards apart, you kept three yards apart. When I was in France, there was a Canadian regiment there, and this platoon of Canadians had to cross a field. Well, they walked across this bloody field like they were on a Sunday stroll. Close? They could have been hand in hand. When they got to the other side, I don't suppose there was more than three of them left. In the war, you played by the rules and regs. If you didn't you were strawberry jam, eh, Jock?'

I think that everybody kept to himself the tacit recognition that his presence here this Christmas was an offence against the rule book – a measure of how far the world had fallen since the days of the Army Manual. The talk shifted in the wind, to memories of city streets in the '30s and '40s.

'Everybody's door was open. You could go in anywhere.'

'If the man was sick, the butcher would slip in an extra pound of mince on the wife's order. You could always count on a helping hand.'

'Well, families had to stick together then, didn't they?'

'No, the family today's not what it was.'

Beyond the window of the bar lounge, a crop of new multi-storey hotels rose like beanstalks among the sandy pines. Cyril stared at them dolefully.

'With these high-rises, they're creating a new breed of animal, aren't they?'

I saw Brenda the Camp Guard watching us through the glass door. She composed her face into an expression of dangerous bonhomie and marched in. 'You men!' she said. 'Ready for the games?'

Jock, who was on the hotel staff, shrank at her entrance. 'Has *he* been going on again?' she enquired of us.

'We were just talking about the war, Brenda,' said Cyril.

'War, war, war. *He* never talks about anything else. I don't know why you put up with it, I really don't.'

There was an odd feeling of general relief at Brenda's nagging. Left to yourself, without a woman to get at you, you never know where you might end up.

'I've spent three hours preparing the competitions,' said Brenda. 'Three hours. Say "Aah".' Everybody said 'Aah' politely. 'That's right,' said Brenda.

Brenda had stuck a lot of photographs cut out of magazines on to ragged sheets of hardboard. 'We'll start with the personalities, shall we?' said Brenda. 'It's very simple. Everybody get their pencil and paper. What we have to do . . . we have to write down the name that goes with the famous face. Got it?'

The bar lounge filled with televiewers and post-prandial nappers. Everybody got their pencil and paper ready, and dutifully filed past Brenda's shabby gallery of faces. Mantovani was there, so were Raquel Welch and Adolf Hitler. Mrs Mason studied the photograph of our current premier and put him down as Harold Winslow.

Then Brenda divided everyone into two teams, and organized a squad of furniture-movers to clear the floor. The two teams stood patiently in line while Brenda busied herself in her box of props and found two empty matchboxes. The teams passed them from nose to nose up and down the line. Team A beat Team B. (Brenda's imagination seemed to desert her when it came to names.) Then Brenda got out a milk bottle. 'This is going to be fun!' she threatened.

The milk bottle had to be gripped between your thighs and passed to the next person up the line without being touched by anyone's hand. There were shrieks and guffaws when Brenda demonstrated this familiar-looking action. Brenda smiled primly. Brenda was a Christian.

The two milk bottles went slowly, jerkily up and down the lines. Elderly women locked with men they'd barely known for one whole day in a ribald parody of copulation. Frances was half smothered by a Birmingham steve-dore with enormous buttocks: as the neck of the bottle penetrated a fold in her skirt, she laughed in a burst of hysterical squeaks. Her face had the same ambiguous cast of simultaneous terror and good humour as those of the apes in the Typhoo Tea ads.

My nerve broke and I fled. The Cliff Court, with its forced intimacies and its building steam pressure of stringent conformity, was becoming all too like a real family. For most people there, the holiday was proving an immense success. As the milk bottles clattered on to the floor from between people's legs, the bar lounge throbbed with delirious, happy laughter. For the moment, everybody was a child again, back in the warm, dirty, claustropho-bic bosom of a family. There was no place for me there. I'd started as an intruder with a secret purpose and a notebook; I was fast turning into a rebellious child. I'd had enough, and wanted out.

Leaving the hotel, I felt a truant. I slipped round the side, avoiding the picture window of the bar lounge. From the street, the Cliff Court sounded as if it was about to burst with all the brassy whoops and shrieks that were coming from inside. I climbed down the zig-zag path on the West Cliff to the almost empty promenade. It was getting dark. There were three jagged shreds of flame and peach on the horizon. I walked past the empty beach chalets and the blacked-out hulk of Happyland. A scattering of elderly couples were out under their umbrellas, and occasional loners, sunk in hats and coats, mooched on the sand.

By Bournemouth pier, a child and his father were flying a Batman kite under a streetlamp. I walked to the end of the deserted pier to watch the fierce sunset colours fade. It was several minutes before I realized that there was a man below me, hunched on a camp stool on the lower deck of the pier. He was as motionless and black as the heap of rope and iron a few yards further along the deck. The hairline of his outstretched fishing rod was hardly visible against the darkening sea. He must have been there all day. I wondered if he had a family to escape from. Or had he, perhaps, come here to commune moodily with the dabs and wrasse that skulked among the piles? When the fish are biting, you're always in touch with something. I envied him his Christmas. I would have liked to talk, but the rocklike set of his black oilskins was proof against conversation. He flicked his weighted bait out to sea, where it sank without a ripple.

Jonathan Raban, 'Christmas in Bournemouth'

Kitsch in Japan

In Japan, as elsewhere, Christmas comes with a cacophonous vengeance. Throughout December 'Jingle Bells' rings out subdued but clear in hotel lobbies, airport lounges, neighbourhood shopping streets, supermarkets, banks, coffee shops, 24-hour convenience stores – in fact anywhere people go during the last heady weeks of December as they prepare to say farewell to one year and to greet another. Planted firmly in the middle of the year-end *oseibo* gift giving 'season' and just before the few days' respite from work that the Japanese traditionally enjoy over the first days of the New Year, Christmas has its own special place now in the cycle of seasonal events that constitutes Japan's domestic consumer economy.

So, while Japanese pop groups sing '*Merī Kurisumasu*' to one and all, store announcements inform us that Christmas is near and that 'Santa Claus is very busy so get your orders in early'. This busyness is partly to do with the way in which Santa finds himself suddenly obliged to decorate streets, shops, and advertisements all over the country. But this physical splitting of his personality is taken further when it comes to naming the red-suited gift-bearer. As 'Saint Nicholas' – the way in which he is toasted in a French Restaurant in Harajuku – he is still recognizable; as 'Uncle Chimney' in a Ginza department store, he is somewhat less so. A few years ago, he was even found in a nativity scene in another Ginza department store, where he was acting as stand-in model for the newborn Christ. Such transformations of Santa's persona continue apace. This year he takes to the streets as Colonel Sanders outside Kentucky Fried Chicken stores, and even appears disguised as a woman shop assistant in a local bakery.

Christmas, of course, means gifts – of snowman pyjamas, Yves Saint Laurent's heart-shaped compacts, chunky hand-knit sweaters, bottles of *rosé* champagne, strawberry topped cakes, and 'friendly pants' (*nakayoshi pants*). It is the time to buy toy purring cats, singing birds, and 'flower rock' swaying plastic flowers for your friends. But Christmas is also more than just gifts. In Japan, it is an expensive dinner for two on a yacht that cruises around Tokyo Bay, a night out at a luxury hotel lining the Yokohama waterfront, a skiing holiday on candlelit slopes in the Japan Alps. It is also a young lady in blue satin dress who sits down at a grand piano on the third floor of Mitsukoshi Department Store and from time to time trills out a somewhat classical version of numerous well-known carols. It is the music playing in neighbouring Takashimaya's sales pitch for an 'oseibo symphony', in a bank advertisement's 'Bonus carol echoes', and in the ubiquitous phrase 'silent night' (*seiya*) found in both English and Japanese in advertising of all shapes and sizes.

As this hodge-podge of activities suggests, 'silent night' is a far cry from the kind of 'family Christmas' with which the tune is associated in the West. Also referred to by the English word 'eve', silent night conjures up a wide enough range of associations to make the proverbial rabbits on the moon prick up their ears in astonishment. It is true that one English company maintains the family image of Christmas with 'Mother's reminiscences and Wedgwood – Everyone comes back here on Christmas Eve', but for the most part Christmas Eve in advertising takes on different connotations. 'Classic chocolate for silent night' reads the caption to a visual of candles, holly, two cups of coffee, a silver jug and sugar pot, and porcelain statue of Mozart. Two glasses of champagne, red berries on a wreath, and an open box of chocolates (with half a dozen more on a china plate) are all encapsulated by 'Silent night's sweet message for him'. ' "I love you" comes back to life on December 24th' promises a close-up black and white photograph of a boy and girl kissing passionately, with their names – Garray and Vivian – hand-written inside a pink heart across their bodies. 'A night to wear kisses . . .' claim another couple locked in their 'private session' embrace. 'The satisfaction of (Christmas) Eve', smiles a blonde girl who sits demurely on a red suitcase beside three bottles of champagne and some empty wine glasses, with a large axe slung over one shoulder. 'Dreams dance in the forest of the silent night' features Santa Claus astride a reindeer, a wolf standing on its hind legs chewing at a decorated fir tree, and a girl who has tumbled over to the ground, upsetting a basket of fruit and stars.

This strange mixture of fairy-tale elements is echoed in 'Become beautiful, Cinderella Christmas', in which a Japanese girl in gold lamé strapless swimsuit with a coronet on her head, and holding a large gold starred wand, stands at the bottom of a spiralling red-carpeted staircase leading into illuminated spires and castle-like buildings. Is this the 'Urban ecstasy' referred to by a fashion house, or merely an echo of Tokyo Disneyland's 'Christmas fantasy'? A child angel standing on a red rose answers: ' "Oh! My God" God Save the Christmas'.

Brian Moeran and Lise Skov, 'Cinderella Christmas:
Kitsch, Consumerism and Youth in Japan'

All Lit Up

Why is Arkansas millionaire Jennings Osborne so obsessed with celebrating Christmas his way that he'll go to the Supreme Court to defend it?

Probably no child in America looks forward to Christmas with more unbridled passion than William Jennings Bryan Osborne, Jr, a fifty-one-year-old reclusive multimillionaire from Little Rock. Certainly no child in America has as much wherewithal to celebrate that passion. As the owner of the Arkansas Research Medical Testing Center (ARMTC) – a firm that tests new drugs on human beings – Osborne has reaped millions from some of the country's largest pharmaceutical companies. It's a secretive business, and Osborne is a secretive man. He builds walls, literally and figuratively, around himself. But at Christmastime he goes as public as he's ever likely to let himself go. He gives lavish gifts – furs, cars, jewelry – to his family. Until recently, he sent 'fruit baskets', each containing a whole turkey *and* a whole ham, to neighbors he hardly knew. He buys cases of Montblanc pens to pass out to others, especially journalists, who happen to cross his path during this festive season. For Osborne, Christmas is a time of memories, dreams, and excess – three words that go a long way toward defining the man himself.

He would add the word 'giving', and it's true that he gives more than generously to existing charities, needy individuals, and community causes, and does so throughout the year. There is one wrinkle, however: Jennings Osborne has a skewed sense of proportion. He has been quoted as saying, 'If I see something that someone else has that I want, I'm going to want something twice as big.' For example, he lives in a twenty-two-thousand-square-foot house, in West Little Rock, that is surrounded by a wall whose height exceeds the city's current code. He owns more than thirty cars. His fondness for the large-scale infects his gift-giving – sometimes happily, sometimes not. When he takes guests out to eat, he orders six or eight entrées. Recently, he provided dinner at every rehearsal for a group of local lawyers who were at Little Rock's Arkansas Repertory Theater practicing for a biennial spoof of life and politics in Arkansas. On opening night, Osborne sent dinner not just for the cast but for the audience – complete with Dom Pérignon champagne. 'I don't want anybody to be disappointed in anything I do, so you have to keep doing it bigger and better,' he says.

It's this kind of thinking, paired with his love of Christmas, that has ignited a blast of bad feelings in Osborne's neighborhood. The problem has to do with what Osborne considers his 'gift' to the people of Arkansas – a spectacular Christmas-light display. For the past eight holiday seasons, he has progressively, lovingly, obsessively added to the Christmas lights at his family mansion. Finally, last year, the neighbors could stand it no longer. They risked Grinchdom to sue him.

The simple words 'Christmas lights' may be somewhat misleading in this instance. Let me quote from the actual court document. Filing suit in May of 1993, the plaintiffs stated:

The lighted display bedecks the trees and almost every inch of available space on the imposing wall surrounding the Osborne home and the home itself. Strands of lights are also strewn between the structures and the wall to form a canopy. They are raised high into the sky on large metal, shaped sculptures.

In 1990, the display utilized an estimated 800,000 red lights alone; in 1991 1.2 million; and in 1992 approximately 1.6 million.

Features incorporated into the 1992 display included: i. four Christmas-tree-shaped masts, two atop the house, towering at least eighty feet in the air and adorned by massive stars; ii. a three-dimensional world globe, thirty feet in diameter, suspended one-hundred feet in the air with flashing multicolored lights; iii. a calliope (once used in the annual Rose Bowl Parade) tooting repeatedly automated musical tracks; iv. a rotating carousel, twelve feet in diameter suspended at least twenty feet in the air; v. a depiction of a steam engine and three train cars driven atop the west walls by Mickey Mouse; vi. three wise men, three camels, Santa, his sleigh and nine reindeer positioned elsewhere atop the walls; and; vii. a message, suspended overhead approximately fifty feet above ground, Merry Christmas, Happy New Year in letters six feet high.

The plaintiffs claimed that the Osborne display was a public and private nuisance, because it attracts thousands of sightseers, who crawl by in their cars, jamming traffic and blocking the right-of-way not only for the Osbornes' neighbours – who, at the height of the evening, have been forced to spend as much as an hour and a half to fetch a few forgotten items at the grocery store – but for any emergency vehicles that might be needed during that time. 'Everybody has a right to have Christmas lights,' Arleta Power, the spokesperson for the plaintiffs, says. 'It's just a question of how far you go.'

When the case went to trial, in November of 1993, the Osbornes contended that any attempt to block or curtail their light display was a violation of their right of free speech and an affront to their freedom of religion. Jennings is a fallen-away Baptist, who admitted in court that he hadn't been to a Baptist church since 1965. Still, Christmas is Jesus' birthday, and this is the way he chooses to celebrate it.

After a week of tumultuous testimony, Judge Ellen Brantley, of the Pulaski County Chancery Court, found that indeed the spectacle was a nuisance.

And then, restricting Osborne's hours and requiring him to hire security guards, she let him go on with the 1993 light display anyway.

Neither side was happy with this ruling. Osborne responded by doubling his display to three million lights, stretched across his house and the houses on either side, which he had bought without ever having entered them. One pilot reports having seen the glow from Russellville, eighty miles away. But while cars crept and the mothers of wide-eyed children wept – one told Osborne, 'This is the closest to Disney World my little girl will ever get' – both sides knew the battle had just begun. Osborne appealed to the Arkansas Supreme Court. As the Justices wrestled with the legalities, a tantalizing, though nonlegal, question was certain to be hovering over the proceedings: What sort of man wants to put three million Christmas lights on his house anyway?

'I'm a nut,' Osborne says, with the calculated charm of someone who has spent years cultivating his image as an enigma. It's a game he plays, a kind of hide-and-seek. He builds walls around himself – and yet he makes them so ostentatious that no one can help wondering about the man inside. In some respects, he's an odd fit in the role that some people have tried to cast him in – that of Santa Claus. He does have the girth, having ballooned in weight after he quit smoking, around five years ago. But he's too ironic, too inwardly focused, to convince as jolly St Nick: he's Santa as cast by Alfred Hitchcock. His hair style is what you imagine Elvis might wear if he were alive today – thinning but long, one length all over, set off by white sideburns. Though Osborne's family and co-workers say he has a sense of humor that reminds them of George Carlin's, there's an instinctive wariness about him. In photographs of the Osborne family posed before the Christmas lights, Mitzi and Breezy, Osborne's wife and daughter, are inevitably smiling; Jennings stands there poker-faced, looking at the camera through veiled eyes . . .

Mitzi, a handsome, statuesque woman, has been married to Jennings for thirty years. And yet when she is questioned about her husband's visions – especially those concerning the Christmas lights – she responds with a laugh that has the hollow tone of wonder, of bafflement. Clearly, the lights mean more to him than they do to her. She confirms that they spring from his mind in full flower, complete with bright colors and deep dimension. It all began in 1986, when Breezy, then six, asked if they could have a few lights on their house at Christmas. Jennings agreed, and one thing led to another. He has claimed ever since that the Christmas lights are for his daughter. 'I'm just making memories for Breezy,' Osborne explains, his eyes opaque . . .

The Osbornes say they have few friends. At night, Mitzi and Breezy roam around the twenty-two-thousand-square-foot vision of a house, with its tennis court, its swimming pools, its game rooms, its big-screen TVs. Jennings spends most nights at the office. The room that Jennings stays in is small and cluttered, and has a sink but no bathroom or closet. He hangs his clothes on racks just outside the door, below a crumbling ceiling tile. He sleeps in a twin-size bed, which is unmade – a childhood rule broken. The room's other furnishings include two phones, a lamp, a chair with a reindeer-hide throw, and a loveseat with a signed Roy Rogers pillow. There is a television set. And there are four ventriloquist's dummies. One sits on the loveseat, next to the Roy Rogers pillow.

James Morgan

Christmas

Choose the baby's cocktail,
To drink in an eartrumpet.
Deprivation angers; at least
Rejoice in his captivity.

Give Maurice lemons.
He's broken the pottery,
Arses around the attic,
Gorging biscuits and olives.

This is a happy family.
Come, sing of the harbour,
Nights guzzling bouillabaisse.
We'll syringe to the next flat,
Make another party.

Harold Pinter

Yule be Sorry . . .

Every now and then, a woman meets a man and thinks: 'What the Hell?' A few hours later, she thinks: 'Where am I?'

It goes like this. A woman is at a party. She is bored witless. She has run out of her preferred brand of cigarettes. The friend she came with has run into some other friends.

This woman has had a few drinks just to pass the time.

The next day, she *can* remember mooching a Camel Light from someone. She *cannot* remember how it was that, about four and a half minutes later, she was in an unfamiliar bedroom, with an unfamiliar man, on an unfamiliar bed with a lot of unfamiliar coats on it.

Women's 'Where am I?' stories generally involve the following:

Alcohol

Somebody's boss

Somebody else's husband

A mini cab

Christmas. Christmas is a constant.

The key characters in Christmas 'Where am I?' stories tend to keep shtum till well into the New Year and the year after that. It's up to the friend, the cab driver and everybody who went to get their coats to make sure that the beans get spilled.

Christmas has a curious magnifying effect on everything. By the time a Christmas-in-the-coats scenario has done the rounds, there is always a photocopier involved.

Ribald tales of mischief among the mince-pies are so rife, a woman might surmise that the key to Yuletide survival would be one fitted to a chastity belt. But, when pressed on the perils of mistletoe month, most women don't mention gruesome gropes with married blokes from marketing. Most women talk thighs in terms of size. *Weight* is what they worry about. 'I've got to go to some dinner thing again tonight . . . I just don't want to EAT any more.'

It's all crisps and crunchy crab cakes and chocolates with cream centres from the 15th until the first. It's compulsive, they complain. It's repulsive, and relentless, and murder on their middles. The thing is, they say, they're helpless to resist 'cause they're already chock-full of champagne by the time the canapés come their way.

That's the real trouble with this time of year, moans another, with a groan, the morning-afters, the headaches . . . the hangovers (no mention of men). Copious quantities of plonk quaffed at lunch, and again at supper time, add to the evil effects of the food frenzy. They look lousy in the a.m. They feel lousy too. They feel even more lousy when they crawl out of bed, 20 minutes late, and discover they've got Nothing to wear.

'What to Wear' . . . now we're talking real women's woes. (Still not a whisper re coat-room cavorts.) Christmas – crisis and consternation in the wardrobe department.

'I *can't* wear that red jacket again. I wore it to EVERYTHING last year.'

The woman with a What to Wear crisis doesn't usually suffer alone. She calls a friend. As it happens, this friend is having a What to Wear crisis as well. They decide to sort this situation via a spot of shopping.

They meet and do a bit of a trawl for a satiny-pant-suit type job which would be just the thing for straight-from-work functions. Much later, exhausted from the push and shove and general pell-mell in the shops, they stop for a cup of coffee. There's a queue.

'It's hell,' they say, 'trying to get anything done in December.'

The women sit down, at last. They hook bags of clobber over the backs of their chairs. The *crowds*, they complain. Christmas Shoppers . . .

Christmas shopping, there's a right Noel Nasty for you. Why us, women bleat, why are we supposed to remember the size of *his* mother's feet? It's just no Fun, John Lewis, with a list. (Have I missed the bawdy bit about the boss?) It's really the pits, having to figure out which one your god-daughter will fit. And the *lines*, the whines reaching fever pitch now. 'Oh,' women sigh, 'the shopping's the bit I hate the Most.' And it's so Expensive.

Money, you see, most women will say, that's what it all boils down to. Christmas just costs toooo much. THAT'S the worst thing. (As opposed to getting caught in a cupboard with the wrong sort of chap.)

The presents, of course, are the problem. Anybody knows that a satiny-pant-suit type job is a useful year-round thing for straight-from-work functions. Also, a lipstick that lasts all night, and some kind of cream that reduces eye-luggage to mere wrinkles is a must-have. The sticky stuff for over-stressed tresses may have been an extravagance but actually, it was Aunty's pot-holders that tipped the scales and necessitated the overdraft facility.

'It's ALL so draining.' The drinking, and the Dos, and the dressing up, and the going out, and the worrying about wearing red and whether your arms are too white to leave bare at night, and the presents, and the food . . . you're TIRED All The Time.

'It's the lack of sleep that does me in.' (No hints with regard to tarts or parts you shouldn't reach for.)

It comes round so quick and passes so fast. There's Never enough *time*, what with all the above, for frosting pears and painting little deer on cakes. And as for wrapping, *who* finds brown paper and paints their own? There's this pressure to be perfect and all Homes and Gardens.

'*That's* what gets to me,' says she with three kids and a cottage in the Cotswolds. (Not a care about getting her gear off with the gardener, under the influence of home-made mead.)

Sometimes a weary woman, who's had it with December, meets a chum for a quiet evening. They have a right old whinge and whine about their weight and the state of their bank balances. Then they get to the Real Christmas contentious issues. Families. Their moans are myriad. They range from 'They treat me like a child' to 'She treats my child like *she* were her mother'. Relating to relations is the thing they *dread*. A lot more is said. (Nothing about flirts, or hands up skirts.)

December, it seems, can be dicey. Christmas plagued with problems. But bonking doesn't feature on the list of laments. Not a woman, not a girl, worries that she'll be the One they're all making fun of, in the office in January. 'I *swear*, I only went in to get my coat . . .'

So here's a solution to your end of year woes. Simple, slimming and free. A complexion-clearing plan with No Dress Required. Only the Best sort of relations involved.

On December the 15th, all wise women ought to:

(1) Grab themselves a man and drag him into the coats.
(2) Keep him there until the 1st.

(Afterwards, these women should tell the story themselves, remembering to add a photocopier, two mince-pies and a Santa Suit.)

Deborah McKinlay

Hausfrauenchor

'She's younger than I am, almost certainly
blonde, and he sleeps with her once a year . . .
The occasion is the office-party – alcohol,
music, and their formal routine collaboration
suddenly becomes something else. – All over
the country, wives write to the agony columns
for advice. One letter covers thousands
of cases. Of course, you want to allow him
his bit of fun; after working all year for
Germany's *Wirtschaftswunder* and your own.
And it's probably more than you can provide
with your cooking, your meat-and-two-veg sex,
the occasional *Sauerbraten* . . . He deserves it.
The rest of the time, he's faithful to you.
But when he comes home at some godforsaken hour,
lipstuck and dishevelled, drunk as a god, his

dried sperm crackling and flaking in his pants,
then you feel differently about it. You wish
you'd gone to the party and kept an eye on him.
- But then the newspapers don't recommend that:
husbands resent it – what's your business
in an office where you never set foot otherwise?
They tell you the only course is to declare
a general amnesty for this particular offence.
A mass-exemption, like the students of '68,
who no longer have a 'past', and instead hold
positions in the Civil Service: vetting radicals;
checking over photographs of demonstrations,
signatories on petitions; looking for traces
of the ineradicable red paint that is sprayed
over crowds of Communists to identify them . . .
So the best way is to kill them with kindness.
- And it isn't any easier for the secretary:
because she doesn't want to be a cock-teaser,
she gets into trouble with her boyfriend . . .
A week or two later, she gives my husband a tie
for Christmas. The whole family (himself
included) make fun of it, a silly pattern,
awful colours, what a useless garment anyway . . .
But then he wears it all the following year.'

Michael Hofmann

Christmas Triolet

FOR GAVIN EWART

It's Christmas, season of wild bells
And merry carols. On the floor
Are gifts in pretty paper shells.
It's Christmas, season of wild Belle's
Big party. George's stomach swells
With ale; his wife's had even more.
It's Christmas, season of wild belles,
And merry Carol's on the floor.

Wendy Cope

[71]

Adultery

Another horror is not being able to spend Christmas with your lover because he or she is married to someone else. One sees all those couples embracing frantically in telephone booths near Simpson's of Piccadilly, or sobbing drunkenly on each other's necks outside Fortnum's.

'Only nine days till 2 January, Noël darling,' cries Ms Stress: 'You'd better hang on to the bracelet, darling. Gordon's bound to suspect something if I take it home. Promise to ring on Christmas Day: if Gordon's in the room, I'll pretend you're a wrong number.'

Then Ms Stress vanishes into a taxi, and is embarrassingly only five yards away an hour later because the traffic's so frightful.

'There is no doubt,' admitted one girlfriend, 'that my adulterous Christmases were the worst in my whole life, because I was single and he was going back to his wife. Christmas Eve was spent plodding from one West End shop to another, tears pouring down my face, as "Oh Come All Ye Faithful" pealed out over Oxford Street.'

'The unhappiness and sense of rejection of those Christmases when I was divorced,' wrote another woman friend, 'is something I would never wish to live through again.'

'The very mention of "Christmas" would plunge me into despair. I had fallen passionately in love with a married man, which made things even worse. I remember so vividly those nights sitting at home alone knowing that my lover, and, as I thought, the whole world and his wife, were out at pre-Christmas parties. The brooding, pining and imagining would get out of all proportion.

'I sat over the telephone willing it to ring, and when it didn't, I'd go and have a bath, and if it still didn't, I'd have another, then it would ring and, mad with excitement, I'd rush to answer it; only to find it was a girlfriend, who'd been at the same party as my lover, and kindly thought I'd like to know he was fine, a bit drunk but in dazzling form. That was all I needed. How could he? Back to the bath, not only to drown my sorrows but wanting to drown myself.'

As well as loneliness, adultery at Christmas is fraught with hazards because lovers, primed by drink and a feeling that the world is going to end anyway, get much more reckless than usual. One barrister I know was having a Christmas Eve bunk-up with his mistress in his flat in Belgravia, when the front door opened and in marched his mother-in-law, who'd been sent a spare key to deliver the Christmas presents.

Another friend was driving down to the country cottage together with his wife and children and a boot crammed with Christmas Fayre, when the mistress, drunk from the office party, rang up on the car telephone and her tearfully amorous declaration was heard by all.

If a lover gets desperate and rings home at a sticky moment, it is far too lame an excuse to pretend that he's a wrong number. Say it's an obscene telephone call, let it run for five seconds and then slam down the telephone; the disgusting things the caller is alleged to have said should explain your blushes.

Husbands who don't want to get rumbled shouldn't leave Christmas present bills lying around. Scarlett thinks it very odd that a Janet Reger négligé Noël bought for her appears to have got lost in the post. It also seems odd that Noël, having allegedly spent six hours at the office party, returns home at midnight perfectly sober.

Noël, on the other hand, should watch out, if Scarlett suddenly starts buying pink, six-foot, fluffy teddy bears allegedly for herself just before Christmas, or a Janet Reger négligé because she thought it suited her, or, even more sinister, a yearning pop record, on the excuse that she heard it on Radio One and liked the words. Equally, if Scarlett keeps running round the corner to visit some boring girlfriend, she's either using the boring friend's telephone, picking up letters, or admiring the dozen red roses, or the parrot that's being looked after for her. If she suddenly starts looking wonderful over Christmas, and doesn't put on at least seven pounds misery-eating – the marriage is in trouble.

Jilly Cooper, *How to Survive Christmas*

❦ 4 ❧

ORIGINS: PAGAN ROOTS,
CHRISTIAN TREE

The Nativity of the Sun

In the Julian calendar the twenty-fifth of December was reckoned the winter solstice, and it was regarded as the Nativity of the Sun, because the day begins to lengthen and the power of the sun to increase from that turning-point of the year. The ritual of the nativity, as it appears to have been celebrated in Syria and Egypt, was remarkable. The celebrants retired into certain inner shrines, from which at midnight they issued with a loud cry, 'The Virgin has brought forth! The light is waxing!' The Egyptians even represented the newborn sun by the image of an infant which on his birthday, the winter solstice, they brought forth and exhibited to his worshippers. No doubt the Virgin who thus conceived and bore a son on the twenty-fifth of December was the great Oriental goddess whom the Semites called the Heavenly Virgin or simply the Heavenly Goddess; in Semitic lands she was a form of Astarte. Now Mithra was regularly identified by his worshippers with the Sun, the Unconquered Sun, as they called him; hence his nativity also fell on the twenty-fifth of December. The Gospels say nothing as to the day of Christ's birth, and accordingly the early Church did not celebrate it. In time, however, the Christians of Egypt came to regard the sixth of January as the date of the Nativity, and the custom of commemorating the birth of the Saviour on that day gradually spread until by the fourth century it was universally established in the East. But at the end of the third or the beginning of the fourth century the Western Church, which had never recognized the sixth of January as the day of the Nativity, adopted the twenty-fifth of December as the true date, and in time its decision was accepted also by the Eastern Church. At Antioch the change was not introduced till about the year 375 AD.

What considerations led the ecclesiastical authorities to institute the festival of Christmas? The motives for the innovation are stated with great frankness by a Syrian writer, himself a Christian. 'The reason,' he tells us, 'why the fathers transferred the celebration of the sixth of January to the

twenty-fifth of December was this. It was a custom of the heathen to celebrate on the same twenty-fifth of December the birthday of the Sun, at
which they kindled lights in token of festivity. In these solemnities and
festivities the Christians also took part. Accordingly when the doctors of the
Church perceived that the Christians had a leaning to this festival, they took
counsel and resolved that the true Nativity should be solemnized on that day
and the festival of the Epiphany on the sixth of January. Accordingly, along
with this custom, the practice has prevailed of kindling fires till the sixth.'
The heathen origin of Christmas is plainly hinted at, if not tacitly admitted,
by Augustine when he exhorts his Christian brethren not to celebrate that
solemn day like the heathen on account of the sun, but on account of him
who made the sun. In like manner Leo the Great rebuked the pestilent belief
that Christmas was solemnized because of the birth of the new sun, as it was
called, and not because of the nativity of Christ.

Thus it appears that the Christian Church chose to celebrate the birthday
of its Founder on the twenty-fifty of December in order to transfer the
devotion of the heathen from the Sun to him who was called the Sun of
Righteousness.

Sir James George Frazer, The Golden Bough

The Yule Log

If the heathen of ancient Europe celebrated, as we have good reason to
believe, the season of Midsummer with a great festival of fire, of which the
traces have survived in many places down to our own time, it is natural to
suppose that they should have observed with similar rites the corresponding
season of Midwinter; for Midsummer and Midwinter, or, in more technical
language, the summer solstice and the winter solstice, are the two great
turning-points in the sun's apparent course through the sky, and from the
standpoint of primitive man nothing might seem more appropriate than to
kindle fires on earth at the two moments when the fire and heat of the great
luminary in heaven begin to wane or to wax.

In modern Christendom the ancient fire-festival of the winter solstice
appears to survive, or to have survived down to recent years, in the old
custom of the Yule log, clog, or block, as it was variously called in England.
The custom was widespread in Europe, but seems to have flourished
especially in England, France, and among the South Slavs; at least the fullest
accounts of the custom come from these quarters. That the Yule log was only

the winter counterpart of the midsummer bonfire, kindled within doors instead of in the open air on account of the cold and inclement weather of the season, was pointed out long ago by our English antiquary John Brand; and the view is supported by the many quaint superstitions attaching to the Yule log, superstitions which have no apparent connection with Christianity but carry their heathen origin plainly stamped upon them. But while the two solstitial celebrations were both festivals of fire, the necessity or desirability of holding the winter celebration within doors lent it the character of a private or domestic festivity, which contrasts strongly with the publicity of the summer celebration, at which the people gathered on some open space or conspicuous height, kindled a huge bonfire in common, and danced and made merry round it together.

Down to about the middle of the nineteenth century the old rite of the Yule log was kept up in some parts of Central Germany. Thus in the valleys of the Sieg and Lahn the Yule log, a heavy block of oak, was fitted into the floor of the hearth, where, though it glowed under the fire, it was hardly reduced to ashes within a year. When the new log was laid next year, the remains of the old one were ground to powder and strewed over the fields during the Twelve Nights, which was supposed to promote the growth of the crops. In some villages of Westphalia the practice was to withdraw the Yule log (*Christbrand*) from the fire so soon as it was slightly charred; it was then kept carefully to be replaced on the fire whenever a thunderstorm broke, because the people believed that lightning would not strike a house in which the Yule log was smouldering. In other villages of Westphalia the old custom was to tie up the Yule log in the last sheaf cut at harvest.

In several provinces of France, and particularly in Provence, the custom of the Yule log or *tréfoir*, as it was called in many places, was long observed. A French writer of the seventeenth century denounces as superstitious 'the belief that a log called the *tréfoir* or Christmas brand, which you put on the fire for the first time on Christmas Eve and continue to put on the fire for a little while every day till Twelfth Night, can, if kept under the bed, protect the house for a whole year from fire and thunder; that it can prevent the inmates from having chilblains on their heels in winter; that it can cure the cattle of many maladies; that if a piece of it be steeped in the water which cows drink it helps them to calve; and lastly that if the ashes of the log be strewn on the fields it can save the wheat from mildew.'

In some parts of Flanders and France the remains of the Yule log were regularly kept in the house under a bed as a protection against thunder and lightning; in Berry, when thunder was heard, a member of the family used to take a piece of the log and throw it on the fire, which was believed to avert the lightning. Again, in Perigord, the charcoal and ashes are carefully collected and kept for healing swollen glands; the part of the trunk which has not been burnt in the fire is used by ploughmen to make the wedge for their plough, because they allege that it causes the seeds to thrive better; and the women keep pieces of it till Twelfth Night for the sake of their chickens. Some people imagine that they will have as many chickens as there are sparks that fly out of the brands of the log when they shake them; and others place the extinct brands under the bed to drive away vermin. In various parts of France the charred log is thought to guard the house against sorcery as well as against lightning.

In England the customs and beliefs concerning the Yule log used to be similar. On the night of Christmas Eve, says the antiquary John Brand, 'our ancestors were wont to light up candles of an uncommon size, called Christmas Candles, and lay a log of wood upon the fire, called a Yule-clog or Christmas-block, to illuminate the house, and, as it were, to turn night into day'. The old custom was to light the Yule log with a fragment of its predecessor, which had been kept throughout the year for the purpose; where it was so kept, the fiend could do no mischief. The remains of the log were also supposed to guard the house against fire and lightning.

To this day the ritual of bringing in the Yule log is observed with much solemnity among the Southern Slavs, especially the Serbians. The log is usually a block of oak, but sometimes of olive or beech. They seem to think that they will have as many calves, lambs, pigs, and kids as they strike sparks out of the burning log. Some people carry a piece of the log out to the fields to protect them against hail. In Albania down to recent years it was a common custom to burn a Yule log at Christmas, and the ashes of the fire were scattered on the fields to make them fertile. The Huzuls, a Slavonic people of the Carpathians, kindle fire by the friction of wood on Christmas Eve (Old Style, the fifth of January) and keep it burning till Twelfth Night.

It is remarkable how common the belief appears to have been that the remains of the Yule log, if kept throughout the year, had power to protect the house against fire and especially against lightning. As the Yule log was frequently of oak, it seems possible that this belief may be a relic of the old Aryan creed which associated the oak-tree with the god of thunder. Whether the curative and fertilizing virtues ascribed to the ashes of the Yule log, which are supposed to heal cattle as well as men, to enable cows to calve, and to promote the fruitfulness of the earth, may not be derived from the same ancient source, is a question which deserves to be considered.

Sir James George Frazer, *The Golden Bough*

Christmas and the Professors

There is one very vile habit that the pedants have, and that is explaining to a
man why he does a thing which the man himself can explain quite well – and
quite differently. If I go down on all-fours to find sixpence, it annoys me to be
told by a passing biologist that I am really doing it because my remote
ancestors were quadrupeds. I concede that he knows all about biology, or
even a great deal about my ancestors; but I know he is wrong, because he
does not know about the sixpence. If I climb a tree after a stray cat, I am
unconvinced when a stray anthropologist tells me that I am doing it because I
am essentially arboreal and barbaric. I happen to know why I am doing it; and
I know it is because I am amiable and somewhat over-civilized. Scientists will
talk to a man on general guesswork about things that they know no more
about than about his pocket-money or his pet cat. Religion is one of them,
and all the festivals and formalities that are rooted in religion. Thus a man
will tell me that in keeping Christmas I am not keeping a Christian feast, but
a pagan feast. This is exactly as if he told me that I was not feeling furiously
angry, but only a little sad. I know how I am feeling all right; and why I am
feeling it. I know this in the case of cats, sixpences, anger, and Christmas Day.
When a learned man tells me that on the 25th of December I am really
astronomically worshipping the sun, I answer that I am not. I am practising a
particular personal religion, the pleasures of which (right or wrong) are not
in the least astronomical. If he says that the cult of Christmas and the cult of
Apollo are the same, I answer that they are utterly different; and I ought to
know, for I have held both of them. I believed in Apollo when I was quite
little; and I believe in Christmas now that I am very, very big.

Let us not take with such smooth surrender these tenth-truths at tenth
hand, such as the phrase that Christmas is pagan in origin. Let us note
exactly how much it really means. It amounts, so far as our knowledge goes,
solely to this – that primitive Scandinavians did hold a feast in midwinter.
What the dickens else could primitive Scandinavians do, especially in winter?
That they put on the largest log in winter: do the professors expect such
simple pagans to put on the largest log in summer? It amounts to this, again –
that many tribes have either worshipped the sun or (more probably) compared some god or hero to the sun. Just so many a poet has compared his lady
to the sun – without by any means intending that she was a Solar Myth.
Thus, by talking a great deal about the solar solstice, it can be maintained
that Christmas is a sort of sun-worship; to all of which the simple answer

is that it feels quite different. If people profess to feel 'the spirit' behind symbols, the first thing I expect of them is that they shall feel how opposite are the adoration of the sun and the following of the star.

G. K. Chesterton

Mistletoe

The official Christian legend is a charming fiction, invented to bring the plant under the general umbrella of 'pious folklore'. The story is told that originally there were huge mistletoe trees, from one of which Christ's cross was fashioned. After the crucifixion, all the other mistletoe trees shrank with shame and had to live out their lives as tiny parasites growing on other trees. Therefore, by bringing a sprig of mistletoe into our houses at Christmastime we are, in effect, putting up a symbolic crucifix in honour of Jesus Christ.

This was a clever take-over bid for the Christmas rights to mistletoe, but there are rival claims to be considered. To the ancient Druids, mistletoe was also a sacred plant, especially when it was found growing on their most revered tree, the oak. This was a rare event, because the oak is not a typical host. Mistletoe is most commonly found on apple trees. So when the combination of oak and mistletoe was discovered it was an occasion for a special ceremony. An elaborate sacrificial ritual was carried out:

Two white bulls were brought to the place where the mistletoe had been found growing on the oak. One Druid, dressed in a white robe, climbed the tree carrying a golden sickle. While others held a white cloth below to catch the sacred plant, he cut the mistletoe ceremonially from the oak. It was essential that the mistletoe was not cut with iron and that it should never touch the ground, or it would lose its magical powers. The two bulls were then sacrificed, a special feast was prepared, and a potion was made from the mistletoe, to be used as a cure for poisoning and, above all, to ensure the fertility of animals. A sprig of the oak-mistletoe was also carried by women to increase their chances of becoming pregnant.

Among its many supposed magical powers, mistletoe was said to protect against sorcery and witchcraft. A sprig of the plant hung in a house would be sufficient to keep away evil spirits. This has been used as an explanation for the special pagan connection between mistletoe and the midwinter festivals that were later to become known as Christmas. These were periods of great celebration, and it was believed that cheerful events of this kind were precisely the occasions that attracted the Evil Eye and the powers of darkness.

So it was natural to hang up protective devices at just these times. There is, however, no reliable evidence that this connection was ever made, except in the imaginations of students of folklore.

A simpler, if less dramatic, explanation is that mistletoe was just another plant, like holly, ivy and laurel, that remained green at Christmastime and was therefore suitable as one more form of indoor decoration. Greenery of various kinds had been used since long before the birth of Christ to provide a temporary home for the 'vegetation spirits' that required a safe haven during the harsh days of midwinter. In earlier centuries people were apparently not too fussy about which particular plants were employed in this way. According to one early writer on the subject, they used 'whatsoever the season of the year afforded to be green'.

Despite the pagan associations of mistletoe, the British custom of kissing underneath it seems to be purely Christian. It appears to have begun in the following way:

Back in fourteenth-century Britain, it was traditional at Christmastime to hang a small effigy of the Holy Family just inside the door of the house. This little model was put on a small platform and the platform itself was placed inside a wooden hoop. The hoop was decorated with greenery. Anything that remained green at Christmastime would do – holly, ivy, or mistletoe. The precise plants used had no special significance at this early stage. All that mattered initially was that they looked fresh and alive in the dead of winter.

This display of the Holy Family was called a Holy Bough and at Christmas the local priest travelled around his parish and blessed each one. Any person visiting a house during the Christmas period had to be embraced as they crossed the threshold. This was done to demonstrate that, in the holy season, everyone was loved in a Christian way. Performing the embrace beneath the model of the Holy Family made the act more sacred.

As time passed, the use of effigies was frowned upon as idolatrous, and the little model of the Holy Family had to be removed. But old customs die hard and people were reluctant to abandon the decorated hoop altogether. To solve the problem, the Holy Bough was renamed the Holly Bough. The embracing continued even though it was now done under nothing more than hoops decorated with greenery.

In the sixteenth century, the ordinary greeting embrace became more effusive and included kissing. Then, about three hundred years ago, a new element was added to the ritual. Every time a visitor to the house was kissed one of the white berries was removed from the sprig of mistletoe that was included among the greenery. When all the berries had gone, the kissing had to stop.

This idea was probably introduced to limit what was rapidly becoming an excuse for excessive bouts of less-than-holy kissing. Its effect, however, was to create a special link between one of the types of greenery – the mistletoe – and the act of kissing. Previously, despite its strange history, mistletoe had been just another form of evergreen available at Christmastime. Now, suddenly, it was the 'kissing bough'.

As time passed, the hoops were omitted and a simple sprig of mistletoe was all that was left, hanging by itself in the hallway at Christmas.

Mistletoe has retained its kissing role right up to the present day. Its true origin has long been forgotten but as a licence for intimacy it has retained its great popularity, becoming increasingly sexual and less and less sacred as the years have passed.

Whereas many seemingly Christian acts at Christmastime are in reality pagan in origin, this is a seemingly pagan act that appears to be truly Christian, symbolizing the love of Christ for all mankind.

The rival explanation for kissing under the mistletoe, often given, is that the plant's pagan connection with fertility made it ideal for 'blessing' a sexual kiss. Although this may sound convincing, it is pure conjecture and there is no evidence to support it. The fact that the early Christmas kissing was part of a completely non-sexual, social greeting, makes it highly unlikely.

Desmond Morris, *Christmas Watching*

The Roman Saturnalia

We have seen that many peoples have been used to observe an annual period of licence, when the customary restraints of law and morality are thrown aside, when the whole population give themselves up to extravagant mirth and jollity, and when the darker passions find a vent which would never be allowed them in the more staid and sober course of ordinary life. Such outbursts of the pent-up forces of human nature, too often degenerating into wild orgies of lust and crime, occur most commonly at the end of the year, and are frequently associated, as I have had occasion to point out, with one or other of the agricultural seasons, especially with the time of sowing or of harvest. Now, of all these periods of licence the one which is best known and which in modern language has given its name to the rest is the Saturnalia. This famous festival fell in December, the last month of the Roman year, and was popularly supposed to commemorate the merry reign of Saturn, the god of sowing and of husbandry, who lived on earth long ago as a righteous and beneficent king of Italy, drew the rude and scattered dwellers on the mountains together, taught them to till the ground, gave them laws, and ruled in peace. His reign was the fabled Golden Age: the earth brought forth abundantly; no sound of war or discord troubled the happy world; no baleful love of lucre worked like poison in the blood of the industrious and contented peasantry. Slavery and private property were alike unknown: all men had all things in common. At last the good god, the kindly king, vanished suddenly; but his memory was cherished to distant ages, shrines were reared in his honour, and many hills and high places in Italy bore his name. Yet the bright tradition of his reign was crossed by a dark shadow: his altars are said to have been stained with the blood of human victims, for whom a more merciful age afterwards substituted effigies. Of this gloomy side of the god's religion there is little or no trace in the descriptions which ancient writers have left us of the Saturnalia. Feasting and revelry and all the mad pursuit of pleasure are the features that seem to have especially marked this carnival of antiquity, as it went on for seven days in the streets and public squares and houses of ancient Rome from the seventeenth to the twenty-third of December.

But no feature of the festival is more remarkable, nothing in it seems to have struck the ancients themselves more than the licence granted to slaves at this time. The distinction between the free and the servile classes was temporarily abolished. The slave might rail at his master, intoxicate himself like his betters, sit down at table with them, and not even a word of reproof would be administered to him for conduct which at any other season might have been punished with stripes, imprisonment, or death. Nay, more, masters actually changed places with their slaves and waited on them at table; and not till the serf had done eating and drinking was the board cleared and dinner set for his master. So far was this inversion of ranks carried, that each household became for a time a mimic republic in which the high offices of state were discharged by the slaves, who gave their orders and laid down the law as if they were indeed invested with all the dignity of the consulship, the praetorship, and the bench. Like the pale reflection of power thus accorded to bondsmen at the Saturnalia was the mock kingship for which freemen cast lots at the same season. The person on whom the lot fell enjoyed the title of king, and issued commands of a playful and ludicrous nature to his temporary subjects. One of them he might order to mix the wine, another to drink, another to sing, another to dance, another to speak in his own dispraise, another to carry a flute-girl on his back round the house.

Sir James George Frazer, The Golden Bough

The Christmas/Epiphany Cycle

Attempts have been made to see Epiphany as the Christianization of the Feast of Tabernacles, the third great Jewish feast. Both celebrations included the all-night vigil, the lighting of fires and the procession of lights, the waters of life, the palm branches and the allusions to the sacred marriage, but the theory is by no means proved.

Both Christmas and Epiphany are, partly at any rate, an attempt to counter pagan festivities connected with the winter solstice, which in the West was reckoned to be on 25 December, and in the East, in Alexandria, on 6 January. December 25 had been fixed as the date for observing the birthday of the sun, *Natalis solis invicti*, in 274, only sixty-two years before the first evidence of the Christian celebration of Christmas in Rome (Philocalian Calendar). Constantine encouraged the adaptation by the Church of various features of sun-worship, and the institution of the feast may owe something to him and to his building of St Peter's on the Vatican Hill, where the sun was already worshipped in the Mithras-cult. In the East 6 January was connected with the virgin-birth of Aion/Dionysus and with legends of epiphanies in which gods made themselves known to men. Pliny the Elder even tells of Dionysus revealing his presence on that day by changing the water in springs and fountains into wine.

Christmas and Epiphany became widely celebrated only in the fourth century and their popularity undoubtedly owes much to the contemporary Christological controversies and the need to combat Arianism.

Epiphany is almost certainly the older of the two festivals and was probably from its origin a celebration both of Christ's nativity and the events connected with it, and of his baptism and first miracle at Cana. The fragment of a sermon, possibly by Hippolytus, preserved at the end of the *Ep. of Diognetus* [may indicate] that such a unitive festival existed as early as the end of the second century or the beginning of the third. Although the name indicates its Greek origin, the first indisputable reference to it, in Ammianus Marcellinus' *History*, is to its celebration in Gaul in *c.* 361. The reference unfortunately, however, provides no evidence as to the content of the celebration. At Jerusalem, according to Egeria's account (which is, however, incomplete), the main content was the nativity; there is no reference to the baptism or to the miracle at Cana, yet Jerome (d. 420), who spent forty-five years in the East, twenty-four of them in Bethlehem, says that baptism was the main content. By the time of his death, however, Christmas had been introduced into the East, in Antioch by 386, in Cappadocia by 370, and in Constantinople itself by 380.

Unlike the feast of the Epiphany, Christmas originated in the West, probably at Rome itself, where Epiphany does not seem to have been celebrated before the early fifth century, although it was well established by the time of Leo. Christmas also seems to have been the original feast in North Africa. Augustine in 412 complains that the Donatists have not added the festival of the Epiphany like everyone else. The Epiphany was, however, known earlier in Gaul and Spain and even in north Italy, where it was a three-fold commemoration of the Adoration of the Magi, our Lord's baptism and the miracle at Cana, whereas in Rome the Magi seem to have been its only theme in the mid-fifth century.

It would seem then that an originally unitive festival has become divided in different ways in East and West: Christmas is the feast of the nativity in both, to which the East adds a commemoration of the adoration of the Magi; Epiphany is a celebration of the Lord's baptism in the East and of the visit of the Magi in the West. The other two themes associated with Epiphany, the baptism and the marriage at Cana, are commemorated on the Sundays after Epiphany in the West. In the Byzantine liturgy there is no mention of Cana but nuptial imagery is used of baptism.

In the East, as early as the Cappadocian Fathers, Epiphany became a normal day for baptism, whilst in the West, at least up to the time of Leo, baptism was never administered then, although Leo did preach on the subject at Christmas. In Gaul, however, which was much influenced by the East, Christmas/Epiphany did become a baptismal season, and it is significant that it is in Gaul that we first hear of a forty-day period of preparation for it.

Peter G. Cobb, 'The Calendar'

'All the World should be Taxed'

And it came to pass in those days, that there went out a decree from Cæsar Augustus, that all the world should be taxed. (*And* this taxing was first made when Cyrenius was governor of Syria.) And all went to be taxed, every one into his own city.

And Joseph also went up from Galilee, out of the city of Nazareth, into Judaea, unto the city of David, which is called Bethlehem; (because he was of the house and lineage of David): to be taxed with Mary his espoused wife, being great with child.

And so it was, that, while they were there, the days were accomplished that she should be delivered. And she brought forth her firstborn son, and wrapped him in swaddling clothes, and laid him in a manger; because there was no room for them in the inn.

And there were in the same country shepherds abiding in the field, keeping watch over their flock by night. And, lo, the angel of the Lord came upon them, and the glory of the Lord shone round about them: and they were sore afraid. And the angel said unto them, Fear not: for, behold, I bring you good tidings of great joy, which shall be to all people. For unto you is born this day in the city of David a Saviour, which is Christ the Lord. And this *shall be* a sign unto you; Ye shall find the babe wrapped in swaddling clothes, lying in a manger.

And suddenly there was with the angel a multitude of the heavenly host praising God, and saying, Glory to God in the highest, and on earth peace, good will toward men.

And it came to pass, as the angels were gone away from them into heaven, the shepherds said one to another, Let us now go even unto Bethlehem, and see this thing which is come to pass, which the Lord hath made known unto us. And they came with haste, and found Mary, and Joseph, and the babe lying in a manger. And when they had seen *it*, they made known abroad the saying which was told them concerning this child. And all they that heard *it* wondered at those things which were told them by the shepherds. But Mary kept all these things, and pondered *them* in her heart. And the shepherds returned, glorifying and praising God for all the things that they had heard and seen, as it was told unto them.

Luke 2:1–20

From a Sermon Preached at Bexterly, on Christmas Day, 1552

LUKE 2:7

This gospel maketh special mention of the nativity of our Saviour Jesus Christ, declaring how Mary, with her husband Joseph, came after the commandment of the emperor, from Nazareth unto Bethlehem, the city of David, of whose lineage and tribe she was; what miseries and calamities she suffered by the way, and how poor and miserable she was, having nothing that pertained to a woman being in her case, you may right well consider: and as touching his nativity, his poverty, how he was born in a stable among beasts, lacking all manner of necessary things which appertained to young children: insomuch that he had neither cradle nor clouts. Wherefore Mary his mother wrapped him, as it is most like, in her own apparel, and laid him in a manger, where he was shewed, not to the rulers of this world, neither to kings, potentates, or bishops; but rather to simple shepherds, and poor servants keeping their sheep in the field. To these poor wretches the angel of God was sent which proclaimed these great things unto them; saying, 'Be not afraid, for behold I bring you tidings of great gladness that shall come to all people: for unto you is born this day in the city of David a Saviour, which is Christ the Lord, &c.'

This is the greatest comfort in the world, to know that our Saviour is born, that he is abroad, and at hand unto every one that calleth upon him. What greater gladness can be unto a man that feeleth his sin, and seeth his damnation before his eyes; unto such a man nothing is more acceptable than to hear that there is a Saviour which will help him and heal his sores. Therefore this message of the angel was very joyful tidings.

The angel bad them go unto Bethlehem and to search for the child: and forthwith a great many of angels came together rejoicing, singing, and praising God for our sakes, that the Redeemer of mankind was born into the world. For without him nothing availeth in the sight of God the Father; without him no man can praise God, because it hath pleased God for his Son's sake only, to show himself favourable and loving unto mankind, and to receive only that prayer which is made unto him in the name of Christ our Saviour. Therefore all those which come without him before God, shall be rejected as persons rebellious against God and his constitutions. For the will, pleasure, and counsel of God is, to receive only those which come to him in the name of his Son our Saviour, which know themselves, lament their own sins, and confess their own naughtiness and wickedness, and put their whole trust and confidence only in the Son of God the redeemer of mankind, as the angels themselves testify.

Here in this gospel note, that here was singing and rejoicing, for the great and unspeakable goodness and mercy of Almighty God the Father, whom it pleased to redeem mankind through the death of his only, natural, and most dearly beloved Son our Saviour and Redeemer, Jesus Christ, very God and very man, the son of God after his godhead, the son of Mary after his manhood; which he hath taken upon him for man's sake, to redeem and deliver the same from all misery, and to set him at unity with God the Father, and finally to bring him to everlasting life . . .

Now let us come to the shepherds.

'The shepherds said one to another, Let us go unto Bethlehem, and see these things which we hear say is happened, that the Lord hath shewed unto us.' Here note the faith of these poor shepherds which believed the saying of the angels so stedfastly, that they were ready to go and do after the commandment of the said angels. They did not as many of us do, which are so slothful that we will scant abide one hour to hear the word of God. And when we have heard the same, we believe it not, we regard it not, it goeth in at one ear and out at the other. Wherefore it is not to be marvelled that God is angry with us, seeing we are so forgetful and unthankful for his great and exceeding benefits shewed unto us in these latter days of the world.

This is a comfortable place for servants which should be more diligent in their business than they be, considering that God regardeth them so much, that he is content to open his great and high mysteries unto servants first, setting aside all kings and rulers in this world, which are only esteemed in the sight of men. Here therefore, learn, O ye servants, and consider that God no less regardeth you than the greatest lords in the world, if you live after his commandments, which is, that you shall serve your masters truly and uprightly, and not with a feigned heart.

'Let us go to Bethlehem, saith the shepherds.' Here is to be noted in these shepherds a great charity among themselves, in that one exhorteth another to go to follow the word of God. Many folks nowadays agree and exhort themselves to do wickedly, to steal, to pick, and to do all lewdness: but to exhort their neighbours to do any goodness as those shepherds did, they will not agree. Therefore let us not be ashamed to learn of these poor shepherds, to follow their examples. When we hear the word of God let us exhort one another to follow the same, and let us agree in goodness, to seek Christ and to follow him according to his word, and then we shall find him. Let the curate exhort his parishioners, to follow the commandments of God: let the householder exhort his wife, children, servants, and family to the seeking of Christ; let every neighbour exhort another to goodness, yea let every one consider that no one person is born into the world for his own sake, but for the commonwealth sake. Let us therefore walk charitably, not seeking our own commodities, but the honour and glory of God, and the wealth of all Christians, with exhortations, admonitions and prayers one for another, that the name of God may be magnified among us, and his will known and fulfilled. Of these poor shepherds we may learn much goodness, yea the best doctor of divinity need not be ashamed to learn of them, and to follow their examples, which are now saints in heaven, and the inheritors of everlasting life.

But yet we must beware that we go not too far. For we may not make gods of them, nor call upon them, as we have been taught in times past, because God will be called upon, honoured, and worshipped alone.

Hugh Latimer

Shepherd

They say I'm old, that I should give up my flock,
stay back with the women in the warm.
They say the cold is bad for me, and hiking

over hills to find a lost sheep, sitting up
all night to nurse a lamb are young men's jobs.
When I tell my story, I see glances and disbelief.

Yet none would dare deny my flock's
the best-kept in the region, my memory
still sharp as winter wind. It was a night

much like this. We huddled round the fire,
and passed a cup for warmth. I was youngest.
Now the rest are gone, so when I die

there'll be no one to remember.
Each of us heard a voice that gave commands.
(Afterwards, we couldn't recall

what words were said, but all agreed
we had been instructed to go somewhere,
for a reason we didn't understand.)

While it spoke, winter seemed
to withdraw, and it was spring
(though still cold, dark, and wind blowing bitterly).

When the voice stopped, we didn't like to catch
our neighbour's eye: each thought
perhaps he should keep this to himself.

But there was a burst of light, that blinded us
as sunlight does when you
come out of a dark cave into the morning.

We had no doubt then, packed up our things,
and went, without much talking,
to where we had been directed.

At length, we stood, and saw. Just for a moment
it occurred to me that it was me that had been chosen
out of the whole world. Me, to stand here

and be a witness. Not kings, or lords or the village mayor,
but me. A warmth crept up like an August breeze,
or a woollen coat, or more like long thin fingers

trying to curl round me and drag me away.
Then it was gone, and I knew my thought
had been wrong, despicable. That is why

I'll tend my sheep, welcome the bitterest nights,
tell my story to anyone with half an ear,
and one day I will have atoned.

Peter Howard

'When They Saw the Star'

Now the birth of Jesus Christ was on this wise: When as his mother Mary
was espoused to Joseph, before they came together, she was found with child
of the Holy Ghost. Then Joseph her husband, being a just *man*, and not
willing to make her a publick example, was minded to put her away privily.
But while he thought on these things, behold, the angel of the Lord appeared
unto him in a dream, saying, Joseph, thou son of David, fear not to take unto
thee Mary thy wife: for that which is conceived in her is of the Holy Ghost.
And she shall bring forth a son, and thou shalt call his name JESUS: for he
shall save his people from their sins.

Now all this was done, that it might be fulfilled which was spoken of the
Lord by the prophet, saying, Behold, a virgin shall be with child, and shall

bring forth a son, and they shall call his name Emmanuel, which being interpreted is, God with us. Then Joseph being raised from sleep did as the angel of the Lord had bidden him, and took unto him his wife: and knew her not till she had brought forth her firstborn son: and he called his name JESUS.

Now when Jesus was born in Bethlehem of Judaea in the days of Herod the king, behold, there came wise men from the east to Jerusalem, saying, Where is he that is born King of the Jews? for we have seen his star in the east, and are come to worship him. When Herod the king had heard *these things*, he was troubled, and all Jerusalem with him. And when he had gathered all the chief priests and scribes of the people together, he demanded of them where Christ should be born. And they said unto him, In Bethlehem of Judæa: for thus it is written by the prophet, And thou Bethlehem, *in* the land of Juda, art not the least among the princes of Juda: for out of thee shall come a Governor, that shall rule my people Israel.

Then Herod, when he had privily called the wise men, inquired of them diligently what time the star appeared. And he sent them to Bethlehem, and said, Go and search diligently for the young child; and when ye have found *him*, bring me word again, that I may come and worship him also.

When they had heard the king, they departed; and, lo, the star, which they saw in the east, went before them, till it came and stood over where the young child was. When they saw the star, they rejoiced with exceeding great joy. And when they were come into the house, they saw the young child with Mary his mother, and fell down, and worshipped him: and when they had opened their treasures, they presented unto him gifts; gold, and frankincense, and myrrh. And being warned of God in a dream that they should not return to Herod, they departed into their own country another way.

And when they were departed, behold, the angel of the Lord appeareth to Joseph in a dream, saying, Arise, and take the young child and his mother, and flee into Egypt, and be thou there until I bring thee word: for Herod will seek the young child to destroy him. When he arose he took the young child and his mother by night, and departed into Egypt: and was there until the death of Herod: that it might be fulfilled which was spoken of the Lord by the prophet, saying, Out of Egypt have I called my son. Then Herod, when he saw that he was mocked of the wise men, was exceeding wroth, and sent forth, and slew all the children that were in Bethlehem, and in all the coasts thereof, from two years old and under, according to the time which he had diligently inquired of the wise men.

Matthew 1:18–2:16

From a Sermon Preached before The King's Majesty at Whitehall, on Christmas Day 1622

Now to *venimus*, their coming itself. And it follows well. For it is not a star only, but a load-star; and whither should *stella Ejus ducere*, but *ad Eum*? 'Whither lead us, but to Him Whose the star is?' The star to the star's Master.

All this while we have been at *dicentes*, 'saying' and seeing; now we shall come to *facientes*, see them do somewhat upon it. It is not saying nor seeing will serve St James; he will call, and be still calling for *ostende mihi*, 'shew me thy faith by some work'. And well may he be allowed to call for it this day; it is the day of *vidimus*, appearing, being seen. You have seen His star, let Him now see your star another while. And so they do. Make your faith to be seen; so it is – their faith in the steps of their faith. And so was Abraham's first by coming forth of his country; as these here do, and so 'walk in the steps of the faith of Abraham', do his first work.

It is not commended to stand 'gazing up into Heaven' too long; not on Christ Himself ascending, much less on His star. For they sat not still gazing on the star. Their *vidimus* begat *venimus*; their seeing made them come, come a great journey. *Venimus* is soon said, but a short word; but many a wide and weary step they made before they could come to say *Venimus*, Lo, here 'we are come'; come, and at our journey's end. To look a little on it. In this their coming we consider, (1) First, the distance of the place they came from. It was not hard by as the shepherds – but a step to Bethlehem over the fields; this was riding many a hundred miles, and cost them many a day's journey. (2) Secondly, we consider the way that they came, if it be pleasant, or plain and easy; for if it be, it is so much the better. (1) This was nothing pleasant, for through deserts, all the way waste and desolate. (2) Nor secondly, easy neither; for over the rocks and crags of both Arabias, specially Petraea, their journey lay. (3) Yet if safe – but it was not, but exceeding dangerous, as lying through the midst of the 'black tents of Kedar', a nation of thieves and cut-throats; to pass over the hills of robbers, infamous then, and infamous to this day. No passing without great troop or convoy. (4) Last we consider the time of their coming, the season of the year. It was no summer progress. A cold coming they had of it at this time of the year, just the worst time of the year to take a journey, and specially a long journey in. The ways deep, the weather sharp, the days short, the sun farthest off, *in solstitio brumali*, 'the very dead of winter'. *Venimus*, 'we are come', if that be one, *venimus*, 'we are now come', come at this time, that sure is another.

And these difficulties they overcame, of a wearisome, irksome, troublesome, dangerous, unseasonable journey; and for all this they came. And came it cheerfully and quickly, as appeareth by the speed they made. It was but *vidimus, venimus,* with them; 'they saw', and 'they came'; no sooner saw, but they set out presently. So as upon the first appearing of the star, as it might be last night, they knew it was Balaam's star; it called them away, they made ready straight to begin their journey this morning. A sign they were highly conceited of His birth, believed some great matter of it, that they took all these pains, made all this haste that they might be there to worship Him with all the possible speed they could. Sorry for nothing so much as that they could not be there soon enough, with the very first, to do it even this day, the day of His birth. All considered, there is more in *venimus* than shews at the first sight. It was not for nothing it was said in the first verse, *ecce venerunt*; their coming hath an *ecce* on it, it well deserves it.

And we, what should we have done? Sure these men of the East shall rise in judgment against the men of the West, that is us, and their faith against ours in this point. With them it was but *vidimus, venimus*; with us it would have been but *veniemus* at most. Our fashion is to see and see again before we stir a foot, specially if it be to the worship of Christ. Come such a journey at such a time? No; but fairly have put it off to the spring of the year, till the days longer, and the ways fairer, and the weather warmer, till better travelling to Christ. Our Epiphany would sure have fallen in Easter-week at the soonest.

But then for the distance, desolateness, tediousness, and the rest, any of them were enough to mar our *venimus* quite. It must be no great way, first, we must come; we love not that. Well fare the shepherds, yet they came but hard by; rather like them than the Magi. Nay, not like them neither. For with us the nearer, lightly the farther off; our proverb is you know, 'The nearer the Church, the farther from God.'

Nor it must not be through no desert, over no Petraea. If rugged or uneven the way, if the weather ill-disposed, if any never so little danger, it is enough to stay us. To Christ we cannot travel, but weather and way and all must be fair. If not, no journey, but sit still and see farther. As indeed, all our religion is rather *vidimus*, a contemplation, than *venimus*, a motion, or stirring to do ought.

But when we do it, we must be allowed leisure. Ever *veniemus*, never *venimus*; ever coming, never come. We love to make no very great haste. To other things perhaps; not to *adorare*, the place of the worship of God. Why

should we? Christ is no wild-cat. What talk ye of twelve days? And if it be
forty days hence, ye shall be sure to find His Mother and Him; she cannot
be churched till then. What needs such haste? The truth is, we conceit Him
and His birth but slenderly, and our haste is even thereafter. But if we be at
that point, we must be out of this *venimus*; they like enough to leave us
behind. Best get us a new Christmas in September; we are not like to come to
Christ at this feast. Enough for *venimus*.

Lancelot Andrewes

Journey of the Magi

'A cold coming we had of it,
Just the worst time of the year
For a journey, and such a long journey;
The ways deep and the weather sharp,
The very dead of winter.'
And the camels galled, sore-footed, refractory,
Lying down in the melting snow.
There were times we regretted
The summer palaces on slopes, the terraces,
And the silken girls bringing sherbet.
Then the camel men cursing and grumbling
And running away, and wanting their liquor and women,
And the night-fires going out, and the lack of shelters,
And the cities hostile and the towns unfriendly
And the villages dirty and charging high prices:
A hard time we had of it.
At the end we preferred to travel all night,
Sleeping in snatches,
With the voices singing in our ears, saying
That this was all folly.

    Then at dawn we came down to a temperate valley,
Wet, below the snow line, smelling of vegetation,
With a running stream and a water-mill beating the darkness,
And three trees on the low sky.
And an old white horse galloped away in the meadow.
Then we came to a tavern with vine-leaves over the lintel,

Six hands at an open door dicing for pieces of silver,
And feet kicking the empty wine-skins.
But there was no information, so we continued
And arrived at evening, not a moment too soon
Finding the place; it was (you may say) satisfactory.

    All this was a long time ago, I remember,
And I would do it again, but set down
This set down
This: were we led all that way for
Birth or Death? There was a Birth, certainly,
We had evidence and no doubt. I had seen birth and death,
But had thought they were different; this Birth was
Hard and bitter agony for us, like Death, our death.
We returned to our places, these Kingdoms,
But no longer at ease here, in the old dispensation,
With an alien people clutching their gods.
I should be glad of another death.

                                            T. S. Eliot

A Botticelli Nativity

Before the entry of the Kings,
their horses, caparisoned and fettled,
the peacock got itself settled

on a crumbling wall,
where the stones sprout flowers
through long Italian hours.

Much lather at the bit is slavered,
and steam coils off the stallions' bared
backs. We enter at the point where

discussion across the empty saddles
is hushed, and one of the Kings unfurls,
from beneath a golden band, a head of curls.

This gives an opportunity for drapery
to swing in the direction of a baby,
ruling from a crimson knee.

The peacock spreads its cards
behind its back. The Kings unleash
their homage. All the haberdashery is hushed.

This Medici Bethlehem is squaring up
to its Christ, with the beautiful and shy
Madonna, and the peacock preens the sky.

David Scott

From a Sermon Preached at Grimsthorpe, on Twelfth Day, 1553

MATTHEW 2:1–2

The evangelist Matthew in this gospel, goeth about to prove, that Jesus was
the Messias which was spoken of so much beforetimes by the prophets; and
this he doth, by the place where he was born, namely, at Bethlehem, and also
by the time, namely, when Herod was king over the Jews. But here be no
Jews, therefore it needeth not to entreat of this matter.

Here we shall note the simplicity, and heartiness of these men, which came
a great way out of their countries, where the prophet Daniel had been
beforetimes; for no doubt but they had learned of Daniel, that there should a
Messias come. Therefore now when they perceived by the star that he was
born, they are ready to forsake their countries, and come into Jewry, being a
great way, to make inquisition for him: and there go very simply to work,
casting no peril. They ask openly at Jerusalem for him, saying, *Ubi est Rex?*
'Where is he that is born king of the Jews?' Here you must understand, that
after Pompey the Great had subdued the Jews, in process of time, Herod had
gotten the rule over them, by the means and appointment of the emperor.
Which Herod was not a Jew, but an Idumean: a cruel, wicked, and forecast-
ing man; for he trusted not constantly upon the Jews. He was ever afraid he
should be deprived of his kingdom. Now at that time when this wicked man
had the rule, these wise men came into the city, and inquired for the king of
the Jews, and openly protested their faith which they had in Christ. They

were nothing afraid of Herod, for they had such a trust and confidence in God, that they were sure he would deliver them from his hands.

But worldly wise men will say, they were but fools to put themselves in such danger without need; they might have asked for him secretly, so that the king might not have heard of it: such is the wisdom of those which have no faith nor confidence in God, they will not abide any peril for God's sake, they will seek all corners to hide themselves in, rather than they will profess God's word openly. I pray you note and mark well their words, they say, 'We are come to worship him'; to do him homage, to acknowledge him to be our Lord. Then again note the words of Herod, he saith unto them, 'Go and search diligently for the child, and when you have found him, bring me word, that I may come and worship him also.' Lo, here what a fox this Herod was. Who can judge of man's words, except God which knoweth the hearts of men?

Note another thing, which is this: as soon as this was published, that these strangers were come, asking for the king of the Jews, 'Herod was troubled,' saith the text, 'and all Jerusalem with him.' This was a strange thing, that Jerusalem should be troubled, which longed so long time for a king, for that Messias, for that Saviour. But they were even as we are, they cared not for God's word, they sought nothing but their cease, and to be at rest; they cared not greatly for religion: they thought, if we receive him, we shall have trouble with him, therefore it is better for us to leave him, and to let him alone, rather than to disquiet ourselves: they were even right merchantmen, they sought nothing but to save their substance in this world, this was all they looked for; therefore they were troubled when they heard that Christ was born.

Now what doth Herod? Forsooth he calleth all the bishops and learned men, and inquireth of them the time at the which Christ should be born. They were well seen in the law and the prophets after the letter, and there-fore by and by made answer unto him, saying, 'At Bethlehem Judah he shall be born'; for so it is written in the fifth chapter of Micah, *Et tu Bethlehem Juda*, 'And thou, Bethlehem Judah, thou art not the least concerning the princes of Judah; for out of thee shall come the captain that shall govern my people Israel.' After that Herod had heard this, he called the wise men, and bade them that they should 'go and search out the child, and when they had found him, they should bring him word again, that he might come and worship him also'. O what a fox is this! There hath been many such foxes in England, specially in the time of persecution, which pretended great holi-ness, and zeal to God-ward with their mouth, but their hearts are poisoned with the cruelty of Herod.

Hugh Latimer

Innocent's Song

Who's that knocking on the window,
Who's that standing at the door,
What are all those presents
Lying on the kitchen floor?

Who is the smiling stranger
With hair as white as gin,
What is he doing with the children
And who could have let him in?

Why has he rubies on his fingers,
A cold, cold crown on his head,
Why, when he caws his carol,
Does the salty snow run red?

Why does he ferry my fireside
As a spider on a thread,
His fingers made of fuses
And his tongue of gingerbread?

Why does the world before him
Melt in a million suns,
Why do his yellow, yearning eyes
Burn like saffron buns?

Watch where he comes walking
Out of the Christmas flame,
Dancing, double-talking:

Herod is his name.

Charles Causley

'The Story Circumstantially Belies Itself'

The story of Herod destroying all the children under two years old belongs altogether to the writer of the book of Matthew; and not one of the rest mentions anything about it. Had such a circumstance been true, the universality of it must have made it known to all the writers; and the thing would have been too striking to have been omitted by any. The writer tells us that Jesus escaped this slaughter because Joseph and Mary were warned by an angel to flee with him into Egypt; but he forgot to make provision for John, who was then under two years of age. John, however, who stayed behind, fared as well as Jesus, who fled; and therefore the story circumstantially belies itself.

Thomas Paine, *The Age of Reason*

'In the Beginning was the Word'

In the beginning was the Word, and the Word was with God, and the Word was God. The same was in the beginning with God. All things were made by him; and without him was not any thing made that was made. In him was life; and the life was the light of men. And the light shineth in darkness; and the darkness comprehended it not.

There was a man sent from God, whose name *was* John. The same came for a witness, to bear witness of the Light, that all *men* through him might believe. He was not that Light, but *was sent* to bear witness of that Light. *That* was the true Light, which lighteth every man that cometh into the world.

He was in the world, and the world was made by him, and the world knew him not. He came unto his own, and his own received him not. But as many as received him, to them gave he power to become the sons of God, *even* to them that believe on his name: Which were born, not of blood, nor of the will of the flesh, nor of the will of man, but of God.

And the Word was made flesh, and dwelt among us (and we beheld his glory, the glory as of the only begotten of the Father,) full of grace and truth.

John 1:1–14

Holy Sonnets

ANNUNCIATION

Salvation to all that will is nigh,
That All, which alwayes is All every where,
Which cannot sinne, and yet all sinnes must beare,
Which cannot die, yet cannot chuse but die,
Loe, faithfull Virgin, yeelds himselfe to lye
In prison, in thy wombe; and though he there
Can take no sinne, nor thou give, yet he'will weare
Taken from thence, flesh, which deaths force may trie.
Ere by the spheares time was created, thou
Wast in his minde, who is thy Sonne, and Brother,
Whom thou conceiv'st, conceiv'd; yea thou art now
Thy Makers makers, and thy Fathers mother,
Thou'hast light in darke; and shutst in little roome,
Immensity cloysterd in thy deare wombe.

NATIVITIE

Immensitie cloysterd in thy deare wombe,
Now leaves his welbelov'd imprisonment,
There he hath made himselfe to his intent
Weake enough, now into our world to come;
But Oh, for thee, for him, hath th'Inne no roome?
Yet lay him in this stall, and from th'Orient,
Starres, and wisemen will travell to prevent
Th'effect of *Herods* jealous generall doome.
Seest thou, my Soule, with thy faiths eyes, how he
Which fils all place, yet none holds him, doth lye?
Was not his pity towards thee wondrous high,
That would have need to be pittied by thee?
Kisse him, and with him into Egypt goe,
With his kinde mother, who partakes thy woe.

John Donne

The Angels for the Nativity of Our Lord

Run, shepherds, run where Bethlem blest appears,
We bring the best of news, be not dismayed,
A Saviour there is born more old than years,
Amidst heaven's rolling heights this earth who stayed:
In a poor cottage inned, a virgin maid
A weakling did him bear, who all upbears;
There is he, poorly swaddled, in manger laid,
To whom too narrow swaddlings are our spheres:
Run, shepherds, run, and solemnize his birth,
This is that night – no, day, grown great with bliss,
In which the power of Satan broken is;
In heaven be glory, peace unto the earth!
    Thus singing, through the air the angels swam,
    And cope of stars re-echoèd the same.

William Drummond

Hymn

Lord when the wise men came from farr,
Led to thy Cradle by a Starr,
Then did the shepheards too rejoyce,
Instructed by thy Angells voyce:
Blest were the wisemen in their skill,
And shepheards in their harmlesse will.

Wisemen in tracing Natures lawes
Ascend unto the highest cause,
Shepheards with humble fearefulnesse
Walke safely, though their light be lesse:
Though wisemen better know the way
It seems noe honest heart can stray.

Ther is noe merrit in the wise
But love, (the shepheards sacrifice).

Wisemen all wayes of knowledge past,
To th'shepheards wonder come at last:
To know, can only wonder breede,
And not to know, is wonders seede.

A wiseman at the Altar bowes
And offers up his studied vowes
And is received; may not the teares,
Which spring too from a shepheards feares,
And sighs upon his fraylty spent,
Though not distinct, be eloquent?

'Tis true, the object sanctifies
All passions which within us rise,
But since noe creature comprehends
The cause of causes, end of ends,
Hee who himselfe vouchsafes to know
Best pleases his creator soe.

When then our sorrowes wee applye
To our owne wantes and poverty,
When wee looke up in all distresse
And our owne misery confesse,
Sending both thankes and prayers above,
Then though wee doe not know, we love.

Sidney Godolphin

The Burning Babe

As I in hoary winter's night
    Stood shivering in the snow,
Surprised I was with sudden heat
    Which made my heart to glow;
And lifting up a fearful eye
    To view what fire was near,
A pretty Babe all burning bright
    Did in the air appear;
Who, scorchèd with excessive heat,

Such floods of tears did shed,
As though His floods should quench His flames,
  Which with His tears were fed.
'Alas!' quoth He, 'but newly born
  In fiery heats I fry,
Yet none approach to warm their hearts
  Or feel my fire but I!

'My faultless breast the furnace is;
  The fuel, wounding thorns;
Love is the fire, and sighs the smoke;
  The ashes, shames and scorns;
The fuel Justice layeth on,
  And Mercy blows the coals,
The metal in this furnace wrought
  Are men's defilèd souls:
For which, as now on fire I am
  To work them to their good,
So will I melt into a bath,
  To wash them in my blood.'
With this He vanish'd out of sight
  And swiftly shrunk away,
And straight I callèd unto mind
  That it was Christmas Day.

                                        Robert Southwell

Christmas

All after pleasures as I rid one day,
  My horse and I, both tir'd, bodie and minde,
  With full crie of affections, quite astray,
I took up in the next inne I could finde.
There when I came, whom found I but my deare,
  My dearest Lord, expecting till the grief
  Of pleasures brought me to him, readie there
To be all passengers most sweet relief?
O Thou, whose glorious, yet contracted light,
  Wrapt in nights mantle, stole into a manger;

Since my dark soul and brutish is thy right,
To Man of all beasts be not thou a stranger:
    Furnish & deck my soul, that thou mayst have
    A better lodging then a rack or grave.

The shepherds sing; and shall I silent be?
        My God, no hymne for thee?
My soul's a shepherd too; a flock it feeds
        Of thoughts, and words, and deeds.
The pasture is thy word: the streams, thy grace
        Enriching all the place.
Shepherd and flock shall sing, and all my powers
        Out-sing the day-light houres.
Then we will chide the sunne for letting night
        Take up his place and right:
We sing one common Lord; wherefore he should
        Himself the candle hold.
I will go searching, till I finde a sunne
        Shall stay, till we have done;
A willing shiner, that shall shine as gladly,
        As frost-nipt sunnes look sadly.
Then we will sing, and shine all our own day,
        And one another pay:
His beams shall cheer my breast, and both so twine,
Till ev'n his beams sing, and my musick shine.

George Herbert

❧ 5 ❧

CAROLS

A Christmas Carol

In the bleak midwinter
    Frosty wind made moan,
Earth stood hard as iron,
    Water like a stone;
Snow had fallen, snow on snow,
    Snow on snow,
In the bleak midwinter
    Long ago.

Our God, Heaven cannot hold Him,
    Nor earth sustain;
Heaven and earth shall flee away
    When He comes to reign:
In the bleak midwinter
    A stable-place sufficed
The Lord God Almighty
    Jesus Christ.

Enough for Him whom cherubim
    Worship night and day,
A breastful of milk
    And a mangerful of hay;
Enough for Him whom angels
    Fall down before,
The ox and ass and camel
    Which adore.

Angels and archangels
    May have gathered there,

Cherubim and seraphim
　　Throng'd the air,
But only His mother
　　In her maiden bliss
Worshipped the Beloved
　　With a kiss.

What can I give Him,
　　Poor as I am?
If I were a shepherd
　　I would bring a lamb,
If I were a wise man
　　I would do my part,
Yet what I can I give Him,
　　Give my heart.

Christina Rossetti

As It Was

The week before Christmas, when snow seemed to lie thickest, was the moment for carol-singing; and when I think back to those nights it is to the crunch of snow and to the lights of the lanterns on it. Carol-singing in my village was a special tithe for the boys, the girls had little to do with it. Like hay-making, blackberrying, stone-clearing, and wishing-people-a-happy-Easter, it was one of our seasonal perks.

By instinct we knew just when to begin it; a day too soon and we should have been unwelcome, a day too late and we should have received lean looks from people whose bounty was already exhausted. When the true moment came, exactly balanced, we recognized it and were ready.

So as soon as the wood had been stacked in the oven to dry for the morning fire, we put on our scarves and went out through the streets, calling loudly between our hands, till the various boys who knew the signal ran out from their houses to join us.

One by one they came stumbling over the snow, swinging their lanterns around their heads, shouting and coughing horribly.

'Coming carol-barking then?'

We were the Church Choir, so no answer was necessary. For a year we had praised the Lord out of key, and as a reward for this service – on top of the

Outing – we now had the right to visit all the big houses, to sing our carols and collect our tribute.

To work them all in meant a five-mile foot journey over wild and generally snowed-up country. So the first thing we did was to plan our route; a formality, as the route never changed. All the same, we blew on our fingers and argued; and then we chose our Leader. This was not binding, for we all fancied ourselves as Leaders, and he who started the night in that position usually trailed home with a bloody nose.

Eight of us set out that night. There was Sixpence the Tanner, who had never sung in his life (he just worked his mouth in church); the brothers Horace and Boney, who were always fighting everybody and always getting the worst of it; Clergy Green, the preaching maniac; Walt the bully, and my two brothers. As we went down the lane other boys, from other villages, were already about the hills, bawling 'Kingwenslush', and shouting through keyholes 'Knock on the knocker! Ring at the Bell! Give us a penny for singing so well!' They weren't an approved charity as we were, the Choir; but competition was in the air.

Our first call as usual was the house of the Squire, and we trouped nervously down his drive. For light we had candles in marmalade-jars suspended on loops of string, and they threw pale gleams on the towering snowdrifts that stood on each side of the drive. A blizzard was blowing, but we were well wrapped up, with Army puttees on our legs, woollen hats on our heads, and several scarves around our ears.

As we approached the Big House across its white silent lawns, we too grew respectfully silent. The lake near by was stiff and black, the waterfall frozen and still. We arranged ourselves shuffling around the big front door, then knocked and announced the Choir.

A maid bore the tidings of our arrival away into the echoing distances of the house, and while we waited we cleared our throats noisily. Then she came back, and the door was left ajar for us, and we were bidden to begin. We brought no music, the carols were in our heads. 'Let's give 'em "Wild Shepherds",' said Jack. We began in confusion, plunging into a wreckage of keys, of different words and tempo; but we gathered our strength; he who sang loudest took the rest of us with him, and the carol took shape if not sweetness.

This huge stone house, with its ivied walls, was always a mystery to us. What were those gables, those rooms and attics, those narrow windows veiled by the cedar trees. As we sang 'Wild Shepherds' we craned our necks, gaping into that lamplit hall which we had never entered; staring at the muskets and untenanted chairs, the great tapestries furred by dust – until suddenly, on the stairs, we saw the old Squire himself standing and listening with his head on one side.

He didn't move until we'd finished; then slowly he tottered towards us, dropped two coins in our box with a trembling hand, scratched his name in the book we carried, gave us each a long look with his moist blind eyes, then turned away in silence.

As though released from a spell, we took a few sedate steps, then broke into a run for the gate. We didn't stop till we were out of the grounds. Impatient, at last, to discover the extent of his bounty, we squatted by the cowsheds, held our lanterns over the book, and saw that he had written 'Two Shillings'. This was quite a good start. No one of any worth in the district would dare to give us less than the Squire.

So with money in the box, we pushed on up the valley, pouring scorn on each other's performance. Confident now, we began to consider our quality and whether one carol was not better suited to us than another. Horace, Walt said, shouldn't sing at all; his voice was beginning to break. Horace disputed this and there was a brief token battle – they fought as they walked, kicking up divots of snow, then they forgot it, and Horace still sang.

Steadily we worked through the length of the valley, going from house to house, visiting the lesser and the greater gentry – the farmers, the doctors, the merchants, the majors, and other exalted persons. It was freezing hard and blowing too; yet not for a moment did we feel the cold. The snow blew into our faces, into our eyes and mouths, soaked through our puttees, got into our boots, and dripped from our woollen caps. But we did not care. The collecting-box grew heavier, and the list of names in the book longer and more extravagant, each trying to outdo the other.

Mile after mile we went, fighting against the wind, falling into snowdrifts, and navigating by the lights of the houses. And yet we never saw our audience. We called at house after house; we sang in courtyards and porches, outside windows, or in the damp gloom of hallways; we heard voices from hidden rooms; we smelt rich clothes and strange hot food; we saw maids bearing in dishes or carrying away coffee-cups; we received nuts, cakes, figs, preserved ginger, dates, cough-drops, and money; but we never once saw our patrons. We sang as it were at the castle walls, and apart from the Squire, who had shown himself to prove that he was still alive, we never expected it otherwise.

As the night drew on there was trouble with Boney. 'Noël', for instance, had a rousing harmony which Boney persisted in singing, and singing flat. The others forbade him to sing it at all, and Boney said he would fight us. Picking himself up, he agreed we were right, then he disappeared altogether.

He just turned away and walked into the snow and wouldn't answer when we called him back. Much later, as we reached a far point up the valley, somebody said 'Hark!' and we stopped to listen. Far away across the fields from the distant village came the sound of a frail voice singing, singing 'Noël', and singing it flat – it was Boney, branching out on his own.

We approached our last house high up on the hill, the place of Joseph the farmer. For him we had chosen a special carol, which was about the other Joseph, so that we always felt that singing it added a spicy cheek to the night. The last stretch of country to reach his farm was perhaps the most difficult of all. In these rough bare lanes, open to all winds, sheep were buried and wagons lost. Huddled together, we tramped in one another's footsteps, powdered snow blew into our screwed-up eyes, the candles burnt low, some blew out altogether, and we talked loudly above the gale.

Crossing, at last, the frozen mill-stream – whose wheel in summer still turned a barren mechanism – we climbed up to Joseph's farm. Sheltered by trees, warm on its bed of snow, it seemed always to be like this. As always it was late; as always this was our final call. The snow had a fine crust upon it, and the old trees sparkled like tinsel.

We grouped ourselves round the farmhouse porch. The sky cleared, and broad streams of stars ran down over the valley and away to Wales. On Slad's white slopes, seen through the black sticks of its woods, some red lamps still burned in the windows.

Everything was quiet; everywhere there was the faint crackling silence of the winter night. We started singing, and we were all moved by the words and the sudden trueness of our voices. Pure, very clear, and breathless we sang:

> As Joseph was a walking
> He heard an angel sing;
> 'This night shall be the birth-time
> Of Christ the Heavenly King.
>
> He neither shall be bornèd
> In Housen nor in hall,
> Nor in a place of paradise
> But in an ox's stall . . .'

And two thousand Christmases became real to us then; the houses, the halls, the places of paradise had all been visited; the stars were bright to guide the Kings through the snow; and across the farmyard we could hear the beasts in their stalls. We were given roast apples and hot mince-pies, in

our nostrils were spices like myrrh, and in our wooden box, as we headed
back for the village, there were golden gifts for all.

Laurie Lee, *Cider with Rosie*

I Sing of a Maiden

I sing of a maiden
   That is makèless;
King of all kings
   To her son she ches.

He came all so still
   Where his mother was,
As dew in April
   That falleth on the grass.

He came all so still
   To his mother's bowr,
As dew in April
   That falleth on the flower.

He came all so still
   Where his mother lay,
As dew in April
   That falleth on the spray.

Mother and maiden
   Was never none but she;
Well may such a lady
   Godès mother be.

14th century

Adam Lay Ybounden

Adam lay ybounden,
   Bounden in a bond;
Four thousand winter
   Thought he not too long.

And all was for an apple,
   An apple that he took,
As clerkès finden written
   In their book.

Ne had the apple taken been,
   The apple taken been,
Ne had never our lady
   A-been heavenè queen.

Blessèd be the time
   That apple taken was.
Therefore we moun singen
   Deo gracias!

15th century

The Holly and the Ivy

The holly and the ivy,
When they are both full grown,
Of all the trees that are in the wood,
The holly bears the crown:

   The rising of the sun
   And the running of the deer,
   The playing of the merry organ,
   Sweet singing in the choir.

The holly bears a blossom,
As white as the lily flower,
And Mary bore sweet Jesus Christ,
To be our sweet Saviour:

The holly bears a berry,
As red as any blood,
And Mary bore sweet Jesus Christ
To do poor sinners good:

The holly bears a prickle,
As sharp as any thorn,
And Mary bore sweet Jesus Christ
On Christmas day in the morn:

The holly bears a bark,
As bitter as any gall,
And Mary bore sweet Jesus Christ
For to redeem us all:

The holly and the ivy,
When they are both full grown,
Of all the trees that are in the wood,
The holly bears the crown:

14th century

The Cherry Tree Carol

This ballad elaborates a story told in *Pseudo-Matthew*, a Gospel that once formed part of the Church Canon. St Joseph became very unpopular in consequence; there being a widely held superstition that when an expectant mother feels a craving – technically called a *pica* – for any particular food, she must be indulged, or else the child will come to harm.

Joseph was an old man
And an old man was he,
When he married Maid Mary
The Queen of Galilee.

Joseph and Mary walkèd
Through an orchard green,
Where was berries and cherries
As thick as might be seen.

O then bespoke Mary
So meek and so mild,
'Pluck me a cherry, Joseph,
For I am with child.'

O then bespoke Joseph
So wilful and wild,
'Let him pluck thee cherries
That got thee with child.'

[111]

O then bespoke the Babe
  Within his mother's womb,
'Bow down, then, the tallest tree,
  For my mother to have some.'

Then bowed down the tallest tree
  Unto his mother's hand;
Then she cried: 'See, Joseph,
  I have cherries at command!'

As Joseph was a-walking
  He heard angels sing:
'This night shall be born to us
  Our heavenly king.

'He neither shall be born to us
  In house nor in hall,
Nor in the place of Paradise,
  But in an ox's stall.

'He neither shall be clothèd
  In purple nor in pall,
But all in fair linen
  Such as wear babies all.

'He neither shall be rockèd
  In silver nor in gold
But all in a wooden cradle
  That stands on the mould.'

Then Mary took her babe
  Up on her left knee:
With 'Dear Child, I pray thee now,
  Tell how this world shall be.'

'On the fifth day of January
  Three kings shall draw near,
While the stars in the Heaven
  Do tremble for fear.

'Upon the Good Friday
I will hang on a rood
And all the seed of Adam
I'll buy with my blood.

'For I shall be so dead, Mother
As the stones in the wall:
O the stones in the street, Mother
Shall mourn for me all.

'Upon Easter Day, Mother,
My rising shall be:
O, the sun and the moon then
Shall uprise with me.'

Traditional

A Small, Dry Voice

And I remember that we went singing carols once, a night or two before Christmas Eve, when there wasn't the shaving of a moon to light the secret, white-flying streets. At the end of a long road was a drive that led to a large house, and we stumbled up the darkness of the drive that night, each one of us afraid, each one holding a stone in his hand in case, and all of us too brave to say a word. The wind made through the drive-trees noises as of old and unpleasant and maybe web-footed men wheezing in caves. We reached the black bulk of the house.

'What shall we give them?' Dan whispered.

' "Hark the Herald"? "Christmas comes but Once a Year"?'

'No,' Jack said: 'We'll sing "Good King Wenceslas". I'll count three.'

One, two, three, and we began to sing, our voices high and seemingly distant in the snow-felted darkness round the house that was occupied by nobody we knew. We stood close together, near the dark door.

Good King Wenceslas looked out
On the Feast of Stephen.

And then a small, dry voice, like the voice of someone who has not spoken for a long time, suddenly joined our singing: a small, dry voice from the other side of the door: a small, dry voice through the keyhole. And when we stopped running we were outside *our* house; the front room was lovely and bright; the gramophone was playing; we saw the red and white balloons hanging from the gas-bracket; uncles and aunts sat by the fire; I thought I smelt our supper being fried in the kitchen. Everything was good again, and Christmas shone through all the familiar town.

'Perhaps it was a ghost,' Jim said.

'Perhaps it was trolls,' Dan said, who was always reading.

'Let's go in and see if there's any jelly left,' Jack said. And we did that.

Dylan Thomas, 'Memories of Christmas.'

Good King Wenceslas

Good King Wenceslas looked out,
　　On the Feast of Stephen,
When the snow lay round about,
　　Deep, and crisp, and even:
Brightly shone the moon that night,
　　Though the frost was cruel,
When a poor man came in sight,
　　Gathering winter fuel.

'Hither, page, and stand by me,
　　If thou know'st it, telling,
Yonder peasant, who is he?
　　Where and what his dwelling?'
'Sire, he lives a good league hence,
　　Underneath the mountain,
Right against the forest fence,
　　By Saint Agnes' fountain.'

'Bring me flesh, and bring me wine,
　　Bring me pine-logs hither;
Thou and I will see him dine,
　　When we bear them thither.'
Page and monarch, forth they went,
　　Forth they went together;
Through the rude wind's wild lament
　　And the bitter weather.

'Sire, the night is darker now,
    And the wind blows stronger;
Fails my heart, I know not how;
    I can go no longer.'
'Mark my footsteps, good my page;
    Tread thou in them boldly:
Thou shalt find the winter's rage
    Freeze thy blood less coldly.'

In his master's steps he trod,
    Where the snow lay dinted;
Heat was in the very sod
    Which the Saint had printed.
Therefore, Christian men, be sure,
    Wealth or rank possessing,
Ye who now will bless the poor,
    Shall yourselves find blessing.

                                        J. M. Neale

Stille Nacht! Heilige Nacht!

Silent night! Holy night!
    All is calm, all is bright.
See the gentle mother and Child,
    (Holy infant so tender and mild),
Rest in heav'nly peace,
    Rest in heav'nly peace.

Silent night! Holy night!
    Guiding star, lend thy light!
See the eastern wise men bring
    Gifts and homage to our King!
Jesus Christ is born,
    Jesus Christ is born.

Silent night! Holy night!
    Wondrous star, lend thy light!
With the angels let us sing

Alleluya to our King!
Jesus Christ is here,
    Jesus Christ is here.

J. Moier

A Carol at Auschwitz

December 1942 was a busy month for the men who administered Auschwitz. In the first place, Christmas was coming; and, while the birth of the Infant Jesus was scarcely an event hallowed in Nazi gospels, the SS, nevertheless, like so many who wallow in cruelty, wallowed also in sentimentality. They would burn without scruples, indeed with patriotic fervour, one thousand children; but their eyes would grow misty when they swapped pictures of their own loved ones at home.

Therefore Christmas could not be ignored, particularly when they were surrounded by a bunch of bloody Jews who did not believe in Santa Claus and whose barbaric forefathers had crucified the Saviour in the first place. The problem was how they could acknowledge the event without relaxing what they called euphemistically discipline; and this they solved simply by making it compulsory that in every barracks, prisoners should sing in chorus 'Silent Night'. Those who sang badly, it was decreed, were sent to bed without supper.

So every evening after work we stood before Block Senior Polzakiewicz. A violinist, borrowed from the orchestra, drew gently on his bow and we began to bawl out the words of this fine old carol. For those of us who spoke German, of course, it was not a particularly onerous duty; but those who did not, most of the Poles, for instance, had a hard time.

Polzakiewicz would tear his hair as they mangled the beautiful old German words. Then he would churn down among the ranks, trying to beat the words into their thick skulls with his club, as a result of which few of them slept, to quote the carol, in heavenly peace.

Rudolf Vrba and Alan Bestic, *I Cannot Forgive*

I Saw Three Ships

I saw three ships come sailing in,
  On Christmas Day, on Christmas Day,
I saw three ships come sailing in,
  On Christmas Day in the morning.

And what was in those ships all three?

Our Saviour Christ and his lady.

Pray, whither sailed those ships all three?

O, they sailed into Bethlehem.

And all the bells on earth shall ring,

And all the angels in Heaven shall sing,

And all the souls on earth shall sing,

Then let us all rejoice amain!

14th century

❦ 6 ❦

CARDS

Victoriana

The Christmas card was modest enough in its beginnings. Yet this excellent and cheap means of assuring friends and relatives once a year of your affection changed soon enough the straightforward 'Compliments of the Season' into something that looked more like all sorts of compliments for every conceivable season. Allegories ranging from the sublime to the ridiculous and even obscene invaded the cards during the seventies. No wonder that the Christmas card soon outpassed the popularity of the Valentine – then just one hundred years old. The more varied the greetings, the more proof they bore of how carefully you had chosen your card to suit the recipient's taste. Add to this the continuous hankering after something new, the idea of progress which always demanded more and better cards, and it will be easily understood why the Victorian card after a promising start degenerated into the most tawdry suburban stationery.

The sentimental Victorian enjoyed an enormous variety of designs: cats, kittens, dogs, sometimes carrying mistletoe, children feeding birds in winter and manikins dressed in period costume. There were various reasons for this intrusion of motives not really connected with Christmas. One certainly was the zeal for instruction. The Christmas card very often supplanted the earlier Christmas book. Christmas joy and teaching are combined when pictures of birds, fish and butterflies are introduced, drawn with so high a degree of accuracy that school-books could have benefited a great deal by using such illustrations. Special studies of flowers were very popular also. A beautiful spray of oleander by Thomas Crane – a brother of Walter Crane – is a fine example.

Pictures illustrating scenes from one period of the past or another have been favourites for nearly two hundred years. In Christmas cards they also appear very frequently. Sometimes the period chosen is the dateless though vaguely medieval time of the 'good old days' of the Christmas story, with cheer and wassail, sometimes the jollity of the eighteenth-century squire.

The end of the century warmed towards the stage-coach, the traditional vehicle of Christmas. No doubt it was of happier memory when looked at from the great days of the railway than from those of its own slow, cold and clumsy creakings. It makes a bright and cheery show in innumerable wintry countrysides, through countless half-timbered snow-laden streets, and halts before thousands of welcome inns with hot punch and hearty ostlers.

The country house, the destination of the early nineteenth-century traveller, is also the subject of many cards of all periods. The wealthy send private cards showing their own mansions, but the ordinary suburban householder and rent-payer has to be content with the picture of the castle or manor of his dreams. Of recent years the mansion tends to be Georgian, but the vicarious enjoyment of wealth seems to persist.

Another favourite from the early years has been the ship. It appears as an emblem of luck. Ships of all kinds grace the cards, but by far the most common is the galleon with its associations with the old days of the sea dogs. The design varies from a colourful seascape to a more artistic formalized pattern. Perhaps the most interesting example of the ship motive on a Christmas card is the photogravure of the *Endeavour* sent by Sir Ernest Shackleton to his friends in 1910.

Topical allusions like that of Shackleton's card make some cards an interesting subject of study. There was a card celebrating the end of the Boer War, while William Lockyer, the pioneer balloonist, had a card for 1909 which, suitably enough, employed the novel technique of a montage of aerial photographs. On the Lord Mayor of Birmingham's card for that year Santa Claus arrives in a primitive aeroplane to distribute over the 'Forward' city not toys but the gifts of a benevolent corporation – trams, electric lights, dust-carts, baths and policemen.

But surely the most interesting and certainly the most amusing of these topical cards was one noted by *The Times* in its annual card review in 1882. This card, presumably commemorating the defeat of the Egyptian mutiny in September of that year by Lord Wolseley at Tel-el-Kebir, showed those most incompatible queens, Cleopatra and Victoria, the former welcoming her successor as mistress of Egypt. Where else in any world have these two met, where else could they meet save in the general amnesty and good will of a nineteenth-century Christmas card?

The same sentiment is often a saccharine disguise for sex appeal. What a curious *fin de siècle* mentality is revealed by cards showing a fashionable *décolletée* young lady gambolling with a whole bevy of cupids against a background of mistletoe or flowering South Sea plants? The Christmas message is banished to a small frame artistically unconnected with the rest of the picture. Or what can be said of a card showing a number of nude or scantily clad young maidens shown against a background of mountains, luscious tropical fruit and lily ponds? *Punch* at once spotted this chance of a parody and published a drawing of naked maidens and boys meeting Father Christmas in a blizzard.

Can we discover any reason behind this variety of subjects, from Shackleton's *Endeavour* to the pretty semi-nude? A certain narrative element seems common to most Victorian cards. No proof is needed for the statement that the second half of the nineteenth century was the age of the 'narrative picture'. The catalogues of the Royal Academy of that time read like publishers' lists of cheap fiction. Whether heroic or trivial the subject matter was so treated as to make a story. It is the same with the illustrations of the popular art periodicals like the *Graphic* and the colour print. Only the narrative has been adapted to the mentality of the less-sophisticated classes. The Victorian Christmas card was heir to the colour print in form and content. It has a lot in common with the pictorial press of the day.

The paraphernalia of the 'good old days' as popularized by the Christmas literature brought the narrative element. It was the interest in the anecdote which made designers forget the seasonal associations – consequently a colour print alone remained. It is characteristic that when this happened inscriptions of good wishes vanished from the front and found room only on the back where a poem often had to evoke the Christmas sentiments which the picture could not possibly hope to conjure up. Thus senders of Christmas cards made it plain that they did remember their friends not only in the spirit of the season but were also bestowing on them a picture fit to be preserved in an album together with Valentines, reward-tickets and press-cuttings.

L. D. Ettlinger and R. G. Holloway, *Compliments of the Season*

Verse or Worse

I do not receive many Christmas cards. This is not surprising as I never remember to send any out. The most I have ever done, when feeling most strenuous, was to scramble out a few New Year's cards to people who had sent me Christmas cards, and whose remembrance of me stirred my gratitude. But I do always get some, and I got a few this year.

I have just been looking at them all before cremating them. Those which come from the more intellectual of my friends have no longer anything peculiarly Christmas cardy about them. They are in good taste, designed by or for the senders, admirably printed, and, in point of language, ready for the scrutiny of the most fastidious critic of style. Nothing could be more refined. There are no sprigs of holly on these, no claspings of amputated hands, no squat village towers amid snowy landscapes. They have brown collotype pictures of the owners' houses, choice etchings after Rembrandt, or exquisite coloured reproductions of St Vincent and a Donor by Melozzo da Forli in the Palazzo Doria-Pamphili at Rome. Each card of them is a silent protest against the old kind of card. As I look at them I hear them saying, 'What an improvement we are! How clearly we demonstrate that Christmas greetings can be conveyed without vulgarity. What careful consideration we betray! The men and women who chose *us* really wished to send their friends something worth having.' There is a beautiful woodcut on yellowish hand-made paper, with 'A Happy Christmas' as only inscription. There is a page from an illuminated manuscript. There is a card specially written out by an expert calligrapher. There is another displaying choice specimens of seventeenth-century typographical ornament. All very chaste, and not one of them (I need scarcely say) bearing a line of verse, even of good verse.

Yet from the more old-fashioned and less aspiring remnant of my acquaintance there still come a few tokens of the old Victorian sorts, freely powdered with Robin Redbreasts and mistletoe, and carrying quatrains to a card. It was one of these quatrains that checked me in the middle of my campaign of destruction and made me begin these reflections. It runs as follows:

> Glad Christmas to you on this day,
> Good Fortune ever find you,
> Life's Sunlight be before you aye,
> Its shadows all behind you.

Well, you will say, there is nothing very odd about that: it is precisely like thousands of others. Wait a moment. The odd thing is that under those verses is printed the name 'Browning'.

I stand open to correction. I have, I admit, not searched Robert Browning's works for this sequence of elegant sentiments. But I really cannot suppose that he wrote it. Nor can I believe that his wife wrote it. Nor can I even believe that Mr Oscar Browning wrote it, and with him is exhausted the catalogue of the Brownings known to fame or me. There have been, no doubt, other Brownings. John Browning or Nicodemus Browning may have been the author of this composition; or George Bernard Browning, or J. Pierpont Browning, or some inglorious but not altogether mute Ella Wheeler Browning. But if Robert Browning was really the author he must certainly have had a bad off day, on which his style was indistinguishable from that of any other Christmas card poet. And the common style of the Christmas card poets reaches the lowest known or conceivable level of banality in conception and tameness in execution.

I look through some of the other missives which have been sent to me in the hope (I must presume) of cheering me up, of inducing merriment and an optimistic outlook. Here are some of the verses on them – if I am committing breaches of copyright I must apologize:

(1)

To you and those within your home
This Christmas day may blessings come,
And may good luck, good health, good cheer
Be guests of yours for all the year.

(2)

As on Life's tide the seasons come and go
May sorrow ebb and gladness ever flow.

(3)

Milestones of olden memories
   Along sweet friendship's way;
Oh! how they brighten up the past,
   And cheer the coming day.

(4)

Greeting just to say we all unite,
In wishing you and yours a Christmas bright.

(5)

Deck out the walls with garlands gay,
And let the kindly laughter play.
List! the chimes are sweetly sounding
Xmas happiness abounding:
All that's good and true be thine
At this merry festive time.

(6)

This is the time for sweet remembrance,
   For thoughts of friends both old and new;

The words will not express the wishes
Sent within this card for you.

If Browning wrote one of them why not the lot? There is, I admit, a touch of *Mrs* Browning about the rhyme of 'time' and 'thine' in number five, and the elaborate maritime image in number two has perhaps a touch of Swinburne. But except for these very slight local differences the whole of these, not to mention thousands of others, all that you have ever seen and all that your Aunt Maria has ever seen, might have come from one pen. It is amazing that every publisher of Christmas cards should have 'on tap' a bard so skilful that he can turn out hundreds of these poems without ever introducing a touch of individuality or novelty. For somebody must write them, even if it be only the chairman of the manufacturing company or the compositor who does the type-setting. Who are these mysterious people? Are they scattered amateurs everywhere? Or is it here that we find the explanation of how our professional and justly celebrated poets earn their living? Or is this one of those industries which are the hereditary monopoly of a few families like flint-knapping, violin-making and gold-beating? Does Mr Jones, of Putney, whose neighbours know him for one who 'goes up to the City' every morning on some vague but presumably respectable business, really immure himself for eight hours per diem in an office in Chancery Lane and compose those verses which he never mentions at home, his father having left him a very valuable connection with the makers? Or – this is another solution – is it really that nobody has written any new ones for years?

Our enlightened capitalists are always said to be exploring new methods of eliminating waste. May it not be that it long ago occurred to one of them that a sufficient accumulation of Christmas verses was now in existence, that there was no difference between old ones and new ones, that nobody could even remember if he had seen one of them before, and that it was criminally extravagant to go on employing labour in the fabrication of a constant supply of new goods before the old were worn out? Surely if these truths were not grasped by keen business minds in the old days of fat and plenty they must have occurred to somebody during the war when every ounce of effort had to be put into war-work, and he who mis-employed labour was helping the Germans. If not, are we to understand that the composers of Christmas verses, after five years' inactivity, have actually been set to work again at their own trade – or (awful thought) that some of those extraordinary tribunals exempted them as indispensable?

J. C. Squire, 'Christmas Cards'

Annual Ritual

Miss Margaret Waters and her sister Mary were quietly at work in their cottage in the village street. They sat, one each side of the big round table in the living room, penning their Christmas cards in meticulous copperplate. Music tinkled from the large old-fashioned wireless set on the dresser by the fireplace, vying with the noise of the bells outside. Mary's grey curls began to nod in time to a waltz, and putting her pen between her teeth, she rose to increase the volume of the music. At that moment an excruciating clashing of St Patrick's peal informed the world of Fairacre that at least three of the six bell-ringers were hopelessly awry in their order.

'Switch it off, Mary, do! Them dratted bells drowns anything else. We may as well save the electric!' exclaimed Margaret, looking over the top of her gold-rimmed spectacles.

Mary obeyed, as she always did, and returned to her seat. It would have been nice, she thought privately, to hear 'The Merry Widow' waltz all the way through, but it was not worth upsetting Margaret – especially with Christmas so near. After all, it was the season of goodwill. She picked up a card from the central pile and surveyed it with affection.

'All right for Uncle Toby?' she queried, her head on one side. 'He's partial to a robin.'

Her sister looked up from her writing and studied the card earnestly. Sending just the right card to the right person was something which both sisters considered with the utmost care. Their Christmas cards had been chosen from the most modestly priced counter at Bell's, the Caxley stationer's, but even so the amount had been a considerable sum from the weekly pension of the two elderly sisters.

'You don't feel it's a mite spangly? That glitter on the icicles don't look exactly *manly* to me. I'd say the coach and horses myself.'

Mary set aside the robin reluctantly, and began to inscribe the card with the coach and horses: *From your affectionate nieces, Margaret and Mary.*

The ancient mahogany clock, set four-square in the middle of the mantelpiece, ticked steadily as it had done throughout their parents' married life and their own single one. A log hissed on the small open fire, and the black kettle on the trivet began to hum. By bedtime it would be boiling, ready for the sisters' hot-water bottles. It was very peaceful and warm in the cottage and Mary sighed with content as she tucked in the flap of Uncle Toby's envelope. It was the time of day she loved best, when the work was done, the curtains were drawn, and she and Margaret sat snugly and companionably by the fire.

'That seems to be the lot,' she observed, putting the envelopes into a neat stack. Margaret added her last one. Three, including the rejected robin, remained unused.

'There's bound to be someone we've forgot,' said Margaret. 'Put 'em all on the dresser, dear, and we'll post 'em off tomorrow.'

'Miss Read' (Dora Jessie Saint), *Village Christmas*

The Computer's First Christmas Card

jollymerry
hollyberry
jollyberry
merryholly
happyjolly
jollyjelly
jellybelly
bellymerry
hollyheppy
jollyMolly
marryJerry
merryHarry
hoppyBarry
heppyJarry
boppyheppy
berryjorry
jorryjolly
moppyjelly
Mollymerry
Jerryjolly
bellyboppy
jorryhoppy
hollymoppy
Barrymerry
Jarryhappy
happyboppy
boppyjolly

jollymerry
merrymerry
merrymerry
merryChris
ammerryasa
Chrismerry
asMERRYCHR
YSANTHEMUM

Edwin Morgan

Real Life Christmas Card

Robin, I watch you. You are perfect robin –
except, shouldn't you be perched on a spade handle?

Robin, you watch me. Am I perfect man – except,
shouldn't I have a trap in my pocket, a gun in my hand?

I, too, am in my winter plumage, not unlike yours,
except, the red is in my breast, not on it.

You sing your robin song, I my man song. They're different,
but they mean the same: winter, territory, greed.

Will we survive, bold eyes, to pick
the seeds in the ground, the seeds in my mind?

The snow man thinks so. Look at his silly smile
slushily spilling down the scarf I gave him.

Norman MacCaig

Grievous Greetings

24 December I am a poor man, but I would gladly give ten shillings to find out who sent me the insulting Christmas card I received this morning. I never insult people; why should they insult me? The worst part of the transaction is, that I find myself suspecting all my friends. The handwriting on the envelope is evidently disguised, being written sloping the wrong way. I cannot think either Gowing or Cummings would do such a mean thing. Lupin denied all knowledge of it, and I believe him; although I disapprove of his laughing and sympathizing with the offender. Mr Franching would be above such an act; and I don't think any of the Mutlars would descend to such a course. I wonder if Pitt, that impudent clerk at the office, did it? Or Mrs Birrell, the charwoman, or Burwin-Fosselton? The writing is too good for the former.

Christmas Day   We caught the 10.20 train at Paddington, and spent a pleasant day at Carrie's mother's. The country was quite nice and pleasant, although the roads were sloppy. We dined in the middle of the day, just ten of us, and talked over old times. If everybody had a nice, *un*interfering mother-in-law, such as I have, what a deal of happiness there would be in the world. Being all in good spirits, I proposed her health; and I made, I think, a very good speech.

I concluded, rather neatly, by saying: 'On an occasion like this – whether relatives, friends, or acquaintances – we are all inspired with good feelings towards each other. We are of one mind, and think only of love and friendship. Those who have quarrelled with absent friends should kiss and make up. Those who happily have *not* fallen out, can kiss all the same.'

I saw the tears in the eyes of both Carrie and her mother, and must say I felt very flattered by the compliment. That dear old Reverend John Panzy Smith, who married us, made a most cheerful and amusing speech, and said he should act on my suggestion respecting the kissing. He then walked round the table and kissed all the ladies, including Carrie. Of course one did not object to this: but I was more than staggered when a young fellow named Moss, who was a stranger to me, and who had scarcely spoken a word through dinner, jumped up suddenly with a sprig of mistletoe, and exclaimed: 'Hulloh! I don't see why I shouldn't be in on this scene.' Before one could realize what he was about to do, he kissed Carrie and the rest of the ladies.

Fortunately the matter was treated as a joke, and we all laughed; but it was a dangerous experiment, and I felt very uneasy for a moment as to the result. I subsequently referred to the matter to Carrie, but she said: 'Oh, he's not much more than a boy.' I said that he had a very large moustache for a boy. Carrie replied: 'I didn't say he was not a nice boy.'

26 December   I did not sleep very well last night; I never do in a strange bed. I feel a little indigestion, which one must expect at this time of year. Carrie and I returned to Town in the evening. Lupin came in late. He said he enjoyed his Christmas, and added: 'I feel as fit as a Lowther Arcade fiddle, and only require a little more "oof" to feel as fit as a £500 Stradivarius.' I have long since given up trying to understand Lupin's slang, or asking him to explain it.

27 December   I told Lupin I was expecting Gowing and Cummings to drop in tomorrow evening for a quiet game. I was in hope the boy would volunteer to stay in, and help to amuse them. Instead of which, he said: 'Oh, you had better put them off, as I have asked Daisy and Frank Mutlar to come.' I said I could not think of doing such a thing. Lupin said: 'Then I will send a wire, and put off Daisy.' I suggested that a post-card or letter would reach her quite soon enough, and would not be so extravagant.

Carrie, who had listened to the above conversation with apparent annoyance, directed a well-aimed shaft at Lupin. She said: 'Lupin, why do you object to Daisy meeting your father's friends? Is it because they are not good enough for her, or (which is equally possible) *she* is not good enough for them?' Lupin was dumbfounded, and could make no reply. When he left the room, I gave Carrie a kiss of approval.

28 December   Lupin, on coming down to breakfast, said to his mother: 'I have not put off Daisy and Frank, and should like them to join Gowing and Cummings this evening.' I felt very pleased with the boy for this. Carrie said in reply: 'I am glad you let me know in time, as I can turn over the cold leg of mutton, dress it with a little parsley, and no one will know it has been cut.' She further said she would make a few custards, and stew some pippins, so that they would be cold by the evening.

Finding Lupin in good spirits, I asked him quietly if he really had any personal objection to either Gowing or Cummings. He replied: 'Not in the least. I think Cummings looks rather an ass, but that is partly due to his patronizing "the three-and-six-one-price hat company", and wearing a reach-me-down frockcoat. As for that perpetual brown velveteen jacket of Gowing's – why, he resembles an itinerant photographer.'

I said it was not the coat that made the gentleman; whereupon Lupin, with a laugh, replied: 'No, and it wasn't much of a gentleman who made their coats.'

We were rather jolly at supper, and Daisy made herself very agreeable, especially in the earlier part of the evening, when she sang. At supper, however, she said: 'Can you make tee-to-tums with bread?' and she commenced rolling pieces of bread, and twisting them round on the table. I felt this to be bad manners, but of course said nothing. Presently Daisy and Lupin, to my disgust, began throwing bread-pills at each other. Frank followed suit, and so did Cummings and Gowing, to my astonishment. They then commenced throwing hard pieces of crust, one piece catching me on the forehead, and making me blink. I said: 'Steady, please; steady!' Frank jumped up and said: 'Tum, tum; then the band played.'

I did not know what this meant, but they all roared, and continued the bread-battle. Gowing suddenly seized all the parsley off the cold mutton, and threw it full in my face. I looked daggers at Gowing, who replied: 'I say, it's no good trying to look indignant, with your hair full of parsley.' I rose from the table, and insisted that a stop should be put to this foolery at once. Frank Mutlar shouted: 'Time, gentlemen, please! time!' and turned out the gas, leaving us in absolute darkness.

I was feeling my way out of the room, when I suddenly received a hard intentional punch at the back of my head. I said loudly: 'Who did that?' There was no answer; so I repeated the question, with the same result. I struck a match, and lighted the gas. They were all talking and laughing, so I kept my own counsel; but, after they had gone, I said to Carrie: 'The person who sent me that insulting post-card at Christmas was here tonight.'

29 December   I had a most vivid dream last night. I woke up, and on falling asleep, dreamed the same dream over again precisely. I dreamt I heard Frank Mutlar telling his sister that he had not only sent me the insulting Christmas card, but admitted that he was the one who punched my head last night in the dark. As fate would have it, Lupin, at breakfast, was reading extracts from a letter he had just received from Frank.

I asked him to pass the envelope, that I might compare the writing. He did so, and I examined it by the side of the envelope containing the Christmas card. I detected a similarity in the writing, in spite of the attempted disguise. I passed them on to Carrie, who began to laugh. I asked her what she was laughing at, and she said the card was never addressed to me at all. It was 'L. Pooter', not 'C. Pooter'. Lupin asked to look at the direction and the card, and exclaimed with a laugh: 'Oh yes, Guv, it's meant for me.' I said: 'Are you in the habit of receiving insulting Christmas cards?' He replied: 'Oh yes, and of *sending* them, too.'

In the evening Gowing called, and said he enjoyed himself very much last night. I took the opportunity to confide in him, as an old friend, about the vicious punch last night. He burst out laughing, and said: 'Oh, it was *your head*, was it? I know I accidentally hit something, but I thought it was a brick wall.' I told him I felt hurt, in both senses of the expression.

George and Weedon Grossmith, *The Diary of a Nobody*

Christmas Card

You have anti-freeze in the car, yes,
   But the shivering stars wade deeper.
Your scarf's tucked in under your buttons,
   But a dry snow ticks through the stubble.
Your knee-boots gleam in the fashion,
   But the moon must stay

         And stamp and cry
         As the holly the holly
         Hots its reds.

Electric blanket to comfort your bedtime
   The river no longer feels its stones.
Your windows are steamed by dumpling laughter
   The snowplough's buried on the drifted moor.
Carols shake your television
   And nothing moves on the road but the wind

         Hither and thither
         The wind and three
         Starving sheep.

Redwings from Norway rattle at the clouds
   But comfortless sneezers puddle in pubs.
The robin looks in at the kitchen window
   But all care huddles to hearths and kettles.
The sun lobs one wet snowball feebly
   Grim and blue

         The dusk of the coombe
         And the swamp woodland
         Sinks with the wren.

See old lips go purple and old brows go paler.
   The stiff crow drops in the midnight silence.
Sneezes grow coughs and coughs grow painful.

The vixen yells in the midnight garden.
You wake with the shakes and watch your breathing
Smoke in the moonlight – silent, silent.

Your anklebone
And your anklebone
Lie big in the bed.

Ted Hughes

❧ 7 ❧

THE CHRISTMAS TREE

The Christmas Tree

Put out the lights now!
Look at the Tree, the rough tree dazzled
In oriole plumes of flame,
Tinselled with twinkling frost fire, tasselled
With stars and moons – the same
That yesterday hid in the spinney and had no fame
Till we put out the lights now.

Hard are the nights now:
The fields at moonrise turn to agate,
Shadows are cold as jet;
In dyke and furrow, in copse and faggot
The frost's tooth is set;
And stars are the sparks whirled out by the north wind's fret
On the flinty nights now.

So feast your eyes now
On mimic star and moon-cold bauble:
Worlds may wither unseen,
But the Christmas Tree is a tree of fable,
A phoenix in evergreen,
And the world cannot change or chill what its mysteries mean
To your hearts and eyes now.

The vision dies now
Candle by candle: the tree that embraced it
Returns to its own kind,
To be earthed again and weather as best it
May the frost and the wind.

Children, it too had its hour – you will not mind
If it lives or dies now.

C. Day Lewis

Prince Albert's Legacy

I have been looking on, this evening, at a merry company of children
assembled round that pretty German toy, a Christmas Tree. The tree was
planted in the middle of a great round table, and towered high above their
heads. It was brilliantly lighted by a multitude of little tapers; and everywhere sparkled and glittered with bright objects. There were rosy-cheeked
dolls, hiding behind the green leaves; and there were real watches (with
movable hands, at least, and an endless capacity of being wound up) dangling
from innumerable twigs; there were French-polished tables, chairs, bed-
steads, wardrobes, eight-day clocks, and various other articles of domestic
furniture (wonderfully made, in tin, at Wolverhampton), perched among the
boughs, as if in preparation for some fairy housekeeping; there were jolly,
broad-faced little men, much more agreeable in appearance than many real
men – and no wonder, for their heads took off, and showed them to be full of
sugar-plums; there were fiddles and drums; there were tambourines, books,
work-boxes, paint-boxes, sweetmeat boxes, peep-show boxes, and all kinds of
boxes; there were trinkets for the elder girls, far brighter than any grown-up
gold and jewels; there were baskets and pincushions in all devices; there were
guns, swords, and banners; there were witches standing in enchanted rings of
pasteboard, to tell fortunes; there were tee-totums, humming-tops, needle-
cases, pen-wipers, smelling-bottles, conversation-cards, bouquet-holders;
real fruit, made artificially dazzling with gold leaf; imitation apples, pears,
and walnuts, crammed with surprises; in short, as a pretty child, before me,
delightedly whispered to another pretty child, her bosom friend, 'There was
everything, and more.' This motley collection of odd objects, clustering on
the tree like magic fruit, and flashing back the bright looks directed towards it
from every side – some of the diamond-eyes admiring it were hardly on a
level with the table, and a few were languishing in timid wonder on the
bosoms of pretty mothers, aunts, and nurses – made a lively realization of
the fancies of childhood; and set me thinking how all the trees that grow and
all the things that come into existence on the earth, have their wild adorn-
ments at that well-remembered time.

Being now at home again, and alone, the only person in the house awake, my thoughts are drawn back, by a fascination which I do not care to resist, to my own childhood. I begin to consider, what do we all remember best upon the branches of the Christmas Tree of our own young Christmas days, by which we climbed to real life.

Straight, in the middle of the room, cramped in the freedom of its growth by no encircling walls or soon-reached ceiling, a shadowy tree arises; and, looking up into the dreamy brightness of its top – for I observe in this tree the singular property that it appears to grow downwards towards the earth – I look into my youngest Christmas recollections!

All toys at first, I find. Up yonder, among the green holly and red berries, is the Tumbler with his hands in his pockets, who wouldn't lie down, but whenever he was put upon the floor, persisted in rolling his fat body about, until he rolled himself still, and brought those lobster eyes of his to bear upon me – when I affected to laugh very much, but in my heart of hearts was extremely doubtful of him. Close beside him is that infernal snuff-box, out of which there sprang a demoniacal Counsellor in a black gown, with an obnoxious head of hair, and a red cloth mouth, wide open, who was not to be endured on any terms, but could not be put away either; for he used suddenly, in a highly magnified state, to fly out of Mammoth Snuff-boxes in dreams, when least expected. Nor is the frog with cobbler's wax on his tail, far off; for there was no knowing where he wouldn't jump; and when he flew over the candle, and came upon one's hand with that spotted back – red on a green ground – he was horrible. The cardboard lady in a blue-silk skirt, who was stood up against the candlestick to dance, and whom I see on the same branch, was milder, and was beautiful; but I can't say as much for the larger cardboard man, who used to be hung against the wall and pulled by a string; there was a sinister expression in that nose of his; and when he got his legs round his neck (which he very often did), he was ghastly, and not a creature to be alone with.

When did that dreadful Mask first look at me? Who put It on, and why was I so frightened that the sight of it is an era in my life? It is not a hideous visage in itself; it is even meant to be droll; why then were its stolid features so intolerable? Surely not because it hid the wearer's face. An apron would have done as much; and though I should have preferred even the apron away, it would not have been absolutely insupportable, like the mask. Was it the immovability of the mask? The doll's face was immovable, but I was not afraid of *her*. Perhaps that fixed and set change coming over a real face, infused into my quickened heart some remote suggestion and dread of the universal change that is to come on every face, and make it still? Nothing reconciled me to it. No drummers, from whom proceeded a melancholy chirping on the turning of a handle; no regiment of soldiers, with a mute band, taken out of a box, and fitted, one by one, upon a stiff and lazy little set of lazy-tongs; no old woman, made of wires and a brown-paper composition, cutting up a pie for two small children; could give me a permanent comfort, for a long time. Nor was it any satisfaction to be shown the Mask, and see that it was made of paper, or to have it locked up and be assured that no one wore it. The mere recollection of that fixed face, the mere knowledge of its existence anywhere, was sufficient to awake me in the night all perspiration and horror, with, 'O I know it's coming! O the mask!'

I never wondered what the dear old donkey with the panniers – there he is! was made of, then! His hide was real to the touch, I recollect. And the great black horse with the round red spots all over him – the horse that I could even get upon – I never wondered what had brought him to that strange condition, or thought that such a horse was not commonly seen at Newmarket. The four horses of no colour, next to him, that went into the wagon of cheeses, and could be taken out and stabled under the piano, appear to have bits of fur-tippet for their tails, and other bits for their manes, and to stand on pegs instead of legs, but it was not so when they were brought home for a Christmas present. They were all right, then; neither was their harness unceremoniously nailed into their chests, as appears to be the case now. The tinkling works of the music-cart, I *did* find out, to be made of quill toothpicks and wire; and I always thought that little tumbler in his shirt-sleeves, perpetually swarming up one side of a wooden frame, and coming down, head foremost, on the other, rather a weak-minded person – though good-natured; but the Jacob's Ladder, next him, made of little squares of red wood, that went flapping and clattering over one another, each developing a different picture, and the whole enlivened by small bells, was a mighty marvel and a great delight.

Ah! The Doll's house! – of which I was not proprietor, but where I visited. I don't admire the Houses of Parliament half so much as that stone-fronted mansion with real glass windows, and doorsteps, and a real balcony – greener than I ever see now, except at watering places; and even they afford but a poor imitation. And though it *did* open all at once, the entire house-front (which was a blow, I admit, as cancelling the fiction of a staircase), it was but to shut it up again, and I could believe. Even open, there were three distinct rooms in it: a sitting-room and bedroom, elegantly furnished, and best of all, a kitchen, with uncommonly soft fire-irons, a plentiful assortment of diminutive utensils – oh, the warming-pan! – and a tin man-cook in profile, who was always going to fry two fish. What Barmecide justice have I done to the noble feasts wherein the set of wooden platters figured, each with its own peculiar delicacy, as a ham or turkey, glued tight on to it, and garnished with something green, which I recollect as moss! Could all the Temperance Societies of these later days, united, give me such a tea-drinking as I have had through the means of yonder little set of blue crockery, which really would hold liquid (it ran out of the small wooden cask, I recollect, and tasted of matches), and which made tea, nectar. And if the two legs of the ineffectual little sugar-tongs did tumble over one another, and want purpose, like Punch's hands, what does it matter? And if I did once shriek out, as a poisoned child, and strike the fashionable company with consternation, by reason of having drunk a little teaspoon, inadvertently dissolved in too hot tea, I was never the worse for it, except by a powder!

Upon the next branches of the tree, lower down, hard by the green roller and miniature gardening-tools, how thick the books begin to hang. Thin books, in themselves, at first, but many of them, and with deliciously smooth covers of bright red or green. What fat black letters to begin with! 'A was an archer, and shot at a frog.' Of course he was. He was an apple-pie also, and there he is! He was a good many things in his time, was A, and so were most of his friends, except X, who had so little versatility, that I never knew him to get beyond Xerxes or Xantippe – like Y, who was always confined to a Yacht or a Yew Tree; and Z condemned for ever to be a Zebra or a Zany. But, now, the very tree itself changes, and becomes a bean-stalk – the marvellous bean-stalk up which Jack climbed to the Giant's house! And now, those dreadfully interesting, double-headed giants, with their clubs over their shoulders, begin to stride along the boughs in a perfect throng, dragging knights and ladies home for dinner by the hair of their heads. And Jack – how noble, with his sword of sharpness, and his shoes of swiftness! Again those old meditations come upon me as I gaze up at him; and I debate within myself whether there was more than one Jack (which I am loth to believe possible), or only one genuine original admirable Jack, who achieved all the recorded exploits.

Good for Christmastime is the ruddy colour of the cloak, in which – the tree making a forest of itself for her to trip through, with her basket – Little Red Riding-Hood comes to me one Christmas Eve to give me information of the cruelty and treachery of that dissembling Wolf who ate her grandmother, without making any impression on his appetite, and then ate her, after making that ferocious joke about his teeth. She was my first love. I felt that if I could have married Little Red Riding-Hood, I should have known perfect bliss. But, it was not to be; and there was nothing for it but to look out the Wolf in the Noah's Ark there, and put him late in the procession on the table, as a monster who was to be degraded. O the wonderful Noah's Ark! It was not found seaworthy when put in a washing-tub, and the animals were crammed in at the roof, and needed to have their legs well shaken down before they could be got in, even there – and then, ten to one but they began to tumble out at the door, which was but imperfectly fastened with a wire latch – but what was *that* against it! Consider the noble fly, a size or two smaller than the elephant: the lady-bird, the butterfly – all triumphs of art! Consider the goose, whose feet were so small, and whose balance was so indifferent, that he usually tumbled forward, and knocked down all the animal creation. Consider Noah and his family, like idiotic tobacco-stoppers; and how the leopard stuck to warm little fingers; and how the tails of the larger animals used gradually to resolve themselves into frayed bits of string!

Hush! Again a forest, and somebody up in a tree – not Robin Hood, not Valentine, not the Yellow Dwarf (I have passed him and all Mother Bunch's wonders, without mention), but an Eastern King with a glittering scimitar and turban. By Allah! two Eastern Kings, for I see another, looking over his shoulder! Down upon the grass, at the tree's foot, lies the full length of a coal-black Giant, stretched asleep, with his head in a lady's lap; and near them is a glass box, fastened with four locks of shining steel, in which he keeps the lady prisoner when he is awake. I see the four keys at his girdle now. The lady makes signs to the two kings in the tree, who softly descend. It is the setting-in of the bright Arabian Nights.

Oh, now all common things become uncommon and enchanted to me. All lamps are wonderful; all rings are talismans. Common flower-pots are full of treasure, with a little earth scattered on the top; trees are for Ali Baba to hide in; beefsteaks are to throw down into the Valley of Diamonds, that the precious stones may stick to them, and be carried by the eagles to their nests, whence the traders, with loud cries, will scare them. Tarts are made, according to the recipe of the Vizier's son of Bussorah, who turned pastrycook after he was set down in his drawers at the gate of Damascus; cobblers are all Mustaphas, and in the habit of sewing up people cut into four pieces, to whom they are taken blindfold.

Any iron ring let into stone is the entrance to a cave which only waits for the magician, and the little fire, and the necromancy, that will make the earth shake. All the dates imported come from the same tree as that unlucky date, with whose shell the merchant knocked out the eye of the genie's invisible son. All olives are of the stock of that fresh fruit, concerning which the Commander of the Faithful overheard the boy conduct the fictitious trial of the fraudulent olive merchant; all apples are akin to the apple purchased (with two others) from the Sultan's gardener for three sequins, and which the tall black slave stole from the child. All dogs are associated with the dog, really a transformed man, who jumped upon the baker's counter, and put his paw on the piece of bad money. All rice recalls the rice which the awful lady, who was a ghoule, could only peck by grains, because of her nightly feasts in the burial-place. My very rocking-horse – there he is, with his nostrils turned completely inside-out, indicative of Blood! – should have a peg in his neck, by virtue thereof to fly away with me, as the wooden horse did with the Prince of Persia, in the sight of all his father's Court.

Yes, on every object that I recognize among those upper branches of my Christmas Tree, I see this fairy light! When I wake in bed, at daybreak, on the cold dark winter mornings, the white snow dimly beheld, outside, through the frost on the window-pane, I hear Dinarzade. 'Sister, sister, if you are yet awake, I pray you finish the history of the Young King of the Black Islands.' Scheherazade replies, 'If my lord the Sultan will suffer me to live another day, sister, I will not only finish that, but tell you a more wonderful story yet.' Then, the gracious Sultan goes out, giving no orders for the execution, and we all three breathe again.

At this height of my tree I begin to see, cowering among the leaves – it may be born of turkey, or of pudding, or mince-pie, or of these many fancies, jumbled with Robinson Crusoe on his desert island, Philip Quarll among the monkeys, Sandford and Merton with Mr Barlow, Mother Bunch, and the Mask – or it may be the result of indigestion, assisted by imagination and over-doctoring – a prodigious nightmare. It is so exceedingly indistinct, that I don't know why it's frightful – but I know it is. I can only make out that it is an immense array of shapeless things, which appear to be planted on a vast exaggeration of the lazy-tongs that used to bear the toy soldiers, and to be slowly coming close to my eyes, and receding to an immeasurable distance. When it comes closest, it is worse. In connection with it I descry remembrances of winter nights incredibly long; of being sent early to bed, as a punishment for some small offence, and waking in two hours, with a sensation of having been asleep two nights; of the laden hopelessness of morning ever dawning; and the oppression of a weight of remorse.

Charles Dickens, 'A Christmas Tree'

Certain London Spiritualists for some years past have decked out a Christmas tree with presents that have each the names of some dead child upon it, and sitting in the dark on Christmas night they hear the voice of some grown-up person, who seems to take the presents from the tree, and the clamorous voices of the children as they are distributed. Yet the presents still hang there and are given next day to an hospital.

W. B. Yeats, *A Vision*

To a Young Wretch

(*Boethian*)

As gay for you to take your father's ax
As take his gun – rod – to go hunting – fishing.
You nick my spruce until its fiber cracks,
It gives up standing straight and goes down swishing.
You link an arm in its arm and you lean
Across the light snow homeward smelling green.

I could have bought you just as good a tree
To frizzle resin in a candle flame,
And what a saving 'twould have meant to me.
But tree by charity is not the same
As tree by enterprise and expedition.
I must not spoil your Christmas with contrition.

It is your Christmases against my woods.
But even where, thus, opposing interests kill,
They are to be thought of as opposing goods
Oftener than as conflicting good and ill;
Which makes the war god seem no special dunce
For always fighting on both sides at once.

And though in tinsel chain and popcorn rope
My tree, a captive in your window bay,
Has lost its footing on my mountain slope
And lost the stars of heaven, may, oh, may
The symbol star it lifts against your ceiling
Help me accept its fate with Christmas feeling.

Robert Frost

The Christmas Life

> If you don't have a real tree, you don't
> bring the Christmas life into the house.
> *Josephine Mackinnon, aged 8*

Bring in a tree, a young Norwegian spruce,
Bring hyacinths that rooted in the cold,
Bring winter jasmine as its buds unfold:
Bring the Christmas life into this house.

Bring red and green and gold, bring things that shine,
Bring candlesticks and music, food and wine.
Bring in your memories of Christmas past,
Bring in your tears for all that you have lost.

Bring in the shepherd boy, the ox and ass,
Bring in the stillness of an icy night,
Bring in a birth, of hope and love and light:
Bring the Christmas life into this house.

Wendy Cope

❦ 8 ❦

CHRISTMAS LEGENDS

Saint Brandan

Saint Brandan sails the northern main;
The brotherhoods of saint are glad.
He greets them once, he sails again;
So late! – such storms! The Saint is mad!

He heard, across the howling seas,
Chime convent-bells on wintry nights;
He saw, on spray-swept Hebrides,
Twinkle the monastery-lights.

But north, still north, Saint Brandan steered –
And now no bells, no convents more!
The hurtling Polar lights are neared,
The sea without a human shore.

At last – it was the Christmas night;
Stars shone after a day of storm –
He sees float past an iceberg white,
And on it – Christ! – a living form.

That furtive mien, that scowling eye,
Of hair that red and tufted fell –
It is – Oh, where shall Brandan fly? –
The traitor Judas, out of hell!

Palsied with terror, Brandan sate;
The moon was bright, the iceberg near.
He hears a voice sigh humbly: 'Wait!
By high permission I am here.

'One moment wait, thou holy man!
On earth my crime, my death, they knew;
My name is under all men's ban –
Ah, tell them of my respite too!

'Tell them, one blessed Christmas-night –
It was the first after I came,
Breathing self-murder, frenzy, spite,
To rue my guilt in endless flame –

'I felt, as I in torment lay
'Mid the souls plagued by heavenly power,
An angel touch mine arm, and say:
Go hence and cool thyself an hour!

' "Ah, whence this mercy, Lord?" I said.
The Leper recollect, said he,
*Who asked the passers-by for aid,
In Joppa, and thy charity.*

'Then I remembered how I went,
In Joppa, through the public street,
One morn when the sirocco spent
Its storms of dust with burning heat;

'And in the street a leper sate,
Shivering with fever, naked, old;
Sand raked his sores from heel to pate,
The hot wind fevered him five-fold.

'He gazed upon me as I passed,
And murmured: *Help me, or I die!*
To the poor wretch my cloak I cast,
Saw him look eased, and hurried by.

'Oh, Brandan, think what grace divine,
What blessing must full goodness shower,
When fragment of it small, like mine,
Hath such inestimable power!

'Well-fed, well-clothed, well-friended, I
Did that chance act of good, that one!
Then went my way to kill and lie –
Forgot my good as soon as done.

'The germ of kindness, in the womb
Of mercy caught, did not expire;
Outlives my guilt, outlives my doom,
And friends me in the pit of fire.

'Once every year, when carols wake,
On earth, the Christmas-night's repose,
Arising from the sinners' lake,
I journey to these healing snows.

'I stanch with ice my burning breast,
With silence balm my whirling brain.
O Brandan! to this hour of rest
That Joppan leper's ease was pain.'

Tears started to Saint Brandan's eyes;
He bowed his head, he breathed a prayer –
Then looked, and lo, the frosty skies!
The iceberg, and no Judas there!

Matthew Arnold

Saint Steven

Saint Steven was a clerk in King Herowdes halle,
And served him of bred and cloth, as every king befalle.

Steven out of kichoun cam with bores hed on hande;
He saw a sterre was fair and bright over Bedlem stande.

He kest adown the bores hed and went into the halle:
'I forsake thee, King Herowdes, and they werkes all.

I forsake thee, King Herowdes, and they werkes all;
Ther is a child in Bedlem born is beter than we alle.'

'What aileth thee, Steven? What is thee befalle?
Lakketh thee either mete or drink in King Herowdes halle?'

'Lakketh me neither mete ne drink in King Herowdes halle;
Ther is a child in Bedlem born is beter than we alle.'

'What aileth thee, Steven? art thou wood, or thou ginnest to brede?
Lakketh thee either gold or fee or any riche wede?'

'Lakketh me neither gold ne fee, ne non riche wede;
Ther is a child in Bedlem born shall help us at our nede.'

'That is al so sooth, Steven, al so sooth, y-wis,
As this capoun crowe shal that lith here in myn dish.'

That word was not so soone said, that word in that halle,
The capoun crew *Christus natus est* among the lordes alle.

Riseth up, myn tormentoures, by two and al by one,
And ledeth Steven out of this town and stoneth him with stone.

Tooken he Steven and stoned him in the way;
And therefor is his even on Cristes owen day.

15th century

The Sword in the Stone

Thenne stood the reame in grete jeopardy long whyle, for every lord that was myghty of men maade hym stronge, and many wende to have ben kyng. Thenne Merlyn wente to the Archebisshop of Caunterbury and counceilled hym for to sende for all the lordes of the reame and alle the gentilmen of armes, that they shold to London come by Cristmas upon payne of cursynge, and for this cause, that Jesu, that was borne on that nyghte, that He wold of His grete mercy shewe some myracle, as He was come to be Kynge of mankynde, for to shewe somme myracle who shold be rightwys kynge of this reame. So the Archebisshop, by the advys of Merlyn, send for alle the lordes and gentilmen of armes that they shold come by Crystmasse even unto London; and many of hem made hem clene of her lyf, that her prayer myghte be the more acceptable unto God.

Soo in the grettest chirch of London – whether it were Powlis or not the Frensshe booke maketh no mencyon – alle the estates were longe or day in the chirche for to praye. And whan matyns and the first masse was done there was sene in the chircheyard ayenst the hyhe aulter a grete stone four square, lyke unto a marbel stone, and in myddes therof was lyke an anvylde of stele a foot on hyghe, and theryn stack a fayre swerd naked by the poynt, and letters there were wryten in gold about the swerd that saiden thus: 'WHOSO PULLETH OUTE THIS SWERD OF THIS STONE AND ANVYLD IS RIGH-TWYS KYNGE BORNE OF ALL ENGLOND.' Thenne the peple merveilled and told it to the Archebisshop.

'I commande,' said th'Archebisshop, 'that ye kepe yow within your chirche and pray unto God still; that no man touche the swerd tyll the hyhe masse be all done.'

So whan all masses were done all the lordes wente to beholde the stone and the swerd. And whan they sawe the scripture som assayed suche as wold have ben kyng, but none myght stere the swerd nor meve hit.

'He is not here,' said the Archebisshop, 'that shall encheve the swerd, but doubte not God will make hym knowen. But this is my counceill,' said the Archebisshop, 'that we lete purvey ten knyghtes, men of good fame, and they to kepe this swerd.'

So it was ordeyned, and thenne ther was made a crye that every man shold assay that wold for to wynne the swerd. And upon Newe Yeers day the barons lete maake a justes and a tournement, that alle knyghtes that would juste or tourneye there myght playe. And all this was ordeyned for to kepe the lordes togyders and the comyns, for the Archebisshop trusted that God wold make hym knowe that shold wynne the swerd.

So upon New Yeres day, whan the servyce was done, the barons rode unto the feld, some to juste and som to torney. And so it happed that syre Ector that had grete lyvelode aboute London rode unto the justes, and with hym rode syr Kaynus, his sone, and yong Arthur that was hys nourisshed broder; and syr Kay was made knyght at Alhalowmas afore. So as they rode to the justes-ward sir Kay had lost his suerd, for he had lefte it at his faders lodgyng, and so he prayd yong Arthur for to ryde for his swerd.

'I wyll wel,' said Arthur, and rode fast after the swerd.

And whan he cam home the lady and al were out to see the joustyng. Thenne was Arthur wroth and saide to hymself, 'I will ryde to the chirche-

yard and take the swerd with me that stycketh in the stone, for my broder sir
Kay shal not be without a swerd this day.' So whan he cam to the chircheyard
sir Arthur alight and tayed his hors to the style, and so he wente to the tent
and found no knyghtes there, for they were atte justyng. And so he handled
the swerd by the handels, and lightly and fiersly pulled it out of the stone,
and took his hors and rode his way untyll he came to his broder sir Kay and
delyverd hym the swerd. And as sone as sir Kay saw the swerd he wist wel it
was the swerd of the stone, and so he rode to his fader syr Ector and said,

'Sire, loo here is the swerd of the stone, wherfor I must be kyng of thys
land.'

When syre Ector beheld the swerd he retorned ageyne and cam to the
chirche, and there they alighte al thre and wente into the chirche, and anon
he made sir Kay to swere upon a book how he came to that swerd.

'Syr,' said sir Kay, 'by my broder Arthur, for he brought it to me.'

'How gate ye this swerd?' said sir Ector to Arthur.

'Sir, I will telle you. When I cam home for my broders swerd I fond
nobody at home to delyver me his swerd. And so I thought my broder syr
Kay should not be swerdles, and so I cam hyder egerly and pulled it out of
the stone withoute ony payn.'

'Found ye ony knyghtes about this swerd?' seid sir Ector.

'Nay,' said Arthur.

'Now,' said sir Ector to Arthur, 'I understande ye must be kynge of this
land.'

'Wherfore I?' sayd Arthur, 'and for what cause?'

'Sire,' saide Ector, 'for God wille have hit soo, for ther shold never man
have drawen oute this swerde but he that shal be rightwys kyng of this land.
Now lete me see whether ye can putte the swerd theras it was and pulle hit
oute ageyne.'

'That is no maystry,' said Arthur, and soo he put it in the stone. Therwithalle sir Ector assayed to pulle oute the swerd and faylled.

'Now assay', said syre Ector unto syre Kay. And anon he pulled at the
swerd with alle his myghte, but it wold not be.

'Now shal ye assay,' said syre Ector to Arthur.

'I wyll wel,' said Arthur, and pulled it out easily.

And therwithalle syre Ector knelyd doune to the erthe and syre Kay.

'Allas!' said Arthur, 'myne own dere fader and broder, why knele ye to me?'

'Nay, nay, my lord Arthur, it is not so. I was never your fader nor of your
blood, but I wote wel ye are of an hyher blood than I wende ye were.' And
thenne syre Ector told hym all how he was bitaken hym for to nourisshe hym
and by whoos commandement, and by Merlyns delyveraunce.

Thenne Arthur made grete doole whan he understood that syre Ector was not his fader.

'Sir,' said Ector unto Arthur, 'woll ye be my good and gracious lord when ye are kyng?'

'Els were I to blame,' said Arthur, 'for ye are the man in the world that I am most beholdyng to, and my good lady and moder your wyf that as wel as her owne hath fostred me and kepte. And yf ever hit be Goddes will that I be kynge as ye say, ye shall desyre of me what I may doo and I shalle not faille yow. God forbede I shold faille yow.'

'Sir,' said sire Ector, 'I will aske no more of yow but that ye wille make my sone, your foster broder syre Kay, seneceall of alle your landes.'

'That shalle be done,' said Arthur, 'and more, by the feith of my body, that never man shalle have that office but he whyle he and I lyve.'

Therewithall they wente unto the Archebisshop and told hym how the swerd was encheved and by whome. And on twelfth day alle the barons cam thyder and to assay to take the swerd who that wold assay, but there afore hem alle ther myghte none take it out but Arthur. Wherfor ther were many lordes wroth, and saide it was grete shame unto them all and the reame to be overgovernyd with a boye of no hyghe blood borne. And so they fell oute at that tyme, that it was put of tyll Candelmas, and thenne all the barons shold mete there ageyne; but alwey the ten knyghtes were ordeyned to watche the swerd day and nyght, and so they sette a pavelione over the stone and the swerd, and fyve alwayes watched.

Soo at Candalmasse many moo grete lordes came thyder for to have wonne the swerde, but there myghte none prevaille. And right as Arthur dyd at Cristmasse he dyd at Candelmasse, and pulled oute the swerde easely, wherof the barons were sore agreved and put it of in delay till the hyghe feste of Eester. And as Arthur sped afore so dyd he at Eester. Yet there were some of the grete lordes had indignacion that Arthur shold be kynge, and put it of in a delay tyll the feest of Pentecoste. Thenne the Archebisshop of Caunterbury by Merlyns provydence lete purveye thenne of the best knyghtes that they myghte gete, and suche knyghtes as Uther Pendragon loved best and moost trusted in his dayes. And suche knyghtes were put aboute Arthur as syr Bawdewyn of Bretayn, syre Kaynes, syre Ulfyus, syre Barsias; all these with many other were alweyes about Arthur day and nyghte till the feste of Pentecost.

And at the feste of Pentecost alle maner of men assayed to pulle at the swerde that wold assay, but none myghte prevaille but Arthur, and he pulled it oute afore all the lordes and comyns that were there. Wherfore alle the comyns cryed at ones,

'We wille have Arthur unto our kyng! We wille put hym no more in delay, for we all see that it is Goddes wille that he shalle be our kynge, and who that holdest ageynst it, we wille slee hym.

Sir Thomas Malory, *Le Morte D'Arthur*

Christmas Knight

On the ground the Green Knight graciously stood,
With head slightly slanting to expose the flesh.
His long and lovely locks he laid over his crown,
Neatly showing the naked neck, nape and all.
Gawain gripped his axe and gathered it on high,
Advanced the left foot before him on the ground,
And slashed swiftly down on the exposed part,
So that the sharp blade sheared through, shattering the bone,
Sank deep in the sleek flesh, split it in two,
And the scintillating steel struck the ground.
The fair head fell from the neck. On the floor it rolled.
So that people spurned and parried it as it passed their feet.
Then blood spurted from the body, bright against the green.
Yet the fellow did not fall, nor falter one whit,
But stoutly strode forward on legs still sturdy
To where the worthy knights stood, weirdly reached out,
Seized his splendid head and straightway lifted it.
Then he strode to his steed, snatched the bridle,
Stepped into the stirrup and swung aloft,
Holding his head by the hair in his hand.
He settled himself in the saddle as steadily
As if nothing had happened to him, though he had
    No head.
      He twisted his trunk about,
      That gruesome body that bled;
      He caused much dread and doubt
      By the time his say was said.

For of a truth he held up the head in his hand,
Pointed the face at the fairest in fame on the dais:
And it lifted its eyelids and looked glaringly,

And menacingly said with its mouth as you may now hear:
'Be prepared to perform what you promised, Gawain;
Seek faithfully till you find me, my fine fellow,
According to your oath in this hall in these knights' hearing.
Go to the Green Chapel without gainsaying to get
– And gladly will it be given in the gleaming New Year –
Such a stroke as you have struck. Strictly you deserve it.
As the Knight of the Green Chapel I am known to many;
Therefore if you ask for me, I shall be found.
So come, or else be called coward accordingly!'
Then he savagely swerved, sawing at the reins,
Rushed out at the hall door, his head in his hand,
And the flint-struck fire flew up from the hooves.
What place he departed to no person there knew,
Nor could any account be given of the country he had come from.
　　　　What then?
　　　At the Green Knight Gawain and King
　　　Grinned and laughed again;
　　　But plainly approved the thing
　　　As a marvel in the world of men.

Though honoured King Arthur was at heart astounded,
He let no sign of it be seen, but said clearly
To the comely queen in courtly speech,.
'Do not be dismayed, dear lady, today:
Such cleverness comes well at Christmastide,
Like the playing of interludes, laughter and song,
And making fine music meet for lords and ladies.
However, I am now able to eat the repast,
Having seen, I must say, a sight to wonder at.'
He glanced at Sir Gawain, and graciously said,
'Now sir, hang up your axe: you have hewn enough.'
And on the backcloth above the dais it was boldly hung
Where all men might mark it and marvel at it
And with truthful testimony tell the wonder of it.
Then to the topmost table the two went together,
The King and the constant knight, and keen men served them
Double portions of each dainty in dignified style,
All manner of meat, and minstrelsy too.

Daylong they delighted till darkness came
    To their shores.
  Now Gawain, give a thought,
For peril lest you pause,
To seeking out the sport
That you have claimed as yours.

        Anon., *Sir Gawain and the Green Knight* (trans. Brian Stone)

The Silent Knight

He went into a huff at Christmas,
there in the crowded church
with the choir behind him, singing hymns
about kings, and mangers
and a holy, silent *night*!

So he became a silent *knight*,
and stormed from the church
to don his armour, mount his horse
and head for his castle home
where he brooded in the bedroom

then pinned up a notice
sacking all the servants,
advertising for dumb replacements,
and warning his wife
never to speak to him again.

And each month at the joust
he was invincible,
his lance became a tin-opener
leaving the meat of knights
for maggots to gobble,

while he never boasted
or cried out in triumph,
just galloped home to his silent castle
where harpists were barred
and monks went on the fire.

        Matthew Sweeney

Per Gynt

It was now Christmas, and Per Gynt, having heard of a farm in the Dovre country where so many Trolls were accustomed to congregate on Christmas Eve that the people who lived there had to flee and find places to stay at other farms, decided to go there: for he thought he would like to see these Trolls. He put on torn clothing, and took with him a tame bear which belonged to him, together with an awl, some pitch, and some wire. When he reached the farm he went in and asked for shelter.

'God help us,' cried the farmer, 'We cannot shelter you. We have to leave the house ourselves, for the place is alive with Trolls every Christmas Eve!'

But Per thought he could manage to clear the farm of Trolls, so they told him to stay, and gave him a pig's skin in the bargain. Then the bear lay down behind the hearth, and Per took his awl, his pitch, and his wire, and made a large shoe out of the pig's skin, drawing a thick rope through it for a shoelace, having also at hand two wagon-spokes for wedges. Suddenly the Trolls arrived with fiddles and fiddlers, and began to dance and to eat their Christmas dinner on the table, some eating fried bacon, some fried frogs and toads and things of that kind; for they had brought their Christmas dinner with them. In the meantime some of them noticed the shoe Per Gynt had made, and since it was evidently intended for a large foot, all the Trolls wanted to try it on. When every one of them had thrust in his foot Per Gynt laced it, forced in a wedge, and drew the lace so tight that at last every one of them was caught and held in the shoe. But now the bear thrust forth his snout and sniffed the roast.

'Would you like some cake, little white cat?' said one of the Trolls, and threw a burning hot roasted frog into the bear's jaws.

'Thump them, Master Bruin!' cried Per Gynt: and the bear, very angry, rushed on the Trolls, raining blows and scratching on every side, Per Gynt hewed into the crowd with his spare wagon-spoke as though he meant to break their skulls. The Trolls soon had to make themselves scarce, but Per remained and feasted on Christmas fare all the week, while for many a year no more was heard of the Trolls.

P. C. Asbjörnsen, *Per Gynt*

Saint Nicholas

Nicholas, a citizen of Patera, was born of rich and pious parents. His father was named Epiphanes, his mother, Johanna. When, in the flower of their youth, they had brought him into the world, they adopted the celibate life thenceforth. While the infant was being bathed on the first day of his life, he stood straight up in the bath. From then on he took the breast only once on Wednesdays and Fridays. As a youth he avoided the dissolute pleasures of his peers, preferring to spend time in churches; and whatever he could under-stand of the Holy Scriptures he committed to memory.

After the death of his parents he began to consider how he might make use of his great wealth, not in order to win men's praise but to give glory to God. At the time a certain fellow townsman of his, a man of noble origin but very poor, was thinking of prostituting his three virgin daughters in order to make a living out of this vile transaction. When the saint learned of this, abhorring the crime he wrapped a quantity of gold in a cloth and, under cover of darkness, threw it through a window of the other man's house and withdrew unseen. Rising in the morning the man found the gold, gave thanks to God, and celebrated the wedding of his eldest daughter. Not long thereafter the servant of God did the same thing again. This time the man, finding the gold and bursting into loud praises, determined to be on the watch so as to find out who had come to the relief of his penury. Some little time later Nicholas threw a double sum of gold into the house. The noise awakened the man and he pursued the fleeing figure, calling out, 'Stop! Stop! Don't hide from me!' and ran faster and faster until he saw that it was Nicholas. Falling to the ground he wanted to kiss his benefactor's feet, but the saint drew away and exacted a promise that the secret would be kept until after his death.

Some time later the bishop of Myra died, and all the bishops of the region gathered to choose a successor. Among them was one bishop of great authority, upon whose opinion the decision of the others would depend. This prelate exhorted the others to fast and pray: and that very night he heard a voice telling him to post himself at the doors of the church in the morning, and to consecrate as bishop the first man he saw coming in, whose name would be Nicholas. In the morning he made this known to his colleagues and went outside the church to wait. Meanwhile Nicholas, miraculously guided by God, went early to the church and was the first to enter. The bishop, coming up to him, asked his name; and he, filled with the simplicity of a dove, bowed his head and answered, 'Nicholas, the servant of your holiness.'

Then all the bishops led him in and installed him on the episcopal throne. But he, amidst his honors, always preserved his former humility and gravity of manner. He passed the night in prayer, mortified his body, and shunned the society of women. He was humble in his attitude toward others, persuasive in speech, forceful in counsel, and strict when reprimands were called for. A chronicle also states that Nicholas took part in the Council of Nicaea.

The Golden Legend

Saint Nicholas money used to give to maidens secretly.
Who that be still may use his wonted liberality;
The mothers all their children on the eve do cause to fast,
And when they every one at night in senseless sleep are cast,
Both apples, nuts, and pears they bring, and other things beside,
As caps, and shoes and petticoats, with other things they hide,
And in the morning found, they say, 'Saint Nicholas this brought.'

Barnabe Googe *Popish Kingdom*

FATHER CHRISTMAS/
SANTA CLAUS

How Santa and His Reindeer got so High

The culture and folklore which brought us our favourite fairytales
may owe as much to magic mushrooms as to imagination.

I am going to tell you the story of Father Christmas. A long time ago, the
dark Siberian winters froze the earth deep down. The mystic nomads who
lived there dug holes in the ground to bear out the long freeze. They were
simple homes – the doors doubled up as smokeholes. Each tribe of nomads
owned a shaman – a leader who looked after the spiritual health of his people,
charged with the tasks of divination. At the right season he would hunt out
and eat a fly agaric toadstool. Fly agaric toadstools are hallucinogenic (but
very dangerous). Climbing out of the smokehole the shaman would take an
hallucinatory flight across the skies, returning through the opening in the
roof of his home, bearing the gifts of knowledge from the gods.

He might have been accompanied outside, for the nomads had noticed that
reindeer in the region also sought out and ate the fly agaric, whereupon they
seemed to suffer from unnatural sight: making them feel perhaps, that
they were flying.

George Monbiot

Trance

My mother opens the scullery door
on Christmas Eve, 1954,
to empty the dregs
of the tea-pot on the snowy flags.
A wind out of Siberia

carries such voices as will carry
through to the kitchen –

Someone mutters a flame from lichen
and eats the red-and-white Fly Agaric
while the others hunker in the dark,
taking it in turn
to drink his mind-expanding urine.
One by one their reindeer
nuzzle in.

My mother slams the door
on her star-cluster of dregs
and packs me off to bed.
At 2 a.m. I will clamber downstairs
to glimpse the red-and-white
up the chimney, my new rocking-horse
as yet unsteady on its legs.

Paul Muldoon

Believer

And so I awaited Christmas Eve, and the always exciting advent of fat Santa.
Of course, I had never seen a weighted, jangling, belly-swollen giant flop
down a chimney and gaily dispense his largesse under a Christmas tree. My
cousin Billy Bob, who was a mean little runt but had a brain like a fist made
of iron, said it was a lot of hooey, there was no such creature.

'My foot!' he said. 'Anybody would believe there was any Santa Claus
would believe a mule was a horse.' This quarrel took place in the tiny
courthouse square. I said: '*There is a Santa Claus because what he does is the
Lord's will and whatever is the Lord's will is the truth.*' And Billy Bob, spitting
on the ground, walked away: 'Well, looks like we've got another preacher on
our hands.'

Truman Capote, One Christmas

Ho, Ho, Who?

Crash! Besides the door into the passage, the nursery had two other doors leading into bedrooms. Lionel had tiptoed through the sacred Howliboo night-nursery and now bounced in upon us again screaming, 'Pumpkin Eater! Pumpkin Eater!'

The nursery-maids rose from their places and chased him out, but as fast as they slammed one door behind him he rushed in at another. There were no keys, and he tore through the room again and again, the nursery-maids trying to hold the doors but never knowing which he was going to attack next. In the middle of the uproar, and just as Lionel had thrown a cushion into the middle of the food, there came a heavy knock on the door which led into the passage.

No one had heard any footsteps so we all jumped, and Lionel popped under the table where he was well hidden by the long tablecloth.

Slowly, slowly the door opened and, to our astonishment, who should come in but Father Christmas.

We big ones naturally guessed at once that it must be someone dressed up; but it didn't look like anyone we knew and it did look exactly like Father Christmas. Betty was sitting opposite to me and I saw her round face go absolutely white as if she were about to faint, while Peter blushed purple.

'It's Mr O'Sullivan,' said Rosamund uncertainly.

'Or is it . . . ? Can it be . . . ?'

Father Christmas now raised his hand and began counting the children in a queer deep voice.

'One, two, three, four, five, six, seven, eight, nine, ten . . . ten?' Here he stopped. As Lionel was under the table of course we were one short. Father Christmas counted again, but it still came to ten.

Then he pronounced in a slow, solemn voice:

> 'The child under the table,
> I give you fair warning,
> Will find nothing in his stocking
> On Christmas morning.'

This was too much for Lionel who suddenly scrambled out and slunk on to his chair, trying to pretend he had been there all the time.

'Eleven!' said Father Christmas and slipped out of the room, shutting the door behind him.

'Quick!' cried Rosamund. 'Which way did he go?'

There was a rush to the door, but by the time we had got it open there was no one to be seen in the passage.

'I think it was Mr O'Sullivan,' said Rosamund again.

'I think it was Grandmama,' said Peggy.

'Grandmama doesn't have a beard.'

'Neither does Mr O'Sullivan.'

'If it wasn't really Father Christmas,' said Peter, 'how did he know that Lionel was under the table?'

How, indeed? We were all puzzled and turned to the grown-ups.

'Nana, who was it?' 'Minnie, May, who was it?' 'You've *got* to tell us who it was.'

But they only laughed, and I can't tell you anything more about it because the mystery was never solved.

Mary Clive, *Christmas with the Savages*

Father Christmas Executed

Christmas of 1951 in France was marked by a controversy – of great interest to press and public alike – that gave the generally festive atmosphere an unusual note of bitterness. A number of the clergy had for several months expressed disapproval of the increasing importance given by both families and the business sector to the figure of Father Christmas. They denounced a disturbing 'paganization' of the Nativity that was diverting public spirit from the true Christian meaning of Christmas to the profit of a myth devoid of religious value. Attacks spread just before Christmas; with more discretion, but just as much conviction, the Protestant Church chimed in with the Catholic Church. A number of articles and letters in the press bore witness to a keen public interest in the affair and showed general hostility to the Church's position. It came to a head on Christmas Eve with a demonstration that a reporter from *France-soir* described as follows:

SUNDAY SCHOOL CHILDREN WITNESS FATHER CHRISTMAS
BURNT IN DIJON CATHEDRAL PRECINCT

Dijon, 24 December

Father Christmas was hanged yesterday afternoon from the railings of Dijon Cathedral and burnt publicly in the precinct. This spectacular execution took place in the presence of several hundred Sunday school children. It was a decision made with the agreement of the clergy who had condemned Father Christmas as a usurper and heretic. He was accused of 'paganizing' the Christmas festival and installing himself like a cuckoo in the nest, claiming more and more space for himself. Above all he was blamed for infiltrating all the state schools from which the crib has been scrupulously banished.

On Sunday, at three o'clock in the afternoon, the unfortunate fellow with the white beard, scapegoated like so many innocents before him, was executed by his accusers. They set fire to his beard and he vanished into smoke.

At the time of the execution a communiqué was issued to the following effect:

'Representing all Christian homes of the parish keen to struggle against lies, 250 children assembled in front of the main door of Dijon Cathedral and burned Father Christmas.

'It wasn't intended as an attraction, but as a symbolic gesture. Father Christmas has been sacrificed. In truth, the lies about him cannot arouse religious feeling in a child and are in no way a means of education. Others may say and write what they want about Father Christmas, but the fact is he is only the counterweight of a modern-day Mr Bogeyman.

'For Christians the festivity of Christmas must remain the annual celebration of the birth of the Saviour.'

Father Christmas's execution in the Cathedral precinct got a mixed response from the public and provoked lively commentaries even from Catholics.

The affair has divided the town into two camps.

Dijon awaits the resurrection of Father Christmas, assassinated yesterday in the cathedral precinct. He will arise this evening at six o'clock in the Town Hall. An official communiqué announced that, as every year, the children of Dijon are invited to Liberation Square where Father Christmas will speak to them from the floodlit roof of the Town Hall.

Canon Kir, deputy-mayor of Dijon, will not take part in this delicate affair.

The same day, the torture of Father Christmas became front-page news. Not one newspaper missed an article on it, some – like *France-soir*, which has the highest circulation of all French papers – even went so far as to make it the subject of an editorial. There was general disapproval towards the attitude of the Dijon clergy. It would seem that the religious authorities were right to withdraw from the battle, or at least to keep silent. Yet they are apparently divided on the issue. The tone of most of the articles was one of tactful sentimentality: it's so nice to believe in Father Christmas, it doesn't harm anyone, the children get such satisfaction from it and store up such delicious memories for their adulthood, etc.

They are, in fact, begging the question. It is not a matter of rationalizing why children like Father Christmas, but rather, why adults invented him in the first place. Widespread reaction to the issue, however, clearly suggests a rift between public opinion and the Church. The incident is important, despite its apparent pettiness; since the war there has been a growing reconciliation in France between a largely non-believing public and the Church: the presence of a political party as distinctly denominational as the MRP[1] on government committees is proof of this. The anti-clerical faction was well aware of the unexpected opportunity offered to them: they are the ones in Dijon and elsewhere who are acting as protectors of the threatened Father Christmas. Father Christmas, symbol of irreligion – what a paradox! For in this case everything is happening as if it were the Church adopting an avidly critical attitude on honesty and truth, while the rationalists act as guardians of superstition. This apparent role reversal is enough to suggest that the whole naïve business is about something much more profound. We are in fact witnessing an important example of a very rapid shift of customs and beliefs both in France and elsewhere. It is not every day that an anthropologist gets the chance to observe in his own society the sudden growth of a rite, even a cult; to research its causes and study its impact on other forms of religious life; and, finally, to understand how both mental and social transformations relate to the seemingly superficial issue on which the Church, so experienced in these matters, has in fact been right to point out a deeper significance.

In the past few years the celebration of Christmas has expanded in a way unknown since before the war. This development, in both form and content, is undoubtedly the direct result of the influence and prestige of the USA. Thus we have simultaneously witnessed the appearance of large illuminated and decorated Christmas trees at crossroads and along motorways; decorated wrapping paper for Christmas presents; illustrated Christmas cards and the custom of displaying them on the mantelpiece during the fateful week; pleas for contributions from the Salvation Army with their great begging bowls on squares and streets; and finally, people dressed up as Father Christmas listening to the requests of children in department stores. All these customs which just a few years ago seemed so puerile and weird to French visitors in the USA, showing clear evidence of a basic incompatibility of mentality between the two cultures, have been introduced to, and spread through, France with an ease that offers food for thought to cultural historians.

In this case we are witnessing a huge process of diffusion, similar to remote examples of ancient technological innovations in fire-lighting or boat-building techniques. Yet it is both easier and more difficult to analyse events that are happening before our very eyes in our own society. It is easier because ongoing experience is protected in all its moments and nuances. Yet

[1] Mouvement Républicain et Populaire, a left-wing Catholic political party of the period.

it is harder because it is on such rare occasions that we can see the extreme complexity of even the most subtle social transformations; and because the obvious explanations of events in which we ourselves are involved are very different from the real causes.

Thus it would be too easy to explain the development of the celebration of Christmas in France simply in terms of influence from the USA. This alone is inadequate. Consider briefly the obvious explanations along these lines: there are more Americans in France celebrating Christmas according to their own customs; the cinema, 'digests' and American novels, articles in the national press have all introduced American customs that are backed up with American economic and military power. It is even possible that the Marshall Plan, directly or indirectly, may have encouraged the import of various products linked to the rites of Christmas. But none of that is enough to explain the phenomenon. Customs imported from the USA influence strata of the population that do not realize their origin. Thousands of workers for whom communist influence would discredit anything marked *Made in USA*, are adopting them as readily as others. In addition to simple diffusion we need to recall the important process first identified by Kroeber called *stimulus diffusion*, whereby an imported practice is not assimilated but acts as a catalyst. In other words, its mere presence stimulates the appearance of a similar practice which had already existed in a nascent state in the secondary environment. To illustrate this with an example from our subject: a paper manufacturer goes to the USA, at the invitation of American colleagues or a member of an economic mission, and notices that they make special wrapping paper for Christmas. He borrows the idea: that is an example of diffusion. A Parisian housewife goes to her local paper shop to buy some wrapping paper and notices some paper on display that she finds more attractive than the sort she usually buys. She is not aware of American customs, but the paper pleases her aesthetically and expresses an existing emotional state which previously lacked expression. In using it, she is not directly borrowing a foreign custom (as the paper manufacturer was), but the behaviour, as soon as it catches on, stimulates the spread of an identical custom.

Second, it should be remembered that before the war the celebration of Christmas was on the increase both in France and in the rest of Europe. Though this is most obviously linked to a general rise in the standard of living, there are also more subtle causes. Christmas as we know it is essentially a modern festival in spite of archaic characteristics. The use of mistletoe is not a direct survival from Druid times. Rather, it seems to have come back in fashion in the Middle Ages. The Christmas tree is only mentioned for the first time in some seventeenth-century German texts. It appears in England in the eighteenth century and not in France until the nineteenth century. Littré hardly seemed to know of it at all, or only in a form quite different from the one we know. As he says: 'in some countries a branch of pine or holly, decorated in different ways, covered with sweets and toys for the children, makes up the festival'. The variety of names given to the person who distributes the children's toys – Father Christmas, Saint Nicholas, Santa Claus – shows that it is a result of a process of convergence and not an ancient prototype preserved everywhere intact.

Yet the contemporary development is not an invention either: it is an old celebration pieced together with various fragments which have not quite been forgotten. If, for Littré, the Christmas tree seems an almost exotic institution, Cheruel notes, significantly, in his *Historic Dictionary of French Institutions, Customs and Practices* (in the author's opinion, a revision of the Dictionary of National Antiquities of Sainte Palaye, 1697–1781): 'Christmas . . . was for several centuries and *up until recently* (author's emphasis) an occasion for family festivities'. There follows a description of eighteenth-century Christmas festivities which seem to bear no resemblance to ours. So the importance of our ritual has already fluctuated through the course of history; it has had its ups and downs. The American version is just its most recent form.

Let it be said in passing that these brief indicators are enough to show how in problems of this sort we must beware of overly easy explanations by an automatic appeal to 'relics' and 'survivals'. If in prehistoric times there had never been a cult of tree worship that continued in a variety of folklore customs, modern Europe would no doubt not have invented the Christmas tree. Yet – as shown above – it is also a recent invention. None the less, this invention was not born from nothing. Other medieval practices testify to this perfectly: the yule log (turned into cakes in Paris) made from a log big enough to burn through the night; Christmas candles, large enough to achieve the same result; the decoration of buildings (a custom in existence since the Roman Saturnalia, which we will return to) with green branches of ivy, holly, pine. Finally, and with no relation to Christmas, stories of the Round Table refer to a supernatural tree all covered in lights. In this context the Christmas tree seems to be a syncretic response, that is to say, it focuses on one object previously scattered attributes of others: magic tree, fire, long-lasting light, enduring greenness. Conversely, Father Christmas is, in his actual form, a modern invention. Even more recent is the belief (which makes Denmark run a special postal service to answer the letters from children all over the world) that he lives in Greenland, a Danish possession, and travels in a sleigh harnessed to reindeer. Some say this aspect of the legend arose during the last war because of American troops stationed in Iceland and Greenland. And yet the reindeer are not there by chance, for English texts from the Renaissance mention the display of antlers during Christmas dances long before any belief in Father Christmas, much less the development of his legend.

Very old elements are thus shuffled and reshuffled, others are introduced, original formulas perpetuate, transform, or revive old customs. There is nothing specifically new in what might be called (no pun intended) the rebirth of Christmas. Then why does it arouse such emotion and why is Father Christmas the focus for hostility from some?

Father Christmas is dressed in scarlet: he is a king. His white beard, his furs and his boots, the sleigh in which he travels evoke winter. He is called 'Father' and he is an old man, thus he incarnates the benevolent form of the authority of the ancients. That is quite clear, yet in what category can he be placed from the point of view of religious typology? He is not a mythic being, for there is no myth that accounts for his origin or his function. Nor is he a legendary figure, as there is no semi-historical account attached to him. In fact, this supernatural and immutable being, eternally fixed in form and defined by an exclusive function and a periodic return, belongs more properly to the family of the gods. Moreover, children pay him homage at certain times of the year with letters and prayers; he rewards the good and punishes the wicked. He is the deity of an age group of our society, an age group that is in fact defined by belief in Father Christmas. The only difference between Father Christmas and a true deity is that adults do not believe in him, although they encourage their children to do so and maintain this belief with a great number of tricks.

Father Christmas thus first of all expresses the difference in status between little children on the one hand, and adolescents and adults on the other. In this sense he is linked to a vast array of beliefs and practices which anthropologists have studied in many societies to try and understand rites of passage and initiation. There are, in fact, few societies where, in one way or another, children (and at times also women) are not excluded from the company of men through ignorance of certain mysteries or their belief – carefully fostered – in some illusion that the adults keep secret until an opportune moment, thus sanctioning the addition of the younger generation to the adult world. At times these rites bear a surprising resemblance to those considered here. For example, there is a startling analogy between Father Christmas and the *katchina* of the Indians of the south-west United States.

These costumed and masked beings are gods and ancestors become incarnate who return periodically to visit their village and dance. They also come to punish or reward children, who do not recognize their elders in their traditional disguise. Father Christmas certainly belongs to the same family as now long-forgotten associates: Croquemitaine, Père Fouettard, etc. Significantly, the same educational trends which today forbid appeal to these punitive 'katchina' have succeeded in exalting the benevolent character of Father Christmas instead of – as the development of rationalism would have us suppose – dismissing him in a similar way. Education is in this sense not so rational as it might seem, for Father Christmas is no more 'rational' than Père Fouettard – the Church is right about this. Rather, what we are witnessing is a shift of myth and it is this that needs explaining.

Initiation rites and myths have a practical function in human societies: they help the elders to keep the younger generation in order and disciplined. All through the year we tell children Father Christmas is coming, to remind them that his generosity is in proportion to their good behaviour. Giving presents only at certain times is a useful way of disciplining children's demands, reducing to a brief period the time when they really have the *right* to demand presents. This simple explanation alone is enough to challenge the tenets of utilitarian explanations. For where do children get rights in the first place, and how is it these rights are imposed so imperiously on adults that they are obliged to work out an expensive and complex ritual in order to satisfy them? It can be seen straight away that belief in Father Christmas is not just a *hoax* imposed by adults on children for fun; it is, to a large extent, the result of a very onerous *transaction* between the two generations. He is part of a complete ritual, like the evergreens – pine, holly, ivy, mistletoe – with which we decorate our homes. Today a simple luxury, in some regions they were once the object of an *exchange* between two social groups. On Christmas Eve in England up until the end of the eighteenth century women used to go *gooding*, that is, begging from house to house and offering evergreen branches in return. We find children in the same bargaining position and it is worth noting here that when they beg on Saint Nicholas's Eve, children sometimes dress up as women – women, children: in both cases, the uninitiated.

Now, there is a very important aspect of initiation rituals which has not always been given adequate attention but which clarifies their nature far better than the utilitarian models discussed above. Consider the example of the katchina ritual of the Pueblo Indians mentioned earlier. If children are kept in the dark about the human nature of the people incarnating the katchina, is this simply to get them to fear, respect, and behave well? Of course, but that is only a secondary function of the ritual. There is another explanation which the myth of origin clarifies perfectly. This myth explains that the katchina are souls of the first native children who were dramatically drowned in a river at the time of the ancestral migrations. So the katchina are simultaneously proof of death and evidence of life after death. Moreover, when the Indians' ancestors finally settled in their village, the myth relates how the katchina used to come every year to visit them and, when they left, took away the children. The Indians, desperate at losing their offspring, made a deal with the katchina that they would stay in the other world in exchange for promising to honour them every year with masked dances. If the children are excluded from the secret of the katchina it is not primarily to intimidate them. I would say just the opposite: it's because they *are* the katchina. They are kept out of the mystery because they represent the reality with which the mystery constitutes a kind of compromise. Their place is elsewhere – not with the masks and the living, but with the gods and the dead – with the gods who are the dead. And the dead are the children.

Arguably this interpretation can be extended to all initiation rites and even to all occasions when society is divided into two groups. 'Non-initiation' is not just a state of deprivation defined in terms of ignorance, illusion, or other negative connotations. There is a positive aspect to the relationship between initiates and non-initiates. It is a complementary relationship between two groups where one represents the dead and the other the living. Moreover, even during the course of a ritual the roles are often reversed, for the duality engenders a reciprocity of perspectives which, like a reflection in a mirror, can be endlessly repeated. If the uninitiated are the dead, they are also the super-initiated. And if, as also often happens, it is the initiates who personify the spirits of the dead to scare the novices, it will be their responsibility at a later stage of the ritual to disperse them and warn of their return. Without pushing the argument too much further, it should still be pointed out that, to the extent that rituals and beliefs linked to Father Christmas relate to a sociology of initiation (and that is beyond doubt), it reveals that beyond the conflict between children and adults lies a deeper dispute between the living and the dead.

I reached this conclusion by a synchronic analysis of the function of certain rituals and the content of myths that give rise to them. Yet a diachronic analysis would have produced the same result. For historians of religion and folklorists both generally agree that the distant origin of Father Christmas is to be found in the Abbé de Liesse, *Abbas Stultorum*, Abbé de la Malgouverné, a replica of the English Lord of Misrule, all characters who rule for a set period as kings of Christmas and who are all heirs of the King of the Roman Saturnalia. Now the Saturnalia was the festival of the *larvae*, those who died a violent death or were left unburied. The aged Saturn, devourer of his children, is the prototype for a number of similar figures: Father Christmas, benefactor of children; the Scandinavian Julebok, horned demon from the underworld who brings presents to the children; Saint Nicholas, who revives them and inundates them with presents; finally, the katchina, prematurely dead children who renounce their role as child murderers to become dispensers of punishments and presents. It should be added that, like the katchina, the ancient prototype of Saturn is a god of germination. In fact, the contemporary character of Santa Claus or Father Christmas is a result of a syncretic fusion of several different characters: Abbé de Liesse, child bishop elected by Saint Nicholas; Saint Nicholas himself from whose festival beliefs in stockings, shoes, and chimneys originated. The Abbé de Liesse reigned on 25 December, Saint Nicholas on 6 December, the child-bishops were elected on Holy Innocents Day, i.e. 28 December. The Scandinavian Jul was celebrated in December. This leads us straight back to the *libertas decembris* of which Horace speaks and which du Tillot cited as early as the eighteenth century linking Christmas with the Saturnalia.

Explanations in terms of survivals are always inadequate. Customs neither disappear nor survive without a reason. When they do survive, the reason is less likely to be found in the vagaries of history than in the permanence of a function which analysing the present allows us to discover. The reason for giving so much prominence in this discussion to the Pueblo Indians is precisely because there is a lack of any conceivable historical link between their institutions and ours (with the exception of some late Spanish influence in the seventeenth century). This demonstrates that with the Christmas rituals we are witness not just to historical relics but to forms of thought and behaviour which illustrate the most general conditions of social life. The Saturnalia and the medieval celebration of Christmas do not contain the ultimate explanation for an otherwise inexplicable ritual devoid of meaning, but they do provide useful comparative material for making sense of the survival of institutions.

It is not surprising that non-Christian aspects of Christmas resemble the Saturnalia, as there are good reasons to suppose the Church fixed the date of the Nativity on 25 December (instead of March or January) to substitute its commemoration for the pagan festival that originally began on 17 December, but which at the end of the empire spread out over seven days, i.e. until the 24th. In fact, from antiquity up until the Middle Ages the 'festivals of December' show similar characteristics. First, the decoration of buildings with evergreens; next, the exchange, or giving to children, of gifts; gaiety and feasting; and finally, fraternization between rich and poor, masters and servants.

Looking more closely at the facts, certain structural analogies become strikingly evident. Like the Roman Saturnalia, medieval Christmas had two syncretic and opposite traits. It was first of all a gathering and a communion: distinction between class and status was temporarily abolished. Slaves and servants sat next to masters, and these became their servants. Richly stocked tables were open to everybody. There was cross-dressing. Yet at the same time the social group split into two. Youth formed itself into an autonomous group, elected a sovereign, the Abbot of Youth or, as in Scotland, *Abbot of Unreason*, and, as the title suggests, they indulged in outlandish behaviour taking the form of abuse directed at the rest of the population and which we know, up until the Renaissance, took extreme forms: blasphemy, theft, rape, and even murder. During both Christmas and the Saturnalia society functions according to a double rhythm of *heightened solidarity* and *exaggerated antagonism* and these two aspects act together in balanced opposition. The character of the Abbé de Liesse acts as a kind of mediator between the two extremes. He is recognized and even enthroned by the regular authorities. His mission is to demand excess while at the same time containing it within certain limits. What connection is there between this character and his function, and the character and function of Father Christmas, his distant descendant?

At this point it is important to distinguish between the historical and the structural points of view. Historically, as we have already seen, the Father Christmas of Western Europe, with his partiality for chimneys and stockings, is purely and simply a result of a recent shift from the festival of Saint Nicholas which has been assimilated to the celebration of Christmas, three weeks later. This explains how the young abbot has become an old man, though only in part, for the transformations are more systematic than historical accidents and calendar dates might suggest. A real person has become a mythical person. A figure of youth, symbolizing antagonism to adults, has changed into a symbol of maturity which is favourably disposed towards youth. The Lord of Misrule has taken charge of sanctioning good behaviour. Instead of open adolescent aggression to parents, we now have parents hiding behind false beards to gratify their children with kindness. The imaginary mediator replaces the real mediator, while at the same time as he changes his nature he begins to function in the opposite way.

There is no point in discussing points which are not essential to the debate and which risk confusing the issue. 'Youth' has largely disappeared as an age

[166]

group from contemporary society (although there have been several attempts in recent years to revive it, it is too early to know what the result will be). So far as Christmas is concerned, a ritual that once affected three groups of protagonists – little children, youth, and adults – now only affects two: adults and children. The 'madness' of Christmas has thus largely gone; it has been displaced and at the same time toned down and only survives in adult groups during the Réveillon at nightclubs and, on the night of Saint Sylvester, at Times Square. But let us consider the role of children instead.

In the Middle Ages children did not wait patiently for their toys to come down the chimney. Variously disguised they gathered in groups which were known as 'guisarts' and went from house to house singing and offering their good wishes, in return for fruit and cakes. Significantly, they invoked death to back up their demands. Thus in eighteenth-century Scotland they sang this verse:

> Rise up, good wife, and be no' swier [lazy]
> To deal your bread as long's you're here;
> The time will come when you'll be dead,
> And neither want nor meal nor bread.

Even without this valuable piece of information and the no less significant one of disguises that change the actors into ghosts or spirits, there are still others concerning children's quests. It is known that these are not limited to Christmas. They go on during the whole critical time of autumn when night threatens day just as the dead menace the living. Christmas quests begin several weeks before the Nativity – usually three, thus establishing a link between the similar quests of Saint Nicholas (which also use disguises), when dead children come to life, and the even more clearly defined initial quest of the season, that of Hallow-Even, which was turned into All Saints' Eve by ecclesiastical decision. Even today in Anglo-Saxon countries, children dressed up as ghosts and skeletons hassle adults unless they reward them with small presents. The progress of autumn from its beginning until the solstice, which marks the salvation of light and of life, is accompanied, in terms of rituals, by a dialectical process of which the principal stages are as follows: the return of the dead; their threatening and persecuting behaviour; the establishment of a *modus vivendi* with the living made up of an exchange of services and presents; finally, the triumph of life when, at Christmas, the dead laden with presents leave the living in peace until the next autumn. It is revealing that up until the last century the Latin Catholic countries put most emphasis on Saint Nicholas, in other words, the most *restrained* version, while the Anglo-Saxon countries willingly split it into the two extreme and antithetical forms of Halloween, when children play the part of the dead to make demands on adults, and Christmas, when adults indulge children in celebration of their vitality.

As a result of this, apparently contradictory aspects of the Christmas rites become clear: for three months the visit of the dead among the living becomes more and more persistent and tyrannical. Thus on the day of their departure it becomes permissible to entertain them and give them a last chance *to raise hell*. But who can personify the dead in a society of the living if not those who, one way or another, are incompletely incorporated into the group, who, that is, share the *otherness* which symbolizes the supreme dualism: that of the dead and the living? Therefore it should come as no surprise that foreigners, slaves, and children become the main beneficiaries of the festival. Inferior political or social status becomes equated with age difference. There is in fact a great deal of evidence, especially from Scandinavia and the Slav countries, that the real essence of the Réveillon is a meal offered to the dead, where the guests play the part of the dead, as the children play that of the angels, and the angels themselves, the dead. It is thus not surprising that Christmas and New Year (its double) should be festivals for present-giving. The festival of the dead is basically the festival of the others, while the fact of being other is the nearest image we can get of death.

This brings us back to the two questions posed at the beginning of the essay. Why did the figure of Father Christmas develop, and why has the Church been worried about its development?

It has been shown that Father Christmas is the heir to, as well as the opposite of, the Abbé de Liesse. This transformation primarily indicates an improvement in our relationships with death. We no longer find it necessary to settle our debts with death and allow it periodic transgression of order and laws. The relationship is now dominated by a slightly disdainful spirit of good will. We can allow ourselves to be generous, because this now consists of nothing more than offering presents or toys – that is, symbols. Yet this weakening of the relationship between the living and the dead has not been made at the expense of the character who embodies it. On the contrary, it could even be said to have improved. This contradiction would be inexplicable if it were not that another attitude towards death seems to be gaining sway in our society. It is no longer the traditional fear of spirits and ghosts that prevails, but instead a dread of everything death represents, both in itself and in life: degeneration, desiccation, and deprivation. We should reflect on the tender care we take of Father Christmas, the precautions and sacrifices we make to keep his prestige intact for the children. Is it not that, deep within us, there is a small desire to believe in boundless generosity, kindness without ulterior motives, a brief interlude during which all fear, envy, and bitterness are suspended? No doubt we cannot fully share the illusion, but sharing with others at least gives us a chance to warm our hearts by the flame that burns in young souls. The belief that we help to perpetuate in our children that their toys come from 'out there' gives us an alibi for our own secret desire to offer them to those 'out there' under the pretext of giving them to the children. In this way, Christmas presents remain a true sacrifice to the sweetness of life, which consists first and foremost of not dying.

Salomon Reinach once wrote with much insight that the main difference between ancient and modern religions was that 'pagans prayed to the dead, while Christians prayed for the dead'. No doubt it is a long way from the prayer to the dead to this muddled prayer we increasingly offer each year to little children – traditional incarnations of the dead – in order that they consent, by believing in Father Christmas, to help us believe in life. We have disentangled the threads that testify to a continuity between these two manifestations of the same reality. The Church was certainly not wrong to denounce the belief in Father Christmas, one of the most solid bastions and active centres of paganism in modern humanity. It remains to be seen if modern humanity can defend its right to be pagan. One final remark: it is a long way from the King of the Saturnalia to Father Christmas. Along the way an essential trait – maybe the most ancient – of the first seems to have been definitely lost. For, as Frazer showed, the King of the Saturnalia was himself the heir of an ancient prototype who, having enjoyed a month of unbridled excess, was solemnly sacrificed on the altar of God. Thanks to the *auto-da-fé* of Dijon we have the reconstructed hero in full. The paradox of this unusual episode is that in wanting to put an end to Father Christmas, the clergymen of Dijon have only restored in all his glory, after an eclipse of several thousand years, a ritual figure they had intended to destroy.

Claude Lévi-Strauss (trans. Diana Gittins)

Dancing Dan's Christmas

Now one time it comes on Christmas, and in fact it is the evening before Christmas, and I am in Good Time Charley Bernstein's little speakeasy in West Forty-seventh Street, wishing Charley a Merry Christmas and having a few hot Tom and Jerrys with him.

This hot Tom and Jerry is an old-time drink that is once used by one and all in this country to celebrate Christmas with, and in fact it is once so popular that many people think Christmas is invented only to furnish an excuse for hot Tom and Jerry, although of course this is by no means true.

But anybody will tell you that there is nothing that brings out the true holiday spirit like hot Tom and Jerry, and I hear that since Tom and Jerry goes out of style in the United States, the holiday spirit is never quite the same.

The reason hot Tom and Jerry goes out of style is because it is necessary to use rum and one thing and another in making Tom and Jerry, and naturally when rum becomes illegal in this country Tom and Jerry is also against the law, because rum is something that is very hard to get around town these days.

For a while some people try making hot Tom and Jerry without putting rum in it, but somehow it never has the same old holiday spirit, so nearly everybody finally gives up in disgust, and this is not surprising, as making Tom and Jerry is by no means child's play. In fact, it takes quite an expert to make good Tom and Jerry, and in the days when it is not illegal a good hot Tom and Jerry maker commands good wages and many friends.

Now of course Good Time Charley and I are not using rum in the Tom and Jerry we are making, as we do not wish to do anything illegal. What we are using is rye whisky that Good Time Charley gets on a doctor's prescription from a drug store, as we are personally drinking this hot Tom and Jerry and naturally we are not foolish enough to use any of Good Time Charley's own rye in it.

The prescription for the rye whisky comes from old Doc Moggs, who prescribes it for Good Time Charley's rheumatism in case Charley happens to get any rheumatism, as Doc Moggs says there is nothing better for rheumatism than rye whisky, especially if it is made up in a hot Tom and Jerry. In fact, old Doc Moggs comes around and has a few seidels of hot Tom and Jerry with us for his own rheumatism.

He comes around during the afternoon, for Good Time Charley and I start making this Tom and Jerry early in the day, so as to be sure to have enough to last us over Christmas, and it is now along towards six o'clock, and our holiday spirit is practically one hundred per cent.

Well, as Good Time Charley and I are expressing our holiday sentiments to each other over our hot Tom and Jerry, and I am trying to think up the poem about the night before Christmas and all through the house, which I know will interest Charley no little, all of a sudden there is a big knock at the front door, and when Charley opens the door who comes in carrying a large package under one arm but a guy by the name of Dancing Dan.

This Dancing Dan is a good-looking young guy, who always seems well dressed, and he is called by the name of Dancing Dan because he is a great hand for dancing around and about with dolls in night clubs, and other spots where there is any dancing. In fact, Dan never seems to be doing anything else, although I hear rumours that when he is not dancing he is carrying on in a most illegal manner at one thing and another. But of course you can always hear rumours in this town about anybody, and personally I am rather fond of Dancing Dan as he always seems to be getting a great belt out of life.

Anybody in town will tell you that Dancing Dan is a guy with no Barnaby whatever in him, and in fact he has about as much gizzard as anybody around, although I wish to say I always question his judgment in dancing so much with Miss Muriel O'Neill, who works in the Half Moon night club. And the reason I question his judgment in this respect is because everybody knows that Miss Muriel O'Neill is a doll who is very well thought of by Heine Schmitz, and Heine Schmitz is not such a guy as will take kindly to anybody dancing more than once and a half with a doll that he thinks well of.

This Heine Schmitz is a very influential citizen of Harlem, where he has large interests in beer, and other business enterprises, and it is by no means violating any confidence to tell you that Heine Schmitz will just as soon blow your brains out as look at you. In fact, I hear sooner. Anyway, he is not a guy to monkey with and many citizens take the trouble to advise Dancing Dan that he is not only away out of line in dancing with Miss Muriel O'Neill, but that he is knocking his own price down to where he is no price at all.

But Dancing Dan only laughs ha-ha, and goes on dancing with Miss Muriel O'Neill any time he gets a chance, and Good Time Charley says he does not blame him, at that, as Miss Muriel O'Neill is so beautiful that he will be dancing with her himself no matter what, if he is five years younger and can get a Roscoe out as fast as in the days when he runs with Paddy the Link and other fast guys.

Well, anyway, as Dancing Dan comes in he weighs up the joint in one quick peek, and then he tosses the package he is carrying into a corner where it goes plunk, as if there is something very heavy in it, and then he steps up to the bar alongside of Charley and me and wishes to know what we are drinking.

Naturally we start boosting hot Tom and Jerry to Dancing Dan, and he says he will take a crack at it with us, and after one crack, Dancing Dan says he will have another crack, and Merry Christmas to us with it, and the first thing anybody knows it is a couple of hours later and we are still having cracks at the hot Tom and Jerry with Dancing Dan, and Dan says he never drinks anything so soothing in his life. In fact, Dancing Dan says he will recommend Tom and Jerry to everybody he knows, only he does not know anybody good enough for Tom and Jerry, except maybe Miss Muriel O'Neill, and she does not drink anything with drugstore rye in it.

Well, several times while we are drinking this Tom and Jerry, customers come to the door of Good Time Charley's little speakeasy and knock, but by now Charley is commencing to be afraid they will wish Tom and Jerry, too, and he does not feel we will have enough for ourselves, so he hangs out a sign which says 'Closed on Account of Christmas', and the only one he will let in is a guy by the name of Ooky, who is nothing but an old rum-dum, and who is going around all week dressed like Santa Claus and carrying a sign advertising Moe Lewinsky's clothing joint around in Sixth Avenue.

This Ooky is still wearing his Santa Claus outfit when Charley lets him in, and the reason Charley permits such a character as Ooky in his joint is because Ooky does the porter work for Charley when he is not Santa Claus for Moe Lewinsky, such as sweeping out, and washing the glasses, and one thing and another.

Well, it is about nine-thirty when Ooky comes in, and his puppies are aching, and he is all petered out generally from walking up and down and here and there with his sign, for any time a guy is Santa Claus for Moe Lewinsky he must earn his dough. In fact, Ooky is so fatigued, and his puppies hurt him so much, that Dancing Dan and Good Time Charley and I all feel very sorry for him, and invite him to have a few mugs of hot Tom and Jerry with us, and wish him plenty of Merry Christmas.

But old Ooky is not accustomed to Tom and Jerry, and after about the fifth mug he folds up in a chair, and goes right to sleep on us. He is wearing a pretty good Santa Claus make-up, what with a nice red suit trimmed with white cotton, and a wig, and false nose, and long white whiskers, and a big sack stuffed with excelsior on his back, and if I do not know Santa Claus is not apt to be such a guy as will snore loud enough to rattle the windows, I will think Ooky is Santa Claus sure enough.

Well, we forget Ooky and let him sleep, and go on with our hot Tom and Jerry, and in the meantime we try to think up a few songs appropriate to Christmas, and Dancing Dan finally renders 'My Dad's Dinner Pail' in a nice baritone and very loud, while I do first-rate with 'Will You Love Me in December – As You Do in May?' But personally I always think Good Time Charley Bernstein is a little out of line trying to sing a hymn in Jewish on such an occasion, and it causes words between us.

While we are singing many customers come to the door and knock, and then they read Charley's sign, and this seems to cause some unrest among them, and some of them stand outside saying it is a great outrage, until

Charley sticks his noggin out the door and threatens to bust somebody's beezer if they do not go on about their business and stop disturbing peaceful citizens.

Naturally the customers go away, as they do not wish their beezers busted, and Dancing Dan and Charley and I continue drinking our hot Tom and Jerry, and with each Tom and Jerry we are wishing one another a very Merry Christmas, and sometimes a very Happy New Year, although of course this does not go for Good Time Charley as yet, because Charley has his New Year separate from Dancing Dan and me.

By and by we take to waking Ooky up in his Santa Claus outfit and offering him more hot Tom and Jerry, and wishing him Merry Christmas, but Ooky only gets sore and calls us names, so we can see he does not have the right holiday spirit in him, and let him alone until along about midnight when Dancing Dan wishes to see how he looks as Santa Claus.

So Good Time Charley and I help Dancing Dan pull off Ooky's outfit and put it on Dan, and this is easy as Ooky only has this Santa Claus outfit on over his ordinary clothes, and he does not even wake up when we are undressing him of the Santa Claus uniform.

Well, I wish to say I see many a Santa Claus in my time, but I never see a better-looking Santa Claus than Dancing Dan, especially after he gets the wig and white whiskers fixed just right, and we put a sofa pillow that Good Time Charley happens to have around the joint for the cat to sleep on down his pants to give Dancing Dan a nice fat stomach such as Santa Claus is bound to have.

In fact, after Dancing Dan looks at himself in a mirror awhile he is greatly pleased with his appearance, while Good Time Charley is practically hysterical, although personally I am commencing to resent Charley's interest in Santa Claus, and Christmas generally, as he by no means has any claim on these matters. But then I remember Charley furnishes the hot Tom and Jerry, so I am more tolerant towards him.

'Well,' Charley finally says, 'it is a great pity we do not know where there are some stockings hung up somewhere, because then,' he says, 'you can go around and stuff things in these stockings, as I always hear this is the main idea of a Santa Claus. But,' Charley says, 'I do not suppose anybody in this section has any stockings hung up, or if they have,' he says, 'the chances are they are so full of holes they will not hold anything. Anyway,' Charley says, 'even if there are any stockings hung up we do not have anything to stuff in them, although personally,' he says, 'I will gladly donate a few pints of Scotch.'

Well, I am pointing out that we have no reindeer and that a Santa Claus is bound to look like a terrible sap if he goes around without any reindeer, but Charley's remarks seem to give Dancing Dan an idea, for all of a sudden he speaks as follows:

'Why,' Dancing Dan says, 'I know where a stocking is hung up. It is hung up at Miss Muriel O'Neill's flat over here in West Forty-ninth Street. This stocking is hung up by nobody but a party by the name of Gammer O'Neill, who is Miss Muriel O'Neill's grandmamma,' Dancing Dan says. 'Gammer O'Neill is going on ninety-odd,' he says, 'and Miss Muriel O'Neill tells me she cannot hold out much longer, what with one thing and another, including being a little childish in spots.

'Now,' Dancing Dan says, 'I remember Miss Muriel O'Neill is telling me just the other night how Gammer O'Neill hangs up her stocking on Christmas Eve all her life, and,' he says, 'I judge from what Miss Muriel O'Neill says that the old doll always believes Santa Claus will come along some Christmas and fill the stocking full of beautiful gifts. But,' Dancing Dan says, 'Miss Muriel O'Neill tells me Santa Claus never does this, although Miss Muriel O'Neill personally always takes a few gifts home and pops them into the stocking to make Gammer O'Neill feel better.

'But, of course,' Dancing Dan says, 'these gifts are nothing much because Miss Muriel O'Neill is very poor, and proud, and also good, and will not take a dime off of anybody, and I can lick the guy who says she will, although,' Dancing Dan says, 'between me and Heine Schmitz, and a raft of other guys I can mention, Miss Muriel O'Neill can take plenty.'

Well, I know that what Dancing Dan states about Miss Muriel O'Neill is quite true, and in fact it is a matter that is often discussed on Broadway, because Miss Muriel O'Neill cannot get more than twenty bobs per week working in the Half Moon, and it is well known to one and all that this is no kind of dough for a doll as beautiful as Miss Muriel O'Neill.

'Now,' Dancing Dan goes on, 'it seems that while Gammer O'Neill is very happy to get whatever she finds in her stocking on Christmas morning, she does not understand why Santa Claus is not more liberal, and,' he says, 'Miss Muriel O'Neill is saying to me that she only wishes she can give Gammer O'Neill one real big Christmas before the old doll puts her checks back in the rack.

'So,' Dancing Dan states, 'here is a job for us. Miss Muriel O'Neill and her grandmamma live all alone in this flat over in West Forty-ninth Street, and,' he says, 'at such an hour as this Miss Muriel O'Neill is bound to be working, and the chances are Gammer O'Neill is sound asleep, and we will just hop over there and Santa Claus will fill up her stocking with beautiful gifts.'

Well, I say, I do not see where we are going to get any beautiful gifts at this time of night, what with all the stores being closed, unless we dash into an all-night drug store and buy a few bottles of perfume and a bum toilet set as guys always do when they forget about their ever-loving wives until after store hours on Christmas Eve, but Dancing Dan says never mind about this, but let us have a few more Tom and Jerrys first.

So we have a few more Tom and Jerrys, and then Dancing Dan picks up the package he heaves into the corner, and dumps most of the excelsior out of Ooky's Santa Claus sack, and puts the bundle in, and Good Time Charley turns out all the lights but one, and leaves a bottle of Scotch on the table in front of Ooky for a Christmas gift, and away we go.

Personally, I regret very much leaving the hot Tom and Jerry, but then I am also very enthusiastic about going along to help Dancing Dan play Santa Claus, while Good Time Charley is practically overjoyed, as it is the first time in his life Charley is ever mixed up in so much holiday spirit. In fact, nothing will do Charley but that we stop in a couple of spots and have a few drinks to Santa Claus's health, and these visits are a big success, although everybody is much surprised to see Charley and me with Santa Claus, especially Charley, although nobody recognizes Dancing Dan.

But of course there are no hot Tom and Jerrys in these spots we visit, and we have to drink whatever is on hand, and personally I will always believe that the noggin I have on me afterwards comes of mixing the drinks we get in these spots with my Tom and Jerry.

As we go up Broadway, headed for Forty-ninth Street, Charley and I see many citizens we know and give them a large hello, and wish them Merry Christmas, and some of these citizens shake hands with Santa Claus, not knowing he is nobody but Dancing Dan, although later I understand there is some gossip among these citizens because they claim a Santa Claus with such a breath on him as our Santa Claus has is a little out of line.

And once we are somewhat embarrassed when a lot of little kids going home with their parents from a late Christmas party somewhere gather about Santa Claus with shouts of childish glee, and some of them wish to climb up Santa Claus's legs. Naturally, Santa Claus gets a little peevish, and calls them a few names, and one of the parents comes up and wishes to know what is the idea of Santa Claus using such language, and Santa Claus takes a punch at the parent, all of which is no doubt most astonishing to the little kids who have an idea of Santa Claus as a very kindly old guy. But of course they do not know about Dancing Dan mixing the liquor we get in the spots we visit with his Tom and Jerry, or they will understand how even Santa Claus can lose his temper.

Well, finally we arrive in front of the place where Dancing Dan says Miss

Muriel O'Neill and her grandmamma live, and it is nothing but a tenement house not far back of Madison Square Garden, and furthermore it is a walk-up, and at this time there are no lights burning in the joint except a gas jet in the main hall, and by the light of this jet we look at the names on the letter-boxes, such as you always find in the hall of these joints, and we see that Miss Muriel O'Neill and her grandmamma live on the fifth floor.

This is the top floor, and personally I do not like the idea of walking up five flights of stairs, and I am willing to let Dancing Dan and Good Time Charley go, but Dancing Dan insists we must all go, and finally I agree because Charley is commencing to argue that the right way for us to do is to get on the roof and let Santa Claus go down a chimney, and is making so much noise I am afraid he will wake somebody up.

So up the stairs we climb and finally we come to a door on the top floor that has a little card in a slot that says O'Neill, so we know we reach our destination. Dancing Dan first tries the knob, and right away the door opens, and we are in a little two- or three-room flat, with not much furniture in it, and what furniture there is is very poor. One single gas jet is burning near a bed in a room just off the one the door opens into, and by this light we see a very old doll is sleeping on the bed, so we judge this is nobody but Gammer O'Neill.

On her face is a large smile, as if she is dreaming of something very pleasant. On a chair at the head of the bed is hung a long black stocking, and it seems to be such a stocking as is often patched and mended, so I can see what Miss Muriel O'Neill tells Dancing Dan about her grandmamma hanging up her stocking is really true, although up to this time I have my doubts.

Well, I am willing to pack in after one gander at the old doll, especially as Good Time Charley is commencing to prowl around the flat to see if there is a chimney where Santa Claus can come down, and is knocking things over, but Dancing Dan stands looking down at Gammer O'Neill for a long time.

Finally he unslings the sack on his back, and takes out his package, and unties this package, and all of a sudden out pops a raft of big diamond bracelets, and diamond rings, and diamond brooches, and diamond neck-laces, and I do not know what all else in the way of diamonds, and Dancing Dan and I begin stuffing these diamonds into the stocking and Good Time Charley pitches in and helps us.

There are enough diamonds to fill the stocking to the muzzle, and it is no small stocking, at that, and I judge that Gammer O'Neill has a pretty fair set of bunting sticks when she is young. In fact, there are so many diamonds that we have enough left over to make a nice little pile on the chair after we fill the stocking plumb up, leaving a nice diamond-studded vanity case sticking out the top where we figure it will hit Gammer O'Neill's eye when she wakes up.

And it is not until I get out in the fresh air again that all of a sudden I remember seeing large headlines in the afternoon papers about a five-hundred-G's stick-up in the afternoon of one of the biggest diamond merchants in Maiden Lane while he is sitting in his office, and I also recall once hearing rumours that Dancing Dan is one of the best lone-hand git-'em-up guys in the world.

Naturally I commence to wonder if I am in the proper company when I am with Dancing Dan, even if he is Santa Claus. So I leave him on the next corner arguing with Good Time Charley about whether they ought to go and find some more presents somewhere, and look for other stockings to stuff, and I hasten on home, and go to bed.

The next day I find I have such a noggin that I do not care to stir around, and in fact I do not stir around much for a couple of weeks.

Then one night I drop around to Good Time Charley's little speakeasy, and ask Charley what is doing.

'Well,' Charley says, 'many things are doing, and personally,' he says, 'I am greatly surprised I do not see you at Gammer O'Neill's wake. You know Gammer O'Neill leaves this wicked old world a couple of days after Christmas,' Good Time Charley says, 'and,' he says, 'Miss Muriel O'Neill states that Doc Moggs claims it is at least a day after she is entitled to go, but she is sustained,' Charley says, 'by great happiness on finding her stocking filled with beautiful gifts on Christmas morning.

'According to Miss Muriel O'Neill,' Charley says, 'Gammer O'Neill dies practically convinced that there is a Santa Claus, although of course,' he says, 'Miss Muriel O'Neill does not tell her the real owner of the gifts, an all-right guy by the name of Shapiro, leaves the gifts with her after Miss Muriel O'Neill notifies him of the finding of same.

'It seems,' Charley says, 'this Shapiro is a tender-hearted guy, who is willing to help keep Gammer O'Neill with us a little longer when Doc Moggs says leaving the gifts with her will do it.

'So,' Charley says, 'everything is quite all right, as the coppers cannot figure anything except that maybe the rascal who takes the gifts from Shapiro gets conscience stricken, and leaves them the first place he can, and Miss Muriel O'Neill receives a ten-G's reward for finding the gifts and returning them. And,' Charley says, 'I hear Dancing Dan is in San Francisco and is figuring on reforming and becoming a dancing teacher, so he can marry Miss Muriel O'Neill, and of course,' he says, 'we all hope and trust she never learns any details of Dancing Dan's career.'

Well, it is Christmas Eve a year later that I run into a guy by the name of Shotgun Sam, who is mobbed up with Heine Schmitz in Harlem, and who is a very, very obnoxious character indeed.

'Well, well, well,' Shotgun says, 'the last time I see you is another Christmas Eve like this, and you are coming out of Good Time Charley's joint, and,' he says, 'you certainly have your pots on.'

'Well, Shotgun,' I say, 'I am sorry you get such a wrong impression of me, but the truth is,' I say, 'on the occasion you speak of, I am suffering from a dizzy feeling in my head.'

'It is all right with me,' Shotgun says. 'I have a tip this guy Dancing Dan is in Good Time Charley's the night I see you, and Mockie Morgan and Gunner Jack and me are casing the joint, because,' he says, 'Heine Schmitz is all sored up at Dan over some doll, although of course,' Shotgun says, 'it is all right now, as Heine has another doll.

'Anyway,' he says, 'we never get to see Dancing Dan. We watch the joint from six-thirty in the evening until daylight Christmas morning, and nobody goes in all night but old Ooky the Santa Claus guy in his Santa Claus make-up, and,' Shotgun says, 'nobody comes out except you and Good Time Charley and Ooky.

'Well,' Shotgun says, 'it is a great break for Dancing Dan he never goes in or comes out of Good Time Charley's, at that, because,' he says, 'we are waiting for him on the second-floor front of the building across the way with some nice little sawed-offs, and are under orders from Heine not to miss.'

'Well, Shotgun,' I say, 'Merry Christmas.'

'Well, all right,' Shotgun says, 'Merry Christmas.'

Damon Runyon, Furthermore

❧ 10 ❧

PRESENTS

Hide and Seek

Hilda Effania always left notes for the girls, explaining where their Christmas from Santa was. This practice began the first year Sassafrass had doubted that a fat white man came down her chimney to bring her anything. Hilda solved that problem by leaving notes from Santa Claus for all the children. That way they had to go search the house, high & low, for their gifts. Santa surely had to have been there. Once school chums & reality interfered with this myth, Hilda continued the practice of leaving her presents hidden away. She liked the idea that each child experienced her gift in privacy. The special relationship she nurtured with each was protected from rivalries, jokes, & Christmas confusions. Hilda Effania loved thinking that she'd managed to give her daughters a moment of their own.

My Oldest Darling, Sassafrass,
    In the back of the pantry is something from Santa. In a red box by the attic window is something your father would want you to have. Out by the shed in a bucket covered with straw is a gift from your Mama.

Love to you,
Mama

Darling Cypress,
    Underneath my hat boxes in the 2nd floor closet is your present from Santa. Look behind the tomatoes I canned last year for what I got you in your Papa's name. My own choice for you is under your bed.

XOXOX,
Mama

Sweet Little Indigo,
    This is going to be very simple. Santa left you something outside your violin. I left you a gift by the outdoor stove on the right hand side. Put your coat on

before you go out there. And the special something I got you from your Daddy is
way up in the china cabinet. Please, be careful.

I love you so much,
Mama

In the back of the pantry between the flour & rice, Sassafrass found a
necklace of porcelain roses. Up in the attic across from Indigo's mound of
resting dolls, there was a red box all right, with a woven blanket of mohair,
turquoise & silver. Yes, her father would have wanted her to have a warm
place to sleep. Running out to the shed, Sassafrass knocked over the bucket
filled with straw. There on the ground lay eight skeins of her mother's finest
spun cotton, dyed so many colors. Sassafrass sat out in the air feeling her
yarns.

Cypress wanted her mother's present first. Underneath her bed, she felt
tarlatan. A tutu. Leave it to Mama. Once she gathered the whole thing out
where she could see it, Cypress started to cry. A tutu *juponnage*, reaching to
her ankles, rose & lavender. The waist was a wide sash with the most delicate
needlework she'd ever seen. Tiny toe shoes in white & pink graced brown
ankles tied with ribbons. Unbelievable. Cypress stayed in her room dancing
in her tutu till lunchtime. Then she found *The Souls of Black Folks* by
DuBois near the tomatoes from her Papa's spirit. She was the only one who'd
insisted on calling him Papa, instead of Daddy or Father. He didn't mind. So
she guessed he wouldn't mind now. 'Thank you so much, Mama & Papa.'
Cypress slowly went to the 2nd floor closet where she found Santa'd left her a
pair of opal earrings. To thank her mother Cypress did a complete *port de
bras*, in the Cecchetti manner, by her mother's vanity. The mirrors inspired
her.

Indigo had been very concerned that anything was near her fiddle that she
hadn't put there. Looking at her violin, she knew immediately what her gift
from Santa was. A brand-new case. No second-hand battered thing from
Uncle John. Indigo approached her instrument slowly. The case was of
crocodile skin, lined with white velvet. Plus, Hilda Effania had bought new
rosin, new strings. Even cushioned the fiddle with cleaned raw wool. Indigo
carried her new case with her fiddle outside to the stove where she found a
music stand holding *A Practical Method for Violin* by Nicolas Laoureux. 'Oh,
my. She's right about that. Mama would be real mad if I never learned to read
music.' Indigo looked thru the pages, understanding nothing. Whenever she
was dealing with something she didn't understand, she made it her business
to learn. With great difficulty, she carried her fiddle, music stand, & music
book into the house. Up behind the wine glasses that Hilda Effania rarely

used, but dusted regularly, was a garnet bracelet from the memory of her father. Indigo figured the bracelet weighed so little, she would definitely be able to wear it every time she played her fiddle. Actually, she could wear it while conversing with the Moon.

Ntozake Shange, *Sassafrass, Cypress & Indigo*

Charade

My mother knew well how hurtful a broken illusion could be. The most trifling disappointment took on for her the dimensions of a major disaster. One Christmas Eve, in Vyra, not long before her fourth baby was to be born, she happened to be laid up with a slight ailment and made my brother and me (aged, respectively, five and six) promise not to look into the Christmas stockings that we would find hanging from our bedposts on the following morning but to bring them over to her room and investigate them there, so that she could watch and enjoy our pleasure. Upon awakening, I held a furtive conference with my brother, after which, with eager hands, each felt his delightfully crackling stocking, stuffed with small presents; these we cautiously fished out one by one, undid the ribbons, loosened the tissue paper, inspected everything by the weak light that came through a chink in the shutters, wrapped up the little things again, and crammed them back where they had been. I next recall our sitting on our mother's bed, holding those lumpy stockings and doing our best to give the performance she had wanted to see; but we had so messed up the wrappings, so amateurish were our renderings of enthusiastic surprise (I can see my brother casting his eyes upward and exclaiming, in imitation of our new French governess, '*Ah, que c'est beau!*'), that, after observing us for a moment, our audience burst into tears.

Vladimir Nabokov, *Speak, Memory*

Useful and Useless

SMALL BOY: Get back to the Presents.
SELF: There were the Useful Presents: engulfing mufflers of the old coach days, and mittens made for giant sloths; zebra scarves of a substance like silky gum that could be tug-o-warred down to the goloshes; blinding

tam-o-shanters like patchwork tea-cosies, and bunny-scutted busbies and balaclavas for victims of head-shrinking tribes; from aunts who always wore wool next to the skin, there were moustached and rasping vests that made you wonder why the aunties had any skin left at all; and once I had a little crocheted nose-bag from an aunt now, alas, no longer whinnying with us. And pictureless books in which small boys, though warned, with quotations, not to, *would* skate on Farmer Garge's pond, and did, and drowned; and books that told me everything about the wasp, except why.

SMALL BOY: Get on with the Useless Presents.

SELF: On Christmas Eve I hung at the foot of my bed Bessie Bunter's black stocking, and always, I said, I would stay awake all the moonlit, snowlit night to hear the roof-alighting reindeer and see the hollied boot descend through soot. But soon the sand of the snow drifted into my eyes, and, though I stared towards the fireplace and around the flickering room where the black sack-like stocking hung, I was asleep before the chimney trembled and the room was red and white with Christmas. But in the morning, though no snow melted on the bedroom floor, the stocking bulged and brimmed: press it, it squeaked like a mouse-in-a-box; it smelt of tangerine; a furry arm lolled over, like the arm of a kangeroo out of its mother's belly; squeeze it hard in the middle, and something squelched; squeeze it again – squelch again. Look out of the frost-scribbled window: on the great loneliness of the small hill, a blackbird was silent in the snow.

SMALL BOY: Were there any sweets?

SELF: Of course there were sweets. It was the marshmallows that squelched. Hardboileds, toffee, fudge and allsorts, crunches, cracknels, humbugs, glaciers and marzipan and butterwelsh for the Welsh. And troops of bright tin soldiers who, if they would not fight, could always run. And Snakes-and-Families and Happy Ladders. And Easy Hobbi-Games for Little Engineers, complete with Instructions. Oh, easy for Leonardo! And a whistle to make the dogs bark to wake up the old man next door to make him beat on the wall with his stick to shake our picture off the wall. And a packet of cigarettes: you put one in your mouth and you stood at the corner of the street and you waited for hours, in vain, for an old lady to scold you for smoking a cigarette and then, with a smirk, you ate it. And, last of all, in the toe of the stocking, sixpence like a silver corn. And then downstairs for breakfast under the balloons!

Dylan Thomas, 'Conversation About Christmas'

Gift-Horses

It was only two days before Christmas and the Outlaws stood in Ginger's back garden discussing its prospects, somewhat pessimistically. All except Henry – for Henry, in a spirit of gloomy resignation to fate, had gone to spend the festival season with relations in the North.

'What're *you* goin' to get?' demanded William of Ginger. The Outlaws generally spent the week before Christmas in ascertaining exactly what were the prospects of that day. It was quite an easy task, owing chiefly to the conservative habits of their relatives in concealing their presents in the same place year after year. The Outlaws knew exactly in which drawer or cupboard to pursue their search, and could always tell by some unerring instinct which of the concealed presents was meant for them.

'Nothin' really *'citin'*,' said Ginger, without enthusiasm, 'but nothin' *awful*, 'cept what Uncle George's giv'n me.'

'What's that?' said William.

'An ole *book*,' said Ginger with withering contempt; 'an ole book called *Kings an' Queens of England*. Huh! An' I shall have to say I like it an' thank him an' all that. An' I shan't be able to sell it even, 'cept for about sixpence, 'cause you never can, an' it cost five shillin's. *Five shillin's!* It's got five shillin's on the back. Well, why can't he give me the five shillin's an' let me buy somethin' sensible?'

He spoke with the bitterness of one who airs a grievance of long standing. 'Goin' wastin' their money on things like *Kings an' Queens of England*, 'stead of giv'n it to us to buy somethin' sensible. Think of all the sensible things we could buy with five shillin's – 'stead of stupid things like *Kings an' Queens of England*.'

'Well,' burst out Douglas indignantly. 'S'not so bad as what my Aunt Jane's got for me. She's gotter ole tie. *A tie!*' He spat the word out with disgust. 'I found it when I went to tea with her las' week. A silly ole green tie. Well, I'd rather pretend to be pleased over any ole book than over a silly green tie. An' I can't even sell it, 'cause they'll keep goin' on at me to wear it – a sick'nin' ole green tie!'

William was not to be outdone.

'Well, you don't know what my Uncle Charles is givin' me. I heard him tellin' mother about it. A silly baby penknife.'

'A penknife!' they echoed. 'Well, there's nothin' wrong with a penknife.'

'I'd rather have a penknife than an old *Kings an' Queens of England*,' said Ginger bitterly.

'An' I'd rather have a penknife *or* a *Kings an' Queens of England* than a silly ole green tie,' said Douglas.

'A *Kings an' Queens of England*'s worse than a tie,' said Ginger fiercely, as though his honour were involved in any suggestion to the contrary.

''Tisn't!' said Douglas equally fiercely.

''Tis!' said Ginger.

''Tisn't!' said Douglas.

The matter would have been settled one way or the other by physical contest between the protagonists had not William thrust his penknife (metaphorically speaking) again into the discussion.

'Yes,' he said, 'but you don't know what *kind* of a penknife, an' I do. I've got three penknives, an' one's almost as big as a nornery knife, an' got four blades *an'* a thing for taking stones out of horses' hoofs *an'* some things what I haven't found out what they're meant for yet, an' this what he's given me is a baby penknife – it's only got one blade, an' I heard him tellin' mother that I couldn't do any harm with it. Fancy,' – his voice quivered with indignation – '*fancy* anyone givin' you a penknife what you can't do any harm with.'

Ginger and Douglas stood equally aghast at this news. The insult of the tie and the *Kings and Queens of England* paled before the deadly insult of a penknife you couldn't do any harm with.

William returned home still burning with fury.

Richmal Crompton, *Just William at Christmas*

King John's Christmas

King John was not a good man –
   He had his little ways.
And sometimes no one spoke to him
   For days and days and days.
And men who came across him,
   When walking in the town,
Gave him a supercilious stare,
Or passed with noses in the air-
And bad King John stood dumbly there,
   Blushing beneath his crown.

King John was not a good man,
    And no good friends had he.
He stayed in every afternoon . . .
    But no one came to tea.
And, round about December,
    The cards upon his shelf
Which wished him lots of Christmas cheer,
And fortune in the coming year,
Were never from his near and dear,
    But only from himself.

King John was not a good man,
    Yet had his hopes and fears.
They'd given him no present now
    For years and years and years.
But every year at Christmas,
    While minstrels stood about,
Collecting tribute from the young
For all the songs they might have sung,
He stole away upstairs and hung
    A hopeful stocking out.

King John was not a good man,
    He lived his life aloof;
Alone he thought a message out
    While climbing up the roof.
He wrote it down and propped it
    Against the chimney stack:
'TO ALL AND SUNDRY — NEAR AND FAR —
F. CHRISTMAS IN PARTICULAR.'
And signed it not 'Johannes R.'
    But very humbly, 'JACK.'

'I want some crackers,
    And I want some candy;
I think a box of chocolates
    Would come in handy;
I don't mind oranges,
    I do like nuts!
And I SHOULD like a pocket-knife

[185]

That really cuts.
And, oh! Father Christmas, if you love me at all,
Bring me a big, red India-rubber ball!'

King John was not a good man –
    He wrote this message out,
And gat him to his room again,
    Descending by the spout.
And all that night he lay there,
    A prey to hopes and fears.
'I think that's him a-coming now,'
(Anxiety bedewed his brow.)
'He'll bring one present, anyhow –
    The first I've had for years.'

'Forget about the crackers,
    And forget about the candy;
I'm sure a box of chocolates
    Would never come in handy;
I don't like oranges,
    I don't want nuts,
And I HAVE got a pocket knife
    That almost cuts.
But, oh! Father Christmas, if you love me at all,
Bring me a big, red India-rubber ball!'

King John was not a good man –
    Next morning when the sun
Rose up to tell a waiting world
    That Christmas had begun,
And people seized their stockings,
    And opened them with glee,
And crackers, toys and games appeared,
And lips with sticky sweets were smeared,
King John said grimly: 'As I feared,
    Nothing again for me!'

'I did want crackers,
    And I did want candy;
I know a box of chocolates

Would come in handy;
I do love oranges,
    I did want nuts.
I haven't got a pocket-knife –
    Not one that cuts.
And, oh! If Father Christmas had loved me at all,
He would have brought a big, red India-rubber ball!'

King John stood by the window,
    And frowned to see below
The happy bands of boys and girls
    All playing in the snow.
A while he stood there watching,
    And envying them all . . .
When through the window big and red
There hurtled by his royal head,
And bounced and fell upon the bed,
    An India-rubber ball!

AND OH, FATHER CHRISTMAS,
    MY BLESSINGS ON YOU FALL
        FOR BRINGING HIM
        A BIG, RED,
        INDIA-RUBBER
        BALL!

A. A. Milne

It's the Thought that Counts

And a few days later Quoyle gave Wavey a clear glass teapot, a silk scarf printed with a design of blueberries. He'd ordered them both through the mail from a museum shop in the States. She gave him a sweater the color of oxblood shoe polish. Had knitted it in the evenings. It was not too small. Their faces close enough for breath to mingle. Yet Quoyle was thinking of the only gift that Petal ever gave him. She had opened dozens of presents from him. A turquoise bracelet, a tropical-fish tank, a vest beaded with Elvis Presley's visage, canary eyes and sequin lips. She opened the last box, glanced at him. Sitting with his hands dangling, watching her.

'Wait a minute,' she said and ran into the kitchen. He heard the refriger-
ator open. She came back with her hands behind her back.

'I didn't have a chance to buy you anything,' she said, then held both
closed hands toward him. Uncurled her fingers. In each cupped palm a
brown egg. He took them. They were cold. He thought it a tender, wonderful
thing to do. She had given him something, the eggs, after all, only a symbol,
but they had come from her hands as a gift. To him. It didn't matter that he'd
bought them himself at the supermarket the day before. He imagined she
understood him, that she had to love him to know that it was the outstretched
hands, the giving, that mattered.

E. Annie Proulx, The Shipping News

Monstrous Ingratitude

Gifts as gulfs . . .
Thought prompted by one
from ice ages ago:
a lime-green cardigan,
a garment I've never worn
and never will wear.
I hid it in a drawer
and mainly it stays there,
except when, as today,
on the trail of a lost sock,
I dig it up and feel once more
that sundering shock.

With kept creases
and buttons still done,
it invariably releases
the same terror as when,
tearing the posh paper,
I saw at a glance
how little she understood me.
Well, I covered my inner silence
with mumbled thanks;
yet the rift persists
and even now

pride prevents me
from trying the thing on, somehow.

                                                    Boris Parkin

Reginald on Christmas Presents

I wish it to be distinctly understood (said Reginald) that I don't want a
'George, Prince of Wales' Prayer-book as a Christmas present. The fact
cannot be too widely known.

There ought (he continued) to be technical education classes on the
science of present-giving. No one seems to have the faintest notion of what
anyone else wants, and the prevalent ideas on the subject are not creditable to
a civilized community.

There is, for instance, the female relative in the country who 'knows a tie is
always useful', and sends you some spotted horror that you could only wear
in secret or in Tottenham Court Road. It *might* have been useful had she kept
it to tie up currant bushes with, when it would have served the double
purpose of supporting the branches and frightening away the birds – for it is
an admitted fact that the ordinary tomtit of commerce has a sounder aes-
thetic taste than the average female relative in the country.

Then there are aunts. They are always a difficult class to deal with in the
matter of presents. The trouble is that one never catches them really young
enough. By the time one has educated them to an appreciation of the fact
that one does not wear red woollen mittens in the West End, they die, or
quarrel with the family, or do something equally inconsiderate. That is why
the supply of trained aunts is always so precarious.

There is my Aunt Agatha, *par exemple*, who sent me a pair of gloves last
Christmas, and even got so far as to choose a kind that was being worn and
had the correct number of buttons. But – *they were nines!* I sent them to a boy
whom I hated intimately: he didn't wear them, of course, but he could have –
that was where the bitterness of death came in. It was nearly as consoling as
sending white flowers to his funeral. Of course I wrote and told my aunt that
they were the one thing that had been wanting to make existence blossom like
a rose; I am afraid she thought me frivolous – she comes from the North,
where they live in the fear of Heaven and the Earl of Durham. (Reginald
affects an exhaustive knowledge of things political, which furnishes an excellent excuse for not discussing them.) Aunts with a dash of foreign extraction
in them are the most satisfactory in the way of understanding these things;

but if you can't choose your aunt, it is wisest in the long run to choose the present and send her the bill.

Even friends of one's own set, who might be expected to know better, have curious delusions on the subject. I am *not* collecting copies of the cheaper editions of Omar Khayyam. I gave the last four that I received to the lift-boy, and I like to think of him reading them, with FitzGerald's notes, to his aged mother. Lift-boys always have aged mothers; shows such nice feeling on their part, I think.

Personally, I can't see where the difficulty in choosing suitable presents lies. No boy who had brought himself up properly could fail to appreciate one of those decorative bottles of liqueurs that are so reverently staged in Morel's window – and it wouldn't in the least matter if one did get dupli- cates. And there would always be the supreme moment of dreadful uncer- tainty whether it was *crème de menthe* or Chartreuse – like the expectant thrill on seeing your partner's hand turned up at bridge. People may say what they like about the decay of Christianity; the religious system that produced green Chartreuse can never really die.

And then, of course, there are liqueur glasses, and crystallized fruits, and tapestry curtains, and heaps of other necessaries of life that make really sensible presents – not to speak of luxuries, such as having one's bills paid, or getting something quite sweet in the way of jewellery. Unlike the alleged Good Woman of the Bible, I'm not above rubies. When found, by the way, she must have been rather a problem at Christmastime; nothing short of a blank cheque would have fitted the situation. Perhaps it's as well that she's died out.

The great charm about me (concluded Reginald) is that I am so easily pleased. But I draw the line at a 'Prince of Wales' Prayer-book.

'Saki'

Shopping

'First of all,' began Margaret, 'we must make a list and tick off the people's names. My aunt always does, and this fog may thicken up any moment. Have you any ideas?'

'I thought we would go to Harrods or the Haymarket Stores,' said Mrs Wilcox rather hopelessly. 'Everything is sure to be there. I am not a good shopper. The din is so confusing, and your aunt is quite right – one ought to make a list. Take my notebook, then, and write your own name at the top of the page.'

'Oh, hooray!' said Margaret, writing it. 'How very kind of you to start with me!' But she did not want to receive anything expensive. Their acquaintance was singular rather than intimate, and she divined that the Wilcox clan would resent any expenditure on outsiders; the more compact families do. She did not want to be thought a second Helen, who would snatch presents since she could not snatch young men, nor to be exposed, like a second Aunt Juley, to the insults of Charles. A certain austerity of demeanour was best, and she added: 'I don't really want a Yuletide gift, though. In fact, I'd rather not.'

'Why?'

'Because I've odd ideas about Christmas. Because I have all that money can buy. I want more people, but no more things.'

'I should like to give you something worth your acquaintance, Miss Schlegel, in memory of your kindness to me during my lonely fortnight. It has so happened that I have been left alone, and you have stopped me from brooding. I am too apt to brood.'

'If that is so,' said Margaret, 'if I have happened to be of use to you, which I didn't know, you cannot pay me back with anything tangible.'

'I suppose not, but one would like to. Perhaps I shall think of something as we go about.'

Her name remained at the head of the list, but nothing was written opposite it. They drove from shop to shop. The air was white, and when they alighted it tasted like cold pennies. At times they passed through a clot of grey. Mrs Wilcox's vitality was low that morning, and it was Margaret who decided on a horse for this little girl, a golliwog for that, for the rector's wife a copper warming-tray. 'We always give the servants money.' 'Yes, do you? yes, much easier,' replied Margaret, but felt the grotesque impact of the unseen upon the seen, and saw issuing from a forgotten manger at Bethlehem this torrent of coins and toys. Vulgarity reigned. Public-houses, besides their usual exhortation against temperance reform, invited men to 'Join our Christmas goose club' – one bottle of gin, etc., or two, according to subscription. A poster of a woman in tights heralded the Christmas pantomime, and little red devils, who had come in again that year, were prevalent upon the Christmas cards. Margaret was no morbid idealist. She did not wish this spate of business and self-advertisement checked. It was only the occasion of it that struck her with amazement annually. How many of these vacillating shoppers and tired shop assistants realized that it was a divine event that drew them together? She realized it though, standing outside in the matter. She was not a Christian in the accepted sense; she did not believe that God had ever worked among us as a young artisan. These people, or most of them, believed it, and if pressed, would affirm it in words. But the visible signs of their belief were Regent Street or Drury Lane, a little mud displaced, a little money spent, a little food cooked, eaten, and forgotten. Inadequate. But in public who shall express the unseen adequately? It is private life that holds out the mirror to infinity; personal intercourse, and that alone, that ever hints at a personality beyond our daily vision.

'No, I do not like Christmas on the whole,' she announced. 'In its clumsy way, it does approach Peace and Goodwill. But, oh, it is clumsier every year.'

E. M. Forster, *Howard's End*

To Graham Wallas

Cliveden, Taplow (chez Nancy Astor)
24 December 1927

. . . I finish this on Xmas morning, amid an orgy of presents. The place looks like Gamage's or Hamley's or the Burlington Arcade. They have presented me with a mouth organ! I deserve it. God! how I have talked since my arrival on Friday.

George Bernard Shaw

Presents for the Domestic Staff

Despatch Case in blue morocco, costing about 8*s*. 6*d*.
Gloves lined with fur
A small Tea-set of their own
A comfortable Armchair or Cushion
An Eiderdown in pretty colours
An Umbrella, Goloshes, Mackintosh

Cheaper Presents

Pretty Blotter and Inkpot
(Not handkerchiefs, as they are too hackneyed)
Money in a small purse
Pot of growing flowers

1 doz. pretty Pencils and Notebook for shopping
Cream for their hands, and two pairs of Chamois Gloves
Manicure Set
Pretty Sponge Bag with coloured sponge and face towel
Pretty Bedroom Shoes

Rose Henniker Heaton, *The Perfect Christmas*

To Margaret A. Carlyle

Craigenputtoch, Tuesday Night,
25 December 1832

My Dear Mother,

Your Parcel has come into our hands, quite safe; and only a few hours ago. It was forgotten, or not delivered in time, the first Wednesday; and then the next, as you will probably have heard ere now, we were at Templand: whence we did not return till two o'clock today. We were to have come off on Saturday; but Mrs Welsh was so poorly, that morning, we did not like to leave her; thus we could not travel till Monday, which proved so bad a day that the inside of 'built walls' seemed the only fit place for us. We rolled off, however, this morning; and got home well enough, tho', as you would say, with our noses tolerably 'set up'. I have several things to do; among others a Letter to write to London: so you must take shorter allowance than I would otherwise gladly have given.

The Clogs seem most sufficiently done; the Drawers also are massy sub-stantial-looking things, and will be highly welcome in the frosts I have to expect. But to express the joy that was felt at sight of the *Kipper* is a task my Pen declines; no language just now at my command could do justice to it. A vision of friendly B[r]eakfasts in Edin*r* rises before the female eye, which almost like Isaac Fletcher's 'glents [flashes] fire'; and guests are pressed to eat this savoury fish, and rejoice over it, let it kill them with indigestion after-wards or not. Seriously, Jane thinks it a very excellent piece of goods, and thanks you very heartily for it . . .

Thomas Carlyle

1889

December 29 Christmas-day passed without disaster, and what more can one ask! I had half a dozen giftlets, but the one that hit the bull's-eye was a contribution from the Bachelers costing three pence. I know the price because Nurse took a week to choose it and I had to advance the money, this all unknown to the B's. They were much distressed when they found it had not cost more, as they had calculated upon spending nine-pence. They have planned the investment for a year. They are admirable beings, always send their 'love' to me instead of their 'duty'. Bacheler couldn't wait until Wednesday to bring the object (a little brass tray for pins), but left it on Monday, thereby reminding me of the beloved pater – so the wise and simple meet – who used to spoil our Christmases so faithfully for us, by stealing in with us, when Mother was out, to the forbidden closet and giving up a peep the week or so before. I can't remember whether he used to confess to Mother after, or not, the dear, dear creature! What an ungrateful wretch I was, and how I used to wish he hadn't done it!!

Alice James

𝕸 I I 𝕸

FOOD

1773

25 December   I breakfasted, and slept again in my Rooms – I went to Chapel this morning at 9 o'clock being Christmas Day, and rec^d the Holy Sacrament from the Hands of our Warden who was present. The Warden was on one side of the Altar and myself being Sub-Warden on the other side – I read the Epistle for the day at the Altar and assisted the Warden in going round with the Wine.

For an Offering at the Altar, gave . . . 0.1.0 The Dean of Christchurch who is Bishop of Chester preached this morning at Christchurch, but I did not attend it . . . N.B. The Dean of Christchurch always preaches this day in the morning at Christchurch Cathedral. I dined in the Hall and 14 Senr Fellows with me. I invited the Warden to dine with us as is usual on this day, but his Sister being here, could not. We had a very handsome dinner of my ordering, as I order dinner every day being Sub-Warden.

We had for dinner, two fine Codds boiled with fryed Souls round them and oyster sauce, a fine sirloin of Beef roasted, some peas soup and an orange Pudding for the first course, for the second, we had a lease of Wild Ducks rosted, a fore Qu: of Lamb and sallad and mince Pies. We had a grace cup before the second course brought by the Butler to the Steward of the Hall who was Mr Adams a Senior Fellow, who got out of his place and came to my chair and there drank to me out of it, wishing me a merry Xmas. I then took it of him and drank wishing him the same, and then it went round, three standing up all the time. From the high Table the grace Cup goes to the Batchelors and Scholars. After the second course there was a fine plumb cake brought to the sen^r Table as is usual on this day, which also goes to the Batchelors after. After Grace is said there is another Grace-Cup to drink omnibus Wiccamisis, which is drunk as the first, only the Steward of the Hall does not attend the second Grace Cup . . . We dined at 3 o'clock and were an Hour and ½ at it. We all then went into the Senr Com: Room, where the Warden came to us and sat with us till Prayers. The Wine drunk by the Senr

Fellows, domus pays for. Prayers this evening did not begin till 6 o'clock, at which I attended as did the Warden . . . I supped etc., in the Chequer, we had Rabbits for supper rosted as is usual on this day . . . The Sub-Warden has one to himself; The Bursars each one apiece, the Senr Fellows $^1/_2$ a one each. The Junr Fellows a rabbit between three.

N.B. Put on this Day a new Coat and Waistcoat for the first time.

Revd James Woodforde, *The Diary of a Country Parson*

On the Turkey

The turkey is undoubtedly one of the handsomest presents which the New World has offered to the Old.

Those people who insist on knowing more than anyone else maintain that the Romans were partial to the turkey, that it was served at Charlemagne's wedding-feast, and that it is therefore incorrect to praise the Jesuits for this savoury import.

One could answer these paradoxes with two simple facts:

(1) The French name of the bird, *coq d'Inde*, clearly betrays its origin: for in the old days America was known as the West Indies;
(2) The appearance of the bird, which is clearly outlandish.

No scientist could have any doubts on the question.

However, although for my part I was thoroughly convinced, I conducted extensive research into the subject, which I shall spare the reader, and which led me to the following conclusions:

(1) That the turkey appeared in Europe towards the end of the seventeenth century;
(2) That it was imported by the Jesuits, who bred it in large numbers, especially on one of their farms in the neighbourhood of Bourges;
(3) That from there it gradually spread over the whole of France; which is why in many regions the popular word for turkey was and still is *jésuite*;
(4) That America is the only place where the turkey has been found wild and in a state of nature (there are none in Africa);
(5) That in North America, where it is very common, it is reared either from eggs which are found and hatched out, or from young birds which are caught in the forest and tamed; reared in this way it is nearer to the natural state, and retains its primitive plumage.

Convinced by these points, I would like to observe that we owe a double debt of gratitude to the good Fathers, for they were also responsible for the importation of quinine, which in English is called Jesuit's-bark.

In the course of my researches I also discovered that the acclimatization of the species in France was a gradual process. Enlightened students of the subject have informed me that about the middle of the last century, out of every twenty turkeys hatched, not more than ten grew to maturity; whereas today, all things being equal, the proportion is fifteen in twenty. Rain-storms are particularly fatal to them. The heavy rain-drops, driven by the wind, beat upon their soft, unprotected skulls and kill them.

Jean-Anthelme Brillat-Savarin, *The Philosopher in the Kitchen*
(trans. Anne Drayton)

'I Shall Eat a Great Deal of Turkey'

I do not know whether an animal killed at Christmas has had a better or a worse time than it would have had if there had been no Christmas or no Christmas dinners. But I do know that the fighting and suffering brotherhood to which I belong and owe everything, Mankind, would have a much worse time if there were no such thing as Christmas or Christmas dinners. Whether the turkey which Scrooge gave to Bob Cratchit had experienced a lovelier or more melancholy career than that of less attractive turkeys is a subject upon which I cannot even conjecture. But that Scrooge was better for giving the turkey and Cratchit happier for getting it I know as two facts, as I know that I have two feet. What life and death may be to a turkey is not my business; but the soul of Scrooge and the body of Cratchit are my business. Nothing shall induce me to darken human homes, to destroy human festivities, to insult human gifts and human benefactions for the sake of some hypothetical knowledge which Nature curtained from our eyes. We men and women are all in the same boat, upon a stormy sea. We owe to each other a terrible and tragic loyalty. If we catch sharks for food, let them be killed most mercifully; let any one who likes love the sharks, and pet the sharks, and tie ribbons round their necks and give them sugar and teach them to dance. But if once a man suggests that a shark is to be valued against a sailor, then I would court-martial the man – he is a traitor to the ship.

Meanwhile, it remains true that I shall eat a great deal of turkey this Christmas; and it is not in the least true (as the vegetarians say) that I shall do it because I do not realize what I am doing, or because I do what I know is wrong, or that I do it with shame or doubt or a fundamental unrest of conscience. In one sense I know quite well what I am doing; in another sense

I know quite well that I know not what I do. Scrooge and the Cratchits and I are, as I have said, all in one boat; the turkey and I are, to say the most of it, ships that pass in the night, and greet each other in passing. I wish him well; but it is really practically impossible to discover whether I treat him well. I can avoid, and I do avoid with horror, all special and artificial tormenting of him, sticking pins in him for fun or sticking knives in him for scientific investigation. But whether by feeding him slowly and killing him quickly for the needs of my brethren, I have improved in his own solemn eyes his own strange and separate destiny, whether I have made him in the sight of God a slave or a martyr, or one whom the gods love and who die young – that is far more removed from my possibilities of knowledge than the most abstruse intricacies of mysticism or theology. A turkey is more occult and awful than all the angels and archangels. In so far as God has partly revealed to us an angelic world, he has partly told us what an angel means. But God has never told us what a turkey means. And if you go and stare at a live turkey for an hour or two, you will find by the end of it that the enigma has rather increased than diminished.

G. K. Chesterton

Talking Turkeys!!

Be nice to yu turkeys dis christmas
Cos turkeys jus wanna hav fun
Turkeys are cool, turkeys are wicked
An every turkey has a Mum.
Be nice to yu turkeys dis christmas,
Don't eat it, keep it alive,
It could be yu mate an not on yu plate
Say, Yo! Turkey I'm on your side.

I got lots of friends who are turkeys
An all of dem fear christmas time,
Dey wanna enjoy it, dey say humans destroyed it
An humans are out of dere mind,
Yeah, I got lots of friends who are turkeys
Dey all hav a right to a life,
Not to be caged up an genetically made up
By any farmer an his wife.

Turkeys jus wanna play reggae
Turkeys jus wanna hip-hop
Can yu imagine a nice young turkey saying,
'I cannot wait for de chop'?
Turkeys like getting presents, dey wanna watch christmas TV,
Turkeys hav brains an turkeys feel pain
In many ways like yu an me.

I once knew a turkey called Turkey
He said 'Benji explain to me please,
Who put de turkey in christmas
An what happens to christmas trees?'
I said, 'I am not too sure turkey
But it's nothing to do wid Christ Mass
Humans get greedy an waste more dan need be
An business men mek loadsa cash.'

Be nice to yu turkey dis christmas
Invite dem indoors fe sum greens
Let dem eat cake an let dem partake
In a plate of organic grown beans,
Be nice to yu turkey dis christmas
An spare dem de cut of de knife,
Join Turkeys United an dey'll be delighted
An yu will mek new friends *FOR LIFE*.

Benjamin Zephaniah

Don't Spoil that Pig

'That's our one pig for Christmas,' Mum warned from the scullery door.
'Don't you boys go spoiling him.'

I had worked with Mack before, and we made a quick job of lugging the
beast out and lashing it down with the ropes put ready. It had been done this
way for centuries in Ireland, using the Kilkenny frame.

Hunger suddenly seized hold of me; my gut raging with emptiness, I saw
scarlet lights I mistook for a glimpse of something our ancestors on the far
side of the world had handed down to us. Warlike monks in monasteries
holding off the Viking marauders, Saint Brigid – buried at Downpatrick

beside her dear friend Saint Patrick, and Saint Columba on the other side –
Mary the Gael, as Father Gwilym called her, his voice clouding as it did
when he was teaching Edith Earnshaw the violoncello. Mack walked round
the victim, inspecting it, his pouch of knives, worn like a sporran slipped
sideways on to his hip, clattering, and the steel swung by a cord. He selected
one long, pointed blade. The pig watched him hone it, then watched him
thinking as he stropped, then screamed at the top of its lungs.

Norah, I knew, hid her head indoors. She could never bear the slaughter.
Mum rumbled back to the stove to be sure her great iron kettle kept on the
boil. Young Kate in the peartree peeped through a Venetian lattice of fingers,
trying to laugh. But of all the women, it was Ellen who caught my attention.
From the scullery door she looked at this pig, absorbed in watching it. Even
though Barney put on a tough act to make her notice him, she had eyes only
for the pig.

'I'll do it this year if you like,' I offered, and the hunger in me was a kind of
speed, a kind of concentration.

Far away a wakeful dingo answered the howling pig with a howl of its own:
the one a desperate betrayed outrage, the other a timeless longing. Ellen's
expression changed at that instant from curiosity to what I can only call
recognition.

Why he did so, I don't know. But Mack, who was in charge of the job,
ignored my claim and handed the knife to Barney, whose pleading, irritable
anxiety of a beaten person fell away from him to reveal a champion. He
brandished the knife admiringly, though Ellen still refused to notice. Eager to
snatch glory from a life of defeats, he drew his arm back to drive the blade
home.

'No!' Mack ordered. 'We just puncture the vein. There.'

Barney trembled. I watched his pants quivering. Was this rage or coward-
ice? Mack, shouting over the rumpus made by the sacrificial beast, which he
alone knew the authentic way to kill, explained the art.

'If he doesn't bleed slow, the meat won't be white. And then you'll have
Mrs Murphy herself to deal with.'

'Don't mess about with my pig,' Mum's voice warned from the kitchen.

Barney stepped forward and let the point in through the skin. At first it
wouldn't go. Then suddenly the resistance gave. Blood squirted out all down
his trousers and on to his boots. He jumped back, letting the blade fall. Mack
took a swipe at him but missed, and retrieved his precious knife, which he
then wiped clean between finger and thumb, checking if it had suffered any
damage. I rushed forward to do Ellen's job, now she was no longer needed,
positioning the milk pail to catch the blood. The pig knew what was happen-

ing. He wriggled and clenched, thumping the frame the way Michael thumped his body against the bed when he had misbehaved. But the pig did not have words to curse our house of a tyrant like my brother did, nor the lovely fire of alcohol to brace him or muffle his pain in warmth.

Down along the creek, the blacks came walking, feet sprung like tall birds, till they could see the house and what was going on. I thought they must be too far off to get any clear idea, but they stayed interested, so perhaps their eyes were better than mine. Each year they heard our pig cry, but it was still new to them. Perhaps they couldn't work out why we seemed unable to kill it outright, why it had to go on crying, moaning and sobbing for ten minutes or quarter of an hour. Perhaps they couldn't even see such a simple thing as why we needed to tie the animal on a frame to do the job properly.

Barney apologized to Mack. And again I was reminded of Father Gwilym, but this time of how his voice could change in the middle of my lesson and I knew next minute his white hand would perch on my working boy's scarred brown one. Barney said it was just his clothes and the shock of spoiling them, not the blood that made him jump, no, nor, he shouted over a renewed wail from the beast facing a certainty of death, the pig yelling. 'I suppose it'll wash out,' he added a bit stupidly, ashamed now Ellie began to laugh at him. And even more ashamed when he found she was, more likely, laughing at the pig for making so much fuss too late to be saved.

Mum brought boiling water. She heaved the great weight of the kettle and carried it herself, out down the steps, squinting in the sunshine and steam, to set it on the bench placed ready; and then carried back the bucket of blood for cooking. This was so full that the contents tilted and some streamed down the side, landing with a soft slap in the dust, which instantly soaked it up. Mum glanced back a moment and went on her way.

The pig's cries had guttered out to a hoarse panting, and now we heard again the remote gunfire from the ocean. An eagle's shadow rippled over grass, on to the dirt, up across the pig-frame, fitting itself to the lovable plumpness of dead flesh, then away, rising the full height of a stone chimney, flickering on smoke from Mum's fire, to vanish in the blue heat of the day before the day we must all celebrate. Next time we looked across towards the creek, the Aborigines had gone. There was just a flat plate of water turning silver on its axis at the bend where one bank had collapsed in the previous year's wet.

'Look at the horses!' Kate shrieked, leaping down, prancing round the orchard and climbing an apricot tree full of Christmas apricots.

We hooted at the miserable cluster of them in the farthest corner of their yard, tails swishing the fence posts. Barney, under Mack's direction, had already begun the scalding and scraping.

'See this?' the butcher called to Ellen still at the door like a Sunday. 'When you get him for a husband you ought to have him apprenticed as a butcher. He's got the feel of it, when he doesn't go throwing a man's good knives around in the dirt.'

Ellen laughed. And I laughed also, at the insulting notion of a twenty-two-year-old man going for an apprentice.

As the scalding and scraping progressed, the pig's skin gave out a rasping whistle under the blade, a persistent ghost of the sound the beast's lungs made when it was dying.

The idea had never come to me before that other animals are covered with fir, feathers, or scales but pigs go naked like ourselves. So the screams which I'd heard once a year now made me feel cold. Each Christmas past I had listened to them without realizing why our neighbours looked in during that quarter of an hour of bedlam. This particular year they included Mr and Mrs Earnshaw enjoying a drive, who waved, and the O'Donovans, cantering through the gate and far enough down the track to get a close view while young Clarrie yelled out that they'd come to check, in case you was mur-derin' someone! I couldn't be sure what he said at the time, but I saluted on behalf of the family, needing a part to play now Barney had cut me out of my job.

Kate in the apricot tree heard, being that much closer, and she told me a few days later, when I returned home from punching Barney in the Brian Boru, my memory hot with the loathing I saw in the eyes of men I'd known all my life, men who would not, they said, lay a finger on me if I got out right away.

Rodney Hall, *The Yandilli Trilogy*

Pig's Head, in Imitation of Wild Boar's Head

This you will say is not only a difficult dish to do, but a very expensive one. You are right when you are obliged to buy the pig to possess the head; but in a small farm-house where they kill a pig perhaps once a year at Christmas, the head can be very easily cut off for this purpose. Being on a visit some years since at a farm-house, I had the opportunity of having one, and trying my skill upon it; it was much approved of, both for its ferocious appearance, and its flavour, and it lasted good for three weeks.

The following is the way you should do it: procure the head with as much of the neck attached to it as possible (the hog must have been stabbed in the neck, not hit on the head as that would have broken the skull); then singe it well over the flame of a fire, then wipe it with a cloth, scrape well with a knife without scratching the skin, and place it on a cloth upon its skull; open it very carefully without piercing the skin, leaving no flesh whatever upon the bones; bone the neck of the pig, and cut it into small fillets two inches long, place the head on a board and rub it with half a pound of brown sugar, let it remain for one hour; then place it in a salting tub, and throw over it six pounds of salt, place in two quarts of ale, four bay leaves, half an ounce of peppercorns, a quarter ditto of cloves, six blades of mace, eight sliced onions, ten sprigs of thyme, ten of winter savory, and two sliced carrots; stir it well up, and let it remain for two hours; then pour over the head, which turn every day for eight or ten days, rubbing it well; when sufficiently salted, take it out and dry it on a cloth, lay the head straight before you, skin side upwards; have ready six or eight pounds of forcemeat, but using pork instead of veal, with which cover the head an inch in thickness at the thinnest part; put the fillets cut from the neck in a layer lengthwise in the head, with a long piece of fat bacon, half an inch square, between each, sprinkle a little chopped eschalots, pepper, salt, and grated nutmeg over, and continue filling with forcemeat and the other ingredients until you have used the whole, finishing by covering forcemeat over; join the two cheeks together with the above in the interior, sew it up with packthread, giving it the shape of the head as much as possible, and fold it in one or two large thin cloths, leaving the ears out and upright.

Braise as follows: Put half a pound of butter in a large braising-pan or stock-pot, over which put four pounds of trimmings of pork or knuckle of veal, eight onions, two carrots, four turnips, eight bay-leaves, a tablespoonful of peppercorns, twelve cloves, ten sprigs of thyme, ten of marjoram, four blades of mace, half a bottle of bucellas wine, and four calf's feet, place it upon a sharp fire, stirring it occasionally, until the bottom is covered with a clearish glaze, then add four gallons of water and half a pound of salt; when boiling draw it to the corner of the stove, skim, and put in the head, the ears uppermost, and let simmer seven or eight hours, or according to the size and age of the pig; but the better plan would be to try it with a trussing-needle; if tender it is done; skim the stock, in which leave the head until half cold, when take it out, partly undo the cloths, and tie it again tighter if possible, and press it in a cover or upon a baking-sheet with three flat pieces of wood, one at each side, with a weight against them, and one upon the top between the ears, on which place a fourteen pounds weight; let it remain all night until quite cold, when take it out of the cloths, detach the thread it was sewn up with, cut a piece an inch in thickness from behind the ears, (from which part it must be carved in as thin slices as possible,) it will have a marbled appearance; trim the head a little, setting the ears in a proper position, glaze it with a brownish glaze, form the eyes with a little lard and a few black currants round, and the tusks with paste, baking them; have some very fresh tulips and roses, which stick tastefully in the ears and some around, but leaving space to carve; garnish boldly with croutons, aspic, made from the clarified stock; the meat and the calf's foot may be used for different dishes.

The second one I had I boiled plainer, merely a little salt and a few vegetables; it was very good, but not so rich in flavour as the other; thus saving expense and trouble. They should be eaten with the following sauce:

Boar's Head Sauce – Cut the rind (free from pith) of two Seville oranges into very thin strips half an inch in length, which blanch in boiling water, drain them upon a sieve, and put them into a basin, with a spoonful of mixed English mustard, four of currant jelly, a little pepper, salt (mix well together), and half a pint of good port wine.

Alexis Soyer, *The Modern Housewife*

King George I's Christmas Pudding

(This is not to be listed as an economy recipe; nor do Sandringham kitchens prepare it nowadays. But we include it to represent the rich old Christmas tradition.)

King George I, sometimes called the 'Pudding King', ate this pudding at six o'clock on December 25, 1714 – his first Christmas in England. Practically the same ingredients were mixed in huge earthenware bowls at Sandringham for his descendants:

1½ lb finely shredded suet
1 lb eggs, weighed in their shells
1 lb each dried plums, stoned and halved;
mixed peel, cut in long strips; small raisins;
sultanas; currants; sifted flour; sugar and brown crumbs

1 teaspoonful (heaped) of mixed spice
½ nutmeg, grated
2 teaspoonfuls salt
½ pint new milk
Juice of 1 lemon
A very large wineglassful brandy

Mix the dry ingredients, moisten with eggs, beaten to a froth, and the milk, lemon juice and brandy mixed. Stand for at least 12 hours in a cool place, then turn into buttered moulds. Boil for 8 hours at first, then for 2 hours before serving. This quantity makes 3 puddings of about 3 lb each.

Country recipes collected by *The Farmers Weekly*

Perilous Pudding

(*Enter* FATHER CHRISTMAS *with Christmas Pudding,*
Turkey, Flagons, etc.)
FATHER CHRISTMAS: I will not drink; let the great flagon here
Till the great toasts are drunk, stand where it is.
But Christmas pudding comes but once a year
But many times a day. And none amiss. (*cuts off a piece*)
The Christmas Pudding, round as the round sky,
Speckled with better things than stars.
DOCTOR: (*rushes in and arrests his hand*) Forgive
My haste. But men who eat that pudding die.
FATHER CHRISTMAS: And men who do not eat it do not live (*eats*).
DOCTOR: Our last proofs show, for perils that appal
A Christmas pudding is a cannon ball.

G. K. Chesterton, 'The Turkey and the Turk: The Mummer's Play'

The Defossilized Plum-Pudding

'Have some more of that stuff?' asked Simpson, hoisting his club-foot on to a vacant chair, and passing his long, bony fingers down the scar that runs vertically from his forehead to his chin.

'I don't mind if I do,' I answered, and he gave me another help.

I do not exactly know why I always dine with Simpson on Christmas Day. Neither of us likes the other. He thinks me a dreamer, and for some reason I never trust him, though he is undoubtedly the most brilliant Pantaeschrologist of his day, and we had been contemporaries at the FRZS. It is possible that he dislikes me, and I him, less than does anybody else. And to this may be due our annual festivity in his luxurious rooms in Gower Street.

'Have some of this sherry,' muttered Simpson, pushing towards me a decanter which his deformed butler had placed before him. 'You'll find it middling.'

I helped myself to a glass and smoothing out my shirt-front, (Simpson is one of those men who 'dress'), settled myself in my chair.

'Notice anything odd about that pudding?' he asked, with a searching glance through his double-convex glasses.

'No,' I said simply, 'I thought it very good.'

A gleam of grim pleasure came out of his face. I knew from this that the annual yarn was coming. Simpson is the most enthralling talker I ever met, but somehow I always go to sleep before he is half-way through. I did so, the year before, when he told me about 'The Carnivorous Mistletoe', and the year before that, when he told me 'The Secret of the Sinister Crackers', and another time, when his theme was 'The Microbes in the Yule Log'. It vexed him very much every time, and he pooh-poohed my excuses. I was determined it should not occur again.

'I am glad you liked the pudding,' he said. 'Pardon my inhospitality in not keeping your company, while you ate. Tobacco is a good preventive against indigestion. You can light up.'

I did so.

'You have heard of fossilized substances?' Simpson began, in that rasping voice so familiar to his pupils at the SVP.

I nodded across my briar.

'Well,' he continued, 'it has always been a pet theory of mine that, just as a substance can, by the action of certain alkaloids operating in the course of time, become, to all purposes, metallic, so – you follow me – it can, in like manner, be restored to its previous condition. You have heard of plum-puddings being kept for twenty-one years?'

I nodded; less, I am afraid, in assent than owing to a physical cause.

'Well,' I heard him saying, 'the stuff that you have eaten tonight is about two hundred and fifty years old and may be much more than that, at a very moderate computation.'

I started. Simpson had raised his voice rather suddenly. He took my start for surprise and continued wagging his crippled forefinger at me. 'That pudding was originally a cannon ball. It was picked up on the field of Naseby. Never mind how I came by it. It has been under treatment in my laboratory for the last ten years.'

'Ten years,' I muttered. 'Ten . . . seems almost impossible.'

'For ten years,' he resumed, 'I have been testing, acidizing . . . thing began to decompose under my very . . . at length . . . brown, pulpy substance, such as you might . . . sultanas . . . Now comes in the curious part of the . . .'

How long after I don't know, I was awoken by a vicious kick from Simpson's club-foot.

'You brute!' I cried, 'you drugged that sherry!'

'Faugh!' he sneered, 'you say that every year!'

Max Beerbohm (after H. G. Wells)

An Empire Christmas Pudding

(With accompanying SAUCE, according to a recipe supplied by the King's Chef, MR CEDARD, with Their Majesties' gracious consent.)

1 lb of Currants – Australia
1 lb of Sultanas – Australia or South Africa
1 lb of stoned Raisins – Australia or South Africa
5 oz of Minced Apple – United Kingdom or Canada
1 lb of Breadcrumbs – United Kingdom
1 lb of Beef Suet – United Kingdom
6½ oz of cut Candied Peel – South Africa
8 oz of Flour – United Kingdom
8 oz of Demerara Sugar – British West Indies or British Guiana
5 eggs – United Kingdom or Irish Free State
½ oz Ground Cinnamon – India or Ceylon
¼ oz Ground Cloves – Zanzibar
¼ oz Ground Nutmegs – British West Indies
¼ teaspoonful Pudding Spice – India or British West Indies
*¼ gill Brandy – Australia, South Africa, Cyprus or Palestine
*½ gill Rum – Jamaica or British Guiana
*1 pint Old Beer – England, Wales, Scotland or Ireland

*These ingredients may be regarded as optional provided some other liquid such as milk is substituted – in which case, however, the pudding will lose its keeping qualities.

SAUCE SABAYON

Put into a whipping bowl the yolks of 2 eggs, ¼ oz castor sugar, ¼ gill South African white wine, ¼ gill water. Set bowl over a slow gas. Whip continuously until quite frothy as whipped cream. Serve immediately. Before serving, a few drops of Cyprus brandy or Jamaica rum may be sprinkled over.

Rose Henniker Heaton, The Perfect Christmas

Scruts (by Arn*ld B*nn*tt)

I

Emily Wrackgarth stirred the Christmas pudding till her right arm began to ache. But she did not cease for that. She stirred on till her right arm grew so numb that it might have been the right arm of some girl at the other end of Bursley. And yet something deep down in her whispered 'It is *your* right arm! And you can do what you like with it!'

She did what she liked with it. Relentlessly she kept it moving till it reasserted itself as the arm of Emily Wrackgarth, prickling and tingling as with red-hot needles in every tendon from wrist to elbow. And still Emily Wrackgarth hardened her heart.

Presently she saw the spoon no longer revolving, but wavering aimlessly in the midst of the basin. Ridiculous! This must be seen to! In the down of dark hairs that connected her eyebrows there was a marked deepening of that vertical cleft which, visible at all times, warned you that here was a young woman not to be trifled with. Her brain despatched to her hand a peremptory message – which miscarried. The spoon wabbled as though held by a baby. Emily knew that she herself as a baby had been carried into this very kitchen to stir the Christmas pudding. Year after year, as she grew up, she had been allowed to stir it 'for luck'. And those, she reflected, were the only cookery lessons she ever got. How like Mother!

Mrs Wrackgarth had died in the past year, of a complication of ailments.[1] Emily still wore on her left shoulder that small tag of crape which is as far as the Five Towns go in the way of mourning. Her father had died in the year previous to that, of a still more curious and enthralling complication of ailments.[2] Jos, his son, carried on the Wrackgarth Works, and Emily kept house for Jos. She with her own hand had made this pudding. But for her this pudding would not have been. Fantastic! Utterly incredible! And yet so it was. She was grown-up. She was mistress of the house. She could make or unmake puddings at will. And yet she was Emily Wrackgarth. Which was absurd.

She would not try to explain, to reconcile. She abandoned herself to the exquisite mysteries of existence. And yet in her abandonment she kept a

[1] See *The History of Sarah Wrackgarth*, pp. 345–482.
[2] See *The History of Sarah Wrackgarth*, pp. 231–344.

sharp look-out on herself, trying fiercely to make head or tail of her nature. She thought herself a fool. But the fact that she thought so was for her a proof of adult sapience. Odd! She gave herself up. And yet it was just by giving herself up that she seemed to glimpse sometimes her own inwardness. And these bleak revelations saddened her. But she savoured her sadness. It was the wine of life to her. And for her sadness she scorned herself, and in her conscious scorn she recovered her self-respect.

It is doubtful whether the people of southern England have even yet realized how much introspection there is going on all the time in the Five Towns.

Visible from the window of the Wrackgarths' parlour was that colossal statue of Commerce which rears itself aloft at the point where Oodge Lane is intersected by Blackstead Street. Commerce, executed in glossy Doulton-ware by some sculptor or sculptors unknown, stands pointing her thumb over her shoulder towards the chimneys of far Hanbridge. When I tell you that the circumference of that thumb is six inches, and the rest to scale, you will understand that the statue is one of the prime glories of Bursley. There were times when Emily Wrackgarth seemed to herself as vast and as lustrously impressive as it. There were other times when she seemed to herself as trivial and slavish as one of those performing fleas she had seen at the Annual Ladies' Evening Fête organized by the Bursley Mutual Burial Club. Extremist!

She was now stirring the pudding with her left hand. The ingredients had already been mingled indistinguishably in that rich, undulating mass of tawniness which proclaims perfection. But Emily was determined to give her left hand, not less than her right, what she called 'a doing'. Emily was like that.

At mid-day, when her brother came home from the Works, she was still at it.

'Brought those scruts with you?' she asked, without looking up.

'That's a fact,' he said, dipping his hand into the sagging pocket of his coat.

It is perhaps necessary to explain what scruts are. In the daily output of every potbank there are a certain proportion of flawed vessels. These are cast aside by the foreman, with a lordly gesture, and in due course are hammered into fragments. These fragments, which are put to various uses, are called scruts; and one of the uses they are put to is a sentimental one. The dainty and luxurious Southerner looks to find in his Christmas pudding a wedding-ring, a gold thimble, a threepenny-bit, or the like. To such fal-lals the Five Towns would say fie. A Christmas pudding in the Five Towns contains nothing but suet, flour, lemon-peel, cinnamon, brandy, almonds, raisins – and two or three scruts. There is a world of poetry, beauty, romance, in scruts – though you have to have been brought up on them to appreciate it. Scruts have passed into the proverbial philosophy of the district. 'Him's a pudden with more scruts than raisins to 'm' is a criticism not infrequently heard. It implies respect, even admiration. Of Emily Wrackgarth herself people often said, in reference to her likeness to her father, 'Her's a scrut o' the owd basin.'

Jos had emptied out from his pocket on to the table a good three dozen of scruts. Emily laid aside her spoon, rubbed the palms of her hands on the bib of her apron, and proceeded to finger these scruts with the air of a connoisseur, rejecting one after another. The pudding was a small one, designed merely for herself and Jos, with remainder to 'the girl'; so that it could hardly accommodate more than two or three scruts. Emily knew well that one scrut is as good as another. Yet she did not want her brother to feel that anything selected by him would necessarily pass muster with her. For his benefit she ostentatiously wrinkled her nose.

'By the by,' said Jos, 'you remember Albert Grapp? I've asked him to step over from Hanbridge and help eat our snack on Christmas Day.'

Emily gave Jos one of her looks. 'You've asked that Mr Grapp?'

'No objection, I hope? He's not a bad sort. And he's considered a bit of a ladies' man, you know.'

She gathered up all the scruts and let them fall in a rattling shower on the exiguous pudding. Two or three fell wide of the basin. These she added.

'Steady on!' cried Jos. 'What's that for?'

'That's for your guest,' replied his sister. 'And if you think you're going to palm me off on to him, or on to any other young fellow, you're a fool, Jos Wrackgarth.'

The young man protested weakly, but she cut him short.

'Don't think,' she said, 'I don't know what you've been after, just of late. Cracking up one young sawny and then another on the chance of me marrying him! I never heard of such goings on. But here I am, and here I'll stay, as sure as my name's Emily Wrackgarth, Jos Wrackgarth!'

She was the incarnation of the adorably feminine. She was exquisitely vital. She exuded at every pore the pathos of her young undirected force. It is difficult to write calmly about her. For her, in another age, ships would have been launched and cities besieged. But brothers are a race apart, and blind. It is a fact that Jos would have been glad to see his sister 'settled' – preferably in one of the other four Towns.

She took up the spoon and stirred vigorously. The scruts grated and squeaked together around the basin, while the pudding feebly wormed its way up among them.

II

Albert Grapp, ladies' man though he was, was humble of heart. Nobody knew this but himself. Not one of his fellow clerks in Clither's Bank knew it. The general theory in Hanbridge was 'Him's got a stiff opinion o' hisself.' But this arose from what was really a sign of humility in him. He made the most of himself. He had, for instance, a way of his own in the matter of dressing. He always wore a voluminous frock-coat, with a pair of neatly striped vicuna trousers, which he placed every night under his mattress, thus preserving in perfection the crease down the centre of each. His collar was of the highest, secured in front with an aluminium stud, to which was attached by a patent loop a natty bow of dove-coloured sateen. He had two caps, one of blue serge, the other of shepherd's plaid. These he wore on alternate days. He wore them in a way of his own – well back from his forehead, so as not to hide his hair, and with the peak behind. The peak made a sort of half-moon over the back of his collar. Through a fault of his tailor, there was a yawning gap between the back of his collar and the collar of his coat. Whenever he shook his head, the peak of his cap had the look of a live thing trying to investigate this abyss. Dimly aware of the effect, Albert Grapp shook his head as seldom as possible.

On wet days he wore a mackintosh. This, as he did not yet possess a greatcoat, he wore also, but with less glory, on cold days. He had hoped there might be rain on Christmas morning. But there was no rain. 'Like my luck,' he said as he came out of his lodgings and turned his steps to that corner of Jubilee Avenue from which the Hanbridge-Bursley trams start every half-hour.

Since Jos Wrackgarth had introduced him to his sister at the Hanbridge Oddfellows' Biennial Hop, when he danced two quadrilles with her, he had seen her but once. He had nodded to her, Five Towns fashion, and she had nodded back at him, but with a look that seemed to say 'You needn't nod next time you see me. I can get along well enough without your nods.' A frightening girl! And yet her brother had since told him she seemed 'a bit gone, like' on him. Impossible! He, Albert Grapp, make an impression on the brilliant Miss Wrackgarth! Yet she had sent him a verbal invite to spend Christmas in her own home. And the time had come. He was on his way. Incredible that he should arrive! The tram must surely overturn, or be struck by lightning. And yet no! He arrived safely.

The small servant who opened the door gave him another verbal message from Miss Wrackgarth. It was that he must wipe his feet 'well' on the mat. In obeying this order he experienced a thrill of satisfaction he could not account for. He must have stood shuffling his boots vigorously for a full minute. This, he told himself, was life. He, Albert Grapp, was alive. And the world was full of other men, all alive; and yet, because they were not doing Miss Wrackgarth's bidding, none of them really lived. He was filled with a vague melancholy. But his melancholy pleased him.

In the parlour he found Jos awaiting him. The table was laid for three.

'So you're here, are you?' said the host, using the Five Towns formula. 'Emily's in the kitchen,' he added. 'Happen she'll be here directly.'

'I hope she's tol-lol-ish?' asked Albert.

'She is,' said Jos. 'But don't you go saying that to her. She doesn't care about society airs and graces. You'll make no headway if you aren't blunt.'

'Oh, right you are,' said Albert, with the air of a man who knew his way about.

A moment later Emily joined them, still wearing her kitchen apron. 'So you're here, are you?' she said, but did not shake hands. The servant had followed her in with the tray, and the next few seconds were occupied in the disposal of the beef and trimmings.

The meal began, Emily carving. The main thought of a man less infatuated than Albert Grapp would have been 'This girl can't cook. And she'll never learn to.' The beef, instead of being red and brown, was pink and white. Uneatable beef! And yet he relished it more than anything he had ever tasted. This beef was her own handiwork. Thus it was because she had made it so . . . He warily refrained from complimenting her, but the idea of a second helping obsessed him.

'Happen I could do with a bit more, like,' he said.

Emily hacked off the bit more and jerked it on to the plate he had held out to her.

'Thanks,' he said; and then, as Emily's lip curled, and Jos gave him a warning kick under the table, he tried to look as if he had said nothing.

Only when the second course came on did he suspect that the meal was a calculated protest against his presence. This a Christmas pudding? The litter of fractured earthenware was hardly held together by the suet and raisins. All his pride of manhood – and there was plenty of pride mixed up with Albert Grapp's humility – dictated a refusal to touch that pudding. Yet he soon found himself touching it, though gingerly, with his spoon and fork.

In the matter of dealing with scruts there are two schools – the old and the new. The old school pushes its head well over its plate and drops the scrut straight from its mouth. The new school emits the scrut into the fingers of its left hand and therewith deposits it on the rim of the plate. Albert noticed that Emily was of the new school. But might she not despise as affectation in him what came natural to herself? On the other hand, if he showed himself as a prop of the old school, might she not set her face the more stringently against him? The chances were that whichever course he took would be the wrong one.

It was then that he had an inspiration – an idea of the sort that comes to a man once in his life and finds him, likely as not, unable to put it into practice. Albert was not sure he could consummate this idea of his. He had indisputably fine teeth – 'a proper mouthful of grinders' in local phrase. But would they stand the strain he was going to impose on them? He could but try them. Without a sign of nervousness he raised his spoon, with one scrut in it, to his mouth. This scrut he put between two of his left-side molars, bit hard on it, and – eternity of that moment! – felt it and heard it snap in two. Emily also heard it. He was conscious that at sound of the percussion she started forward and stared at him. But he did not look at her. Calmly, systematically, with gradually diminishing crackles, he reduced that scrut to powder, and washed the powder down with a sip of beer. While he dealt with the second scrut he talked to Jos about the Borough Council's proposal to erect an electric power station on the site of the old gasworks down Hillport way. He was aware of a slight abrasion inside his left cheek. No matter. He must be more careful. There were six scruts still to be negotiated. He knew that what he was doing was a thing grandiose, unique, epical; a history-making thing; a thing that would outlive marble and the gilded monuments of princes. Yet he kept his head. He did not hurry, nor did he dawdle. Scrut by scrut, he ground slowly but he ground exceeding small. And while he did so he talked wisely and well. He passed from the power station to a first edition of Leconte de Lisle's *Parnasse Contemporain* that he had picked up for sixpence in Liverpool, and thence to the Midland's proposal to drive a tunnel under the Knype Canal so as to link up the main-line with the Critchworth and Suddleford loop-line. Jos was too amazed to put in a word. Jos sat merely gaping – a gape that merged by imperceptible degrees into a grin. Presently he ceased to watch his guest. He sat watching his sister.

Not once did Albert himself glance in her direction. She was just a dim silhouette on the outskirts of his vision. But there she was, unmoving, and he could feel the fixture of her unseen eyes. The time was at hand when he would have to meet those eyes. Would he flinch? Was he master of himself?

The last scrut was powder. No temporizing! He jerked his glass to his mouth. A moment later, holding out his plate to her, he looked Emily full in the eyes. They were Emily's eyes, but not hers alone. They were collective eyes – that was it! They were the eyes of stark, staring womanhood. Her face had been dead white, but now suddenly up from her throat, over her cheeks, through the down between her eyebrows, went a rush of colour, up over her temples, through the very parting of her hair.

'Happen,' he said without a quaver in his voice, 'I'll have a bit more, like.'

She flung her arms forward on the table and buried her face in them. It was a gesture wild and meek. It was the gesture foreseen and yet incredible. It was recondite, inexplicable, and yet obvious. It was the only thing to be done – and yet, by gum, she had done it.

Her brother had risen from his seat and was now at the door. 'Think I'll step round to the Works,' he said, 'and see if they banked up that furnace aright.'

Max Beerbohm, A Christmas Garland

His Excellency Entertains

'But quite the most illuminating example of this sort of thing occurred on the evening when Polk-Mowbray swallowed a moth. I don't think I ever told you about it before. It is the sort of thing one only talks about in the strictest confidence. It was at a dinner party given to the Communist People's Serbian Trade and Timber Guild sometime during Christmas week back in '52. Yugoslavia at that time had just broken with Stalin and was beginning to feel that the West was not entirely populated by "capitalist hyenas" as the press said. They were still wildly suspicious of us, of course, and it was a very hot and embarrassed little group of peasants dressed in dark suits who accepted Polk-Mowbray's invitation to dinner at the Embassy. Most of them spoke only their mother tongue. Comrade Bobok, however, the leader of the delegation, spoke a gnarled embryonic English. He was a huge sweating Bosnian peasant with a bald head. His number two, Pepic, spoke the sort of French that one imagines is learned in mission houses in Polynesia. From a diplomatist's point of view they were Heavy Going.

'I shall say nothing about their messy food habits; Drage the butler kept circling the table and staring at them as if he had gone out of his senses. We were all pretty sweaty and constrained by the time the soup plates were removed. The conversation was early cave-man stuff consisting of growls and snarls and weird flourishes of knife and fork. Bobok and Pepic sat on Polk-

Mowbray's right and left respectively; they were flanked by Spalding the Commercial Attaché and myself. We were absolutely determined to make the evening a success. De Mandeville for some curious reason best known to himself had decreed that we should eat turkey with mustard and follow it up with plum pudding. I suppose it was because it was Christmas week. Comrade Bobok fell foul of the mustard almost at once and only quenched himself by lengthy potations which, however, were all to the good as they put him into a good temper.

'The whole thing might have been carried off perfectly well had it not been for this blasted moth which had been circling the Georgian candlesticks since the start of the dinner-party and which now elected to get burnt and crawl on to Polk-Mowbray's side-plate to die. Polk-Mowbray himself was undergoing the fearful strain of decoding Comrade Bobok's weighty pleasantries which were full of corrupt groups and he let his attention wander for one fatal second.

'As he talked he absently groped in his side-plate for a piece of bread. He rolls bread balls incessantly at dinner, as you know. Spalding and I saw in a flash of horror something happen for which our long diplomatic training had not prepared us. Mind you, I saw a journalist eat a wine-glass once, and once in Prague I saw a Hindu diplomat's wife drain a glass of vodka under the impression that it was water. She let out a moan which still rings in my ears. But never in all my long service have I seen an Ambassador eat a moth – and this is precisely what Polk-Mowbray did. He has a large and serviceable mouth and into it Spalding and I saw the moth disappear. There was a breathless pause during which our poor Ambassador suddenly realized that something was wrong; his whole frame stiffened with a dreadful premonition. His large and expressive eye became round and glassy with horror.

'This incident unluckily coincided with two others; the first was that Drage walked on with a blazing pudding stuck with holly. Our guests were somewhat startled by this apparition, and Comrade Bobok, under the vague impression that the blazing pud must be ushering in a spell of diplomatic toasts, rose to his feet and cried loudly: "To Comrade Tito and the Communist People's Serbian Trade and Timber Guild. *Jiveo!*" His fellow Serbs rose as one man and shouted: "*Jiveo!*"

'By this time, however, light had begun to dawn on Polk-Mowbray. He let out a hoarse jarring cry full of despair and charred moth, stood up, threw up his arms and groped his way to the carafe on the sideboard, shaken by a paroxysm of coughing. Spalding and I rocked, I am sorry to say, with hysterical giggles, followed him to pat him on the back. To the startled eyes of the Yugoslavs we must have presented the picture of three diplomats laughing ourselves to death and slapping each other on the back at the sideboard, and utterly ignoring the sacred toast. Worse still, before any of us could turn and explain the situation Spalding's elbow connected with Drage's spinal cord. The butler missed his footing and scattered the pudding like an incendiary bomb all over the table and ourselves. The Yugoslav delegation sat there with little odd bits of pudding blazing in their laps or on their waistcoats, utterly incapable of constructive thought. Spalding, I am sorry to say, was racked with guffaws now which were infectious to a degree. De Mandeville who was holding the leg of the table and who had witnessed the tragedy also started to laugh in a shrill feminine register.

'I must say Polk-Mowbray rallied gamely. He took an enormous gulp of wine from the carafe and led us all back to table with apologies and excuses which sounded, I must say, pretty thin. What Communist could believe a capitalist hyena when he says that he has swallowed a moth? Drage was flashing about snuffing out pieces of pudding.

'We made some attempt to save the evening, but in vain. The awful thing was that whenever Spalding caught De Mandeville's eye they both subsided into helpless laughter. The Yugoslavs were in an Irremediable Huff and from then on they shut up like clams, and took their collective leave even before the coffee was served.

'It was quite clear that Spalding's Timber Pact was going to founder in mutual mistrust once more. The whole affair was summed up by the *Central Balkan Herald* in its inimitable style as follows: "We gather that the British Embassy organized a special dinner at which the Niece de Resistance was Glum Pudding and a thoroughly British evening was enjoyed by all." You couldn't say fairer than that, could you?'

Lawrence Durrell, Esprit de Corps

The Worst Christmas Dinner, Ever

I did not think we would ever get to the South Seas; Graham [Greene] always seemed committed to dashing off somewhere else. 'I can see now,' he was to write later, 'that my travels, as much as the act of writing, were ways of escape', and he quoted Auden: 'Man needs escape as he needs food and deep sleep.' But that autumn of 1959 he began to make plans for our journey, and on 20 December we set off from Heathrow. We travelled first class; I think my ticket, right round the globe, cost around £650. Graham had apologized for not being able to leave earlier, saying in his defence: 'We don't need to waste time in Singapore and Bangkok and such places' – rather a blasé observation, I thought, for I would have loved to revisit them in his company, and also to see a little of Australia, where I had never been. But no; we had to be in Tahiti by Christmas. The only place *en route* where I managed to persuade him to leave the airport was Sydney, where we had a couple of hours to spare, ate a fine lobster lunch at the Rex Hotel in King's Cross, and took a taxi ride round the city, admiring the wooden trams and the Victorian wrought-iron balconies. We drove past the cricket ground, at which Graham stared glumly, expressing his relief that there was no match being played which I might have bullied him into watching for a few overs. I am still embarrassed when Australians ask me if I have been to their country and I have to reply: 'For three hours.' (We had also had an hour at Darwin airport, watching the sun rise.)

Graham had an idea that we might recoup much of the difference between our fares and that for tourist class by our consumption of free drinks, and from the time we left Heathrow he kept a note of all we had, calculating what each drink would have cost had we had to pay for it. But although we availed ourselves of every offer, the resultant sum mounted so slowly that he stopped keeping a record after we left Jakarta. The first night we spent out of the plane was at Fiji, where we admired the landscape as we drove into the capital, Suva ('Tahiti'll have to be good to be more beautiful than this,' he remarked), but spent a dull evening. A young American in the hotel, recognizing Graham and evidently unaware of his tastes, took us for a gay couple and attempted to strike up an intimacy, explaining that he was a friend of Terence Rattigan, a writer whose work Graham particularly disliked; nor did he much like Rattigan as a man. (Graham once said to me that he thought talking to Rattigan was like walking on very slippery parquet flooring. I thought this an unfair judgement, since Rattigan had been kind and helpful to me in my early days, although he knew I was not of his persuasion.) We then enjoyed the unusual luxury of three Christmas Eves and two Christmas Days.

To get to Tahiti from Fiji, we had to take a New Zealand Airways flying-boat to Samoa and spend a night there, a prospect that pleased Graham, since he was a remote relation and an admirer of Robert Louis Stevenson, who had spent his last years there. This involved crossing the International Date Line and so going back a day. On Christmas Eve we departed from Fiji and crossed into 23 December, but then the pilot learned that the sea was too rough for us to land at Satapuala, so we turned and, in due course, found ourselves back in Fiji for our second Christmas Eve. Next morning a huge chambermaid woke us with cries of 'Merry Christmas!' Off we went again in the seaplane, entered our third Christmas Eve, and in due course landed successfully at Satapuala. *En route*, we had been given a particularly disgusting meal, the worst Christmas lunch that either of us had ever eaten, though it was not to retain that distinction for long.

We had been advised in Fiji that the best hotel in Samoa was the White Horse Inn. Graham and I both liked the sound of this, but the New Zealand cabin attendant told us that we should not stay there but at Aggie Grey's. This recommendation was confirmed by the pilot when he came round to chat with the passengers. Aggie Grey, he explained, was one of the great characters of the South Seas. Now aged, she had known Somerset Maugham and many great writers of an even older vintage, though unfortunately, not being much of a reader, he could not remember their names. We told him we had already wired for rooms at the White Horse Inn, but he said he could telegraph a message to Samoa cancelling the reservation and booking us in at Aggie's if she had any vacancies, which was, however, doubtful since her hotel was so famous and consequently in great demand. But luck, it seemed, was with us. Aggie could fit us in.

Our hearts did not exactly rise when the taxi deposited us at Aggie Grey's, still less when we entered. We had been told by the pilot that Aggie was an eccentric and that her hotel was not like other hotels, but it looked run-down and sordid to a degree. There was no air-conditioning, or if there was it was not working, and no mosquito nets over the beds, which were hard and lumpy. When we went down for a drink before dinner, the only lounge was furnished with a miscellany of ancient chairs, many of them with broken springs showing through the upholstery. These lined the four walls, so that we and the other guests sat staring at each other across the intervening space as though awaiting a performance of something in the round. One large and comparatively comfortable-looking chair was vacant. This, it was explained to us, was Aggie's.

After an impressive delay, Aggie entered, a rather tall old lady, or do I remember her as tall because she was so daunting? A kind of agreed hush fell over the guests; it was as though we were in the presence of royalty, and, as with royalty, we nodded assent to whatever she said and asked no questions. We had a nasty dinner, and a bad night on the uncomfortable beds, devoured by mosquitoes. If this was the best hotel in Samoa, we wondered, what could the White Horse Inn be like? Next morning we were woken, for the second successive day, with cries of: 'Merry Christmas!' It was pelting with rain, and there was nothing to do but read until lunch, which Aggie had hinted the previous evening would be something special. Graham said: 'At least it can't be as bad as New Zealand Airways.'

In due course, and with ceremony, the feast began. The starter was a tinned–crab cocktail, tasting mainly of tin with an undertone of rust, swathed in an evil bottled mayonnaise. This was followed by an indeterminate, dark-fleshed and sinewy bird. Graham said: 'Do you think we'll get anything to drink?' I said I feared not, since otherwise we would surely have been offered something with the crab, but now the waitresses reappeared with bottles and began to fill glasses, beginning at the far end of the table where Aggie sat. The liquid they were pouring was plum-coloured, like the linoleum at Earleywood, and the labels seemed to have only a single word on them. 'Can you read that?' Graham asked (it was a long table). I said: 'I think it says Armagnac.' 'Don't be silly, Armagnac isn't that colour.' 'I know, but that's what it says.' Graham's expression as it was poured into his glass was something to behold. It tasted like syrup of figs, a laxative much prescribed in his and my childhood, when all medicines were nasty to discourage malingering. Then the pudding arrived. This was a sickly white, like spotted dick, under-cooked and suety. Graham and I agreed that we could not remember a nastier meal, even at school or during the war (though New Zealand Airways must have surpassed themselves next day, for in a little paperback volume of Gauguin's paintings which he bought me as a New Year's gift, Graham wrote: '. . . in memory of a terrible Christmas at Aggie Grey's and a worse Christmas meal Samoa-Papeete').

Michael Meyer, *Not Prince Hamlet*

❦ 12 ❦

FAMILY

The Blue Ball

There was a large, brilliant evening star in the early twilight, and underfoot the earth was half frozen. It was Christmas Eve. Also the war was over, and there was a sense of relief that was almost a new menace. A man felt the violence of the nightmare released now into the general air. Also there had been another wrangle among the men on the pit-bank that evening.

Aaron Sisson was the last man on the little black railway-line climbing the hill home from work. He was late because he had attended a meeting of the men on the bank. He was secretary to the Miners' Union for his colliery, and had heard a good deal of silly wrangling that left him nettled.

He strode over a stile, crossed two fields, strode another stile, and was in the long road of colliers' dwellings. Just across was his own house: he had built it himself. He went through the little gate, up past the side of the house to the back. There he hung a moment, glancing down the dark, wintry garden.

'My father – my father's come!' cried a child's excited voice, and two little girls in white pinafores ran out in front of his legs.

'Father, shall you set the Christmas tree?' they cried. 'We've got one!'

'Afore I have my dinner?' he answered amiably.

'Set it now. Set it now. We got it through Fred Alton.'

'Where is it?'

The little girls were dragging a rough, dark object out of a corner of the passage into the light of the kitchen door.

'It's a beauty!' exclaimed Millicent.

'Yes, it is,' said Marjory.

'I should think so,' he replied, striding over the dark bough. He went to the back kitchen to take off his coat.

'Set it now, Father. Set it now,' clamoured the girls.

'You might as well. You've left your dinner so long, you might as well do it

[220]

now before you have it,' came a woman's plangent voice, out of the brilliant light of the middle room.

Aaron Sisson had taken off his coat and waistcoat and his cap. He stood bare-headed in his shirt and braces, contemplating the tree.

'What am I to put it in?' he queried. He picked up the tree, and held it erect by the topmost twig. He felt the cold as he stood in the yard coatless, and he twitched his shoulders.

'Isn't it a beauty!' repeated Millicent.

'Ay! – lop-sided though.'

'Put something on, you two!' came the woman's high imperative voice, from the kitchen.

'We aren't cold,' protested the girls from the yard.

'Come and put something on,' insisted the voice.

The man started off down the path; the little girls ran grumbling indoors. The sky was clear; there was still a crystalline, non-luminous light in the under air.

Aaron rummaged in his shed at the bottom of the garden, and found a spade and a box that was suitable. Then he came out to his neat, bare, wintry garden. The girls flew towards him, putting the elastic of their hats under their chins as they ran. The tree and the box lay on the frozen earth. The air breathed dark, frosty, electric.

'Hold it up straight,' he said to Millicent, as he arranged the tree in the box. She stood silent and held the top bough; he filled in round the roots.

When it was done, and pressed in, he went for the wheelbarrow. The girls were hovering excited round the tree. He dropped the barrow and stooped to the box. The girls watched him hold back his face – the boughs pricked him.

'Ay!' he replied, with a little grunt.

Then the procession set off – the trundling wheelbarrow, the swinging, hissing tree, the two excited little girls. They arrived at the door. Down went the legs of the wheelbarrow on the yard. The man looked at the box.

'Where are you going to have it?' he called.

'Put it in the back kitchen,' cried his wife.

'You'd better have it where it's going to stop. I don't want to hawk it about.'

'Put it on the floor against the dresser, Father. Put it there,' urged Millicent.

'You come and put some paper down, then,' called the mother hastily.

The two children ran indoors; the man stood contemplative in the cold, shrugging his uncovered shoulders slightly. The open inner door showed a bright linoleum on the floor, and the end of a brown sideboard on which stood an aspidistra.

Again with a wrench Aaron Sisson lifted the box. The tree pricked and stung. His wife watched him as he entered staggering, with his face averted.

'Mind where you make a lot of dirt,' she said.

He lowered the box with a little jerk on to the spread-out newspaper on the floor. Soil scattered.

'Sweep it up,' he said to Millicent.

His ear was lingering over the sudden, clutching hiss of the tree-boughs.

A stark white incandescent light filled the room and made everything sharp and hard. In the open fireplace a hot fire burned red. All was scrupulously clean and perfect. A baby was cooing in a rockerless wicker cradle by the hearth. The mother, a slim, neat woman with dark hair, was sewing a child's frock. She put this aside, rose, and began to take her husband's dinner from the oven.

'You stopped confabbing long enough tonight,' she said.

'Yes,' he answered, going to the back kitchen to wash his hands.

In a few minutes he came and sat down to the table. The doors were shut close, but there was a draught, because the settling of the mines under the house made the doors not fit. Aaron moved his chair, to get out of the draught. But he still sat in his shirt and trousers.

He was a good-looking man, fair, and pleasant, about thirty-two years old. He did not talk much, but seemed to think about something. His wife resumed her sewing. She was acutely aware of her husband, but he seemed not very much aware of her.

'What were they on about today, then?' she said.

'About the throw-in.'

'And did they settle anything?'

'They're going to try it – and they'll come out if it isn't satisfactory.'

'The butties won't have it, I know,' she said.

He gave a short laugh, and went on with his meal.

The two children were squatted on the floor by the tree. They had a wooden box, from which they had taken many little newspaper packets which they were spreading out like wares.

'Don't open any. We won't open any of them till we've taken them all out – and then we'll undo one in our turns. Then we s'll both undo equal,' Millicent was saying.

'Yes, we'll take them *all* out first,' re-echoed Marjory.

'And what are they going to do about Job Arthur Freer? – Do they want him?'

A faint smile came on her husband's face.

'Nay, I don't know what they want. Some of 'em want him – whether they're a majority, I don't know.'

She watched him closely.

'Majority! I'd give 'em majority. They want to get rid of you, and make a fool of you, and you want to break your heart over it. Strikes me you need something to break your heart over.'

He laughed silently.

'Nay,' he said. 'I s'll never break my heart.'

'You'll go nearer to it over that, than over anything else: just because a lot of ignorant monkeys want a monkey of their own sort to do the Union work, and jabber to them, they want to get rid of you, and you eat your heart out about it. More fool you, that's all I say – more fool you. If you cared for your wife and children half what you care about your Union, you'd be a lot better pleased in the end. But you care about nothing but a lot of ignorant colliers, who don't know what they want except it's more money just for themselves. Self, self, self – that's all it is with them – and ignorance.'

'You'd rather have self without ignorance?' he said, smiling finely.

'I would, if I've got to have it. But what I should like to see is a man that has thought for others, and isn't all self and politics.'

Her colour had risen, her hand trembled with anger as she sewed. A blank look had come over the man's face, as if he did not hear or heed any more. He drank his tea in a long draught, wiped his moustache with two fingers, and sat looking abstractedly at the children.

They had laid all the little packets on the floor, and Millicent was saying:

'Now I'll undo the first, and you can have the second. I'll take this – '

She unwrapped the bit of newspaper and disclosed a silvery ornament for a Christmas tree; a frail thing like a silver plum, with deep rosy indentations on each side.

'Oh!' she exclaimed. 'Isn't it *lovely*!'

Her fingers cautiously held the long bubble of silver and glowing rose, cleaving to it with a curious, irritating possession. The man's eyes moved away from her. The lesser child was fumbling with one of the little packets.

'Oh' – a wail went up from Millicent – 'You've taken one! – You didn't wait.' Then her voice changed to a motherly admonition, and she began to interfere. 'This is the way to do it, look! Let me help you.'

But Marjory drew back with resentment.

'Don't, Millicent! – Don't!' came the childish cry. But Millicent's fingers itched.

At length Marjory had got out her treasure – a little silvery bell, with a glass drop hanging inside. The bell was made of frail glassy substance, light as air.

'Oh, the bell!' rang out Millicent's clanging voice. 'The bell! It's my bell. My bell! It's mine! Don't break it, Marjory. Don't break it, will you?'

Marjory was shaking the bell against her ear. But it was dumb, it made no sound.

'You'll break it, I know you will. You'll break it. Give it *me* – ' cried Millicent, and she began to take away the bell. Marjory set up an expostulation.

'*Let her alone!*' said the father.

Millicent let go as if she had been stung, but still her brassy, impudent voice persisted:

'She'll break it. She'll break it. It's *mine* – '

'You undo another,' said the mother, politic.

Millicent began with hasty, itching fingers to unclose another package.

'Aw – aw, Mother, my peacock – aw, my peacock, my green peacock!' Lavishly she hovered over a sinuous greenish bird, with wings and tail of spun glass, pearly, and body of deep electric green.

'It's *mine* – my green peacock! It's mine, because Marjory's had one wing off, and mine hadn't. My green peacock that I love! I love it!' She swung it softly from the little ring on its back. Then she went to her mother.

'Look, Mother, isn't it a beauty?'

'Mind the ring doesn't come out,' said her mother. 'Lovely!'

The girl passed on to her father.

'Look, Father, don't you love it!'

'Love it?' he re-echoed, ironical over the word love.

She stood for some moments, trying to force his attention. Then she went back to her place.

Marjory had brought forth a golden apple, red on one cheek, rather garish.

'Oh!' exclaimed Millicent feverishly, instantly seized with desire for what she had not got, indifferent to what she had. Her eye ran quickly over the packages. She took one.

'Now!' she exclaimed loudly, to attract attention. 'Now! What's this? – What's this? What will this beauty be?'

With finicky fingers she removed the newspaper. Marjory watched her wide-eyed. Millicent was self-important.

'The blue ball!' she cried in a climax of rapture. 'I've got *the blue ball.*'

She held it gloating in the cup of her hands. It was a little globe of hardened glass, of a magnificent full dark blue colour. She rose and went to her father.

'It was *your* blue ball, wasn't it, Father?'

'Yes.'

'And you had it when you were a little boy, and now I have it when I'm a little girl.'

'Ay,' he replied drily.

'And it's never been broken all those years.'

'No, not yet.'

'And perhaps it never will be broken?'

To this she received no answer.

'Won't it break?' she persisted. 'Can't you break it?'

'Yes, if you hit it with a hammer,' he said.

'Aw!' she cried. 'I don't mean that. I mean if you just drop it. It won't break if you drop it, will it?'

'I daresay it won't.'

'But *will* it?'

'I sh'd think not.'

'Should I try?'

She proceeded gingerly to let the blue ball drop. It bounced dully on the floor-covering.

'Oh – h – h!' she cried, catching it up. 'I love it.'

'Let *me* drop it,' cried Marjory, and there was a performance of admonition and demonstration from the elder sister.

But Millicent must go further. She became excited.

'It won't break,' she said, 'even if you toss it up in the air.'

She flung it up, it fell safely. But her father's brow knitted slightly. She tossed it wildly: it fell with a little splashing explosion: it had smashed. It had fallen on the sharp edge of the tiles that protruded under the fender.

'*Now* what have you done!' cried the mother.

The child stood with her lip between her teeth, a look, half of pure misery and dismay, half of satisfaction, on her pretty, sharp face.

'She wanted to break it,' said the father.

'No, she didn't! What do you say that for!' said the mother. And Millicent burst into a flood of tears.

He rose to look at the fragments that lay splashed on the floor.

'You must mind the bits,' she said, 'and pick 'em all up.' He took one of the pieces to examine it. It was fine and thin and hard, lined with pure silver, brilliant. He looked at it closely. So – this was what it was. And this was the end of it. He felt the curious soft explosion of its breaking still in his ears. He threw his piece in the fire.

'Pick all the bits up,' he said. 'Give over! give over! Don't cry any more.'

The good-natured tone of his voice quieted the child, as he intended it should.

He went away into the back kitchen to wash himself. As he was bending his head over the sink before the little mirror, lathering to shave, there came from outside the dissonant voices of boys, pouring out the dregs of carol-singing.

'While Shep – ep – ep – ep herds watched – '

He held his soapy brush suspended for a minute. They called this singing! His mind flitted back to early carol music. Then again he heard the vocal violence outside.

'Aren't you off there!' he called out in masculine menace. The noise stopped, there was a scuffle. But the feet returned and the voices resumed. Almost immediately the door opened, boys were heard muttering among themselves. Millicent had given them a penny. Feet scraped on the yard, then went thudding along the side of the house, to the street.

To Aaron Sisson this was home, this was Christmas: the unspeakably familiar. The war over, nothing was changed. Yet everything changed. The scullery in which he stood was painted green, quite fresh, very clean, the floor was red tiles. The wash-copper of red bricks was very red, the mangle with its put-up board was white-scrubbed, the American oilcloth on the table had a gay pattern, there was a warm fire; the water in the boiler hissed faintly. And in front of him, beneath him as he leaned forward shaving, a drop of water fell with strange, incalculable rhythm from the bright brass tap into the white enamelled bowl, which was not half full of pure, quivering water. The war was over, and everything just the same. The acute familiarity of this house, which he had built for his marriage twelve years ago, the changeless pleasantness of it all seemed unthinkable. It prevented his thinking.

When he went into the middle room to comb his hair he found the Christmas tree sparkling, his wife was making pastry at the table, the baby was sitting up propped in cushions.

'Father,' said Millicent, approaching him with a flat blue-and-white angel of cotton-wool, and two ends of cotton – 'tie the angel at the top.'

'Tie it at the top?' he said, looking down.

'Yes. At the very top – because it's just come down from the sky.'

'Ay, my word!' he laughed. And he tied the angel.

Coming downstairs after changing he went into the icy cold parlour, and took his music and a small handbag. With this he retreated again to the back kitchen. He was still in trousers and shirt and slippers: but now it was a clean white shirt, and his best black trousers, and new pink-and-white braces. He sat under the gas-jet of the back kitchen, looking through his music. Then he opened the bag, in which were sections of a flute and a piccolo. He took out the flute, and adjusted it. As he sat he was physically aware of the sounds of the night: the bubbling of water in the boiler, the faint sound of the gas, the sudden crying of the baby in the next room, then noises outside, distant boys shouting, distant rags of carols, fragments of voices of men. The whole country was roused and excited.

The little room was hot. Aaron rose and opened a square ventilator over the copper, letting in a stream of cold air which was grateful to him. Then he cocked his eye over the sheet of music spread out on the table before him. He tried his flute. And then at last, with the odd gesture of a diver taking a plunge, he swung his head and began to play. A stream of music, soft and rich and fluid, came out of the flute. He played beautifully. He moved his head and his raised bare arms with slight, intense movements, as the delicate music poured out. It was sixteenth-century Christmas melody, very limpid and delicate.

The pure, mindless, exquisite motion and fluidity of the music delighted him with a strange exasperation. There was something tense, exasperated to the point of intolerable anger, in his good-humoured breast, as he played the finely spun peace-music. The more exquisite the music, the more perfectly he produced it, in sheer bliss; and at the same time, the more intense was the maddened exasperation within him.

Millicent appeared in the room. She fidgeted at the sink. The music was a bugbear to her, because it prevented her from saying what was on her own mind. At length it ended, her father was turning over the various books and sheets. She looked at him quickly, seizing her opportunity.

'Are you going out, Father?' she said.

'Eh?'

'Are you going out?' She twisted nervously.

'What do you want to know for?'

He made no other answer, and turned again to the music. His eye went down a sheet – then over it again – then more closely over it again.

'Are you?' persisted the child, balancing on one foot. He looked at her, and his eyes were angry under knitted brows.

'What are you bothering about?' he said.

'I'm not bothering – I only wanted to know if you were going out,' she pouted, quivering to cry.

'I expect I am,' he said quietly.

She recovered at once, but still with timidity asked:

'We haven't got any candles for the Christmas tree – shall *you* buy some, because Mother isn't going out?'

'Candles!' he repeated, setting his music and taking up the piccolo.

'Yes – shall you buy us some, Father? Shall you?'

'Candles!' he repeated, putting the piccolo to his mouth and blowing a few piercing, preparatory notes.

'Yes, little Christmas-tree candles – blue ones and red ones, in boxes – shall you, Father?'

'We'll see – if I see any – '

'But *shall* you?' she insisted desperately. She wisely mistrusted his vagueness.

But he was looking unheeding at the music. Then suddenly the piccolo broke forth, wild, shrill, brilliant. He was playing Mozart. The child's face went pale with anger at the sound. She turned, and went out, closing both doors behind her to shut out the noise.

The shrill, rapid movement of the piccolo music seemed to possess the air, it was useless to try to shut it out. The man went on playing to himself, measured and insistent. In the frosty evening the sound carried. People passing down the street hesitated, listening. The neighbours knew it was Aaron practising his piccolo. He was esteemed a good player: was in request at concerts and dances, also at swell balls. So the vivid piping sound tickled the darkness.

He played on till about seven o'clock: he did not want to go out too soon, in spite of the early closing of the public houses. He never went with the stream, but made a side current of his own. His wife said he was contrary. When he went into the middle room to put on his collar and tie, the two little girls were having their hair brushed, the baby was in bed, there was a hot smell of mince-pies baking in the oven.

'You won't forget our candles, will you Father?' asked Millicent, with assurance now.

'I'll see,' he answered.

His wife watched him as he put on his overcoat and hat. He was well-dressed, handsome-looking. She felt there was a curious glamour about him. It made her feel bitter. He had an unfair advantage – he was free to go off, while she must stay at home with the children.

'There's no knowing what time you'll be home,' she said.

'I shan't be late,' he answered.

'It's easy to say so,' she retorted, with some contempt. He took his stick, and turned towards the door.

'Bring the children some candles for their tree, and don't be so selfish,' she said.

'All right,' he said, going out.

'Don't say *All right* if you never mean to do it,' she cried, with sudden anger, following him to the door.

His figure stood large and shadowy in the darkness.

'How many do you want?' he said.

'A dozen,' she said. 'And holders, too, if you can get them,' she added, with barren bitterness.

'Yes – all right,' he turned and melted into the darkness. She went indoors, worn with a strange and bitter flame.

He crossed the fields towards the little town, which once more fumed its lights under the night. The country ran away, rising on his right hand. It was no longer a great bank of darkness. Lights twinkled freely here and there, though forlornly, now that the war-time restrictions were removed. It was no glitter of pre-war nights, pit-heads glittering far-off with electricity. Neither was it the black gulf of the war darkness: instead, this forlorn sporadic twinkling.

Everybody seemed to be out of doors. The hollow dark countryside re-echoed like a shell with shouts and calls and excited voices. Restlessness and nervous excitement, nervous hilarity were in the air. There was a sense of electric surcharge everywhere, frictional, a neurasthenic haste for excitement.

Every moment Aaron Sisson was greeted with Good-night – Good-night, Aaron – Good-night, Mr Sisson. People carrying parcels, children, women, thronged home on the dark paths. They were all talking loudly, declaiming loudly about what they could and could not get, and what this or the other had cost.

When he got into the main street, the only street of shops, it was crowded. There seemed to have been some violent but quiet contest, a subdued fight, going on all the afternoon and evening: people struggling to buy things, to get things. Money was spent like water, there was a frenzy of money-spending. Though the necessities of life were in abundance, still the people struggled in frenzy for cheese, sweets, raisins, pork-stuff, even for flowers and holly, all of which were scarce, and for toys and knick-knacks, which were sold out. There was a wild grumbling, but a deep satisfaction in the fight, the struggle. The same fight and the same satisfaction in the fight was witnessed whenever a tramcar stopped, or when it heaved its way into sight. Then the struggle to mount on board became desperate and savage, but stimulating. Souls surcharged with hostility found now some outlet for their feelings.

As he came near the little market-place he bethought himself of the Christmas-tree candles. He did not intend to trouble himself. And yet, when he glanced in passing into the sweet-shop window, and saw it bare as a board, the very fact that he probably *could not* buy the things made him hesitate, and try.

'Have you got any Christmas-tree candles?' he asked as he entered the shop.

'How many do you want?'

'A dozen.'

'Can't let you have a dozen. You can have two boxes – four in a box – eight. Sixpence a box.'

'Got any holders?'

'Holders? Don't ask. Haven't seen one this year.'

'Got any toffee –?'

'Cough-drops – twopence an ounce – nothing else left.'

'Give me four ounces.'

He watched her weighing them in the little brass scales.

'You've not got much of a Christmas show,' he said.

'Don't talk about Christmas, as far as sweets is concerned. They ought to have allowed us six times the quantity – there's plenty of sugar, why didn't they? We s'll have to enjoy ourselves with what we've got. We mean to, anyhow.'

'Ay,' he said.

'Time we had a bit of enjoyment, *this* Christmas. They ought to have made things more plentiful.'

'Yes,' he said, stuffing his package in his pocket.

D. H. Lawrence, *Aaron's Rod*

Complex

On the subject of all feasts of the Church he held views of an almost grotesque peculiarity. He looked upon each of them as nugatory and worthless, but the keeping of Christmas appeared to him by far the most hateful, and nothing less than an act of idolatry. 'The very word is Popish,' he used to exclaim, 'Christ's Mass!' pursing up his lips with the gesture of one who tastes asafœtida by accident. Then he would adduce the antiquity of the so-called feast, adapted from horrible heathen rites, and itself a soiled relic of the abominable Yule-Tide. He would denounce the horrors of Christmas until it almost made me blush to look at a holly-berry.

On Christmas Day of this year 1857 our villa saw a very unusual sight. My father had given strictest charge that no difference whatever was to be made in our meals on that day: the dinner was to be neither more copious than usual nor less so. He was obeyed, but the servants, secretly rebellious, made a small plum-pudding for themselves. (I discovered afterwards, with pain, that Miss Marks received a slice of it in her boudoir.) Early in the afternoon, the maids – of whom we were now advanced to keeping two – kindly remarked that 'the poor dear child ought to have a bit, anyhow', and wheedled me into the kitchen, where I ate a slice of plum-pudding. Shortly I began to feel that pain inside which in my frail state was inevitable, and my conscience smote me violently. At length I could bear my spiritual anguish no longer, and bursting into the study I called out: 'Oh! Papa, Papa, I have eaten of flesh offered to idols!' It took some time, between my sobs, to explain what had happened. Then my father sternly said: 'Where is the accursed thing?' I explained that as much as was left of it was still on the kitchen table. He took me by the hand, and ran with me into the midst of the startled servants, seized what remained of the pudding, and with the plate in one hand and me still tight in the other, ran till we reached the dust-heap, when he flung the idolatrous confectionery on to the middle of the ashes, and then raked it deep down into the mass. The suddenness, the violence, the velocity of this extraordinary act made an impression on my memory which nothing will ever efface.

Edmund Gosse, *Father and Son*

Halbert and Hob

Here is a thing that happened. Like wild beasts whelped, for den,
In a wild part of North England, there lived once two wild men
Inhabiting one homestead, neither a hovel nor hut,
Time out of mind their birthright: father and son, these – but –
Such a son, such a father! Most wildness by degrees
Softens away: yet, last of their line, the wildest and worst were these.

Criminals, then? Why, no: they did not murder and rob;
But, give them a word, they returned a blow – old Halbert as young Hob:
Harsh and fierce of word, rough and savage of deed,
Hated or feared the more – who knows? – the genuine wild-beast breed.

Thus were they found by the few sparse folk of the country-side;
But how fared each with other? E'en beasts couch, hide by hide,
In a growling, grudged agreement: so, father and son aye curled
The closelier up in their den because the last of their kind in the world.

Still, beast irks beast on occasion. One Christmas night of snow,
Came father and son to words – such words! more cruel because the blow
To crown each word was wanting, while taunt matched gibe, and curse
Competed with oath in wager, like pastime in hell, – nay, worse:
For pastime turned to earnest, as up there sprang at last
The son at the throat of the father, seized him and held him fast.

'Out of this house you go!' – (there followed a hideous oath) –
'This oven where now we bake, too hot to hold us both!
If there's snow outside, there's coolness: out with you, bide a spell
In the drift and save the sexton the charge of a parish shell!'

Now, the old trunk was tough, was solid as stump of oak
Untouched at the core by a thousand years: much less had its seventy broke
One whipcord nerve in the muscly mass from neck to shoulder-blade
Of the mountainous man, whereon his child's rash hand like a feather
            weighed.

Nevertheless at once did the mammoth shut his eyes,
Drop chin to breast, drop hands to sides, stand stiffened – arms and thighs
All of a piece – struck mute, much as a sentry stands,
Patient to take the enemy's fire: his captain so commands.

Whereat the son's wrath flew to fury at such sheer scorn
Of his puny strength by the giant eld thus acting the babe new-born:
And 'Neither will this turn serve!' yelled he. 'Out with you! Trundle, log!
If you cannot tramp and trudge like a man, try all-fours like a dog!'

Still the old man stood mute. So, logwise, – down to floor
Pulled from his fireside place, dragged on from hearth to door –
Was he pushed, a very log, staircase along, until
A certain turn in the steps was reached, a yard from the house-door-sill.

Then the father opened eyes – each spark of their rage extinct, –
Temples, late black, dead-blanched, – right-hand with left-hand linked –
He faced his son submissive; when slow the accents came,
They were strangely mild though his son's rash hand on his neck lay all the
      same.

'Hob, on just such a night of a Christmas long ago,
For such a cause, with such a gesture, did I drag – so –
My father down thus far: but, softening here, I heard
A voice in my heart, and stopped: you wait for an outer word.

'For your own sake, not mine, soften you too! Untrod
Leave this last step we reach, nor brave the finger of God!
I dared not pass its lifting: I did well. I nor blame
Nor praise you. I stopped here: and, Hob, do you the same!'

Straightway the son relaxed his hold of the father's throat.
They mounted, side by side, to the room again: no note
Took either of each, no sign made each to either: last
As first, in absolute silence, their Christmas-night they passed.

At dawn, the father sat on, dead, in the self-same place,
With an outburst blackening still the old bad fighting-face:
But the son crouched all a-tremble like any lamb new-yeaned.

When he went to the burial, someone's staff he borrowed – tottered and
      leaned.
But his lips were loose, not locked – kept muttering, mumbling. 'There!
At his cursing and swearing!' the youngsters cried: but the elders thought
      'In prayer.'
A boy threw stones: he picked them up and stored them in his vest.

So tottered, muttered, mumbled he, till he died, perhaps found rest.
'Is there a reason in nature for these hard hearts?' O Lear
That a reason out of nature must turn them soft, seems clear!

Robert Browning

The Wishbone

Maureen in England, Joseph in Guelph,
my mother in her grave.

*

At three o'clock in the afternoon
we watch the Queen's
message to the Commonwealth
with the sound turned off.

*

He seems to favour *Camelot*
over *To Have and Have Not*.

*

Yet we agree, my father and myself,
that here is more than enough
for two; a frozen chicken,
spuds, sprouts, *Paxo* sage and onion.

*

The wishbone like a rowelled spur
on the fibula of Sir— or Sir—.

Paul Muldoon

A Christmas Childhood

I

One side of the potato-pits was white with frost –
How wonderful that was, how wonderful!
And when we put our ears to the paling-post
The music that came out was magical.

The light between the ricks of hay and straw
Was a hole in Heaven's gable. An apple tree
With its December-glinting fruit we saw –
O you, Eve, were the world that tempted me

[234]

To eat the knowledge that grew in clay
And death the germ within it! Now and then
I can remember something of the gay
Garden that was childhood's. Again

The tracks of cattle to a drinking-place,
A green stone lying sideways in a ditch
Or any common sight the transfigured face
Of a beauty that the world did not touch.

II

My father played the melodeon
Outside at our gate;
There were stars in the morning east
And they danced to his music.

Across the wild bogs his melodeon called
To Lennons and Callans.
As I pulled on my trousers in a hurry
I knew some strange thing had happened.

Outside in the cow-house my mother
Made the music of milking;
The light of her stable-lamp was a star
And the frost of Bethlehem made it twinkle.

A water-hen screeched in the bog,
Mass-going feet
Crunched the wafer-ice on the pot-holes,
Somebody wistfully twisted the bellows wheel.

My child poet picked out the letters
On the grey stone,
In silver the wonder of a Christmas townland,
The winking glitter of a frosty dawn.

Cassiopeia was over
Cassidy's hanging hill,
I looked and three whin bushes rode across
The horizon – the Three Wise Kings.

An old man passing said:
'Can't he make it talk' –
The melodeon. I hid in the doorway
And tightened the belt of my box-pleated coat.

I nicked six nicks on the door-post
With my penknife's big blade –
There was a little one for cutting tobacco.
And I was six Christmases of age.

My father played the melodeon,
My mother milked the cows,
And I had a prayer like a white rose pinned
On the Virgin Mary's blouse.

Patrick Kavanagh

1846

25 *December*   Christmas Day! – to me always a day of poetry & pious musing!

I hate the vulgar revelry which usually accompanies it – the fat beef, the gross turkeys, the stuffed sausage, as evidences of human joy at the Salvation of Christ – are to me utterly disgusting! – But my boys will consider me a brute if I don't eat till I can't see, to prove my joy at their presence.

Benjamin Robert Haydon

Ding-Dong Farely Merily for Xmas

Xmas all grown ups sa is the season for the kiddies but this do not prevent them from taking a tot or 2 from the bot and having, it may seme, a beter time than us. For children in fact Xmas is often a bit of a strane wot with pretending that everything is a surprise. Above all father xmas is a strane. You canot so much as mention that there is no father xmas when some grown-sa Hush not in front of wee tim. So far as i am concerned if father xmas use langwage like that when he tripped over the bolster last time we had beter get a replacement.

CRISTMAS EVE

Hurra for Xmas Eve wot a scurrying there was in the molesworth household. First of all mr molesworth issued jovially with the hamer to hang the decorations – red white purple streemers holly mistletoe lights candles snow Mery Xmas All: mrs molesworth is in the kitchen with the mince pies, all rosy and shining: and judge of the excitement of the 2 boys!

In fact, it is a proper SHAMBLES.

Pop drop the hamer on the cat in the kitchen the xmas puding xplode with a huge crash and the cat spring up the curtains. Outside the sno lie deep and crisp and ect. and just as pop fall off the steplader the WATES arive.

WATES are 3 litle gurls with a torch who go as folows:
HEE HEE HEE NOEL NOEL GO ON GURT
NO-ELL NO-ELL NO YOU RING the KING of
IS-RAY-ER-ELL.
PING! PING!
TANNER FOR THE WATES, PLEASE.

This of course is money for jam but grown ups are so intoxicated with xmas they produce a shiling. Imagine a whole weeks poket money just for that when you can get it all on the wireless anyway if you want it. Or whether you want it or not.

molesworth 2 is very amusing about carols i must sa he hav a famous carol

> *While shepherds washed their socks by night*
> *All seated on the ground*
> *A bar of sunlight soap came down ect.*

He think this is so funy he roar with larffter whenever he think of it and as he spend most of the night thinking of it i do not get much slepe chiz. i sa SHUTUP molesworth 2 SHUTUP i want to go to slepe but in vain the horid zany go cakling on. It is not as if it is funy i mean a bar of sunlight soap ha-ha well it is not ha-ha-ha-ha a bar of ha-ha-ha-ha . . . .

Oh well.

Another thing about xmas eve is that your pater always reads the xmas carol by c. dickens. You canot stop this aktually although he pretend to ask you whether you would like it. He sa:

Would you like me to read the xmas carol as it is xmas eve, boys?

We are listening to the space serial on the wireless, daddy.

But you canot prefer that nonsense to the classick c. dickens?

Be quiet. He is out of control and heading for jupiter.

But –

He's had it the treen space ships are ataking him ur-ur-ur-*whoosh*. Out of control limping in the space vacuum for evermore unless they can get the gastric fuel compressor tampons open.

I –

Why don't they try Earth on the intercom? They will never open those tampons with only a z-ray griper. They will –

Father thwarted strike both boys heavily with loaded xmas stoking and tie their hands behind their backs. He cart them senseless into the sitting room and prop both on his knees. Then he begin:

THE XMAS CAROL by C. DICKENS

(published by grabber and grabber)

Then he rub hands together and sa You will enjoy this boys it is all about ghosts and goodwill. It is tip-top stuff and there is an old man called scrooge who hates xmas and canot understand why everyone is so mery. To this you sa nothing except that scrooge is your favourite character in fiction next to tarzan of the apes. But you can sa anything chiz. Nothing in the world in space is ever going to stop those fatal words:

Marley was dead

Personaly i do not care a d. whether Marley was dead or not it is just that there is something about the xmas Carol which makes paters and grown-ups read with grate XPRESION, and this is very embarassing for all. It is all right for the first part they just roll the r's a lot but wate till they come to scrooge's nephew. When he sa Mery Christmas uncle it is like an H-bomb xplosion and so it go on until you get to Tiny Tim chiz chiz chiz he is a weed. When Tiny Tim sa God bless us every one your pater is so overcome he burst out blubbing. By this time boys hav bitten through their ropes and make good their escape so 9000000000 boos to bob cratchit.

XMAS NITE

At last the tiny felows are tucked up snug in their beds with 3 pilow slips awaiting santa claus. As the lite go off a horid doubt assale the mind e.g. suposing there *is* a santa claus. Zoom about and lay a few traps for him.

Determin to lie awake and get him but go to slepe in the end chiz and dream of space ships. While thus employed something do seem to be hapning among the earthmen.

CRASH!

Be quiet you will wake them up. Hav you got the mecano his is the one with 3 oranges if you drop that pedal car agane i shall scream where are the spangles can you not tie a knot for heavens sake ect. ect.

It would seem that the earthmen are up to something but you are far to busy with the treens who are defending the space palace with germ guns. So snore on, fair child, snore on with thy inocent dreams and do not get the blud all over you.

THE DAY

Xmas day always start badly becos molesworth 2 blub he hav not got the reel rools-royce he asked for. We then hav argument that each hav more presents than the other. A Mery Xmas everybode sa scrooge in the end but we just call each other clot-faced wets so are you you you you pointing with our horny fingers it is very joly i must sa. In the end i wear molesworth 2's cowboy suit and he pla with my air gun so all is quiet.

Then comes DINNER.

This is super as there are turkey crackers nuts cream plum puding jely and everything. We wash it down with a litle ginger ale but grown ups all drink wine ugh and this make all the old lades and grans very sprightly i must sa. They sa how sweet we are they must be dotty until pater raps the table and look v. solemn. He holds up his glass and sa in a low voice

The QUEEN. Cheers cheers cheers for the queen we all drink and hurra for england.

Then pater sa in much lower voice ABSENT FRIENDS and everyone else sa absent friends absent friends absent friends ect. and begin blubbing. In fact it do not seme that you can go far at xmas time without blubbing of some sort and when they listen to the wireless in the afternoon all about the lonely shepherd and the lighthousemen they are in floods of tears.

Still xmas is a good time with all those presents and good food and i hope it will never die out or at any rate not until i am grown up and hav to pay for it all. So ho skip and away the next thing we shall be taken to peter pan for a treat so brace up brace up.

The Molesworth Self-Adjusting Thank-You Letter

As an after xmas wheeze n. molesworth presents his self-adjusting thank-you letter.

Cut out hours of toil pen biting wear on elbows blotches and staring out of windows.

Strike Out words which do not apply.

Dear {
Aunt ....
Uncle..............................
Stinker...........................
Gran ....
Clot ....
Pen-Pal ....
}

Thank you very much for the {
train. tractor. germ gun. kite.
delicious present.* sweets.
space pistol. toy socks.
}

It was {
lovely. useful.
just as good as the other three.
not bad. super.
}

And I hav {
played with it constantly.
bust it already.
no patience with it.
given it to the poor boys.
dismantled it.
}

I am feeling {
very well
very poorly.
lousy.   I hope you are too.
in tip-top form
sick.
}

My birthday when next present is due is on...

From ....

(*Postage must be prepaid.*)

*When you can't remember what it was

Geoffrey Willans and Ronald Searle, *The Compleet Molesworth*

[240]

1847

25 December   Interchanged with all my dear family the wishes belonging, of usage, to this dear day. Fox and Forster came to dinner and we passed a very pleasant evening. The children repeated Milton's Ode to the Nativity. We had a game at whist. My heart is thankful.

William Charles Macready

White Christmas

For once it is a white Christmas,
so white that the roads are impassable
and my wife is snowbound
in a town untroubled by tractor or snowplough.
In bed, awake, alone. She calls

and we pass on our presents by telephone.
Mine is a watch, the very one
I would have chosen. Hers is a song,
the one with the line *Here come the hills of time*
and it sits in its sleeve,

unsung and unopened. But the dog downstairs
is worrying, gnawing, howling,
so I walk her through clean snow
along the tow-path to the boat-house at a steady pace,
then to my parent's place

where my mother is Marie Curie, in the kitchen
discovering radium, and my father is Fred Flintstone,
and a guest from the past has a look on her face meaning
lie and I'll have your teeth for a necklace, boy,
your eyeballs for earrings,

your bullshit for breakfast,
and my two-year-old niece is baby Jesus,
passing between us with the fruit of the earth
and the light of the world – Christingle – a blood orange
spiked with a burning candle.

We eat, but the dog begs at the table,
drinks from the toilet, sings in the cellar.
Only baby Jesus wanders with me down the stairs
with a shank of meat to see her, to feed her,
Later, when I stand to leave

my father wants to shake me by the hand
but my arms are heavy, made of a base metal,
and the dog wants to take me down the black lane, back
to an empty house again. A car goes by
with my sister inside

and to wave goodnight
she lifts the arm of the sleeping infant Christ,
but I turn my wrist to notice the time. There and then
I'm the man in the joke, the man in a world of friends
where all the clocks are stopped,

synchronizing his own watch.

Simon Armitage

Christmas '33

I turned the balance of the Christmas party by siding with the oppressed classes, Aunt Addie – and, as a result, a very amicable evening with Uncle Win, Aunt Addie, Rosalind, Mother, and myself. Uncle Charley had gone to Esther's Christmas Eve and was excluded as being too gloomy. Aunt Addie and Uncle Win reminisced Eatontown characters and the Davises ('Bring on them eats!') [the Davises were vulgar people who lived across the street from Aunt Addie]; Uncle Win told the story he has always told about taking Will Hurley up the Cape on the Fall River boat; asked him what he thought of it and he said: 'Well, them that ain't never seen nothin' don't know nothin'!'

Uncle Win said that when he went to college, it was still true that you were ostracized if you went into business instead of medicine, law, or the church, but after he'd been hangin' around in New York two years, one day when Reuel was talking to one of the James White partners, he said that he understood that there was a prejudice against college men in business. '*I* haven't any prejudice against them,' said the man. 'I'd take one if I could get him.' Reuel declared, 'You've got one. I'm sending my brother down tomorrow.'

Uncle Win was becoming imbued with Fascist ideas. First he complained about the cheap Jewish comedians on the radio – then said that somebody who had come back from Germany had been telling him, even before Hitler, that you couldn't get a job in a German university, you couldn't practice as a lawyer in Germany, unless you were a Jew. 'We'll have trouble with 'em over here, too. Roosevelt's got a lot of Jews at Washington. We can't have them with their ideas.' When I said that the persecution of the Jews by the Nazis was a terrible thing, he hedged: 'Of course it is, but – ' His point was that I had only seen the nice Jews – I didn't know the ones downtown. The Warburgs and the Schiffs were all right [they were among Reuel's patients and friends], but the others! (He had once spoken to me sarcastically about 'your friend Frankfurter'.) Aunt Addie asked him what he thought of the state of the world – were dividends going to come back? He hoped so – he hoped that Roosevelt knew what he was doing, but three economists said that Roosevelt was right and all the rest said he was wrong. He deplored Scripps-Howard's attack on Douglas: 'I think Douglas is one of the soundest men Roosevelt's got.'

Uncle Win on Exeter: old man Wentworth got him up in class one day – he evidently still remembered with horror his shyness when obliged to recite in those big classes of fifty or sixty – and said, 'Where are you going from here, Kimball?' 'Princeton.' 'Boys (turning to the class), we've got to get Kimball into Princeton! – we've got to get him there! – the climate up here doesn't agree with him: it's too cold! – we've got to get him into Princeton right away!' – The story about Hibben coming into the Princeton Club, looking desperately worried about losing the track meet at Yale – they said, 'Why don't you clean 'em out?' – he replied, 'That's just what I'd like to do!' – About the time Uncle Win began refusing to go to the Hartshornes' for Christmas was about the time he began paying for Sandy's asylum expenses. – The story about Father's speaking at the meeting of protest at Princeton about professors' being sent to spy on students (one boy also revealed that he had been paid to spy) – Father made a speech counseling moderation, but they rusticated him for speaking at the meeting and the strike took place anyway. – George M. Cohan: never a dirty line – Fred Stone had said that George Cohan always put on clean plays and he didn't see him having any failures – this was funny because Cohan used to hang around the Hotel Metropole with the worst-looking bunch you ever saw in your life – and the characters in his plays were always people that were around: the racetrack tout, etc. – Cohan was taking care of every broken-down actor in New York.

Aunt Addie's late sophistication: wisecracks learned from Tammany circles [by way of her daughter Adeline, who had married Joe Moran]: 'Dorothy calls her bed her workbench.' Talking of Aunt Laura's late marriage: 'You'd think it was last call for dinner in the dining car.' – She had attained through Dorothy and Adeline a new dignity [her daughters had married rich men], which made it possible for her to dispense with her attitude of humility toward the rest of the family. She was no longer a poor relation.

Anna. She slapped me on the bare stomach when I had my eyes shut, and it gave me a sudden nervous shudder. She said, 'Can't take it, huh? – I used to do that with Sam and it would make-um so sore at me he'd forget he wan'ed it.'

'So nervous – like when I'm here – I think I want to get home and I rush away right away.' Her aunt who had had her ovaries out said that that was what it was – she'd been the same way before she was operated on.

'You don't know how low and common they [the Polish boarders] are!' Twice somebody had done his business and wrapped it up in a paper and put it behind the closet. That's their idea of a joke!

She came in in her red dress, looking somehow very fine, I thought – less cowed, more sense of her own dignity. I noticed it as she sat on the bed, smoking and leaning up against the wall, her legs showing attractively through the red skirt, as I had never seen her do – even her hair seemed more abundant somehow, more of a coiffure.

Edmund Wilson, *The Thirties*

❦ 13 ❦

ENTERTAINMENTS

Ere scenes were played by many a reverend Clerk
(What harm, if David danced before the Ark?)
In Christmas revels, simple country folks
Were pleased with Morrice-mumm'ry, and coarse jokes.

Lord Byron, 'Hints from Horace'

from The Second Shepherds' Play

2ND SHEPHERD: Rise, Mak, for shame! Thou liest right long.
MAK: Now Christ's holy name be us among!
What is this? By Saint James, I can't get along!
I trust I be the same. Ah! My neck has lain all wrong
In this hole.

They help him.

Many thanks! Since yester-even,
Now by Saint Stephen,
A dream sent from heaven
Struck fear in my soul.

I dreamt Gill in her smock cried out full sad,
Gave birth at the first cock to a young lad,
To add to our flock; then be I never glad.
Of cares I've a stock more than ever I had.
Ah, my head!
Those moans of hunger pains,
The devil knock out their brains!
Woe to him whose brood complains
Of too little bread.

I must go home, by your leave, to Gill, as I thought.
First look up my sleeve that I've stolen nought:
I am loth you to grieve, or from you take ought.

Mak goes home.

3RD SHEPHERD: Go forth, ill-luck achieve! Now would I we sought
    This morn
For the sheep in our care.
1ST SHEPHERD: First I shall fare.
    Let us meet.
2ND SHEPHERD: Where?
3RD SHEPHERD: At the crooked thorn.

The Shepherds part.

MAK: Undo this door! Who is here? How long shall I stand?
MAK'S WIFE: Who roars then out there? Be ye one or a band?
MAK: Ah, Gill, what cheer? It is I, Mak, your husband.
MAK'S WIFE: Ah, then never fear, the devil is at hand
    With guile.
  Lo, he strikes a harsh note,
  As though held by the throat,
  And cares never a groat
    My work to beguile.

MAK: Oh, the fuss that she makes when I stir her repose.
  She feigns all her aches and picks at her toes.
MAK'S WIFE: Why, who works, and who wakes, who comes and who goes?
  Who brews and who bakes? Who darns all your hose?
    And then
  It is sad to behold,
  Or e'er to be told,
  How woeful the household
    That wants a woman.
  But how have you sped with the shepherds, Mak?
MAK: The last word that they said when I turned my back,
  They would count each head of the sheep in their pack.
  Now have we no dread when they their sheep lack,
    Pardy;
  But howe'er the game goes,
  They'll be here, I suppose,

Our theft to disclose,
    And cry out upon me.

Now do as you promised.
MAK'S WIFE: To that I agree,
    I'll swaddle him now, in his crib he will be;
    A fine trick to twist on our poor shepherds three.
    To bed! Come assist. Tuck up!
MAK: Let me.
MAK'S WIFE: Behind.
    Come Coll and his mate
    To pry and to prate,
    For help I'll cry straight
        The sheep if they find.

MAK'S WIFE: Hark now for their call; on the breeze be it blown.
    Come make ready all and sing on thine own;
    Sing lullay you shall, for loud I must groan,
    And cry out by the wall on Mary and Joan
        Full sore.
    Sing lullay quite fast
    When you hear them at last;
    If my part is miscast,
        Trust me no more.

3RD SHEPHERD: Ah, Coll, good morn, why sleepest thou not?
1ST SHEPHERD: Alas that ever I was born! A sad grief we have got.
    Lost! A fat wether unshorn.
3RD SHEPHERD: By God, a foul blot.
2ND SHEPHERD: Who should give us this scorn? It won't be forgot.
1ST SHEPHERD: This he shall rue.
    I have searched with my dogs
    All Horbury shrogs,
    And of fifteen hogs,
        Found I but one ewe.
3RD SHEPHERD: Now trust me, if ye will, by St Thomas of Kent,
    Either Mak or Gill, had a hand in this event.
1ST SHEPHERD: Peace, man, be still! I saw when he went.
    You slander him ill, you ought to repent
        With good speed.
2ND SHEPHERD: Now as ever I might thrive,

As I hope to keep alive,
Only Mak could contrive
   To do that same deed.

3RD SHEPHERD: Then off to his homestead, he brisk on our feet.
  I shall never eat bread till we've proved this deceit.
1ST SHEPHERD: Nor have drink in my head till with him I meet.
2ND SHEPHERD: I will rest in no stead till him I may greet,
   My brother.
  My promise I plight
  Till I have him in sight,
  Shall I ne'er sleep one night.
   May I do no other.

They go to Mak's house – singing within.

3RD SHEPHERD: Do ye hear how they croak? My lord will now croon.
1ST SHEPHERD: Ne'er heard I sing folk so clean out of tune;
  Call him.
2ND SHEPHERD: Mak, may you choke! Undo your door soon!
MAK: Who is that spoke, as if it were noon?
   Who scoffed?
  Who is that I say?
3RD SHEPHERD: Good fellows, were it day!
MAK: As far as ye may,
   Speak soft,

Over a sick woman's head, who is not at her ease,
I had rather be dead than she had a disease.

The Shepherds enter Mak's home.

MAK'S WIFE: Be off from the bed, let me breathe, if you please!
  Each step that you tread from my nose to my knees
   Goes through me.
1ST SHEPHERD: Tell us, Mak, if ye may,
  How fare ye, say?
MAK: But are ye in town today?
   Now how fare ye?
  Ye have run in the mire, and now are all wet.
  I shall make you a fire now we are met.
  A nurse would I hire. Think ye on yet
  My dream which entire has fulfilled its threat

In due season.
I have bairns if ye knew,
Far more than a few,
But we must drink as we brew,
    And that is but reason.

Would ye dined ere ye went? Ye sweat, as I think.
2ND SHEPHERD: Our feelings be vent not for meat nor for drink.
MAK: Is ought then ill meant?
3RD SHEPHERD: Yea, in a wink.
  A sheep lost we lament, borne off ere we blink.
MAK: Drink sirs.
  Had I been there
  Some had suffered full dear.
1ST SHEPHERD: In that is our fear;
    None of us errs.

2ND SHEPHERD: Against you goes the grouse, Mak, thief that ye be,
  Either you or your spouse, and so say we.
MAK: Nay, knit not your brows against my Gill or me.
  Come comb through our house, and then ye may see
    Who had her.
  If any sheep I've got,
  Alive or in the pot –
  And Gill, my wife, rose not
    Here since she laid her.

As I am true as steel, to God here I pray,
That this be the first meal that I shall eat this day.
1ST SHEPHERD: Mak, is such thy zeal! Then be advised, I say:
He learns in time to steal that never could say nay.
MAK'S WIFE: I faint!
  Out thieves from my home,
  Ere I claw with my comb!
MAK: If you marked but her foam,
    You'd show some restraint.

MAK'S WIFE: Out thieves from my cot, step you soft on the floor.
MAK: If ye knew her harsh lot, your hearts would be sore.
  Your behaviour's a blot, here to rant and to roar:
  Gill's plight ye've forgot. But I say no more.

MAK'S WIFE: Ah, my middle!
　　I pray to God so mild,
　　If ere I you beguiled,
　　That I should eat this child
　　　　That lies in this cradle.

MAK: Peace, woman, for God's pain, and cry not so:
　　Thou'lt burst thy brain and make me full of woe.
2ND SHEPHERD: I believe our sheep be slain, and that ye know.
3RD SHEPHERD: Our search has been in vain, now let us go.
　　　　He chatters
　　His way through our mesh.
　　Here's to be found no flesh,
　　Soft nor hard, salt nor flesh,
　　　　But two empty platters.

　　No creature but this, tame or wild,
　　As hope I for bliss, smelt so defiled.
MAK'S WIFE: No, so God me bless, and give me joy of my child!
1ST SHEPHERD: We have aimed amiss; we be but beguiled.
2ND SHEPHERD: Have done!
　　Sir, our Lady him save!
　　Be this a boy brave?
MAK'S WIFE: Any lord might him have.
　　　　This child for his son.

　　When he wakes he smiles that joy is to see.
3RD SHEPHERD: May now the world's wiles this bairn leave be.
　　Who stood at the font that so soon were ready?
MAK: The first folk of these isles.
1ST SHEPHERD: A lie now, hark ye!
MAK: God give them thanks.
　　Parkin and Gibbon Waller, I say,
　　And gentle John Horn in grey.
　　He made such droll display
　　　　With his long shanks.

2ND SHEPHERD: Mak, friends will we be, for we are all one.
MAK: We? count not on me, for amends get I none.
　　Farewell all three! And gladly begone.

They leave the cottage.

3RD SHEPHERD: Fair words there may be, but love there is none
    This year.
1ST SHEPHERD: Gave ye the child anything?
2ND SHEPHERD: Not I, ne'er a farthing.
3RD SHEPHERD: I shall find an offering.
    Wait for me here.

He returns to the cottage.

3RD SHEPHERD: Mak, by your leave, your son may I see?
MAK: A mere mock I believe; his sleep you may mar.
3RD SHEPHERD: This child will not grieve, that little day star.
  Mak, by your leave, thy bairn never bar
    From sixpence.
MAK: Nay, go away, he sleeps.
3RD SHEPHERD: I think he peeps.
MAK: When he wakes he weeps;
    I pray you go hence.

The other shepherds come back.

3RD SHEPHERD: Give me leave to kiss, and once lift him out.
  What the devil is this? He has a long snout!
1ST SHEPHERD: He is marked amiss. Come, best meddle nowt.
2ND SHEPHERD: The ill-spun weft is ever foully turned out.
    Quit talk!
  He is like to our sheep.
3RD SHEPHERD: How, Gib! May I peep?
1ST SHEPHERD: Aye, cunning will creep
    Where it may not walk.

2ND SHEPHERD: A ruse to record, and craftily cast.
  It was a fine fraud.
3RD SHEPHERD: And prettily passed.
  Let's burn this bawd and bind her fast.
  This shrew with a cord will be hanged at last.
    So shalt thou.
  Will you see how they swaddle
  His four feet in the middle.
  Saw I never in a cradle
    A horned lad ere now.
MAK: Peace, I say, what! Let be your blare!

I am he that him got, and yon woman him bare.

1ST SHEPHERD: Have you named him not, nor made him your heir?

2ND SHEPHERD: Now leave him to rot, and God give him care,
    I say.

MAK'S WIFE: A pretty child is he
  As sits on a woman's knee;
  A dillydown dilly,
    To make a man gay.

3RD SHEPHERD: I know him by the ear mark; that is a good token.

MAK: I tell you sirs, hark! His nose here was broken.
  Warned was I by a clerk what such spells did betoken.

1ST SHEPHERD: Do you hear the dog bark? Would fists first had spoken!
    Let be.

MAK'S WIFE: He was witched by an elf;
  I saw it myself:
  When the clock struck twelve,
    Misshapen was he.

2ND SHEPHERD: Both be of ill-spun weft of twisted thread.
  Since they uphold their theft, let's strike them dead.

MAK: I more I thieve, bereft may I be of my head. (*Mak kneels to the shepherds.*)
  At your mercy I am left.

1ST SHEPHERD: Sirs, hear what's said.
    For this trespass
  We will neither curse nor chide,
  No more deride,
  Nor longer bide,
    But toss him in a canvas.

They toss Mak in a canvas, after which Mak and his Wife return home.

1ST SHEPHERD: Lord, but I am sore; to leave now were best.
  In faith I may no more, therefore must I rest.

2ND SHEPHERD: As a sheep of seven score pound he weighed on my chest,
  Now to sleep out of door I'd count myself blest.

3RD SHEPHERD: Then, I pray,
  Lie down on this green.

1ST SHEPHERD: Brisk have these thieves been.

3RD SHEPHERD: Never split your spleen.
    For them, I say.

[252]

They sleep. The ANGEL *sings 'Gloria in Excelsis' then speaks.*

ANGEL: Rise, shepherds, attend! For now is he born
  Who shall fetch from the fiend what from Adam was torn.
  That warlock to end, this night is he born.
  God is made your friend; now at this morn –
    Leave your flocks:
  To Bethlehem go see
  Where he lies so free,
  A child in crib poorly,
    Between ass and ox.

1ST SHEPHERD: This was a sweet sound as ever yet I heard;
  To tell would astound where we this averred.
2ND SHEPHERD: That God's son be unbound from heaven, spoke he word;
  And lightning then crowned the woods as they stirred
    In their fear.
3RD SHEPHERD: He came us to warn,
  In Bethlehem will be born
  A babe.
1ST SHEPHERD: Be we drawn
  By yon star there.
2ND SHEPHERD: Say, what was his song? Heard ye not how it went?
  Three shorts and a long.
3RD SHEPHERD: The very accent.
  With no crochet wrong, and no breath misspent.
1ST SHEPHERD: For to sing us among as he merciful meant,
    I can.
2ND SHEPHERD: Let's see how ye croon.
  Can ye bark at the moon?
3RD SHEPHERD: Hold your tongues full soon!
1ST SHEPHERD: Or sing after, man.

  He sings.

2ND SHEPHERD: To Bethlehem he bad that we should go:
  And sure we be mad to tarry so.
3RD SHEPHERD: Be merry and not sad, our mirth may overflow:
  To be for ever glad is the reward we shall know
    And choose.

1ST SHEPHERD: Then let us hither hie,
  Though we be wet and weary,
  To that child and that lady;
    We have no time to lose.

2ND SHEPHERD: We find by the prophecy – let be your din –
  Of Isaiah and David, and more of their kin,
  They prophesied by clergy that in a virgin
  Should God come to lie, to atone for our sin,
    And abate it.
  Our folk freed from woe,
  Isaiah said so.
  For a maid comes to show
    A child that is naked.

3RD SHEPHERD: Full glad may we be and abide that day,
  That sweet sight to see who all power may sway.
  Lord so bless me, for now and for ay,
  Might I kneel on my knee some word for to say
    To that child.

  But the angel said
  In a crib was he laid;
  He was poorly arrayed,
    Both meek and mild.

1ST SHEPHERD: Patriarchs have been, and prophets have sworn
  They desired to have seen this child that is born,
  Past hope now to glean the gold of his corn.
  To see him we mean now ere it be morn,
    As a token.
1ST SHEPHERD: When I see him and feel,
  Then know I full well
  It is as true as steel
    What prophets have spoken.

  To so poor as we are that he would appear
  First, and to us declare by his messenger.
2ND SHEPHERD: Go we now, let us fare, the place is us near.
3RD SHEPHERD: I am glad to go there; set off in good cheer
    To that mite mild.
  Lord, if thy will be,
  We are unlearned all three,

Grant us thy gracious glee
   To comfort thy child.

1ST SHEPHERD: Hail, comely and clean! Hail, young child!
   Hail, maker, as I mean, of maiden so mild!
   Thou hast crushed in his spleen, the warlock so wild;
   That false traitor has been beyond doubt beguiled.
      Lo, he merry is.
   Lo, he laughs, my sweeting,
   A welcome meeting;
   Take my promised greeting:
      Have a bob of cherries.

2ND SHEPHERD: Hail, sovereign saviour, for thou hast us sought!
   Hail, joyous food and flower, that all things hast wrought!
   Hail, full of favour, that made all of nought.
   Hail, I kneel and I cower. A bird have I brought,
      Bairn that ye are.
   Hail, little tiny mop,
   Of our creed thou art top,
   At your mass I shall stop,
      Little day star.

3RD SHEPHERD: Hail, darling dear, full of godhead!
   I pray thee be near when that I have need.
   Hail, sweet is thy cheer! My heart would bleed
   To see thee sit here in so poor a stead
      With no pennies.
   Hail, hold forth thy hand small;
   I bring thee but a ball:
   Have thou and play withall,
      And go to the tennis.

MARY: The father of heaven, God omnipotent,
   Made all in days seven, his son has he sent.
   My name has he given, his light has me lent.
   Conceived I him even through his might as he meant,
      And now he is born.
   May he keep you from woe!
   I shall pray him do so.
   Tell of him as you go;
      Have mind on this morn.

[255]

1ST SHEPHERD: Farewell, lady, so fair to behold,
  With child on thy knee!
2ND SHEPHERD: But he lies full cold.
  Lord, well is me, now back to our fold.
3RD SHEPHERD: In truth already it seems to be told
    Full oft.
1ST SERVANT: What grace we have found.
2ND SERVANT: Come, now we are unbound.
3RD SERVANT: Let's make a glad sound,
    And sing it not soft.

The Shepherds leave singing.

The Wakefield Mystery Plays

The Bampton Mummers Play

PART ONE

Enter FATHER CHRISTMAS.
FATHER CHRISTMAS: In comes I, old Faather Christmas, welcome, or wel-
  come not.
  I 'ope old Faather Christmas will never be forgot.
  There is a time for work, there is a time for play,
  A time to be melancholy and for to be gay,
  A time to be thrifty, a time to be free,
  And sure enough this Christmas time we all shall jovial be.
  For this is the time when Christ did come, that we might happy be.
  So listen all yet gentiles to what we have to say:
  St George, the Doctor and the Turk, are 'ere together tonight,
  The Doctor has 'is physicks, the Knights have their swords sharp set,
  One will kill the other and the Doctor will raise him up.
  Now all we shall happy be with each 'is Christmas cup,
  And Robin Hood and Little John will pass the beer pot round,
  For two nobler chaps on earth there never yet were found.
  So Ladies an' Gentlemen I pray you give good cheer
  T'old Faather Christmas, he comes but once a year.
  Come in St George the Knight.
Enter ST GEORGE THE KNIGHT.

[256]

ST GEORGE: In comes I, St George the Knight, who with my pagans used to
fight.

With my sword and spear and valiant shield

I'll make an 'ost of adversaries yield.

I'll swear t'is true although I am so pliant in battle

I'm strong as any giant and although I am so slim

I can eat a calf and then not fill my belly. Oh no, not 'arf.

Come in the Turkish Knight.

Enter the TURKISH KNIGHT.

TURKISH KNIGHT: In comes, I the Turkish Knight. I come from Turkey-
land to fight

With bold St George if 'es 'ere, and if 'is 'eart doesn't quake with fear,

I'll cut it out with my shaarp sword and eat it,

That I will upon my word.

Just let 'im come if he be so bowld,

If 'is blood is 'ot, I'll make it cowld.

Fighting. A gasp.

FATHER CHRISTMAS: Is there a Doctor in the land?

Enter DOCTOR GOOD.

DR GOOD: There is a Doctor in the land, skilful both in yead and hand,

And if a man has got a cough, I can cure him without cutting 'is yead off,

And if this pays me well, I'll leave the sinner to each a bunch of thistles for
his dinner,

And if this pays me well, the secret I shall never tell.

Being the case as it was before, rise up they yead and fight once more.

Fighting.

DOCTOR GOOD: Come in bold Robin Hood.

Enter ROBIN HOOD.

ROBIN HOOD: In comes I, bold Robin Hood. With bended bow of yew tree
wood,

And arrows sharp for my quiver, I'll choose an alderman's fat liver.

Under the greenwood tree merrily come with me

To hunt the deer with horn and hound, we take our joyous way,

And when we've done with nut brown ale we'll cheer the hunting day.

With Little John and Friar Tuck we'll roast and eat the slaughtered buck.

Come in bold Little John.

Enter LITTLE JOHN.

LITTLE JOHN: In comes I, bowld Little John. With my quarterstaff I'll play
the don.

[257]

I'm not the man to cheat or cozen, but knock men's brains out by the
dozen.
All I ask you in this quorum, I'll drink your honour in the jorum.
Last Christmas Eve I turned the spit, burnt me fingers, and finds aunt's it.
The sparks fled over the table, the skimmer ran arter the laadle,
I said to the grid iron 'Caan't you two agree,
I'm the justice, bring 'im to me.'

PART TWO

Enter FATHER CHRISTMAS

FATHER CHRISTMAS: Good master and good mistress, I 'ope you're all
within,
For we've come this Merry Christmastime to greet you and your kin,
But if you are offended we'll take it as offence,
And if you do not own us, we'll quickly go you hence.
A room a room to rhyme, please give me and my brave gallant boys a room
To rhyme this Merry Christmastime, active youth, active life,
Life that's never seen or done before upon a common stage,
Stage or no stage, off St George.
Come in the Royal Apprussia King.
Enter the ROYAL APPRUSSIA KING.

ROYAL APPRUSSIA KING: In comes I, the Royal Apprussia King, bound to
defeat all nations.
Cares for no man, neither Austrian, Spanish, French, Dutch nor Turk.
An' I'm sure no man can do me any hurt.
So let all your noble voices ring,
For I'm the Royal Apprussia King.
Come in Soldier bowld.
Enter the SOLDIER BOLD.

SOLDIER BOLD: In comes I, Soldier bowld. Slasher is my name.
With sword and sash hanging by my side, I'll swear I'll win the game.
Who is this man who wi' me stand? I'll swear I'll kill him sword in hand,
Kill 'im and cut 'im and maul 'im into smaller slices,
Send 'im to the cookshop to make mince-pies –
Mince-pies 'ot, Mince-pies cowld,
Send 'im to the cookshop before 'es nine days old.

ROYAL APPRUSSIA KING: Count myself as good a man as thee.

SOLDIER BOLD: Same as I to thee.
Wherein the forelife I value it not,

Must give it up sooner or later or no more room for mortality.
Fighting. A knock.

FATHER CHRISTMAS: Who's there?

DR GOOD (*off stage*): Doctor.

FATHER CHRISTMAS: Come in then good Doctor.
Enter DOCTOR GOOD.

DR GOOD: Italy, t'Italy, Germany, France and Spain,
That's my 'ome and I shall return again.

FATHER CHRISTMAS: What sort of diseases do thy pills cure then good
Doctor?

DR GOOD: All sorts of diseases, the itch, the stitch, the palsy, the gout,
Pains within, pains without, hard carns, soft carns,
Cure a magpie with the toothache.

FATHER CHRISTMAS: How does'th thee do it then good Doctor?

DR GOOD: Cut 'is yead off and chuck 'is body in the ditch.
Also John Jenkins and his wife, I cured they, but they died.
Bring me an old wooman, seventy years of age and lying in her grave,
She'll be able to raise her head and crack one of my imple pimple pills,
I'll be found a Fifty Pound bonfire for her life
If there's another quack doctor in the land
Who can do as well as I can.
Just let 'im come here and raise this dead man.
Come in Jack Finney.
Enter JACK FINNEY.

JACK FINNEY: In comes I as ain't bin 'it, wi' my big yead and little wit.
Me yead's so big, me wits so small, I will endeavour to please you all.
Ladies and gentlemen, my name is not Jack Finney.

FATHER CHRISTMAS: What is thy name then Jack?

JACK FINNEY: Mr Finney. A man of great pains,
Can do more than thee, or any other man.

FATHER CHRISTMAS: What cans't thee do then Jack?

JACK FINNEY: Cure this man if not quite dead,
Being the case as it was before.
Rise up thy yead and fight no more,
Come in old Tom the Tinker.
Enter TOM THE TINKER.

TOM THE TINKER: In comes I, ol' Tom the Tinker. I bean't no small beer
drinker.
I towld the landlord to 'is face, the chimney carner was 'is place.
There us set and dried our face, Old Tom Giles and I.

Me face was black, me beard was long,
Me hat tied on with a leathern thong.
So if you please, all ye ladies and gentlemen,
Will ye give me a copper or two
To get me beard cut to go to church on Sunday?
As I was walking down a wide, narrow, straight, crooked lane
I met a pig with a horse's mane, I went down a little bit faather
I come to a pig sty built with pancakes and thatched wi' apple dumplings.
Now I thought it all very well for trade,
I knocked at the maid, open fled the door,
The pig began to shake and the 'ouse began to roar.
She asked me if I could yet half a pint of ale
And drink a piece of bread and cheese.
I said, 'No thankee, but just if thee please.'
I went down a little bit faarther, I came to two owld women, snipper
    snapping.
One cut a barley corn through a ten foot wall,
Knocked the bottom out of a caste iron pot,
And killed a poor dead dog.
Now I had pity on this poor dead dog.
DR GOOD: What was it Tom, a pedigree?
TOM THE TINKER: No a bitch.
I turn 'im inside outerds, slap bang outerds,
Set 'im at the top of Buckland Hill barking back'ards.
ALL SING: Now for the music and now for the fun,
The feast is ready and Christmas is come,
So welcome us now, and give us a cheer,
For Ol' Faather Christmas comes once in a year.

from *Christmas His Masque*

(*As it was presented at court, 1616*)

Enter CHRISTMAS *with two or three of the guard. He is attired in round hose,
long stockings, a close doublet, a high-crowned hat with a brooch, a long thin
beard, a truncheon, little ruffs, white shoes, his scarfs and garters tied cross, and
his drum beaten before him.*

CHRISTMAS: Why gentlemen, do you know what you do? Ha! would you ha' kept me out? Christmas, old Christmas? Christmas of London, and Captain Christmas? Pray you let me be brought before my lord chamberlain; I'll not be answered else: 'tis merry in hall when beards wag all. I ha' seen the time you ha' wished for me for a merry Christmas, and now you ha' me, they would not let me in; I must come another time! A good jest, as if I could come more than once a year. Why, I am no dangerous person, and so I told my friends o' the guard. I am old Gregory Christmas still, and though I come out of Pope's Head Alley, as good a Protestant as any i' my parish. The troth is, I ha' brought a masque here out o' the city, o' my own making, and do present it by a set of my sons that come out of the lanes of London, good dancing boys all. It was intended, I confess, for Curriers' Hall, but because the weather has been open, and the livery were not at leisure to see it till a frost come that they cannot work, I thought it convenient, with some little alterations and the groom of the revels' hand to't, to fit it for a higher place, which I have done; and though I say it, another manner of device than your New Year's night. Bones o' bread, the king! Son Rowland, son Clem, be ready there in a trice; quick, boys!

Enter his SONS AND DAUGHTERS, *being ten in number, led in a string by* CUPID, *who is attired in a flat cap and a prentice's coat, with wings at his shoulders.*

The Names of His Children, with Their Attires:

Misrule   In a velvet cap with a sprig, a short cloak, great yellow ruff like a reveler, his torchbearer bearing a rope, a cheese and a basket.

Carol   A long tawny coat with a red cap and a flute at his girdle, his torchbearer carrying a songbook open.

Minced Pie   Like a fine cook's wife, dressed neat, her man carrying a pie, dish and spoons.

Gambol   Like a tumbler, with a hoop and bells, his torchbearer armed with a cowlstaff and a blinding cloth.

Post and Pair   With a pair-royal of aces in his hat, his garment all done over with pairs and purs, his squire carrying a box, cards and counters.

New Year's Gift   In a blue coat, serving-man like, with an orange and a sprig of rosemary gilt on his head, his hat full of brooches, with a collar of gingerbread, his torchbearer carrying a Marchpane, with a bottle of wine on either arm.

Mumming   In a masquing pied suit with a visor, his torchbearer carrying the box, and ringing it.

Wassail   Like a neat sempster and songster, her page bearing a brown bowl dressed with ribands and rosemary before her.

[261]

Offering   In a short gown, with a porter's staff in his hand, a withe borne before him, and a basin, by his torchbearer.
Baby Cake   Dressed like a boy, in a fine long coat, biggin, bib, muckender and a little dagger; his usher bearing a great cake with a bean and a peas.
They enter singing:

> Now God preserve, as you well do deserve,
> Your majesties all two there;
> Your highness small, with my good lords all,
> And ladies, how do you do there?
> Gi' me leave to ask, for I bring you a masque
> From little little little little London;
> Which say the king likes, I ha' passed the pikes;
> If not, old Christmas is undone.

Noise outside

Ben Jonson

Not to Like Pantomime

He that says he does not like a pantomime, either says what he does not think, or is not so wise as he fancies himself. He should grow young again, and get wiser . . . Not to like pantomimes is not to like animal spirits: it is not to like motion; not to like love; not to like a jest upon dullness and formality; not to smoke one's uncle; not to like to see a thump in the face; not to laugh; not to fancy; not to like a holiday; not to know the pleasure of sitting up at Christmas; not to sympathize with one's children; not to remember that we have been children ourselves; nor that we shall grow old, and be as gouty as Pantaloon, if we are not as wise and as active as they.

James Henry Leigh Hunt, 'Pantomimes'

Peace and Goodwill to Managers

The Babes in the Wood. The Children's Grand Pantomime.
By Arthur Sturgess and Arthur Collins. Music by J. M. Glover.
Theatre Royal, Drury Lane, 27 December 1897.

1 *January* 1898

I am sorry to have to introduce the subject of Christmas in these articles. It is an indecent subject; a cruel, gluttonous subject; a drunken, disorderly subject; a wasteful, disastrous subject; a wicked, cadging, lying, filthy, blasphemous, and demoralizing subject. Christmas is forced on a reluctant and disgusted nation by the shopkeepers and the press: on its own merits it would wither and shrivel in the fiery breath of universal hatred; and anyone who looked back to it would be turned into a pillar of greasy sausages. Yet, though it is over now for a year, and I can go out without positively elbowing my way through groves of carcases, I am dragged back to it, with my soul full of loathing, by the pantomime.

The pantomime ought to be a redeeming feature of Christmas, since it professedly aims at developing the artistic possibilities of our Saturnalia. But its professions are like all the other Christmas professions: what the pantomime actually does is to abuse the Christmas toleration of dullness, senselessness, vulgarity, and extravagance to a degree utterly incredible by people who have never been inside a theatre. The manager spends five hundred pounds to produce two penn'orth of effect. As a shilling's worth is needed to fill the gallery, he has to spend three thousand pounds for the 'gods', seven thousand five hundred for the pit, and so on in proportion, except that when it comes to the stalls and boxes he caters for the children alone, depending on their credulity to pass off his twopence as a five-shilling piece. And yet even this is not done systematically and intelligently. The wildest superfluity and extravagance in one direction is wasted by the most sordid niggardliness in another. The rough rule is to spend money recklessly on whatever can be seen and heard and recognized as costly, and to economize on invention, fancy, dramatic faculty – in short, on brains. It is only when the brains get thrown in gratuitously through the accident of some of the contracting parties happening to possess them – a contingency which managerial care cannot always avert – that the entertainment acquires sufficient form or purpose to make it humanly apprehensible. To the mind's eye and ear the modern pantomime, as purveyed by the late Sir Augustus Harris, is neither visible nor audible. It is a glittering, noisy void, horribly wearisome and enervating, like all performances which worry the physical senses without any recreative appeal to the emotions and through them to the intellect.

I grieve to say that these remarks have lost nothing of their force by the succession of Mr Arthur Collins to Sir Augustus Harris. In Drury Lane drama Mr Collins made a decided advance on his predecessor. In pantomime he has, I think, also shewn superior connoisseurship in selecting pretty dummies for the display of his lavishly expensive wardrobe; but the only other respect in which he has outdone his late chief is the cynicism with which he has disregarded, I will not say the poetry of the nursery tale, because poetry is unthinkable in such a connection, but the bare coherence and common sense of the presentation of its incidents. The spectacular scenes exhibit Mr Collins as a manager to whom a thousand pounds is as five shillings. The dramatic scenes exhibit him as one to whom a crown-piece is as a million. If Mr Dan Leno had asked for a hundred-guinea tunic to wear during a single walk across the stage, no doubt he would have got it, with a fifty-guinea hat and sword-belt to boot. If he had asked for ten guineas' worth of the time of a competent dramatic humorist to provide him with at least one line that might not have been pirated from the nearest Cheap Jack, he would, I suspect, have been asked whether he wished to make Drury Lane bankrupt for the benefit of dramatic authors. I hope I may never again have to endure anything more dismally futile than the efforts of Mr Leno and Mr Herbert Campbell to start a passable joke in the course of their stumblings and wanderings through barren acres of gag on Boxing night. Their attempt at a travesty of *Hamlet* reached a pitch of abject resourcelessness which could not have been surpassed if they really had been a couple of school children called on for a prize-day Shakespearean recitation without any previous warning.

An imitation of Mr Forbes Robertson and Mrs Patrick Campbell would have been cheap and obvious enough; but even this they were unequal to. Mr Leno, fortunately for himself, was inspired at the beginning of the business to call Hamlet 'Ham'. Several of the easily amused laughed at this; and thereafter, whenever the travesty became so frightfully insolvent in ideas as to make it almost impossible to proceed, Mr Leno said 'Ham', and saved the situation . . .

It is piteous to see the wealth of artistic effort which is annually swamped in the morass of purposeless wastefulness that constitutes a pantomime . . . If I were Mr Collins I should reduce the first four scenes to one short one, and get some person with a little imagination, some acquaintance with the story of the Babes in the Wood, and at least a rudimentary faculty for amusing people, to write the dialogue for it. I should get Messrs Leno and Campbell to double the parts of the robbers with those of the babes, and so make the panorama scene tolerable. I should reduce the second part of the race-course scene, which is fairly funny, with just one front scene, in which full scope might be allowed for Mr Leno's inspiration, and the final transformation. I should either cut the harlequinade out, or, at the expense of the firms it advertises, pay the audience for looking at it . . . And I should fill up the evening with some comparatively amusing play by Ibsen or Browning . . .

George Bernard Shaw, Our Theatres in the Nineties

Harlequin and the Fairy of the Spangled Pocket-handkerchief, or the Prince of the Enchanted Nose

The composer of the Overture of the New Grand Comic Christmas Panto-mime, *Harlequin and the Fairy of the Spangled Pocket-handkerchief, or the Prince of the Enchanted Nose*, arrayed in a brand-new Christmas suit, with his wristbands and collar turned elegantly over his cuffs and embroidered satin tie, takes a place at his desk, waves his stick, and away the Pantomime Overture begins.

I pity a man who can't appreciate a Pantomime Overture. Children do not like it: they say, 'Hang it, I wish the Pantomime would begin.' But for us it is always a pleasant moment of reflection and enjoyment. It is not difficult music to understand, like that of your Mendelssohns and Beethovens, whose symphonies and sonatas Mrs Spec states must be heard a score of times before you can comprehend them. But of the proper Pantomime music I am a delighted connoisseur. Perhaps it is because you meet so many old friends in these compositions consorting together in the queerest manner, and occasioning numberless pleasant surprises. Hark! there goes '*Old Dan Tucker*' wandering into the '*Groves of Blarney*'; our friends the '*Scots wha hae wi' Wallace bled*' march rapidly down '*Wapping Old Stairs*', from which the '*Figlia del Reggimento*' comes bounding briskly, when she is met, embraced, and carried off by '*Billy Taylor*', that brisk young fellow.

All this while you are thinking, with a faint, sickly kind of hope, that perhaps the Pantomime *may* be a good one; something like *Harlequin and the Golden Orange-Tree*, which you recollect in your youth; something like *Fortunio*, that marvellous and delightful piece of buffoonery, which realized the most gorgeous visions of the absurd. You may be happy, perchance; a glimpse of the old days may come back to you. Lives there the man with soul so dead, the being ever so *blasé* and travel-worn, who does not feel some shock and thrill still, just at that moment when the bell (the dear and familiar bell of your youth) begins to tingle, and the curtain to rise, and the large shoes and ankles, the flesh-coloured leggings, the crumpled knees, the gorgeous robes and masks finally, of the actors ranged on the stage to shout the opening chorus?

All round the house you hear a great gasping a-ha-a from a thousand children's throats. Enjoyment is going to give place to Hope. Desire is about to be realized. Oh, you blind little brats! clap your hands, and crane over the boxes, and open your eyes with happy wonder! Clap your hands now. In three weeks more the Reverend Doctor Swishtail expects the return of his young friends to Sugarcane House.

King Beak, Emperor of the Romans, having invited all the neighbouring Princes, Fairies, and Enchanters to the feast at which he celebrated the marriage of his only son, *Prince Aquiline*, unluckily gave the liver-wing of the fowl which he was carving to the Prince's godmother, the *Fairy Bandanna*, while he put the gizzard-pinion on the plate of the *Enchanter Gorgibus*, King of the Maraschino Mountains, and father of the *Princess Rosolia*, to whom the Prince was affianced.

The outraged *Gorgibus* rose from the table in a fury, smashed his plate of chicken over the head of *King Beak*'s Chamberlain, and wished that *Prince Aquiline*'s nose might grow on the instant as long as the sausage before him.

It did so. The screaming Princess rushed away from her bridegroom; and her father, breaking off the match with the House of *Beak*, ordered his daughter to be carried in his sedan by the two giant-porters, *Gor* and *Gogstay*, to his castle in the Juniper Forest, by the side of the bitter waters of the Absinthine Lake, whither, after upsetting the marriage-tables, and flooring *King Beak* in a single combat, he himself repaired.

The latter monarch could not bear to see or even to hear his disfigured son.

When the *Prince Aquiline* blew his unfortunate and monstrous nose, the windows of his father's palace broke; the locks of the doors started; the dishes and glasses of the King's banquet jingled and smashed as they do on board a steamboat in a storm; the liquor turned sour; the Chancellor's wig started off his head; and the Prince's royal father, disgusted with his son's appearance, drove him forth from his palace, and banished him the kingdom.

Life was a burden to him on account of that nose. He fled from a world in which he was ashamed to show it, and would have preferred a perfect solitude, but that he was obliged to engage one faithful attendant to give him snuff (his only consolation), and to keep his odious nose in order.

But as he was wandering in a lonely forest, entangling his miserable trunk in the thickets, and causing the birds to fly scared from the branches, and the lions, stags, and foxes to sneak away in terror as they heard the tremendous booming which issued from the fated Prince whenever he had occasion to use his pocket-handkerchief, the Fairy of the Bandanna Islands took pity on him, and, descending in her car drawn by doves, gave him a kerchief which rendered him invisible whenever he placed it over his monstrous proboscis.

Having occasion to blow his nose (which he was obliged to do pretty frequently, for he had taken cold while lying out among the rocks and morasses in the rainy, miserable nights, so that the peasants, when they heard him snoring fitfully, thought that storms were abroad) at the gates of a castle by which he was passing, the door burst open, and the Irish Giant (afterwards Clown, indeed) came out, and wondering looked about, furious to see no one.

The Prince entered into the castle, and whom should he find there but the *Princess Rosolia*, still plunged in despair. Her father snubbed her perpetually. 'I wish he would snub me!' exclaimed the Prince, pointing to his own monstrous deformity. In spite of his misfortune, she still remembered her Prince. 'Even with his nose,' the faithful Princess cried, 'I love him more than all the world besides!'

At this declaration of unalterable fidelity, the Prince flung away his handkerchief, and knelt in rapture at the Princess's feet. She was a little scared at first by the hideousness of the distorted being before her; but what will not woman's faith overcome? Hiding her head on his shoulder (and so losing sight of his misfortune), she vowed to love him still (in those broken verses which only Princesses in Pantomimes deliver).

At this instant *King Gorgibus*, the Giants, the King's Household, with clubs and battle-axes, rushed in. Drawing his immense scimitar, and seizing the Prince by his too prominent feature, he was just on the point of sacrificing him, when – when, I need not say, the *Fairy Bandanna* (Miss Bendigo), in her amaranthine car drawn by Paphian doves, appeared, and put a stop to the massacre. *King Gorgibus* became Pantaloon, the two Giants first and second Clowns, and the Prince and Princess (who had been, all the time of the Fairy's speech, and actually while under their father's scimitar, unhooking their dresses) became the most elegant Harlequin and Columbine that I have seen for many a long day. The nose flew up to the ceiling, the music began a jig, and the two Clowns, after saying, 'How are you?' went and knocked down Pantaloon.

William Makepeace Thackeray, *Sketches and Travels in London*

At a Pantomime

(By a bilious one)

An actor sits in doubtful gloom,
His stock-in-trade unfurled,
In a damp funereal dressing-room
In the Theatre Royal, World.

He comes to town at Christmastime
    And braves its icy breath,
To play in that favourite pantomime,
    Harlequin Life and Death.

A hoary flowing wig his weird,
    Unearthly cranium caps;
He hangs a long benevolent beard
    On a pair of empty chaps.

To smooth his ghastly features down
    The actor's art he cribs;
A long and a flowing padded gown
    Bedecks his rattling ribs.

He cries, 'Go on – begin, begin!
    Turn on the light of lime;
I'm dressed for jolly Old Christmas in
    A favourite pantomime!'

The curtain's up – the stage all black –
    Time and the Year nigh sped –
(Time as an advertising quack)
    The Old Year nearly dead.

The wand of Time is waved, and lo!
    Revealed Old Christmas stands,
And little children chuckle and crow,
    And laugh and clap their hands.

The cruel old scoundrel brightens up
    At the death of the Olden Year,
And he waves a gorgeous golden cup,
    And bids the world good cheer.

The little ones hail the festive King –
    No thought can make them sad;
Their laughter comes with a sounding ring,
    They clap and crow like mad!

They only see in the humbug old
    A holiday every year,
And handsome gifts, and joys untold,
    And unaccustomed cheer.

The old ones, palsied, blear, and hoar,
    Their breasts in anguish beat –
They've seen him seventy times before,
    How well they know the cheat!

They've seen that ghastly pantomime,
    They've felt its blighting breath,
They know that rollicking Christmastime
    Meant cold and want and death –

Starvation – Poor Law Union fare,
    And deadly cramps and chills,
And illness – illness everywhere –
    And crime, and Christmas bills.

They know Old Christmas well, I ween,
    Those men of ripened age;
They've often, often, often seen
    That actor off the stage.

They see in his gay rotundity
    A clumsy stuffed-out dress;
They see in the cup he waves on high
    A tinselled emptiness.

Those aged men so lean and wan,
    They've seen it all before;
They know they'll see the charlatan
    But twice or three times more.

And so they bear with dance and song,
    And crimson foil and green;
They wearily sit, and grimly long
    For the Transformation Scene.

                       W. S. Gilbert

Panto

Tonight I am a child, hating Christmas,
making my face roar,
walking the tightrope of happiness
under theatre lights,
as the tribe stamps its applause
and party-hats circulate.

Perform! Perform! urge the sudden,
pleading, loved faces
of these polished women,
as from cave to Purley semi
with pantomime brio
they flap at the hearth-flames their men feed,
conjuring feverfew at a pinch
to blast vacant fears
or grasping at heart's-ease,
rounding the glow of happiness
behind which the night soars.

Martin Turner

The Five Uncles

One year, at the Christmas party, all the five uncles were there; and among
uncles I include my father. A father is only a specialized kind of uncle anyhow.

Uncle William, Uncle George, Uncle Frank, Uncle Leonard and Uncle
Horace; a solid block of uncles, each more adorable than the other. There was
a great family likeness among them; and when I was quite small, the chief
difference between them, to my short-sighted eyes, was that three of them
had short beards, and the other two only rudimentary whiskers. At a little
distance I even found it difficult to tell the three bearded ones apart – and
they included my own father! For they all had the same kind of presence; the
same flavour, and the same family voice – a warm, flexible, very moving
voice; the same beautiful hands, and, of course, the same permanently chilly
feet.

So that year we five nieces, with affectionate impudence, acted a short scene, in which we each took the part of one of our uncles.

The plot was simple: we came into the room one by one, making some characteristic remark; then, each in turn, took off our shoes and sat down to warm our feet at an imaginary fire. Margaret, as Uncle William, stumped into the room (he had a wooden leg), whistling under her breath his theme tune: 'Girls and Boys come out to Play', and produced *one* sock out of her pocket to warm at the fire; I, as my father, made some mild complaint about the crowing of the cocks, which waked him so early of a morning. I cannot remember what Uncle Lenny and Uncle Horace did; but Ruth, as Uncle Frank, captured the show. She came in humming an air of Handel's; the real Uncle Frank was kneeling up on a chair, and then moving about near the chimney-place; and Ruth began imitating every movement he made as he watched us. And for quite a long time he had not the faintest idea that he was being copied; and kept on saying, 'Who *is* she acting? What *is* she doing?' Till at last we all laughed so much at them both that the scene came to an end.

Gwen Raverat, *Period Piece*

Carol (to the tune of 'We Three Kings')

Come to our Nativity Play
Raggy doll asleep on the hay
Itchy knickers, bogey-pickers,
I've got a bit to say.

> *O, I'm the star as you can tell.*
> *I'm the Angel Gabriel.*
> *Silver wings and halo thing and*
> *Glittery tights as well.*

They two kings of Orient are
Kevin Jones and Dominic Barr.
Barry Bright has tonsilitis –
Sick in his father's car.

See the shepherds watching their sheep.
Amber Cardy's gone off to sleep.
She was snogging Nathaniel Hogg in a
Cupboard and he's a creep!

Mary, Mary, good as can be
Thinks she's always better than me
Till my candle burns her sandal
Quite accidentally.

Adam's Herod, up on a chair
In his robe and underwear.
It's so rude, he's nearly NUDE
And I saw his pants, so there.

Mums and Grandmas sit in a row,
Toddlers want to be in the show,
Dads who are able to stand on a table to
Get it on video.

John Whitworth

❦ 14 ❦

GROUSES, GOSSIP AND GREETINGS

Greetings from the Dean

London, 24 December 1710. You will have a merryer Christmas Eve than we here. I went up to Court before church, and in one of the rooms, there being but little company, a fellow in a red coat without a sword came up to me, and after words of course, askt me how the ladies did. I askt what ladies? He said, Mrs Dingley and Mrs Johnson: Very well, said I, when I heard from them last: and pray, when came you from thence, sir? Said he, I never was in Ireland; and just at that word lord Winchelsea comes up to me, and the man went off: as I went out I saw him again, and recollected him; it was Vedeau with a pox . . . When I came from church I went up to Court again, where sir Edm. Bacon told me the bad news from Spain, which you will hear before this reaches you; as we have it now, we are undone there, and it was odd to see the whole countenances of the Court changed so in two hours. Lady Mountjoy carried me home to dinner, where I staid not long after, and came home early, and now am got into bed, for you must always write to your MD's in bed, that's a maxim.

> Mr White and Mr Red, write to MD when abed;
> Mr Black and Mr Brown, write to MD when you're down;
> Mr Oak and Mr Willow, write to MD on your pillow.

What's this? faith I smell fire; what can it be? this house has a thousand stinks in it. I think to leave it on Thursday, and lodge over the way. Faith I must rise, and look at my chimney, for the smell grows stronger; stay – I have been up, and in my room, and found all safe, only a mouse within the fender to warm himself, which I could not catch. I smelt nothing more, but now in my bed-chamber I smell it again; I believe I have singed the woolen curtain, and that's all, though I cannot smoak it. Presto's plaguy silly tonight; an't he? Yes, and so he be. Ay, but if I should wake and see fire. Well; I'll venture; so good-night, &c.

25   Pray, young women, if I write so much as this every day, how will this

paper hold a fortnight's work, and answer one of yours into the bargain? You never think of this, but let me go on like a simpleton. I wish you a merry Christmas, and many, many a one with poor Presto at some pretty place . . .

26 By the lord Harry I shall be undone here with Christmas-boxes. The rogues at the coffee-house have raised their tax, every one giving a crown, and I gave mine for shame, besides a great many half-crowns, to great men's porters, &c.

30 Morning. The weather grows cold, you sauce-boxes. Sir Andrew Fountain, they bring me word, is better. I'll go rise, for my hands are starving while I write in bed – Night . . . Well, but when shall we answer this letter, No. 8, of MD's? Not till next year, faith . . . Pray, pray, Dingley, let me go to sleep; pray, pray, Stella, let me go slumber, and put out my wax-candle.

31 Morning. It is now seven, and I have got a fire, but am writing a-bed in my bed-chamber. 'Tis not shaving day, so I shall be ready to go before church to Mr St John, and tomorrow I will answer our MD's letter.

> Would you answer MD's letter,
> On New Year's-day you'll do it better;
> For when the year with MD 'gins,
> It without MD never lins.

(These proverbs have always old words in them; *lins* is leaves off.)

> But if on New-year you write nones,
> MD then will bang your bones –

But Patrick says I must rise – Night. I was early this morning with secretary St John, and gave him a memorial to get the queen's letter for the First-Fruits, who has promised to do it in a very few days. He told me he had been with the Duke of Marlborough, who was lamenting his former wrong steps in joining with the Whigs, and said he was worn out with age, fatigues, and misfortunes. I swear it pitied me; and I really think they will not do well in too much mortifying that man, although indeed it is his own fault. He is covetous as hell, and ambitious as the Prince of it: he would fain have been general for life, and has broken all endeavours for Peace, to keep his greatness and get money . . .

1 January 1711. Morning. I wish my dearest pretty Dingley and Stella a happy new-year, and health, and mirth, and good stomachs, and Fr's company. Faith, I did not know how to write Fr. I wondered what was the matter; but now I remember I always write pdfr. Patrick wishes me a happy New-year, and desires I would rise, for it is a good fire, and faith 'tis cold. I was so politick last night with MD, never saw the like. Get the *Examiners,* and read them; the last nine or ten are full of the reasons for the late change, and of the abuses of the last ministry; and the great men assure me they are all true. I must rise and go see sir Andrew Fountain; but perhaps tonight I may answer MD's letter; so good-morrow, my mistresses all, good-morrow.

> I wish you both a merry new year,
> Roast beef, minced pyes, and good strong beer,
> And me a share of your good cheer;
> That I was there, or you were here,
> And you are a little saucy dear.

Good-morrow again, dear sirrahs . . .

Jonathan Swift, Journal to Stella

1814

Sunday 25 December   Christmas Day – have a very bad side ache in the morning so I rise late – Charles Clairmont comes and dines with us – in the afternoon read Miss Bailie's plays – Hogg spends the evening with us – conversation as usual –

Mary Shelley

Garsington, 1916

Our Christmas party that year (1916) was gay and interesting. The house was made lovely with bright coloured paper garlands and evergreen swags and Chinese lanterns. We acted a play which Katherine Mansfield hurriedly wrote called *The Laurels*. Dr Kite, the chief character, was played by Lytton Strachey, who was a wonderful actor. I don't remember it very vividly, except that he wore a great fur coat and a paper mask with a red worsted beard, made for him by Carrington. Maria and Juliette and Carrington and Clive Bell and the children acted in it. Middleton Murry and Bertie Russell and Aldous and the household and Philip and myself were audience.

Another evening we had a delightful fancy-dress dinner, which Fredigond Shove organized. She was in one of her very witty, wild moods and we were all full of fun. Gerald was King George V bowing pompously with his head,

Clive a fat repulsive old woman. I a Masher in Philip's evening suit and opera hat.

What a work these parties were; to provide food for a large company at this time of food shortage was difficult enough, and the guests, although they had doubtless to put up with meagre diets in their own homes, when at Garsington expected to find food very richly and plentifully supplied, and to have plenty of wine and spirits. There was a dreadful scene one morning at breakfast, when Lytton came down very late and I suppose the appetites of the other guests had been healthy, for he did not find all he required. He lost his temper and turned and rated me angrily for not providing him with sufficient breakfast. Murry and Katherine and several others were present, and we looked at each other surprised and aghast, for there was really ample food. I went to the kitchen and fetched him enough for six men. I know that next day and the succeeding days he had breakfast sent up to his room, piled high with six eggs, ham, fish, scones and everything that could be collected together. It was best to ignore this scene and to heap large hot breakfasts on his head.

I wish I could remember this party in more detail. I know that all the guests were lively and that sparks and currents and cross currents flew about. Carrington began to set her roving eye on Lytton, and shake her sun-bleached, shaggy head of hair at him. Bertie and Katherine had long talks together, so late into the night in the red room, which was under my bedroom, that the sound of their voices kept me awake most of the night. I made them look uncomfortable next day by telling them that I had heard all their conversation, which of course wasn't true.

Long afterwards Bertie told me that Katherine had talked very maliciously against me. Actually what she had said had some effect on him. I did not know this at the time, and was surprised when he warned me against Katherine! He said that she was by nature so jealous that she would try and alienate me from all my friends, so as to be the only one left in possession. Whether this was true I don't know. Bertie certainly seemed to mistrust her after a time.

Lady Ottoline Morrell, *Memoirs*

To Lytton Strachey

Asheham, Rodmell, [Sussex]
Boxing Day [1912]

Dear Lytton,

I meant long ago to write to you, in London, but one can't write in London. In fact we're driven to think that the country is our destiny, partly led thereto by the charms of Mrs Funnell, Old Funnell, their son, and a soldier nephew who served in Egypt, who are all at this moment sitting in the kitchen, eating a great sugar cake, which I bore in and presented, amid subdued cheers. As for the boy he has the figure of a God – a very small, tightly curled head, set upon gigantic shoulders. That's the style I admire; and there he sits speechless, reading the cookery book.

We have just had dinner – Leonard is reading the poems of John Donne: I am half-way through the *Return of the Native*, a novel by Thomas Hardy. We go back tomorrow, alas. Were there time I would tell you about Brighton on Christmas Eve; we spent 2 hours in the Aquarium. The common fish are perfectly wonderful. Soles laid flat on the bottom; cray fish crawling; mackerel shooting endlessly round and round, like torpedo boats; fat white anemones blooming from rocky corners. Then there is the monkey house. For some reason, the mackerel put me in mind of Ottoline and her troupe; she ought to be put in a tank; it's absurd to expect her to stand scrutiny for ways and motives, which is her lot at present . . .

Virginia Woolf

Christmas Numbers

The editors of the magazines bring out their Christmas numbers so long before the time that the reader is more likely to be still lamenting for the turkey of last year than to have seriously settled down to the solid anticipation of the turkey which is to come. Christmas numbers of magazines ought to be tied up in brown paper and kept for Christmas Day. On consideration, I should favour the editors being tied up in brown paper. Whether the leg or arm of an editor should ever be allowed to protrude I leave to individual choice.

G. K. Chesterton, 'Christmas that is Coming'

1762

Friday 24 December   I waited on Louisa. Says she, 'I have been very unhappy since you was here. I have been thinking of what I said to you. I find that such a connection would make me miserable.' 'I hope, Madam, I am not disagreeable to you.' 'No, Sir, you are not. If it was the first duke of England I spoke to, I should just say the same thing.' 'But pray, Madam, what is your objection?' 'Really, Sir, I have many disagreeable apprehensions. It may be known. Circumstances might be very troublesome. I beg it of you, Sir, consider of it. Your own good sense will agree with me. Instead of visiting me as you do now, you would find a discontented, unhappy creature.' I was quite confused. I did not know what to say. At last I agreed to think of it and see her on Sunday. I came home and dined in dejection. Yet I mustered up vivacity, and away I went in full dress to Northumberland House. There was spirit, to lay out a couple of shillings and be a man of fashion in my situation. There was true economy.

Saturday 25 December   The night before I did not rest well. I was really violently in love with Louisa. I thought she did not care for me. I thought that if I did not gain her affections, I would appear despicable to myself. This day I was in a better frame, being Christmas day, which has always inspired me with most agreeable feelings. I went to St. Paul's Church and in that magnificent temple fervently adored the God of goodness and mercy, and heard a sermon by the Bishop of Oxford [John Hume] on the publishing of glad tidings of great joy. I then went to Child's, where little was passing. However, here goes the form of a

Dialogue at Child's

1 CITIZEN: *Why, here is the bill of mortality. Is it right, Doctor?*
PHYSICIAN: *Why, I don't know.*
1 CITIZEN: *I'm sure it is not. Sixteen only died of cholics! I dare say you have killed as many yourself.*
2 CITIZEN: *Ay, and hanged but three! O Lord, ha! ha! ha!*

I then sat a while at Coutts's, and then at Macfarlane's, and then went to Davies's. Johnson was gone to Oxford. I was introduced to Mr Dodsley, a good, jolly, decent, conversable man, and Mr Goldsmith, a curious, odd, pedantic fellow with some genius. It was quite a literary dinner. I had seen no warm victuals for four days, and therefore played a very bold knife and fork.

It is inconceivable how hearty I eat and how comfortable I felt myself after it. We talked entirely in the way of Geniuses.

We talked of poetry. Said Goldsmith, 'The miscellaneous poetry of this age is nothing like that of the last; it is very poor. Why there, now, Mr. Dodsley, is your *Collection*.' DODSLEY: 'I think that equal to those made by Dryden and Pope.' GOLDSMITH: 'To consider them, Sir, as villages, yours may be as good; but let us compare house with house, you can produce me no edifices equal to the *Ode on St Cecilia's Day*, *Absalom and Achitophel*, or *The Rape of the Lock*.' DODSLEY: 'We have poems in a different way. There is nothing of the kind in the last age superior to *The Spleen*.' BOSWELL: 'And what do you think of Gray's odes? Are they not noble?' GOLDSMITH: 'Ah, the rumbling thunder! I remember a friend of mine was very fond of Gray. "Yes," said I, "he is very fine indeed; as thus –

> Mark the white and mark the red,
> Mark the blue and mark the green;
> Mark the colours ere they fade,
> Darting thro' the welkin sheen."

"O, yes," said he, "great, great!" "True, Sir," said I, "but I have made the lines this moment." ' BOSWELL: 'Well, I admire Gray prodigiously. I have read his odes till I was almost mad.' GOLDSMITH: 'They are terribly obscure. We must be historians and learned men before we can understand them.' DAVIES: 'And why not? He is not writing to porters or carmen. He is writing to men of knowledge.' GOLDSMITH: 'Have you seen *Love in a Village*?' BOSWELL: 'I have. I think it is a good, pleasing thing.' GOLD-SMITH: 'I am afraid we will have no good plays now. The taste of the audience is spoiled by the pantomime of Shakespeare. The wonderful changes and shiftings.' DAVIES: 'Nay, but you will allow that Shakespeare has great merit?' GOLDSMITH: 'No, I know Shakespeare very well.' (Here I said nothing, but thought him a most impudent puppy.) BOSWELL: 'What do you think of Johnson?' GOLDSMITH: 'He has exceeding great merit. His *Rambler* is a noble work.' BOSWELL: 'His *Idler* too is very pretty. It is a lighter performance; and he has thrown off the classical fetters very much.' DAVIES: 'He is a most entertaining companion. And how can it be otherwise, when he has so much imagination, has read so much, and digested it so well?'

We had many more topics which I don't remember. I was very well. I then went to Macfarlane's. We were very merry. Erskine and I had some bread and wine and talked for nearly two hours. He told me that he was kept as a blackguard when he was a boy, then went to sea, and then came into the Army. And that he wondered how he had been turned out a tolerable being.

Sunday 26 December I went to Whitehall Chapel, and heard service. I took a whim to go through all the churches and chapels in London, taking one each Sunday.

At one I went to Louisa's. I told her my passion in the warmest terms. I told her that my happiness absolutely depended upon her. She said it was running the greatest risk. 'Then,' said I, 'Madam, you will show the greatest generosity to a most sincere lover.' She said that we should take time to consider of it, and that then we could better determine how to act. We agreed that the time should be a week, and that if I remained of the same opinion, she would then make me blessed. There is no telling how easy it made my mind to be convinced that she did not despise me, but on the contrary had a tender heart and wished to make me easy and happy.

I this day received a letter from the Duke of Queensberry, in answer to one that I had wrote him, telling me that a commission in the Guards was a fruitless pursuit, and advising me to take to a civil rather than a military life. I was quite stupefied and enraged at this. I imagined my father was at the bottom of it. I had multitudes of wild schemes. I thought of enlisting for five years as a soldier in India, of being a private man either in the Horse or Footguards, &c. At last good sense prevailed, and I resolved to be cheerful and to wait and to ask it of Lady Northumberland. At night I sat at Macfarlane's pretty well.

James Boswell, London Journal

To Hannah Macaulay

London, Decr. 26 1832

My love,

I have only time to write a line or two, I am delighted to hear that your cough is better. George assures me that, with proper care on your part, it will soon be removed.

I have no news for you. The papers will tell you that the citadel of Antwerp has fallen, that the elections are going as much against the Tories as ever, and that a most horrible murder has been committed at Enfield. I can give you no private information that you will care to hear. I dined in Bernard Street yesterday, though my Lord Essex begged me to feast with him again. In the evening I went to see Ellis, and found the family keeping their Christmas after the fashion of the old time. They were playing Pope Joan with a pack of cards which, I hear, is produced only once a year, and which, to judge by its appearance, must have been used to celebrate every Christmas Day since the time of Queen Anne. Ellis's beauty is now beyond all description. He can be compared only to the starry heavens. His wife however seems quite content with her speckledy husband. I, however, say with the judicious poet.

> I never thought, in all my life,
> That good could come, I wow,
> Of giving to a Christian
> The diseases of a cow.
> Ellis was waccinated:
> Yet now you see he's peppered,
> And comes out of his bed-room
> As spotty as a leopard.

Perhaps this small-pox is a judgment upon him for allowing card-playing in his house on Christmas Day. If so, you will, I hope, take warning and not go to see Matthews. The great Dr Styles of Brighton, in his book on the stage, pronounces acting to be a far more heinous sin than even card-playing. And you, who are so happy as to be near to that illustrious man, will surely not neglect his admonitions. Remember that beautiful epigram of a Christian poet.

> Ye fools, no longer after Matthews roam.
> Take his example. Be, like him, *at home*.[1]

So now I have made a letter out of nothing at all. Farewell, dearest. Kindest love to Margaret and to our brothers. Is it true that Faithful the member for Brighton is dead. If it is we shall, I trust, be able to find a Hopeful to succeed him. There is a better pun than either of Margaret's.

Ever yours, dearest,

T B M

[Thomas Babington Macaulay]

---

[1] Matthews' 'At Homes' were a series of entertainments, including songs, imitations, recitations, and the like, which began in 1808.

❦ 15 ❦

DEATH, DISASTERS AND DESPAIR

1794

Monday 22 December   Gave to the poor People of Weston against Xmas as usual, 57 in Number at 6ᵈ each 1.8.6. Mr Stoughton of Sparham about 3 o'clock this Afternoon brought us a brace of Partridges, just as we had sat down to dinner, having been shooting at Weston all the Morning, and he dined and spent the Afternoon with us, till near 6 o'clock. We had for dinner to day, a boiled Tongue with Mashed Potatoes and Turnips & a Loin of Veal rosted.

Wednesday 24 December   Last Night was so very cold with a very high rough Easterly Wind and very severe frost besides, that we had but very little Sleep. It froze very sharp within doors all the Night. The Wind being high made our Windows rattle all Night being Easterly. It froze sharp in the back-house this Morn' after 11 o'clock. Water from the Well froze in a few Minutes. I think that I never felt the cold so much before.

Thursday 25 December   Xmas day. We breakfasted, dined, &c. again at home. It was very cold indeed this Morning, and the Snow in many Places quite deep, with an E. Wind. About 11 this Morning I walked to Church and read Prayers & administered the Holy Sacrament. Had but few Communicants the Weather so bad. Gave at the Altar for an Offering 0.2.6. Immediately after the Morning Service so far as before the administration of the H. Sacrament I was attacked with an Epileptic Fit, and fainted away in my Desk, but thank God! soon recovered and went through the remaining part of my duty. Mr & Mrs Girling, Mr & Mrs Howlett, Mr St. Andrews, Mr Hardy &c. &c. were much alarmed and were very kind to Me, during the fit and after. The Weather being so severely cold, which I could never escape from feeling its effect at all times, affected me so much this Morning, that made me faint away, what I always was afraid of for some Winters past, having often had many fears. Mr Howlett after Service, very kindly offered to drive me home in his Cart, but as I was better I declined it, however hope that I shall not forget his civility. After Service was over, I walked into Mr

Stephen Andrews' House, and having warmed myself, I walked home and thank God, got home very well. Mr Stephen Andrews & Family behaved very kindly. After I got home and had something warm to drink, I soon got tolerably well, but could only eat some plumb Pudding & a few Potatoes. Nancy was much alarmed when she first heard of it. Eliz. Case, Widow, Ned Howes, Thos. Atterton Senr., Christ. Dunnell, Robert Downing, and my Clerk Thos. Thurston, all dined at my House to day being Christmas Day, & each had a Shilling o.6.o. A very fine Sirloin of Beef rosted and plenty of plumb Puddings for dinner & strong beer after. Took some Rhubarb going to bed.

Friday 26 December   Thank God! had a pretty good Night last Night, and I hope am something better, but rather languid & low. Could eat but very little for dinner to day. Appetite bad. To Weston Ringers, gave o.2.6. To Christmas Boxes &c. gave o.4.o. Dinner to day, Calfs Fry & Rabbit rosted. I drank plentifully of Port Wine after dinner, instead of one Glass, drank 7 or 8 Wine Glasses, and it seemed to do me much good, being better for it.

Revd James Woodforde, *The Diary of a Country Parson*

Keats's Last Christmas

By the second half of December, his blood-spitting was less, but his mental condition was at its worst. He ran through all his past life, his friends, his love-affair. Tom's death, as always, obsessed him. Again and again, he returned to the notion that he too was dying of a broken heart. Memories of Tom led him into insane delusions of persecution. Long before, in one of his less sane moods, he had himself threatened to poison Wells for what he considered the fatal hoax. Now, by a ghastly distortion of his own threat, he seemed under the firm conviction that poison was administered to him by someone in London. In his delirium, he may have thought that Wells had used his own threatened means of revenge.

Above all, he horrified Severn, who had been at his bedside for all but two hours of the past fortnight, by raging against the comfort of Christian consolation which his friend had, and which was denied him by his own unbelief. On the night of 23/4 December, as Severn sat writing to Taylor, Keats said, 'I think a malignant being must have power over us – over whom the Almighty has little or no influence – yet you know Severn I cannot believe in your book – the Bible.' Denied, so he felt, 'this last cheap comfort – which every rogue and fool have', he exclaimed, 'Here am I with desperation in death which would disgrace the commonest fellow.' He had already given Severn a list of books he would like. These harked back to his religious and philosophical discussions at Oxford with Bailey, the works of Jeremy Taylor, Dacier's Plato, and also *The Pilgrim's Progress*. Severn wrote all night, and when Keats woke on the morning of Christmas Eve, it was to make a macabre bookish joke for his publisher. 'Tell Taylor I shall soon be in a second Edition – in sheets – and cold press.' That afternoon, Keats said it was his last request that no mention should be made publicly of him in any newspaper or magazine, and that no engraving should be made of any picture of him.

Dr Clark could hold out no hope to Severn, nor could even his practised manner conceal from the patient that he was dying. The Italian physician he summoned for consultation on Christmas Eve also gave no hope, and diagnosed a malformation of the chest. Clark believed that, apart from any organic disease, Keats's state of mind alone would soon kill him. Keats, in fact, returned all through the next month to the idea of suicide. At first, he tried to persuade Severn to let him have the bottle of laudanum by appealing to the painter's own interests. He set out, with full medical details, in what Severn called 'the most dreadful scene', the horrors of his own lingering death. It would involve loss of all bodily control, constant diarrhoea, which would need continuous nursing, and which would cut Severn off from all the artistic prospects of his visit to Rome. 'Why not let me die now?' he pleaded. When Severn refused to give him the bottle, Keats swung to the other extreme. For a time he lost all self-respect, and in childish rage would throw away the coffee Severn prepared, bitterly abusing him for keeping him alive against his will, and pouring every sort of mad reproach upon his friend. To keep him quiet, Severn even made a pretence of promising he should have the bottle; in fact, not able to trust himself, the painter had already put it into Clark's safe keeping. When Keats knew this, he transferred his reproaches to the doctor. Fixing Clark with his penetrating sunken eyes, he asked him at every visit, 'How long is this posthumous life of mine to last?'

Robert Gittings, *John Keats*

Upon A Dying Lady[1]

HER FRIENDS BRING HER A CHRISTMAS TREE

Pardon, great enemy,
Without an angry thought
We've carried in our tree,
And here and there have bought
Till all the boughs are gay,
And she may look from the bed
On pretty things that may
Please a fantastic head.
Give her a little grace,
What if a laughing eye
Have looked into your face?
It is about to die.

William Butler Yeats

[1] Mabel Beardsley (1871–1916) (sister of Aubrey Beardsley)

Bereavement

They laid her in the grave – the sweet mother with her baby in her arms – while the Christmas snow lay thick upon the graves. It was Mr Cleves who buried her. On the first news of Mr Barton's calamity, he had ridden over from Tripplegate to beg that he might be made of some use, and his silent grasp of Amos's hand had penetrated like the painful thrill of life-recovering warmth to the poor benumbed heart of the stricken man.

The snow lay thick upon the graves, and the day was cold and dreary; but there was many a sad eye watching that black procession as it passed from the vicarage to the church, and from the church to the open grave. There were men and women standing in that churchyard who had bandied vulgar jests about their pastor, and who had lightly charged him with sin; but now, when they saw him following the coffin, pale and haggard, he was consecrated anew by his great sorrow, and they looked at him with respectful pity.

All the children were there, for Amos had willed it so, thinking that some dim memory of that sacred moment might remain even with little Walter, and link itself with what he would hear of his sweet mother in after-years. He himself led Patty and Dickey; then came Sophy and Fred; Mr Brand had begged to carry Chubby, and Nanny followed with Walter. They made a circle round the grave while the coffin was being lowered. Patty alone of all the children felt that mamma was in that coffin, and that a new and sadder life had begun for papa and herself. She was pale and trembling, but she clasped his hand more firmly as the coffin went down, and gave no sob. Fred and Sophy, though they were only two and three years younger, and though they had seen mamma in her coffin, seemed to themselves to be looking at some strange show. They had not learned to decipher that terrible hand-writing of human destiny, illness and death. Dickey had rebelled against his black clothes, until he was told that it would be naughty to mamma not to put them on, when he at once submitted; and now, though he had heard Nanny say that mamma was in heaven, he had a vague notion that she would come home again tomorrow, and say he had been a good boy, and let him empty her work-box. He stood close to his father, with great rosy cheeks, and wide open blue eyes, looking first up at Mr Cleves and then down at the coffin, and thinking he and Chubby would play at that when they got home.

The burial was over, and Amos turned with his children to re-enter the house – the house where, an hour ago, Milly's dear body lay, where the windows were half-darkened, and sorrow seemed to have a hallowed precinct for itself, shut out from the world. But now she was gone; the broad snow-reflected daylight was in all the rooms; the vicarage again seemed part of the common working-day world, and Amos, for the first time, felt that he was alone – that day after day, month after month, year after year, would have to be lived through without Milly's love. Spring would come, and she would not be there; summer, and she would not be there; and he would never have her again with him by the fireside in the long evenings. The seasons all seemed irksome to his thoughts; and how dreary the sunshiny days that would be sure to come! She was gone from him; and he could never show her his love any more, never make up for omissions in the past by filling future days with tenderness.

Oh, the anguish of that thought that we can never atone to our dead for the stinted affection we gave them, for the light answers we returned to their plaints or their pleadings, for the little reverence we show to that sacred human soul that lived so close to us, and was the divinest thing God had given us to know!

Amos Barton had been an affectionate husband, and while Milly was with him, he was never visited by the thought that perhaps his sympathy with her was not quick and watchful enough; but now he re-lived all their life together, with that terrible keenness of memory and imagination which bereavement gives, and he felt as if his very love needed a pardon for its poverty and selfishness.

George Eliot, *Scenes of Clerical Life*

From 'In Memoriam A. H. H.'

XXVIII

The time draws near the birth of Christ:
   The moon is hid; the night is still;
   The Christmas bells from hill to hill
Answer each other in the mist.

Four voices of four hamlets round,
   From far and near, on mead and moor,
   Swell out and fail, as if a door
Were shut between me and the sound:

Each voice four changes on the wind,
   That now dilate, and now decrease,
   Peace and goodwill, goodwill and peace,
Peace and goodwill, to all mankind.

This year I slept and woke with pain,
   I almost wish'd no more to wake,
   And that my hold on life would break
Before I heard those bells again:

But they my troubled spirit rule,
   For they controll'd me when a boy;
   They bring me sorrow touch'd with joy,
The merry merry bells of Yule.

XXIX

With such compelling cause to grieve
 As daily vexes household peace,
 And chains regret to his decease,
How dare we keep our Christmas-eve;

Which brings no more a welcome guest
 To enrich the threshold of the night
 With shower'd largess of delight
In dance and song and game and jest?

Yet go, and while the holly boughs
 Entwine the cold baptismal font,
 Make one wreath more for Use and Wont,
That guard the portals of the house;

Old sisters of a day gone by,
 Gray nurses, loving nothing new;
 Why should they miss their yearly due
Before their time? They too will die.

XXX

With trembling fingers did we weave
 The holly round the Christmas hearth;
 A rainy cloud possess'd the earth,
And sadly fell our Christmas-eve.

At our old pastimes in the hall
 We gambol'd, making vain pretence
 Of gladness, with an awful sense
Of one mute Shadow watching all.

We paused: the winds were in the beech:
 We heard them sweep the winter land;
 And in a circle hand-in-hand
Sat silent, looking each at each.

Then echo-like our voices rang;
   We sung, tho' every eye was dim,
   A merry song we sang with him
Last year: impetuously we sang:

We ceased: a gentler feeling crept
   Upon us: surely rest is meet:
   'They rest,' we said, 'their sleep is sweet,'
And silence follow'd, and we wept.

Our voices took a higher range;
   Once more we sang: 'They do not die
   Nor lose their mortal sympathy,
Nor change to us, although they change;

'Rapt from the fickle and the frail
   With gather'd power, yet the same,
   Pierces the keen seraphic flame
From orb to orb, from veil to veil.'

Rise, happy morn, rise, holy morn,
   Draw forth the cheerful day from night:
   O Father, touch the east, and light
The light that shone when Hope was born.

                      Alfred, Lord Tennyson

Empty

One day at the vegetarian restaurant a man sitting at the same table began to talk to me. He said he was an Austrian and that he was very lonely in London. I listened for a bit, then realized that though I saw his lips moving I wasn't taking in a word he said. I said, 'Sorry, I must go now,' paid the waitress on my way out and left without looking back. Poor man, he must have been lonely to talk to me. I hope he soon found somebody more lively to keep him company. That was my only adventure in all those months. The days went on, it got colder, and then it was Christmas.

   I sat in the armchair looking out of the window on to the empty street, for London is always very empty at Christmas, wondering how I would get through the day. The vegetarian restaurant was closed, and I was to have lunch in my room. At about twelve o'clock the landlord – it was a landlord, not a landlady, in that house – knocked. 'This came for you by messenger,' he said. He was carrying a Christmas tree about three feet high. He put it on the table, said, 'Very pretty,' and went out. There was no letter with it, only a card with HAPPY CHRISTMAS, but of course I knew the handwriting. I said aloud: 'Oh, he shouldn't have done that, he shouldn't have done that.' I sat in the armchair and stared at the tree. There were little parcels wrapped in gold and silver all over it. I think there were fairy lights on it. There was everything, even a big silver star at the top. I stared at the tree and tried to imagine myself at a party with a lot of people, laughing and talking and happy. But it was no use. I knew in myself that it would never happen. I would never be part of anything. I would never really belong anywhere, and I knew it, and all my life would be the same, trying to belong, and failing. Always something would go wrong. I am a stranger and I always will be, and after all I didn't really care. Perhaps it's my fault, I really can't think far enough for that. But I don't like these people, I thought. I don't hate – they hate – but I don't love what they love. I don't want their lights or the presents in gold and silver paper. The star at the top, I don't want that either. I don't know what I want. And if I did I couldn't say it, for I don't speak their language and I never will.

There was another knock on the door and the landlord came in. The food was chicken instead of beef, and a bit of cake because it was Christmas. I rather liked the landlord. He had a trim white beard and he lived in the basement. He said he was going out that evening but would leave my supper of a glass of milk and bread and cheese on the ledge outside. On this ledge you also put the dirty plates when you had finished eating, and he'd come up and collect them when he wanted to. He looked at the tree but he didn't say anything about it. He wished me a Happy Christmas and I said 'Happy Christmas'. I said: 'I'll be glad of the milk, I get very thirsty at night.'

'Yes, but don't drink too much milk,' he said. 'Too much milk is bad for you.'

'Oh, is it?' I said. 'I never heard that before.'

'Too much milk is binding,' he said.

'Oh, I didn't know that,' I said.

He turned at the door and said: 'Now, don't you believe a word they say.'

I ate the chicken and the cake, put the dirty plates on the ledge outside, then I picked up the Christmas tree and lugged it downstairs and into the street. A taxi came crawling along. I got into the taxi with the tree and told the driver to go to the hospital for sick children in Great Ormond Street.

Here comes a complete blank. The next think I remember clearly is being back in my room. The tree was gone and there was a full, unopened, bottle of gin on the table. Did I take the tree to the hospital, or had I asked the taxi-driver if he had any children, and given it to him? Did I ask him to take me to a place where I could buy a bottle of gin on Christmas Day, or had it been in the cupboard for a long time, unopened? But this is unlikely because I didn't like gin. Anyway, there it was and there I sat, looking at it. I would wait, I thought, until the landlord went out. The people on the floor below had gone out early. The house would be empty, the street would be empty. I sat in the armchair and smoked cigarette after cigarette. There was no hurry, plenty of time. But now I knew what I wanted. I wanted nothing.

I had gone through about half the packet of cigarettes when someone knocked at the door and came in without waiting for me to open it. I didn't recognize her at first, then I remembered that she had been in the crowd in the first film I'd worked in, the one in which the man cheated at cards. During the interminable waits we had talked and had exchanged addresses. She was an artist's model by profession she had told me, and lived in Chelsea.

I didn't mind her coming. She probably wouldn't stay long, I thought, and there was plenty of time, plenty of time. She was carrying a pair of red Turkish slippers as a present, which she had bought in the Caledonian Market.

'I guessed your size,' she said.

'They fit beautifully,' I said. 'How kind of you.'

She stared at the bottle of gin on the table and said, 'Are you giving a party tonight?'

'Oh no,' I said, 'not a party exactly,' and I began to laugh very loud. I said I'd got the gin because if I got too blue I'd drink the lot and then jump out of the window.

'But, my dear, this isn't the right house,' she said. 'Oh no, it isn't high enough. If you jumped out of that window you wouldn't kill yourself. You'd just smash yourself up, and then you'd have to live smashed up and how would you like that? You must look for a very tall house.'

'I never thought of that,' I said.

'Lucky I came along, wasn't it?' she said. 'Let's have a drink on it.'

By the time we'd had a couple of gins we were both giggling. Everything suddenly seemed funny. She said, seriously: 'You know, what's the matter with you is you live in the most depressing part of London. I really hate Bloomsbury. I wouldn't live here for anything. You ought to live in Chelsea, as I do, you'd soon cheer up. I don't live there just because most of the men I sit for do, I really like it. But you know, it's a shame, a lot of rich sugars are flocking to Chelsea, they take all the studios. They grab all the studios and the real artists can't afford them any more. Gosh, if they knew how they were hated they'd stay away.'

We had some more gin. 'You know,' she said, 'if you like, I could easily get a room for you. Would you like me to?'

By this time everything seemed so funny I could only giggle: 'Oh yes, I'd come, why not?' She said she was leaving London for a few weeks but would post me the address when she got it. After she left I had some more gin and went to sleep.

Jean Rhys, Smile Please

1801

Friday 25 December Christmas Day. A very bad day – we drank tea at John Fisher's – we were unable to walk. I went to bed after dinner. The roads very slippery. We received a letter from Coleridge while we were at John Fisher's – a terrible night – little John brought the letter. Coleridge poorly but better – his letter made us uneasy about him. I was glad I was not by myself when I received it.

Dorothy Wordsworth

To Lady Hesketh

The Lodge, Dec. 24, 1787.

My dearest Cousin,

. . . This morning had very near been a tragical one to me, beyond all that have ever risen upon me. Mrs Unwin rose as usual at seven o'clock; at eight she came to me, and showed me her bed-gown with a great piece burnt out of it. Having lighted her fire, which she always lights herself, she placed the candle upon the hearth. In a few moments it occurred to her that, if it continued there, it might possibly set fire to her clothes, therefore she put it out. But in fact, though she had not the least suspicion of it, her clothes were on fire at that very time. She found herself uncommonly annoyed by smoke, such as brought the water into her eyes; supposing that some of the billets might lie too forward, she disposed them differently; but finding the smoke increase, and grow more troublesome (for by this time the room was filled with it), she cast her eye downward, and perceived not only her bed-gown, but her petticoat on fire. She had the presence of mind to gather them in her hand, and plunge them immediately into the basin, by which means the general conflagration of her person, which must probably have ensued in a few moments, was effectually prevented. Thus was that which I have often heard from the pulpit, and have often had occasion myself to observe, most clearly illustrated, – that, secure as we may sometimes seem to ourselves, we are in reality never so safe as to have no need of a super-intending Providence. Danger can never be at a distance from creatures who dwell in houses of clay. Therefore take care of thyself, gentle Yahoo! and may a more vigilant than thou care for thee . . .

Ever thine, most truly,

W[illia]m. Cowper

1711

25 *December* I wish MD a merry Christmas, and many a one; but mine is melancholy: I durst not go to church today, finding myself a little out of order, and it snowing prodigiously, and freezing. At noon I went to Mrs Van, who had this week engaged me to dine there today: and there I received the news, that poor Mrs Long died at Lynn in Norfolk on Saturday last, at four in the morning; she was sick but four hours. We suppose it was the asthma, which she was subject to as well as the dropsy, as she sent me word in her last letter, written about five weeks ago; but then said she was recovered. I never was more afflicted at any death. The poor creature had retired to Lynn two years ago, to live cheap, and pay her debts. In her last letter she told me she hoped to be easy by Christmas; and she kept her word, although she meant it otherwise. She had all sorts of amiable qualities, and no ill ones, but the indiscretion of too much neglecting her own affairs. She had two thousand pounds left her by an old grandmother, with which she intended to pay her debts, and live on an annuity she had of one hundred pounds a year, and Newburg-house, which would be about sixty pounds more. That odious grandmother living so long, forced her to retire; for the two thousand pounds was settled on her after the old woman's death, yet her brute of a brother, Sir James Long, would not advance it for her; else she might have paid her debts, and continued here, and lived still: I believe melancholy helped her on to her grave. I have ordered a paragraph to be put in the *Post-boy*, giving an account

of her death, and making honourable mention of her; which is all I can do to serve her memory: but one reason was spite; for, her brother would fain have her death a secret, to save the charge of bringing her up here to bury her, or going into mourning. Pardon all this, for the sake of a poor creature I had so much friendship for . . .

Jonathan Swift, *Journal to Stella*

🌿 16 🌿

CHRISTMAS CHARITY

In the Workhouse, Christmas Day

It was Christmas Day in the Workhouse,
　And the cold bare walls are bright
With garlands of green and holly,
　And the place is a pleasant sight:
For with clean-washed hands and faces,
　In a long and hungry line
The paupers sit at the tables,
　For this is the hour they dine.

And the guardians and their ladies,
　Although the wind is east,
Have come in their furs and wrappers,
　To watch their charges feast;
To smile and be condescending,
　Put pudding on pauper plates,
To be hosts at the workhouse banquet
　They've paid for – with the rates.

Oh, the paupers are meek and lowly
　With their 'Thank'ee kindly, mum's';
So long as they fill their stomachs,
　What matter it whence it comes?
But one of the old men mutters,
　And pushes his plate aside:
'Great God!' he cries: 'but it chokes me!
　For this is the day *she* died.'

The guardians gazed in horror,
　The master's face went white;

[295]

'Did a pauper refuse their pudding?'
    'Could their ears believe aright?'
Then the ladies clutched their husbands,
    Thinking the man would die,
Struck by a bolt or something,
    By the outraged One on high.

But the pauper sat for a moment,
    Then rose 'mid a silence grim,
For the others had ceased to chatter,
    And trembled in every limb.
He looked at the guardian's ladies,
    Then, eyeing their lords, he said,
'I eat not the food of villains
    Whose hands are foul and red:

'Whose victims cry for vengeance
    From their dank unhallowed graves.'
'He's drunk,' said the workhouse master,
    'Or else he's mad, and raves.'
'Not drunk or mad,' cried the pauper,
    'But only a hunted beast,
Who, torn by the hounds and mangled,
    Declines the vulture's feast.

'I care not a curse for the guardians,
    And I won't be dragged away.
Just let me have the fit out,
    It's only on Christmas Day
That the black past comes to goad me,
    And prey on my burning brain;
I'll tell you the rest in a whisper –
    I swear I won't shout again.

'Keep your hands off me, curse you!
    Hear me right out to the end.
You come here to see how the paupers
    The season of Christmas spend.
You come here to watch us feeding,
    As they watch the captured beast.

Hear why a penniless pauper
    Spits on your paltry feast.

'Do you think I will take your bounty,
    And let you smile and think
You're doing a noble action
    With the parish's meat and drink?
Where is my wife, you traitors –
    The poor old wife you slew?
Yes, by the God above us,
    My Nance was killed by you!

'Last winter my wife lay dying,
    Starved in a filthy den;
I had never been to the parish –
    I came to the parish then.
I swallowed my pride in coming,
    For, ere the ruin came,
I held up my head as a trader,
    And I bore a spotless name.

'I came to the parish, craving
    Bread for a starving wife,
Bread for the woman who'd loved me
    Through fifty years of my life.
And what do you think they told me,
    Mocking my awful grief?
That "the House" was open to us,
    But they wouldn't give "out relief ".

'I slunk to the filthy alley –
    'Twas a cold, raw Christmas Eve –
And the bakers' shops were open,
    Tempting a man to thieve;
But I clenched my fist together,
    Holding my head awry,
So I came to her empty-handed,
    And mournfully told her why.

'Then I told her "the House" was open;
 She had heard of the ways of *that*,
For her bloodless cheeks went crimson,
 And up in her rags she sat,
Crying, "Bide the Christmas here, John,
 We've never had one apart;
I think I can bear the hunger, –
 The other would break my heart."

'All through that eve I watched her,
 Holding her hand in mine,
Praying the Lord, and weeping
 Till my lips were salt with brine.
I asked her once if she hungered,
 And as she answered "No",
The moon shone in at the window
 Set in a wreath of snow.

'Then the room was bathed with glory,
 And I saw in my darling's eyes
The far-away look of wonder
 That comes when the spirit flies;
And her lips were parched and parted,
 And her reason came and went,
For she raved of our home in Devon,
 Where our happiest years were spent.

'And the accents, long forgotten,
 Came back to the tongue once more,
For she talked like the country lassie
 I woo'd by the Devon shore.
Then she rose to her feet and trembled,
 And fell on the rags and moaned.
And, "Give me a crust – I'm famished –
 For the love of God!" she groaned.

'I rushed from the room like a madman,
 And flew to the workhouse gate,
Crying, "Food for a dying woman!"
 And the answer came, "Too late".

They drove me away with curses;
   Then I fought with a dog in the street,
And tore from the mongrel's clutches
   A crust he was trying to eat.

'Back, through the filthy by-lanes!
   Back, through the trampled slush!
Up to the crazy garret,
   Wrapped in an awful hush.
My heart sank down at the threshold,
   And I paused with a sudden thrill,
For there in the silv'ry moonlight
   My Nance lay, cold and still.

'Up to the blackened ceiling
   The sunken eyes were cast –
I knew on those lips all bloodless
   My name had been the last;
She'd called for her absent husband –
   O God! had I but known! –
Had called in vain, and in anguish
   Had died in that den – *alone.*

'Yes, there, in a land of plenty,
   Lay a loving woman dead,
Cruelly starved and murdered
   For a loaf of parish bread.
At yonder gate, last Christmas,
   I craved for a human life.
You, who would feast us paupers,
   What of my murdered wife!

'There, get ye gone to your dinners;
   Don't mind me in the least;
Think of the happy paupers
   Eating your Christmas feast;
And when you recount their blessings
   In your smug parochial way,
Say what you did for *me*, too,
   Only last Christmas Day.'

George R. Sims

[299]

It is a Christmas thought to be heartily glad that George Cannon, the Superintendent of the Casual Ward at St Giles's, who caused the death of a child by refusing to receive it, with its mother, on a vile night, and who stuck to his brutal lie that the mother was drunk, will spend his Christmas Day in gaol, and some three hundred and sixty days after in that edifice; at hard labour. And I hope the officials will take care that it *is* hard.

Punch, 28 December 1872

Chef's Special

Free from regular working hours, Soyer spent even more time than before on charitable work, superintending the running and improvement of soup-kitchens in Ham Yard and Leicester Square. To get funds to support them, he organized a grand ball in Willis's Rooms, at which the *beau monde* danced to Jullien's band, and between dances watched Soyer exhibit all the newest methods of cooking by gas. In Ham Yard a Christmas dinner was served to twenty-two thousand of the poorest of the poor, the *pièce de résistance* of the feast being Soyer's old favourite, an ox roasted whole by gas. Knowing that it was not enough to feed the body alone, he engaged a band to play during the dinner, and knives and forks moved briskly to the 'waltzes, polkas and merry tunes' which were performed . . .

CHRISTMAS DINNER IN HAM YARD TO 22,000 OF THE POOR

9000	pounds of roast and baked meat
178	beef pies
50	hare pies
60	rabbit pies
50	pork and mutton pies

Each weighed between ten and thirty pounds; one of them, the 'monster pie', weighed sixty pounds

20	roast geese
5000	pints of porter
3300	pounds of potatoes
5000	pounds of plum pudding
50	cakes
6000	half-quartern loaves
1	cask of biscuits
18	bushels of Spanish nuts
18	bushels of chestnuts
6	boxes of oranges
3000	two-ounce packages of tea

3000   three-ounce packages of coffee
5000   half-pounds of sugar

and

One whole ox, roasted by gas – the gas supplied by the Western Gas Company, under the gratuitous superintendence of Mr Inspector Davies of that establishment.

Helen Morris, *Portrait of a Chef: the Life of Alexis Soyer*

❧ 17 ❧

CHRISTMAS IN CAPTIVITY

Christmas Day in Prison

On Christmas Day, the prisoners in Newgate, Ludgate, and the two Comp-
ters, amounting together to upwards of nine hundred, were ordered each to
receive one pound of beef, one pint of porter, and half a three-penny loaf; ten
chaldrons of coal were also distributed among them by order of the Right
Honourable The Lord Mayor. – The Sheriffs have ordered a like donation on
New Year's Day.

Lady's Magazine, January 1814

Inside Story

Christmas Day is different in prison. (By the way, have you heard this old
joke? –

'How long did the judge give you this time?'

'Ten days.'

'Gawd, you're lucky, man. Only ten days?'

'Yes, but they're Christmas days.')

Anyway, on Christmas Day you get plum-pudding. And you don't work.
And the Salvation Army band comes and plays a few hymn-tunes in front of
the main-gate about nine o'clock at night. And some of the convicts sing
lustily because the warders don't stop you from singing on Christmas. Other
convicts, who don't like the Salvation Army, get up on to their stools and
shout 'Shut up, you b——s!' through the bars of their cells . . .

The singing on Christmas Day has one or two rather human aspects.
Convicts are not allowed to sing at work or in the cells or at exercise. They
may only sing hymns at the Sunday church services. So they rather let
themselves go on Christmas Day. (They also hold little sing-songs quite
often, in a corner of some yard, at week-ends, but they can't sing very loudly,

and a warder comes round at intervals to shut them up.) But on Christmas it's all in. And it's queer to hear some of the songs the old-timers sing. Songs that were popular when they were last at liberty. I thought it was sad that you could work out how long a man had been in prison when you heard him sing. You could work out the number of years by his repertoire. I wonder if it is the same thing with a caged singing bird: if the bird remembers only the notes that he heard in the woodland, long ago and far away.

But there were other songs that you couldn't guess the length of a man's incarceration by. They were the genuine prison songs, which I had never heard before, and which I have never heard since coming out of prison. These songs could never be sung very loudly. About half-a-dozen convicts would gather together, against a wall or in some corner a good distance away from a warder, and they would sing. And because they had to sing softly, their songs had a quality of nostalgic fragrance and honeysuckle wistfulness that they would not have had, if they were roared out throatily from full lungs. The prison songs fascinated me. I felt they could have been composed only in a prison. And I felt that the right place for singing them was within the walls of a prison. Many of them were dagga rookers' songs. There is something about these prison songs that haunts me. They seem to have been composed only for singing softly, five or six men standing in a corner, and one man standing a little distance off to say 'Edge that' when a warder comes too near.

Herman Charles Bosman, *Cold Stone Jug*

Stuck Here Like Outcasts

Monday 6 December 1943

Dear Kitty,

When St Nicholas Day approached, none of us could help thinking of the prettily decorated basket we had last year and I, specially, thought it would be very dull to do nothing at all this year. I thought a long time about it, until I invented something, something funny.

I consulted Pim, and a week ago we started composing a little poem for each person.

On Sunday evening at a quarter to eight we appeared upstairs with the large laundry basket between us, decorated with little figures, and bows of pink and blue carbon copy paper. The basket was covered with a large piece of brown paper, on which a letter was pinned. Everyone was rather aston-ished at the size of the surprise package.

I took the letter from the paper and read:

> Santa Claus has come once more,
> Though not quite as he came before;
> We can't celebrate his day
> In last year's fine and pleasant way.
> For then our hopes were high and bright,
> All the optimists seemed right,
> None supposing that this year
> We would welcome Santa here.
> Still, we'll make his spirit live,
> And since we've nothing left to give,
> We've thought of something else to do;
> Each please look inside the shoe.

As each owner took his shoe from the basket there was a resounding peal of laughter. A little paper package lay in each shoe with the address of the shoe's owner on it.

Yours, Anne

Wednesday 22 December 1943

Dear Kitty,

A bad attack of 'flu has prevented me from writing to you until today. It's wretched to be ill here. When I wanted to cough – one, two, three – I crawled under the blankets and tried to stifle the noise. Usually the only result was that the tickle wouldn't go away at all; and milk and honey, sugar or lozenges had to be brought into operation. It makes me dizzy to think of all the cures that were tried on me. Sweating, compresses, wet cloths on my chest, dry cloths on my chest, hot drinks, gargling, throat painting, lying still, cushion for extra warmth, hot-water bottles, lemon squashes, and, in addition, the thermometer every two hours!

Can anyone really get better like this? The worst moment of all was certainly when Mr Dussel thought he'd play doctor, and came and lay on my naked chest with his greasy head, in order to listen to the sounds within. Not only did his hair tickle unbearably, but I was embarrassed, in spite of the fact that he once, thirty years ago, studied medicine and has the title of doctor. Why should the fellow come and lie on my heart? He's not my lover, after all! For that matter, he wouldn't hear whether it's healthy or unhealthy inside me anyway; his ears need syringing first, as he's becoming alarmingly hard of hearing.

But that is enough about illness. I'm as fit as a fiddle again, one centimetre taller, two pounds heavier, pale, and with a real appetite for learning.

There is not much news to tell you. We are all getting on well together for a change! There's no quarrelling – we haven't had such peace in the home for at least half a year. Elli is still parted from us.

We received extra oil for Christmas, sweets and syrup; the 'chief present' is a brooch, made out of a two and a half cent piece, and shining beautifully. Anyway, lovely, but indescribable. Mr Dussel gave Mummy and Mrs Van Daan a lovely cake which he had asked Miep to bake for him. With all her work, she has to do that as well! I have also something for Miep and Elli. For at least two months I have saved the sugar from my porridge, you see, and with Mr Koophuis's help I'll have it made into fondants.

It is drizzly weather, the stove smells, the food lies heavily on everybody's tummy, causing thunderous noises on all sides! The war at a standstill, morale rotten.

Yours, Anne

Friday 24 December 1943

Dear Kitty,

I have previously written about how much we are affected by atmosphere here, and I think that in my own case this trouble is getting much worse lately.

'*Himmelhoch jauchzend und zum Tode betrübt*'[1] certainly fits here. I am *Himmelhoch jauchzend* if I only think how lucky we are compared with other Jewish children, and *zum Tode betrübt* comes over me when, as happened today, for example, Mrs Koophuis comes and tells us about her daughter Corry's hockey club, canoe trips, theatrical performances, and friends. I don't think I'm jealous of Corry, but I couldn't help feeling a great longing to have lots of fun myself for once, and to laugh until my tummy ached. Especially at this time of the year with all the holidays for Christmas and the New Year, and we are stuck here like outcasts. Still, I really ought not to write this, because it seems ungrateful and I've certainly been exaggerating. But still, whatever you think of me, I can't keep everything to myself, so I'll remind you of my opening words – 'Paper is patient'.

When someone comes in from outside, with the wind in their clothes and the cold on their faces, then I could bury my head in the blankets to stop

---

[1] A famous tag from Goethe: 'On top of the world, or in the depth of despair.'

myself thinking: 'When will we be granted the privilege of smelling fresh air?' And because I must not bury my head in the blankets, but the reverse – I must keep my head high and be brave – the thoughts will come, not once, but oh, countless times. Believe me, if you have been shut up for a year and a half, it can get too much for you some days. In spite of all justice and thankfulness, you can't crush your feelings. Cycling, dancing, whistling, looking out into the world, feeling young, to know that I'm free – that's what I long for; still, I mustn't show it, because I sometimes think if all eight of us began to pity ourselves, or went about with discontented faces, where would it lead us? I sometimes ask myself, 'Would anyone, either Jew or non-Jew, understand this about me, that I am simply a young girl badly in need of some rollicking fun?' I don't know, and I couldn't talk about it to anyone, because then I know I should cry. Crying can bring such relief . . .

That's enough about that, writing has made my *zum Tode betrübt* go off a bit.

Yours, Anne

Saturday 25 December 1943

Dear Kitty,

During these days, now that Christmas is here, I find myself thinking all the time about Pim, and what he told me about the love of his youth. Last year I didn't understand the meaning of his words as well as I do now. If he'd only talk about it again, perhaps I would be able to show him that I understand.

I believe that Pim talked about it because he who 'knows the secrets of so many other hearts' had to express his own feelings for once; because otherwise Pim never says a word about himself, and I don't think Margot has any idea of all Pim has had to go through. Poor Pim, he can't make *me* think that he has forgotten everything. He will never forget this. He has become very tolerant. I hope that I shall grow a bit like him, without having to go through all that.

Yours, Anne

Monday 27 December 1943

Dear Kitty,

On Friday evening for the first time in my life I received something for Christmas. Koophuis and the Kraler girls had prepared a lovely surprise again. Miep had made a lovely Christmas cake, on which was written 'Peace 1944'. Elli had provided a pound of sweet biscuits of pre-war quality. For Peter, Margot, and me a bottle of Yoghourt, and a bottle of beer for each of the grown-ups. Everything was so nicely done up, and there were pictures stuck on the different parcels. Otherwise Christmas passed by quickly for us,

Yours, Anne

The Diary of Anne Frank

Colditz Comfort

There were about eighty Polish army officers in the camp when we arrived. They were among the cream of the Polish army and some had undoubtedly charged tanks at the head of their troop of horse. Although stripped of much of their military attire, they were always smartly turned out on parade. They wore black riding-boots which they kept in beautiful condition. Their Senior Officer was General Tadensz Piskor, and there was also an Admiral named Joseph Unrug.

The officers had all committed offences against the German Reich and the majority had escaped unsuccessfully at least once. They had been prisoners, of course, since the end of September 1939. So many of them had prison sentences outstanding against them that the half-dozen cells normally set apart for solitary confinement housed about six officers each. The cells were about three yards square and each had one small, heavily barred window. These were the windows we saw, crammed with grimy faces, immediately on entering the prison upon our arrival. Thus nearly half of their contingent was officially in solitary confinement!

Time passed more quickly in the new surroundings and in making new friends. The Germans, after a week or so, gave us permanent quarters: a dormitory with two-tier bunks, a washroom, a kitchen, and a day-room in a wing of the Castle separated from the Poles. The courtyard was the exercise area. At first we were given different hours to exercise, but the Jerries eventually gave up trying to keep us apart. To do so would have meant a sentry at every courtyard door, and there were half a dozen of these. Moreover, the Castle was a maze of staircases and intercommunicating doors, and the latter merely provided lock-picking practice for the Poles. We were so often found in each other's quarters that the Germans would have had to put the whole camp into 'solitary' to carry out their intentions, so they gave it up as a bad job.

A trickle of new arrivals increased the British contingent, until by Christmas we numbered sixteen officers. A few French and Belgian officers appeared. All the newcomers were offenders, mostly escapers, and it was impressed upon us that our Castle was 'the bad boys' camp', the '*Straflager*' or '*Sonderlager*' as the Germans called it. At the same time we also began to appreciate its impregnability from the escape point of view. This was to be the German fortress from which there was no escape, and it certainly looked for a long time as if it would live up to that reputation. As I said in my Prologue, the garrison manning the camp outnumbered the prisoners at all times; the Castle was floodlit at night from every angle despite the blackout, and notwithstanding the sheer drop of a hundred feet or so on the outside from barred windows, sentries surrounded the camp within a palisade of barbed wire. The enemy seemed to have everything in his favour. Escape would be a formidable proposition indeed.

The Poles entertained us magnificently over the Christmas period. They had food parcels from their homes in Poland. We had nothing until, lo and behold, on Christmas Eve Red Cross parcels arrived! The excitement had to be seen to be believed. They were bulk parcels; that is to say, they were not addressed individually, nor did each parcel contain an assortment of food. There were parcels of tinned meat, of tea, of cocoa, and so on. Apart from a bulk consignment which reached Laufen the previous August, these were our first parcels of food from England and we felt a surge of gratitude for this gift, without which our Christmas would have been a pathetic affair. We were also able to return, at least to a limited extent, the hospitality of the Poles, whose generosity was unbounded. We had to ration severely, for we could not count on a regular supply, and we made this first consignment, which we could have eaten in a few days, last for about two months. Our estimate was not far wrong.

Throughout the whole war, in fact, supplies of Red Cross parcels to Colditz were never regular and a reserve had always to be stocked. Parcels were despatched from England at the rate of one per week per person. In Colditz we received normally one, on rare occasions two, parcels per person in three weeks. The parcels both from the United Kingdom and from Canada were excellent in quality and variety. The 'individual' as opposed to the 'bulk' parcels weighed ten and a half pounds each and contained a selection of the following: tinned meat, vegetables, cheese, jam and butter, powdered egg, powdered milk, tea or cocoa, chocolate, sugar and cooking-fat. These parcels were paid for to a large extent by a prisoner's relatives, but it became almost a universal rule at all camps that 'individual' parcels were put into a pool and everybody shared equally.

The Poles prepared a marionette show for Christmas. It was *Snow White and the Seven Dwarfs*. They had the full text of the story, and the characters were taken by persons behind the screen. It was a picturesque show, pro-fessionally produced both as to the acting and the décor. The marionettes were beautifully dressed and the frequently changing scenery was well painted. It lasted about two hours and was a great success. During the interval, sandwiches and beer were served and afterwards a feast was offered. The Poles had saved everything for months for this occasion. The beer was a ration, also saved. It was bottled lager which was handed out by the Jerries against prison money on spasmodic occasions. To begin with, in Colditz, it was not too scarce, but by the middle of 1941 it had disappeared completely.

P. R. Reid, *The Colditz Story*

1943

25 December Christmas Day. Very good spirits prevailing. Visiting of patients in the wards commencing very early. I was shockingly embarrassed by my wards treating me to 'For he's a Jolly Good Fellow'! The height of optimism was reached by one lad who told me that he considered that now the pessimists said February and the optimists March!

I am completely sunk financially owing to repair of my shoes 6 ticals, Christmas presents to the 2/2 CCS of tobacco, cigarettes, tins of meat, 10 ticals, and similar small presents to batmen and ward staffs. But what the hell!

An excellent presentation of *Cinderella* in camp in the afternoon. The audience, which includes most of the Nipponese officers, was seated in the open before an excellent little stage built of bamboo. A gasp went up when the curtain swung back revealing the 'ladies' and elegantly costumed men. It is simply amazing what can be done in the way of dress and costume design by mosquito netting and other scraps of cloth, plus silver foil, tinsel and oddments. A most convincing presentation, the only amusement being caused by the well marked scabies and ulcer marks on the legs of the 'ladies'! I saw only the first hour, then came back to the hospital for the Christmas service at which I read the lesson.

In the evening 'Pop' Vardy as Father Christmas accompanied by a Crazy Gang of Brennan, 'Legs' Leigh, Sydney Pitt, Hazleton and others, did a grand tour of the wards making great revelry and investing the ward masters as sisters with a pair of tin 'pectoral projections', a cowl with a red cross, a shepherd's crook and a bottle with a teat. A lottery was drawn in each ward of 2 ticals first prize; three prizes of 1 tical and a few bars of soap. Sydney Pitt nearly broke his neck several times with acrobatics. Marsh did much of the organizing and finally joined the procession as Nell Gwynne. Finally, the party assembled in the concert area and continued their buffoonery investing other officials: for example Harvey, with a large tin fish; Dunlop, an outsize in knives! Tommy Atkins was the most unceremonial, being treated with a final presentation of a thunderbox which was placed over his shoulders with his head through the hole and a jerry firmly jammed on his head. (Spectacles fortunately still intact!)

Bad feeling against the Con Depot staff (the Con Depot meal was a flop) was increased by them not attending or taking much interest in the men during the day.

E. E. Dunlop, *The War Diaries of Weary Dunlop*

Dancing with Death

'In August I was selected for a transport to go to work at Stutthof. By then I was a member of a small group of girls who looked after each other, and although the rail journey north was unspeakable, our spirits were high – at least for the first day of it. We were leaving Auschwitz. Whatever awaited us had to be better.

'Stutthof itself was a halfway house for us. We just waited there until work was allocated. We were sent to a labour-camp satellite of Stutthof called Kochstädt. We travelled there by open train, and that was actually bliss. It may sound crazy, but just to feel the wind on your face, and see the countryside, was a pleasure beyond price.

'Our work was to level ground for an airstrip. We were close to the Baltic, and the earth was composed of sand-dunes. We had to work fast because the concrete-laying machinery was hot on our heels. We were equipped with shovels with which we loaded the sand on to open trucks. It was backbreaking. I found it bearable as long as the sun shone, but the heat made it worse for some of the other girls, who couldn't take it and fell ill. The SS didn't give us much water.

'None of the 800 men and women at Kochstädt died at work because every second counted. Prisoners who couldn't make it were loaded on to lorries and taken to the gas chambers at Stutthof. The lorries brought fresh people back the same day as replacements. The work we were doing was of actual and urgent importance to the Germans, so we were always kept topped up to 800.

'Life was not made any easier by the SS. There was an *Oberaufseherin* called Emma. She was about thirty-five, I should think. She greeted us when she first met us with the information that prior to Stutthof she had been at Riga, where she had personally been responsible for the deaths of several thousand Jewish children. That was so we'd be under no illusion about what sort of woman she was.

'One evening at roll-call I happened to be standing next to a Hungarian girl who casually mentioned that she hoped it wouldn't last long because it would cut down their rehearsal-time if it did. It transpired that Emma was keen on culture and had encouraged a group of prisoners to put a Christmas show together: music, poetry and dance. I thought they were mad to devote precious rest-hours to rehearsing, but later when I had another conversation with the same girl, it turned out that they were weak on the dance side of their programme. They were trying to do *Coppélia*, and I rashly told her not only that I knew the ballet but that I was a trained dancer.

'The next thing I knew was that I was summoned from my barrack to the barrack where they held their rehearsals. I cursed my big mouth, but when I arrived I found that the barrack was warm and well lit. It was a huge room, and different girls were rehearsing different things in various corners. I saw some half a dozen girls prancing around appallingly to an accordionist who was, sure enough, playing *Coppélia*. No one paid any attention to me, and I sat down, furious that I was losing sleeping time. I watched the dancers until I could stand it no more and then I stood up again and said to them: "You got me to this damned rehearsal; now, do you want me to show you what to do or not?" They were all Hungarian girls and a bit shy, but we soon got over that, bridging the language barrier with German and Czech and French, and I started to choreograph them; and while I was doing it, the old energies took hold of me and I really got to work and the thing began to get pushed into shape. I forgot where I was – and then I realized that everyone else had stopped and they were all watching us. So I told my girls to try the dance from the top again, and it still looked pretty awful, but it had shape. I was high. The girl on the accordion, who was very good, started to play a tango. "Dance!" she called to me. And I started improvising to the tango, right there, in my striped uniform; and I got completely carried away. The Hungarians loved it and they hugged me and kissed me and said, "You are a star! We have a big, big star in our midst!" And someone who worked in the kitchens rushed off and brought me back margarine and a slice of bread. I took the food back to my barracks and woke up my friends to share it with them, and of course I wasn't exhausted any more; I was more alive than I had been in years.

'The next day brought me back to reality harshly and suddenly. The tiredness caught up with me, and it had snowed on the site, and the work was hellish. I knew it was going badly with me, and our overseer that day was one of the most unpleasant SS-men. I could feel him watching me, and finally approaching. I will never forget his words: *Du bist auch schon reif für Stutthof.* (You look just about ready for Stutthof.) The death-sentence. But nothing came of it, and my number wasn't called that evening at roll-call. Instead, I was summoned to the rehearsals again. The others had told Emma that they had found a brilliant dancing star, and she should come and see! I remember she sat on a chair and they ran through the whole programme for her – she sat like a block of wood, arms crossed, terrifying, with eyes like slits. They left me until last.

'When I had finished, there was a dreadful silence, and during it she just stood up and walked out. And I thought, oh God, and everyone was terribly depressed. Emma was displeased. I was dismissed with none of my former glory.

'I passed one of the worst nights of my life. Next morning, at roll-call, I was as usual asleep on my feet, vaguely listening to the usual announcements being made over the loudspeaker system, when suddenly I was wide awake – my number had been called.

'I was not kept in suspense long. By order of the *Oberaufseherin*, who had clearly thought it beneath her dignity the night before to indulge in any public display of enthusiasm – or maybe she just acted tough for effect – I was excused all other duties in order to take charge of rehearsals full-time until the day of the performance. Which meant I would be warm and indoors. There would be little physical labour, and what there was would be enjoyable. I was given an extra soup ration. Because it was dry in the rehearsal barrack, I would be able to wash some of my clothes. The other performers had to go out and work during the day as usual, so rehearsals didn't start until 5 p.m.; until then I was free to do as I chose – which meant resting and sleeping. It was like a holiday; the only thing that marred it was that the performance would just be for the SS, but even that objection was taken away. In the spirit of Christmas, the SS decided to let the whole camp see it. And Emma became very enthusiastic, and organized make-up and costumes.

'When it came, the evening was a great success. I had prepared two dances to do myself – the tango and a slow waltz – and everything else went like clockwork. Everyone applauded like mad and Emma's face was wreathed in smiles – she was barely recognizable, and as proud as Punch to be Little Miss Culture. In the enthusiasm of the moment, she ordered goulash to be made for the whole cast of thirty – though when it came it was very hard to eat it with 770 hungry pairs of eyes watching you. Mind you, it wasn't so rich that it would do us any harm, but it was warm, and there was a bit of meat and potato swimming around in it. We had to earn it again though, because Emma was so delighted that she ordered a New Year's Eve programme. The entire cast was taken off work to knock it together in a week. I shudder to think today what it looked like, but in the circumstances it was considered to be high art. Anyway, it too was thought a great success and Emma once again was very pleased – a fact which led to a horrible moment afterwards, for she decided that there would be a post-performance party dance for the cast. We all danced with each other, of course, but Emma danced, too. Of course she chose her partners, and of course she chose me. And I danced with her. The tango. The foxtrot. I can remember how I felt when she put her arms around me . . .

'But I felt that I had turned a corner. I'd had three weeks indoors, with extra soup, and I was that much stronger. I might even have put on a bit of weight. Now that I had to go into the cold again, I thought I could manage a while longer; but it didn't last long, because the Russians were getting closer.

'We were evacuated on the morning of 27 January. I would certainly not have survived what was to follow without the reprieve my knowledge of dancing had earned me. Dance saved my life.'

Helen Lewis, a Sudetenland Czech, in Anton Gill, *Journey Back from Hell,*
Conversations with Concentration Camp Survivors

CHRISTMAS AT SEA

Christmas at Sea

The sheets were frozen hard, and they cut the naked hand;
   The decks were like a slide, where a seaman scarce could stand.
The wind was a nor'wester, blowing squally off the sea;
   The cliffs and spouting breakers were the only things a-lee.

They heard the surf a-roaring before the break of day;
   But 'twas only with the peep of light we saw how ill we lay.
We tumbled every hand on deck instanter, with a shout,
   And we gave her the maintops'l, and stood by to go about.

All day we tacked and tacked between the South Head and the North;
   All day we hauled the frozen sheets, and got no further forth;
All day as cold as charity, in bitter pain and dread,
   For very life and nature we tacked from head to head.

We gave the South a wider berth, for there the tide-race roared;
   But every tack we made we brought the North Head close aboard:
So's we saw the cliffs and houses, and the breakers running high
   And the coastguard in his garden, with his glass against his eye.

The frost was on the village roofs as white as ocean foam;
   The good red fires were burning bright in every 'longshore home;
The windows sparkled clear, and the chimneys volleyed out;
   And I vow we sniffed the victuals as the vessel went about.

The bells upon the church were rung with a mighty jovial cheer;
   For it's just that I should tell you how (of all days in the year)
This day of our adversity was blessed Christmas morn,
   And the house above the coastguard's was the house where I was born.

O well I saw the pleasant room, the pleasant faces there,
My mother's silver spectacles, my father's silver hair;
And well I saw the firelight, like a flight of homely elves,
Go dancing round the china-plates that stand upon the shelves.

And well I knew the talk they had, they talk that was of me,
Of the shadow on the household and the son that went to sea;
And O the wicked fool I seemed, in every kind of way,
To be here and hauling frozen ropes on blessed Christmas Day.

They lit the high sea-light, and the dark began to fall.
'All hands to loose topgallant sails,' I heard the captain call.
'By the Lord, she'll never stand it,' our first mate, Jackson, cried.
. . . 'It's the one way or the other, Mr Jackson,' he replied.

She staggered to her bearings, but the sails were new and good,
And the ship smelt up to windward just as though she understood.
As the winter's day was ending, in the entry of the night
We cleared the weary headland, and passed below the light.

And they heaved a mighty breath, every soul on board but me,
As they saw her nose again pointing handsome out to sea;
But all that I could think of, in the darkness and the cold,
Was just that I was leaving home and my folks were growing old.

Robert Louis Stevenson

Christmas, 1903

O, the sea breeze will be steady, and the tall ship's going trim,
And the dark blue skies are paling, and the white stars burning dim;
The long night watch is over, and the long sea-roving done,
And yonder light is the Start Point light, and yonder comes the sun.

O, we have been with the Spaniards, and far and long on the sea;
But there are the twisted chimneys, and the gnarled old inns on the quay.
The wind blows keen as the day breaks, the roofs are white with the rime,
And the church-bells ring as the sun comes up to call men in to Prime.

The church-bells rock and jangle, and there is peace on the earth.
Peace and good will and plenty and Christmas games and mirth.
O, the gold glints bright on the wind-vane as it shifts above the squire's
    house,
And the water of the bar of Salcombe is muttering about the bows.

O, the salt sea tide of Salcombe, it wrinkles into wisps of foam,
And the church-bells ring in Salcombe to ring poor sailors home.
The belfry rocks as the bells ring, the chimes are merry as a song,
They ring home wandering sailors who have been homeless long.

John Masefield

From Hull to Danzig

It is always rather a problem how to spend Christmas. Forced festivities can often be as tedious as forced isolation, and over-eating has definite draw-backs. Donald, a stranger in a strange land, found it very difficult to know what to do. He had no relations to visit, and he did not like to thrust himself upon any of the friends who had been so kind to him during the months that he had spent in England. For Christmas is essentially the feast of the Family, and it is the only season of the year in which the Englishman instinctively prefers to be surrounded with his relations rather than with his friends. And Donald had to be very careful about admitting his prospective isolation, for he knew that his English acquaintances would violate even the Yuletide sanctity of the home rather than allow him to be lonely at Christmas. When the Englishman does let himself go, he hates to think that others may not be so fortunately situated.

Donald, therefore, decided that the best thing to do would be to avoid embarrassing these worthy folk either by his presence at their feast or by his absence from any feast, and he saw the solution of the problem in the window of a Haymarket travel-bureau. For the modest sum of ten pounds he could travel in a small steamship from Hull to Danzig, spend one day in Danzig, and return from Danzig to back to Hull, all in seven days. Impulsively he went in and bought a ticket, and at 5 o'clock on a drizzly, foggy winter's afternoon he found himself, with spirits rapidly sinking, in the gloomy city of Kingston-upon-Hull. As he stood in the centre of that dismal spread of squalor and shivered in the cold and listened to the screaming trams, he began to regret bitterly his impulse. The only shred of consolation that he could find for the fact that he was standing – cold, wet, and lonely – in the town of Hull, was that he might be standing cold, wet, and lonely in the town of Goole, which, as seen from the train, looked even bloodier than Hull.

The boat was not due to sail until 8 o'clock; the pubs did not open until 6 o'clock. An hour had to be spent in this desperate wilderness of slate and stone and rain before even a drink could be got. Donald's spirits went lower and lower. He cursed that infernal impulse in the Haymarket. He cursed Hull and the North Sea and Danzig and himself and Christmas, and the insane rules for the opening and shutting of public-houses, and the English and England and the weather. At 6 o'clock he entered the smallest, the squalidest, the smelliest public-house he had ever been in and drank a half-pint of abominable beer and fled, almost in tears, to the ship. The ship itself put the finishing touch to his despair. It was very small and very dirty. It looked, to Donald's feverish and distorted vision, as if it was about three times the size of an ordinary rowing-boat. Actually it was about 1,800 tons, and very old. The crew was Polish, the officers Russian, except the wireless operator, who was German, and there was to be only one other passenger. Donald stood on the quay and looked at the rusty hen-coop in which he was going to spend three days and three nights upon a wintry North Sea. And, what somehow made it worse, he was going to spend them in the hen-coop voluntarily. He was under no sort of compulsion. He had taken his passage of his own free will. Seventy-two hours there, in the company of a parcel of foreigners and a strange Englishman, and seventy-two hours back in the company of God knew who.

In the depths of despondency, he leaned against a warehouse and watched a party of dock labourers helped, or rather hindered, by the Polish sailors, struggling to hoist a queer-shaped engine on to the ship. The operation was superintended by a foreman who was encrusted from head to foot in grit and coal-dust and general grime, and Donald was appalled to learn from the company's agent that this foreman was to be his fellow-passenger in the hen-coop.

At 8 o'clock the tiny ship began to plunge its way laboriously down the Humber, and Donald sat down to a solitary dinner – for the foreman had disappeared with his machine into the hold. Dinner was excellent, and whisky out of bond at five shillings a bottle restored a little of the forlorn traveller's spirits.

By some meteorological caprice the North Sea next day was a sheet of misty steel and, after a large breakfast, Donald leaned on the taffrail and watched the distant fishing-fleets and the timber ships from Russia and Finland, and began to enjoy himself.

[317]

Just before lunch the foreman appeared, wearing a smart grey suit and a stiff collar and blue tie secured with a ring, spruced up to the nines. The removal of the grit and coal-dust revealed a thin, clean-shaven face, close-cut grey hair, and a general appearance of about sixty years of age. He talked in a broad Yorkshire accent that was sometimes a little difficult to understand.

'I'm real glad to meet you, Mister,' he exclaimed, grasping Donald's hand in a huge, thin, bony grip. 'My name is Rhodes, but I'm mostly called William, or Will, or Bill, but mostly William. Shall we go in to dinner? The bell's gone.'

Mr Rhodes proved to be a great conversationalist. In fact he hardly ever stopped talking. Donald, who spoke French and a certain amount of halting German, wondered if he would have to interpret for Mr Rhodes on the ship. He also wondered how Mr Rhodes was going to manage when he reached Poland. He also wondered why on earth the engineering firm, which had made the queer-looking machine, had not sent a more educated caretaker with it. For whatever William's technical efficiency might be, it jumped to the eyes that he had not been educated at Eton.

'I'm taking a machine to Warsaw,' said William, tucking away at the garlic sausages and cold tunny-fish and onions; 'a machine for pumping out sewers. Oh! it's lovely. It'll pump out a five-thousand-gallon sewer in eighty-five seconds, all by steam vacuum. I'm going to teach the fellows how to use it. Our folk built it in the shops, and I had the assembling of it. I drove it down from Leeds yesterday – first time it's ever been on the road. But do you know what, Mister?' He leaned across the table earnestly. 'Have you ever seen the crest of the Corporation of Warsaw? You haven't? Well, you mightn't believe me, but it's the upper half of a woman without any clothes on. Can you beat it? And there it is, painted on both sides of that sewer-pump, and me, William Rhodes, that's known throughout the length and breadth of the East Riding, sitting atop of that machine and driving her to Hull yesterday. I tell you I fair blushed with shame as I came through some of those villages where I'm known. It's indecent, Mister, that's what it is. Downright indecent.'

Mr Rhodes made hay of an omelette and ordered a small bottle of beer and went on.

'Have you ever been in Hungary, Mister?'

'No,' replied Donald, 'but I've got a friend out there who says – '

'I would like right well to hear about him,' said William sincerely. 'I spent two years in Hungary once with a machine for weeding between the rows of fruit-trees. It's a lovely country – Hungary, with miles of peaches and apples and cherries, but they were terrible troubled with weeds. Fine chaps, those

Hungarians; I liked them. It was a lovely machine. I took it out to show those fellows how to use it, and I stayed two years. Queer, wasn't it?'

Donald agreed that it was extremely queer, and started to tell Mr Rhodes about his friend who had a castle in Transylvania.

'Just one moment, Mister,' interposed Mr Rhodes. 'I want very much to hear about your friend, but before we get on to him, Transylvania's in Romania, isn't it?'

'Yes,' replied Donald, 'by the Treaty of Trianon – '

'I was in Romania before the war,' said Mr Rhodes reminiscently, 'with machines for oil-boring. I was teaching those fellows how to use them. Queer folk, the Romanians. I was there nearly three years. Do you know, I got to like those folk quite a lot after a bit. Yes, I liked them quite a lot. Queer, isn't it?'

'Very queer,' said Donald with just a touch of coldness in his voice.

'Russia, now,' pursued Mr Rhodes, 'that is a queer place. I was there before the war, with dredgers. We were to dredge a canal near Petersburg and I went out to show those fellows how to manage the scoops and grapplers. It was mostly grapplers – the canal was full of rocks, you see – and some nob or other had got a contract for supplying barges for the machines, a Grand Duke or Heir Apparent as like as not, and the barges were rotten. Yes, Mister, they were rotten. And every time we grappled a rock and hauled, instead of the rock coming up, the barge went over, and the grappler with it. In another month we'd have had to dredge the canal for dredging-machines. We couldn't use our own barges, because this nob, whoever he was, had bribed everyone right and left. It would have been a scream if we hadn't been working on a time-limit – job not done by a certain date, no money. And then this nob would get the contract himself, fish up our grapplers, and make a packet. My word, but it was business.'

'What happened in the end?' inquired Donald politely.

Mr Rhodes blushed.

'To tell you the truth, Mister, I had to do a thing I didn't like doing. But I had my firm to consider, and I've been with them now for one-and-forty years. I couldn't let them down, now, could I? So what could I do but what I did?'

'And what was that?'

'Well, I bribed the chief engineer to certify that the canal was dredged. It was the only way round that nob. He had bribed everyone except the chief. That's a cardinal rule in life, Mister, and I pass it on to you with pleasure, because I like you. Never bribe if you can possibly help it, but when you do, only bribe the heads. Stick to that and you can't go wrong.'

Donald promised to stick to that, and escaped as soon as possible to the top-deck with a book, and saw no more of William until the evening. By the time the steward was ringing the bell and announcing that dinner was ready, Donald was so bored by his own company, by the unvarying oiliness of the sea, and by the absence of anything to look at except the wintry sun and, once or twice an hour, a timber-ship, that he found himself almost longing for a storm and almost looking forward to William's company at table.

William began to talk even before he had sat down.

'Have you ever travelled in Spain?' he started at once. 'It's a very queer country. I don't know that I've ever been in a queerer; not that Java isn't queer too, but then you expect that from black men. But in Spain they're white and that makes it all the funnier. Bone-lazy, that's the trouble. And when I say bone-lazy, I mean bone-lazy. If a Spaniard doesn't want to work, he won't. Not if you offered him a million pounds. I spent eight months in Spain some years ago, digging irrigation canals. At least I had to do the digging in the end, though it wasn't what I went out for originally. My firm built some canal ploughs, beauties, steam-machines you understand, and fitted with four-foot plough-sheaves, and I went out with them to teach those fellows how to use them. Well, I'd spend a week teaching a fellow, and then, just as I'd got him in good shape, he'd remember that his cousin's aunt had got scarlet fever or something, and off he'd go and I'd have to start again with a new fellow. I stuck it for six weeks and then I ploughed the canals myself and went back to Leeds.'

'How did you manage to make yourself understood to all these people?' asked Donald. 'Do they all talk English?'

'None of them,' said Mr Rhodes, 'until you get up Scandinavia way. But most of them understand a bit of German, and I just talk German to them until I've picked up enough of their lingo to rub along in.'

This unexpected linguistic talent in a working engineer startled Donald.

'Where did you learn your German?' he asked.

'I'm bi-lingual in English and German,' answered the engineer. 'You see, my father was forty years in the same firm and he was their representative in Hamburg when I was born. But I can get along in most languages except French. I never had a job of work to do in France in all my life. But as I was saying, Mister, Demerara is a queer place. Rum's cheaper than water in Demerara. Have you ever drunk rum?'

'During the war – ' began Donald.

'I can tell you a curious thing about Demerara rum,' proceeded William.

'Most of ours came from Jamaica during the war.'

'I was in Demerara ploughing drainage-ways for getting water out of canals,' said William. 'It was a queer job, because I had to make a machine that would go through the water as well as do the ploughing. It took me a time to do it, I can tell you, but I hit on a lovely notion. I made a special carburettor that would take rum instead of petrol. What do you think of that? Rum, ninety overproof, at a penny a gallon and petrol at one and eleven. But do you know what I hadn't reckoned on?'

'I've no idea,' murmured Donald, overwhelmed by this flow of technical wizardry.

'Why!' exclaimed William triumphantly, 'I hadn't reckoned that rum at ninety overproof would eat into ordinary steel just as I'd eat into that cheese,' and he helped himself to a cut at the Camembert that made the steward jump.

'But I beat that rum,' went on William, sinking his voice to an impressive whisper. 'I beat it, and do you know how? I got some old tank-engines that had been sold for scrap, lovely engines, all specially hardened aluminium, and I coppered those engines and I fitted them into my drainage-ploughs, and by gum, Mister, I ploughed drainage-ways eight and a half per cent faster than they'd ever been ploughed before in those parts. By gum, those fellows were surprised. I was teaching them, do you see? And I taught them another thing, too. Do you know that they were sending out their folks on foot to work – two hours there and two hours back? Did you ever hear such silliness? I made them see it though, and before I left Demerara I built them a light railway, plumb through a greenwood savannah, too. I don't know if you've ever built a light railway through a greenwood savannah, Mister?'

Donald was forced to admit that so far this experience had eluded him. He would have liked very much to have indicated that hardly a week passed in which he did not drive railways through greenwood savannahs. It sounded a romantic sort of undertaking. But his native honesty prevented him, although it did occur to him that William would never find out that he was lying because William would not listen to him in any case.

'I had to make them a machine, first of all, for uprooting the trees,' proceeded the inexorable wizard, 'and then I went to them and said, "Look here, Misters," I said, "there's all that fine greenwood timber lying there and going to waste. It all belongs to you, and there's money in it. All you want is a couple of sixty-foot steel barges to bring the trunks down the canal to the sea, and a steam saw-mill to cut it up." And then after we'd got the wood cut up, they gave me a hundred pounds to go back to Leeds. They said if I stayed any longer I'd sell them a machine for hoisting them into bed at night and tucking them up; but of course that was just their joke, because I never heard of any such machine or of anybody asking for tenders for one.'

William spent that evening in the wireless operator's cabin – the operator, or 'Sparks' as William invariably called him, was a German-speaking Pole from Poznań who had served in the German Imperial Navy and been sunk at Jutland – discussing the latest developments in wireless and showing the operator one or two small contrivances of his own invention.

Next morning the good ship *Wilno* chugged doggedly up the Elbe, through the lock-gates at Braunebüttel, and into the Kiel Canal, that mighty witness to an overwhelming imperial ambition. For sixty miles, at ten miles an hour, the *Wilno* steamed between the concrete walls, with flat pasture-land and woods and windmills on each side, passing from time to time reminders of vanished Power, great iron railway bridges raised on vast embankments to allow for the passage of tripod-masts of *Derfflingers* and *Von der Tanns* and *Hindenburgs*; deserted repair-shops on whose crumbling walls was still visible the Black Eagle of Hohenzollern; and ruined quays for the tying-up of small ships to make way for the Hoch See Flotte, now lying derelict, encrusted with seaweed, at the bottom of a far-off Orkney bay.

For mile after mile the *Wilno* met no ship in the Imperial Canal, not even a barge or dredger or skiff, except a single oil-tanker, carrying the hammer and sickle upon its great Red Flag, and a string of timber-ships. Ten miles from Kiel the *Wilno* slowed up, and there was a great running to and fro among the officers and much frenzied talk. William hung about the door of the engine-room, listening to the sound of the engines and excitedly maintaining to Donald that something was up with some fearfully technical apparatus that he seemed to know all about. After a little, his expert diagnosis was confirmed by 'Sparks', who had torn himself away from an account on his loud-speaker of a boxing match in Berlin, to find out what was up, and William darted off to his cabin for his overalls. He spent the next four hours on his back in the engine-room, welding or riveting or performing some such mysterious feat, to the vast admiration of the Polish engineers, and the *Wilno* resumed its normal speed. That night at dinner the captain sent William a bottle of champagne, which distressed William a good deal, for he greatly preferred his small bottle of beer, but did not want to hurt the captain's feelings. He insisted upon Donald helping him out with it, and he related during the meal a queer experience he had once had when, after taking a dozen steam-tractors from Vladivostok to Samarkand, he had been asked to survey the camel-route from Samarkand to the Afghan frontiers to see if it could be made practical for motor-buses with caterpillar wheels.

After dinner that night there was an informal concert and William danced a clog-dance and told mildly improper stories in German and sang 'Ilkley Moor'. By this time Wilhelm, or Weely, was the life and soul of the ship.

On the third afternoon the great towers of the Marienkirche rose above the waters of the Bay of Danzig. William pointed them out to Donald.

'Another journey over,' he said, and then he added unexpectedly, 'I'm getting too old for journeys. Thirty-five years I've been travelling the world, and there's only one place I want to see, and that's Leeds. When I was younger it was different. Take my advice, Mister, and travel when you're young. If you get a chance to go to Honolulu when you're twenty-five, take it, like I did. Because you won't be half so keen to go back at fifty-five, like I did.'

Donald asked him if he ever thought of asking the firm to let him stay at home. William shook his head.

'It's the foreign pay,' he explained. 'That, and the travelling allowances. I've got two sons, and until the second one is fair started, I can't afford to give it up.'

'Are they going into the firm too?' Donald asked. 'You said your father was in it before you.'

'Yes, but my sons won't be,' said William. 'I'm only a working engineer, and when I get back to Leeds after the trip abroad, back I go to the bench in the assembling-shop. I've never known anything except machines. But I've saved enough in forty-and-one years to give them a better chance. They've both been to Leeds University, and that's not bad for the sons of a shop-foreman.'

Donald asked him what they were going to be.

'The eldest is a schoolmaster with a fine job near Birmingham, and the youngest is just finishing to be a parson. A parson! That's queer, isn't it? And him mad on cricket, too. They wanted him to play for Yorkshire, but he wouldn't. '"Tis a great game," he said, "but 'tisn't a life." And I reckon he's right. But I've seen him bat all afternoon for the Chapel, or the Scouts. He doesn't get very many runs, mind you, but there's mighty few in Leeds or Bradford can get him out. And the funny thing is we've called him Parson ever since he was a nipper. Never smoked, never touched a drop. No films or skirts. But put him with Scouts, or Boys' Brigade, or YMCA, and he's as happy as happy. Ay! when he's settled in a parish, I reckon I'll be able to chuck the travelling and stick to Leeds.'

'And chuck the engineering too?'

'Nay, lad,' said William, breaking into his broadest Yorkshire, 'I'll never chuck the shop till the shop chucks me, and that won't be for many a year yet.' He held out his two great thin hands and went on, with perfect simplicity: 'I can make any machine in the world with these two. I'm a craftsman, lad, as good as any in the North Country. And it isn't only that.' He laid one of his hands upon Donald's sleeve and said with earnestness: 'There's poetry in machines. You'll maybe not understand. But that's how I see it. Some folks like books and music and poems, but I get all that out of machines. I take a lot of steel and I put it into different shapes, and it works. It works. D'you see? It works as true as a hair to the thousandth part of an inch just as I made it and meant it. I'll go on making machines till my dying day, even if it's only toy engines for grandchildren. There now,' he broke off, as a bell clanged vehemently in the depths of the ship, and someone shouted in a loud voice, 'I thought we weren't going to round that buoy. The skipper's drunk, you see, and he told me just now on the bridge that he couldn't see the buoy, but that the ship had done the trip often enough and ought to be able to round the buoy on her own.'

There was more shouting and bell-clanging, the first officer ran up to the bridge, the engines slowed, then reversed, and the good ship *Wilno* managed to slip round the right side of the buoy. The pilot-boat came alongside and the pilot stepped aboard. The ancient city of Danzig came steadily towards them. The voyage was at an end.

Donald felt that he was parting from a lifelong friend when he shook hands on the quay with William, once again in his overalls, ready to land his machine.

He had learned a good deal about England upon that rusty Polish hen-coop.

A. G. Macdonell, *England Their England*

Aboard the General Walter

Strange little things happened aboard the *General Walter*. The first morning after breakfast I went into my cabin and found the Polish steward reading my copy of *Time*. He had placed it open in the top drawer of the bureau; as I entered, he pushed the drawer shut with his knee and began to sweep. I offered to lend him the magazine, but that only embarrassed him. He frowned and shook his head. In the Mediterranean, off Cartagena, we hit a dramatic storm in which, during a twenty-four-hour period, we not only made no progress, but actually ended a few kilometers behind the point where we had been on the preceding day. The same cape was there to the west, and the same lighthouse. The sailors had not been very thoroughly indoctrinated with Marxism. They blamed the storm on the presence aboard of the priest. It was a well-known fact, several of them told me, that a priest on a boat often caused shipwreck.

On Christmas Day the sun was hot over the Red Sea where we sailed. The captain chipped paint all day on the fo'c's'le deck, because he was not a party member; the man who made the decisions aboard was a mechanic. In the wretched town of Djibouti at a sidewalk café, surrounded by carrion crows, the unhappy captain drank beer and told me his troubles. It was hard to be a captain, he complained, unless you had command of the ship. Understandably he did not relish the humiliation, in front of his crew, of being singled out to do hard labor all during Christmas Day.

Paul Bowles, *Without Stopping*

Sea-sick

When I returned from Calais last December, after spending Christmas at Boulogne according to my custom, the sea was rough as I crossed to Dover and, having a cold upon me, I went down into the second-class cabin, cleared the railway books off one of the tables, spread out my papers and continued my translation, or rather analysis, of the Iliad. Several people of all ages and sexes were on the sofas and they soon began to be sea-sick. There was no steward, so I got them each a basin and placed it for them as well as I could; then I sat down again at my table in the middle and went on with my translation while they were sick all round me.

Samuel Butler, *The Notebooks of Samuel Butler*

1737

Thursday 22 December　I took my leave of America (though, if it please God, not for ever), going on board the *Samuel*, Captain Percy, with a young gentleman who had been a few months in Carolina, one of my parishioners of Savannah, and a Frenchman, late of Purrysburg, who was escaped thence with the skin of his teeth.

Saturday 24 December　We sailed over Charlestown bar, and about noon lost sight of land.

The next day the wind was fair, but high, as it was on Sunday, 25, when the sea affected me more than it had done in the sixteen weeks of our passage to America. I was obliged to lie down the greatest part of the day, being easy only in that posture.

Monday 26 December   I began instructing a negro lad in the principles of Christianity. The next day I resolved to break off living delicately, and return to my old simplicity of diet; and after I did so, neither my stomach nor my head much complained of the motion of the ship.

Wednesday 28 December   Finding the unaccountable apprehensions of I know not what danger (the wind being small, and the sea smooth), which had been upon me several days, increase, I cried earnestly for help; and it pleased God, as in a moment, to restore peace to my soul.

John Wesley

❦ 19 ❦

WHITE CHRISTMASES

White as Lapland

One Christmas was so much like another, in those years around the sea-town corner now and out of all sound except the distant speaking of the voices I sometimes hear a moment before sleep, that I can never remember whether it snowed for six days and six nights when I was twelve or whether it snowed for twelve days and twelve nights when I was six.

All the Christmases roll down toward the two-tongued sea, like a cold and headlong moon bundling down the sky that was our street; and they stop at the rim of the ice-edged, fish-freezing waves, and I plunge my hands in the snow and bring out whatever I can find. In goes my hand into that wool-white bell-tongued ball of holidays resting at the rim of the carol-singing sea, and out come Mrs Prothero and the firemen.

It was on the afternoon of the day of Christmas Eve, and I was in Mrs Prothero's garden, waiting for cats, with her son Jim. It was snowing. It was always snowing at Christmas. December, in my memory, is white as Lapland, though there were no reindeers. But there were cats. Patient, cold and callous, our hands wrapped in socks, we waited to snowball the cats. Sleek and long as jaguars and horrible-whiskered, spitting and snarling, they would slink and sidle over the white back-garden walls, and the lynx-eyed hunters, Jim and I, fur-capped and moccasined trappers from Hudson Bay, off Mumbles Road, would hurl our deadly snowballs at the green of their eyes.

The wise cats never appeared. We were so still, Eskimo-footed arctic marksmen in the muffling silence of the eternal snows – eternal, ever since Wednesday – that we never heard Mrs Prothero's first cry from her igloo at the bottom of the garden. Or, if we heard it at all, it was, to us, like the far-off challenge of our enemy and prey, the neighbour's polar cat. But soon the voice grew louder. 'Fire!' cried Mrs Prothero, and she beat the dinner-gong.

And we ran down the garden, with the snowballs in our arms, toward the house; and smoke, indeed, was pouring out of the dining-room, and the gong was bombilating, and Mrs Prothero was announcing ruin like a town crier in

Pompeii. This was better than all the cats in Wales standing on the wall in a row. We bounded into the house, laden with snowballs, and stopped at the open door of the smoke-filled room.

Something was burning all right; perhaps it was Mr Prothero, who always slept there after midday dinner with a newspaper over his face. But he was standing in the middle of the room, saying, 'A fine Christmas!' and smacking at the smoke with a slipper.

'Call the fire brigade,' cried Mrs Prothero as she beat the gong.

'They won't be there,' said Mr Prothero, 'it's Christmas.'

There was no fire to be seen, only clouds of smoke and Mr Prothero standing in the middle of them, waving his slipper as though he were conducting.

'Do something,' he said.

And we threw all our snowballs into the smoke – I think we missed Mr Prothero – and ran out of the house to the telephone box.

'Let's call the police as well,' Jim said.

'And the ambulance.'

'And Ernie Jenkins, he likes fires.'

But we only called the fire brigade, and soon the fire engine came and three tall men in helmets brought a hose into the house and Mr Prothero got out just in time before they turned it on. Nobody could have had a noisier Christmas Eve. And when the firemen turned off the hose and were standing in the wet, smoky room, Jim's aunt, Miss Prothero, came downstairs and peered in at them. Jim and I waited, very quietly, to hear what she would say to them. She said the right thing, always. She looked at the three tall firemen in their shining helmets, standing among the smoke and cinders and dissolving snowballs, and she said: 'Would you like anything to read?'

Dylan Thomas, *A Child's Christmas in Wales*

To Mrs Sitwell

Thursday 24 December, 1874

Outside, it snows thick and steadily. The gardens before our house are now a wonderful fairy forest. And O, this whiteness of things, how I love it, how it sends the blood about my body! Maurice de Guérin hated snow; what a fool he must have been! Somebody tried to put me out of conceit with it by saying that people were lost in it. As if people don't get lost in love, too, and die of devotion to art; as if everything worth were not an occasion to some people's end.

What a wintry letter this is! Only I think it is winter seen from the inside of a warm greatcoat. And there is, at least, a warm heart about it somewhere. Do you know, what they say in Xmas stories is true. I think one loves their friends more dearly at this season. Ever your faithful friend,

Robert Louis Stevenson.

1870

Sunday, Christmas Day As I lay awake praying in the early morning I thought I heard a sound of distant bells. It was an intense frost. I sat down in my bath upon a sheet of thick ice which broke in the middle into large pieces whilst sharp points and jagged edges stuck all round the sides of the tub like *chevaux de frise*, not particularly comforting to the naked thighs and loins, for the keen ice cut like broken glass. The ice water stung and scorched like fire. I had to collect the floating pieces of ice and pile them on a chair before I could use the sponge and then I had to thaw the sponge in my hands for it was a mass of ice. The morning was most brilliant. Walked to the Sunday School with Gibbins and the road sparkled with millions of rainbows, the seven colours gleaming in every glittering point of hoar frost. The Church was very cold in spite of two roaring stove fires. Mr V. preached and went to Bettws.

Monday, 26 December Much warmer and almost a thaw. Left Clyro at 11 a.m.

At Chippenham my father and John were on the platform. After dinner we opened a hamper of game sent by the Venables, and found in it a pheasant, a hare, a brace of rabbits, a brace of woodcocks, and a turkey. Just like them, and their constant kindness.

Tuesday, 27 December After dinner drove into Chippenham with Perch and bought a pair of skates at Benk's for 17/6. Across the fields to the Draycot water and the young Awdry ladies chaffed me about my new skates. I had not been on skates since I was here last, 5 years ago, and was very awkward for the first ten minutes, but the knack soon came again. There was a distinguished company on the ice, Lady Dangan, Lord and Lady Royston and Lord George Paget all skating. Also Lord and Lady Sydney and a Mr Calcroft, whom they all of course called the Hangman. I had the honour of being knocked down by Lord Royston, who was coming round suddenly on the outside edge. A large fire of logs burning within an enclosure of wattled hurdles. Harriet Awdry skated beautifully and jumped over a half-sunken punt. Arthur Law skating jumped over a chair on its legs.

Wednesday, 28 December   An inch of snow fell last night and as we walked to Draycot to skate the snow storm began again. As we passed Langley Burrell Church we heard the strains of the quadrille band on the ice at Draycot. The afternoon grew murky and when we began to skate the air was thick with falling snow. But it soon stopped and gangs of labourers were at work immediately sweeping away the new fallen snow and skate cuttings of ice. The Lancers was beautifully skated. When it grew dark the ice was lighted with Chinese lanterns, and the intense glare of blue, green, and crimson lights and magnesium riband made the whole place as light as day. Then people skated with torches.

Revd Francis Kilvert

Hill Christmas

They came over the snow to the bread's
purer snow, fumbled it in their huge
hands, put their lips to it
like beasts, stared into the dark chalice
where the wine shone, felt it sharp
on their tongue, shivered as at a sin
remembered, and heard love cry
momentarily in their hearts' manger.

They rose and went back to their poor
holdings, naked in the bleak light
of December. Their horizon contracted
to the one small, stone-riddled field
with its tree, where the weather was nailing
the appalled body that had not asked to be born.

R. S. Thomas

Cambridgeport Christmas

Ice aches and eases
underfoot:
a luscious pleasure
for the solitary walker,
where morning flings its shadows,

extravagant and pat,
across playground and parking-lot.
Cars are stunned
by a Yuletide smother-love.
Bushes weigh

their meted dollops,
and the boxy clapboard churches
are drenched and cleansed
by a piquant light from the east.
One for every block,

they favour a dapper
domestic garrison air.
Time now to register
pangs of accord
between each yearning object

and its heaven-sent word,
before cars cough and lurch to life,
dislodging snow,
and churches receive
their annual revellers,

the strenuous, frowning carollers.

Christopher Reid

❦ 20 ❧

HOT CHRISTMASES

Christmas in India

Dim dawn behind the tamarisks – the sky is saffron-yellow –
   As the women in the village grind the corn,
And the parrots seek the river-side, each calling to his fellow
   That the Day, the staring Eastern Day, is born.
     O the white dust on the highway! O the stenches in the byway!
      O the clammy fog that hovers over earth!
     And at Home they're making merry 'neath the white and scarlet
       berry –
      What part have India's exiles in their mirth?

Full day behind the tamarisks – the sky is blue and staring –
   As the cattle crawl afield beneath the yoke,
And they bear One o'er the field-path, who is past all hope or caring,
   To the ghat below the curling wreaths of smoke.
     Call on Rama, going slowly, as ye bear a brother lowly –
      Call on Rama – he may hear, perhaps, your voice!
     With our hymn-books and our psalters we appeal to other altars,
      And to-day we bid 'good Christian men rejoice'!

High noon behind the tamarisks – the sun is hot above us –
   As at Home the Christmas Day is breaking wan.
They will drink our healths at dinner – those who tell us how they love us,
   And forget us till another year be gone!
     O the toil that knows no breaking! O the *Heimweh*, ceaseless, aching!
      O the black dividing Sea and alien Plain!
     Youth was cheap – wherefore we sold it. Gold was good – we
      hoped to hold it.
      And to-day we know the fullness of our gain!

Grey dusk behind the tamarisks – the parrots fly together –
  As the Sun is sinking slowly over Home;
And his last ray seems to mock us shackled in a lifelong tether
  That drags us back howe'er so far we roam.
    Hard her service, poor her payment – she in ancient, tattered
      raiment –
      India, she the grim Stepmother of our kind.
    If a year of life be lent her, if her temple's shrine we enter,
      The door is shut – we may not look behind.

Black night behind the tamarisks – the owls begin their chorus –
  As the conches from the temple scream and bray.
With the fruitless years behind us and the hopeless years before us,
  Let us honour, O my brothers, Christmas Day!
    Call a truce, then, to our labours – let us feast with friends and
      neighbours,
      And be merry as the custom of our caste;
    For if 'faint and forced the laughter', and if sadness follow after,
      We are richer by one mocking Christmas past.

Rudyard Kipling

1837

Monday (Christmas Day) 25 December I must go back to my Journal, dearest; but having just come from church, I must begin by wishing you and yours a great many happy Christmases. This is our third Christmas Day, so, however appearances are against it, time does really roll on. I don't know why, but I am particularly *Indianly* low today. There is such a horrid mixture of sights and sounds for Christmas. The servants have hung garlands at the doors of our tents, and (which is very wrong) my soul recoiled when they all assembled, and in their patois wished us, I suppose, a happy Christmas.

Somehow a detestation of the Hindustani language sounding all round us, came over me in a very inexplicable manner.

Then, though nothing could be better than the way in which Mr Y. performed the service, still it was in a tent, and unnatural, and we were kneeling just where the Prince of Lucknow and his son, and their turbaned attendants, were sitting on Saturday at the durbar, and there was nobody except G. with whom I felt any real communion of heart and feelings. So, you see, I just cried for you and some others, and I daresay I shall be better after luncheon.

Emily Eden, *Up the Country*

1897

Christmas Day   The others went shooting very early and I rode out to meet them coming back. I met a lynx and saw a mirage of another beautiful tank with palm trees as I rode away from the water. The *Bankwallah* had to leave us before dinner because of some press of business, which was a pity, and we three sat on the shore in the dusk talking. We had a turkey and plum pudding for dinner and a few holly berries on the table, quite unrecognizable, but they had been sent out from England on the chance that they might retain some semblance of something. We arranged them flat in the centre, where, their leaves having withered, they looked like cherry stones. The tent was small and we sat doubled up and drank many healths. I pictured the Christmas dinner tables, smug at home, and thought how infinitely I preferred the banks of Depalpur.

26 December   Up early and off to Indore. Whilst the tents were coming down I painted *Menyanthes cristata*, which I got near the tank. In the midst of this Trilby and Talisman both broke loose and galloped among the tent ropes till it made one's heart stand still for fear they should break their legs. Pat had started earlier and the *syces* had gone on so we had a dreadful time catching them; I got Trilby at last but had to lay hold of her from behind a tree trunk, she is so vicious. The arab looked very fine, his tail in the air and his neck arched, stepping up to his nose and snorting, but it was no joke. However we got off after some delay and rode six miles at a steady canter without a check and reached Ajnod in time to box the horses before the train came in; at five o'clock we were at Pat's house at Indore where we spent three pleasant days before moving on to the little state of Dewas where we meant to spend the rest of our holiday.

Violet Jacob, *Diaries and Letters from India*

Natal, 1862

Wednesday 24 December   Beautiful day, wagon arrived about mid-day. Great unpacking and overhauling of its contents, made our room like a store. Have had very wet weather in town, and, gratifying fact! some people enquiring what had become of me. Carpenter has made a table, and a sort of rocking unstable-footed bench for a seat gives a furnished look to the establishment! Great preparations for Christmas. Norton set to work as chief baker and a currant cake the consequence, lots of currants and raisins, but when we hunted for salt, which we are just out of, could find it nowhere: a lucky thought suggested the rock salt got for sheep and it was impounded accordingly. Set up the grindstone, Phillip assisting me, etc. Day kept up beautiful, clear and cloudy by turns. Fog at sundown.

Thursday 25 December   CHRISTMAS – dawned clear and bright and kept so all day. Had a great set to, plum-pudding making. Had three visitors come to see sheep. Had a jolly good dinner, boiled corned beef and pudding, then raisins and almonds and a nip, oh dear, it wanted two! I felt quite unfit for any exertion and lay down on the floor of the house. Very warm; Henry rode out with the strangers to see the sheep, when they departed. Day kept fine till sunset, no fog, only a haziness from heat. Couldn't sleep at night, what between heat and pudding!

Sunday 28 December   Wet all day, principal occupations, gun cleaning, touching up sketches and eating! Phillip brought in remains of a sheep that he found in the sluit opposite, head down and all the body eaten bare.

Wednesday 31 December   Sheep shearing begins! Some of the rams from Norton's not having their wool off, all hands set to work and got them done by dinner time, 24 rams to 4 shearers. Backs all very bad! Barking posts and rails in afternoon. Weather been cloudy, ending in thunder and fog. Last night another sheep killed and eaten, supposed to be the foul deed of a leopard or panther, vulgarly called tigers in this country, but on examination pronounced to be jackals. Two jackals have been killed by the poisoned baits laid for them. Footprint found in cowdung however seemed to argufy the point in favour of 'tiger'.

John Sheddon Dobie

1937

Hureidha, 26 December

> *Ah, to touch in the track*
> *Where the pine learnt to roam*
> *Cold girdles and crowns of the sea-gods, cool blossoms of water*
> *and foam.*
> (SWINBURNE, *Atalanta in Calydon*)

The people of the Hadhramaut all say that, in spite of the great heat, the summer is their healthy time. In winter they suffer from a cough which settles with fever on their lungs and is as widespread as influenza in London. We all have suffered, and continue to suffer from it. When I returned from my pilgrimage I, too, went down, as the aeroplane was leaving, decided to hasten matters as I hoped by a week in Aden hospital. Alinur was now well again, and the Archaeologist better; they preferred to convalesce in Seiyun, where Harold and the RAF were temporarily installed, negotiating with the Se'ar in the north. It would be a little while before the Archaeologist was fit to begin her work: I hoped to be with them, or very soon after them, in Hureidha.

But who can predict the course of events, even with the help of mechanics? The hospital refused to relinquish me when the week was up: the aeroplane left alone, and crashed while joy-riding in Tarim, luckily with no damage except to its own machinery and the nerves of the pilot: the Hadhramaut was suddenly removed as it were from the Home Counties to the Antipodes. The kind and pleasant hospital still wished to keep me, but I was naturally anxious to rejoin the marooned expedition, from which of course no news was coming through. So I left in a 4,000–ton pilgrim boat touching at Mukalla.

All day we ploughed along the Arabian coast, watching the changing colour of the sea. From the morning's sapphire to the afternoon, shot silk like a kingfisher's wing and barred with luminous shafts, it grew white in the sunset, its underlying darkness showing only in smooth and oily shadows. The tossing flecks of foam in mid-ocean, like tritons suddenly diving, all subsided. The detail of the coast grew clear of haze, the west a stair of gold. Inland ranges with sharpening tops showed thin as paper above their misty flanks. The seagull's crescent wings against the west were unfathomably dark. The ocean, too, darkened like old black cloth gone green with age.

In the morning at seven we wakened off Mukalla, grey and dove-like in the dawn, to a sea alive with fishing porpoises: their sharp perpendicular fins make the small sudden splashes of foam. Gulls flying low above their heads were fishing too; and so were the men in huris, paddling their round oars. Man here is happy; he joins in the activities of his universe: he lives in a pleasant companionship with the porpoises and gulls. The sailor in his ship is happy too among the gulfs and islands of his round world, whose weathers and vicissitudes he shares; his inventions have not outstripped his mind. But we are now companionless in a universe in which we are unique; our pressing need is to find some harmony which once more may include us with forces equal to our own, greater than those our science has outrun.

There seemed to be no chance of finding a motor car from Mukalla for at least a week. It was Christmas. I had accepted with happy resignation a necessity which obliged me to eat a holiday dinner with my friends, when a small aeroplane appeared making for the landing-ground of Fuwa: the postmaster, the mail-bags and I packed ourselves into a car and found the still nerve-shattered pilot and a small spare plane ready to take us on. The rest of Christmas morning I spent with the surface of the jōl below me, intricate and gnawed by water like a sponge. I lunched at Seiyun, and dined at Qatn, talked about Arab history with Sultan 'Ali, met there my old patriarchal friend, the Mansab of Meshed, and continued the day after for Hureidha.

In this part of the wadi, the stretches of corn are almost continuous on the south, because of the nearness of water in the ground. The sunshine lay upon the green like a yellow garment; the houses stood solitary, peaceful and far apart. The land belongs to the tribes.

Freya Stark, *A Winter in Arabia*

Africa

Bilbow wore an old green towelling shirt with short sleeves and his white cotton jeans which still displayed the dirt scuffs from his encounter with Morgan the night before. At first glance he looked ridiculously young with his tall lean body, blue eyes behind the round spectacle frames and the overall blandness of his near albino colouring – longish straight platinum hair, invisible eyebrows and lashes, pink starlet lips. But a closer inspection revealed the graininess of his skin, the thin lines stretching down from the corners of his nostrils, and others forming brackets round his mouth. His voice, which his panic and distress had made whiny last night, had settled into its normal deeper timbre, and for all its comic-book Yorkshire tones it had a genuinely friendly and quietly relaxed quality.

'Merry Christmas,' he said as Morgan shambled through the screen door on to the verandah. He was sitting at the verandah table with the remains of his breakfast in front of him. He gestured at the sunlit garden. 'Quite bizarre,' he said. 'Here I am in a short-sleeved shirt eating – what's it called? – paw-paw in a temperature of eighty degrees while everyone at home's wrapped up warm watching the telly.'

'Yeah well,' Morgan said surlily through his hangover, thinking of last night's events, 'that's what it's like in Africa: out of the ordinary.'

'I've got a present for you,' Bilbow said. 'Well not so much a present, more of a thank you for last night. Saved me life.' He held out a slim book. Morgan took it. *The Small Carafe and Other Poems* by Greg Bilbow.

'Thanks,' Morgan said gruffly. 'I'll, ah, have a look at it later.' He sat down in front of his bowl of cornflakes. He rubbed his eyes. Merry bloody Christmas. He felt hellish, like the survivor of some week-long battle. Surely things would calm down now? He looked across the table at Bilbow – the fine, centrally parted blond hair, the pinched bespectacled face. He didn't seem to suspect anything about last night, seemed quite happy to accept Morgan's version of events. That, at least, was something.

Morgan pushed his uneaten cornflakes to one side and thought about his Christmas Day ahead. First he had to get rid of the decomposing body in his car boot, then dress up as Santa Claus and hand out presents to kids: the contrast seemed ghoulishly obscene.

Femi Robinson gave a clenched fist salute as Morgan swept past him into the Commission drive. He noted there were no guards at the gate but thought nothing of it. It was Christmas Day after all: a holiday for everyone – except for Robinson. You had to admire the man's stamina, Morgan thought as he stepped out of his car, he could do with a dose of it himself.

Fanshawe was pacing up and down on the Commission steps, his face white and drawn with anger.

'Merry Christmas, Arth . . .'

'It's gone!' Fanshawe exclaimed shrilly. 'Gone. Disappeared in the night. Vanished!'

'Of course she has,' Morgan said calmly. What was the little cretin so upset about? he wondered to himself impatiently. Wasn't that exactly what he wanted?

'What do you mean "of course"?' Fanshawe's face was very close to his own. Morgan backed down the steps.

'For God's sake, Arthur,' he protested. 'You told me – no, you *ordered* me to get rid of Innocence's body. Top priority, sole responsibility, remember? Well I've simply followed my instructions that's all.' He folded his arms across his chest and looked hurt and offended.

'Oh *no*,' Fanshawe groaned. 'Oh God no! Don't tell me she's in the morgue. Disaster. Utter, utter disaster.'

'Well no,' Morgan said, surprised at his vehement chagrin. 'She's not in the morgue, she's in the boot of my car.'

Fanshawe stared very hard at him – as if his face had suddenly turned bright green or smoke was belching from his ears.

'What?' Fanshawe demanded hoarsely.

'In my car.'

'That one?'

'It's the only car I've got.'

'Oh my God.'

'What's the problem?' Morgan asked, quickly losing such small reserves of patience as he had left.

'You've got to put her back.'

Morgan gazed out of his office window at the lone defiant figure of Femi Robinson. Surely there was some sort of lesson for him in the man's stupid perseverance, his stubborn isolation? He looked down at his Peugeot standing in the empty car-park full in the glare of the afternoon sun. He winced. The boot would be like a pressure cooker: Christ alone knew what was happening to Innocence in there. He turned away, stoking up the fires of hatred for Fanshawe. If only the stupid bastard had followed his advice, he thought angrily, but oh no, you couldn't have a decomposing corpse anywhere near the Duchess. So flunky Leafy had removed the body as instructed and what had happened? Every Commission servant had gone on instant strike, had refused to stir from their quarters except to announce their action to a startled Fanshawe over his Christmas breakfast.

Fanshawe had sniffed round the boot of Morgan's car like a suspicious customs officer searching for drugs, stopping every now and then to stare at Morgan in disbelief. The smell and the hovering flies soon convinced him that the body was indeed there.

'You've got to put it back,' he said weakly. 'I almost had a revolt on my hands this morning. A riot. It was frightful.' He leaned against the boot of the car and then leapt back as if the metal was boiling hot. 'How can you drive around,' he said with distasteful curiosity, 'with . . . that in your car?' He looked uncomprehendingly at Morgan. 'Doesn't it upset you?' Morgan ignored him. 'Put it *back*?' he said incredulously. 'What are you talking about? How, for God's sake, how?'

'I don't care,' Fanshawe insisted stridently. 'This strike you've landed us in is an absolute catastrophe. The Duchess is arriving here after lunch and there's not a single Commission servant on duty anywhere.' He looked wildly round the garden as if he expected to see them crouching defiantly behind the trees and bushes. 'And tomorrow,' he went on, 'tomorrow there are two hundred people coming here for a buffet-lunch reception. It'll be a farce. A total disgrace!' He rubbed his forehead vigorously as if to disperse the images of milling, unfed and unwatered dignitaries. 'At least,' he said, 'you haven't delivered her to the morgue. That *is* something in your favour. We have a chance of salvaging some shreds of our reputation. You've *got* to have Inno-cence back where she was by tomorrow, that's all: it's the only way the servants will come back to work. That's all there is to it. We can just cope today, but tomorrow we simply must have everyone back at their posts. It's quite impossible otherwise – we'd never live it down.'

'Hold on a sec,' Morgan said, controlling the urge to seize Fanshawe by his scrawny throat. 'I can't just drive up to the servants' quarters and tip her out of the boot. They'll lynch me, for Christ's sake! What exactly do you expect me to do?'

'I'm having absolutely nothing more to do with it,' Fanshawe exclaimed, his voice getting higher as he grew more excited, waving his hands about in front of his face. 'Nothing. Nothing at all. It's all your doing: you sort the wretched mess out. Get her back, that's all I care. That strike's got to be over by tomorrow.' He flinched visibly at the memory. 'It was positively horrific this morning,' he said. 'There we were sitting happily at breakfast, exchang-ing presents, when this mob turns up outside. Isaac, Joseph, all these men normally quite agreeable pleasant types. They were most aggressive and insulting. Chloe was terribly upset, really distraught. She had to go and lie down and . . .'

'They don't think I did it, do they?' Morgan asked, suddenly worried.

'No. At least I don't think so. But they're convinced we had something to do with it. That's why they're going on strike, until we return the body. Those were the conditions.' Fanshawe scuffed at the gravel with his feet. For a moment Morgan saw him as a perplexed and worried man, not sure if he could cope. Then before his eyes he saw him change: the shoulders stiffened, the jaw was set, the pompous light gleamed in his eye.

'Things have got themselves into a pretty fair mess all round,' he stated accusingly to Morgan. 'The Kingpin project's a shambles, we're having to kow-tow to the present government in apology which is the last thing we wanted. Then there's this appalling death: bodies littering the compound. And now you've landed us with a total strike just when the Duchess is arriving. The whole Nkongsamba part of her visit is going to be one long saga of inefficiency and shoddiness. How do you think our record's going to look after this, eh? I'll tell you: absolutely fifth-rate, totally and unacceptably non-British. Now,' he continued, 'I'm leaving it up to you to rectify things as best as you can. There's nothing we can do to salvage Kingpin at this late stage but we can at the very least make sure the Duchess leaves Nkongsamba with happy memories and no horror-stories to tell the High Commissioner when she gets down to the capital.' His voice dropped a register. 'I'm deeply disappointed in you, Morgan. Deeply. I thought you were a man of experience and ability. Someone I could rely on. But I'm sorry to say you've let me down shockingly on every count, so, let's see what you can do to make amends.'

Morgan had watched him walk away. The black splenetic fury that would normally have erupted had been replaced this time by bleak cynical resignation. The injustice was so towering, so out of proportion that no rage could hope to match it. Fanshawe was scum, he had decided, not worthy even of his most scathing contempt.

He turned away from the window and went back to his desk. There, folded on his chair, were his Santa Claus overalls and a large cotton-wool beard. Beneath the seat were shiny black gumboots. On his desk was a note from Mrs Fanshawe outlining his duties and itinerary.

His stomach rumbled with hunger. He had not returned home but had stayed on at the Commission and moped. Around lunchtime he had telephoned his house and spoken to Bilbow.

'Shame you're tied up,' Bilbow had said. 'Your boys have given me a great loonch. Whopping roast turkey, all the trimmings.'

Morgan's saliva glands surged into action, but 'leave some for me' was all he said. Bilbow was due to take part in some festival of poetry and dance at the university arts theatre on Boxing Day, co-sponsored by the Kinjanjan Ministry of Culture and the British Council as part of the nationwide Independence anniversary celebrations. Morgan vaguely remembered the letter he had signed several days previously telling him the Commission could provide accommodation. Under the circumstances, he thought, it was scarcely surprising it had slipped his mind. He told Bilbow he could stay on with him if he wanted, and to his relief the poet accepted. Morgan thought it as well to keep him away from the Fanshawes.

He looked at his watch: 3.45. According to the timetable he had to be at the club at 4.00, where a landrover would be waiting, laden with the presents he was to distribute. Weighed down with self-pity he began to change into his Santa outfit. He took off his shirt and trousers and put on the red overalls. Mrs Fanshawe had added gold tinsel trimmings and a hood. He put on the gumboots and hooked the beard over his ears. For a second or two he thought he might pass out. There was no let-up, he bitterly reflected, no relief from the succession of Job-like torments he was inflicted with. He wondered what on earth he looked like and went through to the landing bathroom to find a mirror.

Mrs Bryce had clearly been at work. A scrap of carpet had been laid on the scuffed parquet of the landing and flower-filled vases were placed on every window ledge. Morgan peered into the guest suite. All was clean and fresh in readiness for her Grace. In the bathroom the porcelain gleamed from energetic Vimming; small tablets of soap and neatly folded towels were laid out as if for kit inspection. The only tawdry element was the plastic shower curtain with its faded aquatic motifs; obviously Fanshawe's budget didn't stretch to replacing that.

Morgan regarded his reflection in the mirror of the medicine cabinet. He did look suitably Christmassy he thought, though the too-short sleeves seemed an absurdly rakish note, his broad shoulders and thick arms making him appear an aggressively youthful and somehow faintly yobbish Santa. He sighed, causing his spade-like beard to flutter: the things he did for his country.

'Gareth Jones . . . There you are, Merry Christmas . . . Bronwyn Jones. Hello Bronwyn, Merry Christmas . . . Funsho Akinremi? Merry Christmas Funsho . . . Trampus McKrindle. Ah, Trampus? Where's Trampus? . . . There you are, Merry Christmas . . . What have we here? I can't read this . . . Yes, Yvonne and Tracy Patten. Merry Christmas, girls . . .'

It took him almost an hour to distribute the presents from the two immense sacks that were sitting in the open back of the landrover. It was parked on the lawn in front of the club. On the grass below the terrace were long tables where the scores of children had eaten their Christmas tea and which were now covered with the incredible detritus all children's parties seemed to leave behind them. The tables reminded Morgan of unscrubbed surgical trestles from some Crimean War dressing-station, covered in blobs and shreds of multicoloured jelly, flattened cakes, vivid spilt drinks, oozing trifle mush, deliquescent ice-cream. Morgan had called each child out to receive two presents – one donated by their parents expressly for this purpose, the other a tin of sweets ostensibly provided by the Duchess – reading their names out from the cards in a booming ho-ho-ho Santa voice. His cheeks and jawbones ached from the effort of smiling. Despite the disguise of his beard he had found it impossible to convey an impression of geniality with a straight face. On the terrace overlooking the children, the parents and other interested onlookers stood clutching drinks. Morgan could see the Joneses and Dalmire and Priscilla. On a low podium to the right of the landrover sat the Duchess of Ripon herself, flanked by the Fanshawes.

After all the presents had been handed over Dalmire strode on to the lawn, clapped his hands for silence and without the least trace of anxiety gave a short speech thanking the Duchess for hosting the party, honouring the Nkongsamba club with her presence and called on everyone to give three cheers.

As the last hurrah died away Morgan clambered down from the back of the landrover, snatched off his beard and made for the bar at a brisk trot. He saw Fanshawe, however, imperiously beckon him over to their group. Reluctantly he changed course.

'This is Mr Leafy, our First Secretary,' Fanshawe introduced him to the Duchess.

'You made a splendid Santa, Mr Leafy, I'm most grateful.' Morgan looked into the hooded, deeply bored eyes of a stumpy middle-aged woman. She had frosted blonde-grey hair curling from beneath her straw turban and lumpy unpleasant features that shone with decades of insincerity, arrogance and bad manners. As he shook her damp soft hand he noticed the way the loose flesh on her upper arm jiggled to and fro.

'Not at all, ma'am,' he said. 'My pleasure entirely.'

Mrs Fanshawe led her off to the official car while Fanshawe lingered behind. He clutched at Morgan's wrist.

'Luckily, we're dining with the Government tonight,' he hissed, unyielding still in his displeasure. 'But what's happening with Innocence?'

'Ah, I'm working on that, Arthur.'

'Where is she?'

'Ooh, about fifty yards away.'

'Not in your . . .?'

'Yes. I'm afraid the car's the safest place until I can work out a plan.'

Fanshawe had gone pale again. 'I'll never understand you,' he said hollowly, shaking his head. 'Never. Just get her back. That's all. Get her back in place tonight.' Morgan said nothing, all he could think about was the drink that was waiting for him at the bar.

'Nothing else must go wrong, Leafy,' Fanshawe threatened. 'Everything must be settled by tomorrow. I'm warning you,' he added grimly. 'Your future depends on it.'

Morgan watched the last lights go out in the servants' quarters. He sat in his car hugging the gallon-can of petrol to his chest trying to stop the car's interior tilting and swaying like a boat on a rough sea, attempting to get his eyes to focus on objects for more than two seconds at a time. He had stood at the club bar and had drunk steadily all evening, still clad in his Santa costume, looking like some cheap dictator from a banana republic with his rubber jackboots and tinsel epaulettes. He had been the butt of much good-humoured ribbing and had smiled emptily through it all, happily allowing people to buy him drinks. Around eleven o'clock his pickled brain had finally come up with an idea, a way of replacing Innocence's body, and he was now waiting to put the first phase into effect.

At ten past twelve he finally grew tired of sitting around so he left his car and stumbled across the road, correcting his course several times, and made his way in a series of diagonals towards the servants' quarters. He was approaching them from the main road side. Between the road and the first block of the quarters lay a ditch, a patch of scrub waste-land and the sizeable mound of the quarter's rubbish heap. Morgan fell into the ditch, hauled himself out and crossed through the scrub patch as quietly as he could, holding the petrol can in both hands. He was glad he was wearing gumboots as they would protect him from any snake or scorpion he might encounter. He awkwardly scaled the crumbling gamey slope of the dump. He heard things scuttling away from his feet but he tried not to think about them. When he reached the first of the old car-hulks that rested on the top he stopped and crouched down beside it to get his breath back. He was about thirty or forty feet away from the first block of the servants' quarters. All the windows facing him were shuttered. To his left he could just make out the tin roof of the wash-place. The moon obligingly cast the same light as it had done just twenty-four hours or so before. Morgan thought wryly that he had not expected to be back quite so soon. He sat down carefully and listened for any noises. He suspected that Isaac, Joseph and Ezekiel would be far more vigilant tonight, hence the need for the diversion he'd planned. He heard nothing unusual. The moon shone down on the corrugated-iron roofs of the quarters, the smell of rotting vegetables and stale shite rose up sluggishly all about him. Unthinkingly, he unscrewed the cap from the petrol can and poured its contents over the floor of the rusty chassis and across the torn and gaping upholstery of the seats. Stepping back he struck a match and tossed it into the car. Nothing happened. He inched closer, struck another, threw. Nothing happened. Tiring of this game he went up to the car and dropped a match directly on to the remains of the back seat. With a soft *whoomph* the car seemed to explode in a ball of fire before his face. He felt the flames scald his eyeballs and he fell back in fearful horror. The car blazed away furiously, touching everything with orange. Morgan forgot about his face.

'*FAYAH!*' he yelled with hoarse abandon at the servants' quarters. 'YOU GET FAYAH FOR HEAH!'

As he scramble-sprinted back to his car he could hear doors slamming and the first shrill screams of alarm. He jumped into his car and drove speedily up the road a hundred yards before flinging it round in a sharp right-hand turn on to the laterite track up which he and Friday had laboriously pushed it the previous night. He roared up to the end of the track, throwing caution to the winds, assuming that everyone's attention would by now be fully concentrated on the fire. Switching off the lights and crashing the gears, he reversed as far as he could into the allotment grove. Through the trees he could see a tall column of flame shooting up from the blazing car and see dark shapes of rushing figures silhouetted against the glow. Fumbling with his keys he opened the boot and flung it open.

The smell leapt out and hit him with almost palpable force, as if it were some powerful genie suddenly released from the dark recesses of his car. Morgan thought he was going to faint: he gagged and spat several times on the ground. Then with the strength and singlemindedness of a drunk and demonically inspired man he levered and hauled Innocence's body from the boot. The cloying smells seemed to seize his throat like bony fingers as she thumped heavily to the ground. He grabbed her rigid arms and dragged her along the path. He felt his face tense and contort into a twisted sobbing grimace as he heaved and strained at his ghastly burden. He stopped for a moment behind a tree to wipe his sweating hands on his overalls, sour vomit in his throat, his heart thumping timpanically in his ears. He darted into the gable-shadow of the nearest block. People wailed and ran across the laterite square, some carrying buckets of water but most seemed to be around at the back of the far building fighting or observing the blaze. Morgan dashed back to Innocence's body, seized it for the last time and dragged it down the path and into the shadow, leaving it only a few yards from where she had originally been struck down. He glanced at her inflated shapeless corpse.

'Here we are again,' he said with a mad note in his voice, then, like some nameless fiend or apprentice devil, he scurried back from tree to tree to his car.

Morgan stopped the Peugeot some distance up the road and watched the wreck quickly burn itself out. He felt tears trickling from his eyes but put that down to the searing they had received when the car went up. His hands were caked with dust from the verge where he'd rubbed them in a demented Lady Macbethian attempt to drive the clinging feel of Innocence's skin from his palms. He felt very odd indeed, he decided: a freakish macedoine of moods and sensations, still high from the alcohol, his nostrils reeking with the smell of putrefaction, a fist of outraged sadness lodged somewhere in the back of his head, his body quivering from the massive adrenalin dose that had flooded its muscles and tissues. He resolved not to move an inch until everything had calmed down.

A short while later he heard the astonished shout and clamour of excited voices as the body was discovered. And when he drove by after a further ten minutes he saw briefly a cluster of lanterns beyond the wash-place. He drove a couple of hundred yards past the Commission gate then parked his car at the side of the road and walked cautiously back. He wanted to change out of his ridiculously festive Santa uniform and he was also desperately keen to wash his hands. He was glad to see the Commission itself was completely dark, though he noticed Fanshawe's house was brightly lit. He assumed the Duchess was being entertained there as he saw several cars parked in its drive. He wondered if they had been aware of the blaze on the dump.

He quietly let himself into the Commission and crept through the hall and up the stairs. On the landing he decided to clean up first before he changed back into his clothes. He tiptoed into the guest bathroom and softly closed the door behind him. He switched on the light and gave a gasp of horror-struck astonishment when he saw his reflection in the mirror. His face was black with dirt and smoke and scored by tear-tracks. One eyebrow had been singed away leaving a shiny rose stripe and the sparse hair of his widow's peak had been heat-blasted into a frizzy blond quiff, like an atrocious candy-floss perm. His startled eyes stared blearily back at him in angry albino pinkness.

'Oh Sweet bloody Jesus,' he wailed in dismay. 'You poor bloody idiot.' Was it worth it, he asked himself, was it worth it?

He had only begun to wash his hands when he heard the voices in the hall. He heard Chloe Fanshawe's loudly yodelled goodnights and the sound of two people coming up the stairs. He felt panic clench his heart into a tiny pounding ball. He switched off the light in the bathroom and stood nailed to the middle of the floor wondering what to do until some faint instinct of self-preservation steered him towards the bath. He stepped in and drew the shower curtain around him, seeking some form of safety however flimsy.

He heard modulated English voices. Someone said, 'Did you unpack everything, Sylvia?' and Sylvia replied, 'Yes, Ma'am.' Ma'am would be the Duchess, he reasoned, wondering who Sylvia might be: probably a lady-in-waiting, chaperone or first companion of the bedchamber or whatever it was, he decided. He thought hopelessly that perhaps no one would need to use the bathroom . . .

The light went on. Morgan froze behind his shower curtain.

'. . . Ghastly little man I thought,' he heard the Duchess say. 'And his wife! Good Lord, what an extraordinary . . . oh I don't know, the people they send out here.' Morgan's instinctive dislike was strengthened by this general slur. The door was shut and he smelt cigarette smoke. He tried not to breathe. Through the semi-transparent plastic of the curtain he could make out a dim grey shape. He heard a zip being run down, the rustle of a dress being lowered. He saw the shape sit down on the WC, heard the straining grunts, the farts, the splashes. Ah, he thought to himself, a manic giggle chattering in his head, so they do go to the toilet like everyone else. There was the noise of paper crumpling, the flush, clothes being readjusted, the running of water from the taps. He heard the Duchess mutter 'bloody filthy', at the state he'd left the basin in, then the water stopped. The door was opened.

'Sylvia?' came the voice more distantly from the passageway. 'When exactly are we leaving tomorrow?'

Morgan breathed again, perhaps he might make it after all. He wondered if he had the time to clamber out of the bathroom window and make his escape across the back lawn. Maybe Sylvia would only have a pee as well and that would be it. He felt so tense he thought his spine might snap. But he had no time to dwell on the state of his body as there were more steps on the landing outside. Christ, Sylvia arriving, he thought. Some obscure need for disguise made him reach into his pocket for his cotton-wool beard which he quickly put on. He heard the door click shut, smelt cigarette smoke and he knew the Duchess had returned. Please God, he prayed with all the intensity he could muster, please just let her clean her teeth. I'll do anything God, he promised, *anything*. He held his breath in agonized anticipation. He heard a rustle, a snap of elastic, the sound of something soft hit the floor.

He saw a shadow-hand reach for the shower curtain. With a rusty click of metal castors the curtain was twitched back. Morgan and the Duchess stared at each other eye to eye. He had never seen dumbfounded surprise and shock registered on anyone's face quite so distinctly before. After all, the thought flashed through his brain, it's not every day you find Father Christmas in your bath. The Duchess stood there slack and squat, quite naked apart from a pale blue shower cap and a half smoked cigarette in one hand. Morgan saw breasts like empty socks, floppy-jersey fat folds, a grey brillo pad, turkey thighs. Her mouth hung open in paralysed disbelief.

'Evening, Duchess,' Morgan squeaked from behind his beard, stepping from the bath with the falsetto audacity of a Raffles. He flung open the bathroom window, lowered the lid of the WC, stepped up and slung his legs over the window-sill. He glanced back over his shoulder. He didn't care any more. Her mouth was still open but an arm was across her breasts and a hand pressed into her lap.

'Listen,' he said. 'I promise I won't tell if you won't.'

He dropped down six feet on to the tar-paper roof of the rear verandah, crawled to the edge and hung down, falling on to the back lawn. As he tore across the dark grass towards the gate he felt curiously exultant and carefree as he waited for the Duchess's screams to rend the night air. But nothing disturbed the impartial gaze of the stars and the convivial silence of the scene.

Bilbow stuck his head out of the spare bedroom when Morgan let himself into the house twenty minutes later.

'Bloody hell,' Bilbow said, looking at Morgan's face. 'What happened to you, Santa? Reindeers crash? Sledge get shot down in flames?'

Morgan didn't bother to reply – he was too busy pouring himself a huge drink.

William Boyd, *A Good Man in Africa*

Jamaica

I was grumbling in imagination at the incessant clamour of the cocks on the morning of Christmas Day, when my ears were assailed with another sort of music, not much more melodious. This was a chorus of Negroes singing 'Good morning to your night-cap, and health to master and mistress'. They came into the house and began dancing. I slipped on my dressing gown and mingled in their orgies, much to the diversion of the black damsels, as well as of the inmates of the house, who came into the piazza to witness the cere-monies. We gave the fiddler a dollar, and they departed to their grounds to prepare their provisions for two or three days, and we saw no more of them till the evening, when they again assembled on the lawn before the house with their gombays, bonjaws, and an ebo drum, made of a hollow tree, with a piece of sheepskin stretched over it. Some of the women carried small calabashes with pebbles in them, stuck on short sticks, which they rattled in time to the songs, or rather howls of the musicians. They divided themselves into parties to dance, some before the gombays, in a ring, to perform a bolèro or a sort of love-dance, as it is called, where the gentlemen occasionally wiped the perspiration off the shining faces of their black beauties, who, in turn, performed the same service to the minstrel. Others performed a sort of pyrrhic before the ebo drummer, beginning gently and gradually quickening their motions, until they seemed agitated by the furies. They were all dressed in their best; some of the men in long-tailed coats, one of the gombayers in old regimentals; the women in muslins and cambrics, with coloured handker-chiefs tastefully disposed round their heads, and ear-rings, necklaces, and bracelets of all sorts, in profusion. The entertainment was kept up till nine or ten o'clock in the evening, and during the time they were regaled with punch and santa in abundance; they came occasionally and asked for porter and wine. Indeed a perfect equality seemed to reign among all parties; many came and shook hands with their master and mistress, nor did the young ladies refuse this salutation any more than the gentlemen. The merriment became rather boisterous as the punch operated, and the slaves sang satirical philip-pics against their master, communicating a little free advice now and then; but they never lost sight of decorum, and at last retired, apparently quite satisfied with their Saturnalia, to dance the rest of the night at their own habitations.

Cynric R. Williams, *A Tour through the Island of Jamaica in the year 1823*

Chilblains and Camels

The vicar preached his usual Christmas sermon. It was one to which his parishioners were greatly attached.

'How difficult it is for us,' he began, blandly surveying his congregation, who coughed into their mufflers and chafed their chilblains under their woollen gloves, 'to realize that this is indeed Christmas. Instead of the glow-ing log fire and windows tight shuttered against the drifting snow, we have only the harsh glare of an alien sun; instead of the happy circle of loved faces, of home and family, we have the uncomprehending stares of the subjugated, though no doubt grateful, heathen. Instead of the placid ox and ass of Bethlehem,' said the vicar, slightly losing the thread of his comparisons, 'we have for companions the ravening tiger and the exotic camel, the furtive jackal and the ponderous elephant . . .' And so on, through the pages of faded manuscript. The words had temporarily touched the heart of many an obdurate trooper, and hearing them again, as he had heard them year after year since Mr Tendril had come to the parish, Tony and most of Tony's guests felt that it was an integral part of their Christmas festivities; one with which they would find it very hard to dispense. 'The ravening tiger and the exotic camel' had long been bywords in the family, of frequent recurrence in all their games.

Evelyn Waugh, *A Handful of Dust*

Touring

Very nice it was to be on an England side two up in Australia. Never before in my experience had we retained the hundred per cent after two matches. We felt now that the rubber was within our reach, although it was plain that the Australians were improving with every match. And we won the rubber while we could, following up at Melbourne a fortnight later with a three wickets' victory. Before that, however, Christmas came, and my wife and I spent it with friends at Warrnambool. A strange Christmas! – tennis in flannels and picnics in the Bush under the midsummer sun, while your thoughts go roaming – not entirely untinged with homesickness, however happy you are – back to the old country and its roaring Yule-logs and crackers and holly and plum-pudding.

Jack Hobbs, *Playing for England! My Test-Cricket Story*

The next day was Sunday, and the next Christmas Day, so there was a hiatus in the game of forty-eight hours. Our Christmas dinner was a quiet affair in a private room at the hotel, where we were joined by R. W. V. Robins. In the evening most of the chaps went out to be entertained in private houses.

I made no rules and regulations about what time my team should retire for the night. I took the view that they were old enough to look after themselves and I certainly had no intentions of tucking them up in bed. It was up to all of them to look after themselves, and if they should have turned up unfit next morning they knew what my reactions would have been.

On both the Sunday and the Monday the sun scorched down on the wicket, drying it right out and tending to widen the cracks in it. From now on the ball tended to keep low more often.

By lunch time on the third day we were not doing so well . . .

Freddie Brown, *Cricket Musketeer*

Second Test, December 1950

Played at Melbourne Cricket Ground on 22, 23, 26, 27 December, 1950
Toss: Australia. Result: AUSTRALIA won by 28 runs.
Debuts: Australia – K. A. Archer.

This match, which included the unusual feature of a two-days interlude for Sunday and Christmas Day, produced a close and tense contest. England, needing to score 179 runs in just over three days to end Australia's long unbeaten run, eventually failed against a fine display by Lindwall, Johnston, and the 'mystery' slow bowler, Iverson.

AUSTRALIA

K. A. Archer	c Bedser b Bailey	26	c Bailey b Bedser		46
A. R. Morris	c Hutton b Bedser	2	lbw b Wright		18
R. N. Harvey	c Evans b Bedser	42	run out		31
K. R. Miller	lbw b Brown	18	b Bailey		14
A. L. Hassett*	b Bailey	52	c Bailey b Brown		19
S. J. E. Loxton	c Evans b Close	32	c Evans b Brown		2
R. R. Lindwall	lbw b Bailey	8	c Evans b Brown		7
D. Tallon†	not out	7	lbw b Brown		0
I. W. Johnson	c Parkhouse b Bedser	0	c Close b Bedser		23
W. A. Johnston	c Hutton b Bedser	0	b Bailey		6
J. B. Iverson	b Bailey	1	not out		0
Extras	(B 4, LB 2)	6	(B 10, LB 5)		15
Total		194			181

ENGLAND

R. T. Simpson	c Johnson b Miller	4		b Lindwall	23
C. Washbrook	lbw b Lindwall	21		b Iverson	8
J. G. Dewes	c Miller b Johnston	8	(5)	c Harvey b Iverson	5
L. Hutton	c Tallon b Iverson	12		c Lindwall b Johnston	40
W.G.A. Parkhouse	c Hassett b Miller	9	(6)	lbw b Johnston	28
D. B. Close	c Loxton b Iverson	0	(7)	lbw b Johnston	1
F. R. Brown*	c Johnson b Iverson	62	(8)	b Lindwall	8
T. E. Bailey	b Lindwall	12	(3)	b Johnson	0
T. G. Evans†	c Johnson b Iverson	49		b Lindwall	2
A. V. Bedser	not out	4		not out	14
D. V. P. Wright	lbw b Johnston	2		lbw b Johnston	2
Extras	(B 8, LB 6)	14		(B 17, LB 2)	19
Total		197			150

ENGLAND	O	M	R	W	O	M	R	W
Bailey	17.1	5	40	4	15	3	47	2
Bedser	19	3	37	4	16.3	2	43	2
Wright	8	0	63	0	9	0	42	1
Brown	9	0	28	1	12	2	26	4
Close	6	1	20	1	1	0	8	0

AUSTRALIA	O	M	R	W	O	M	R	W
Lindwall	13	2	46	2	12	1	29	3
Miller	13	0	39	2	5	2	16	0
Johnston	9	1	28	2	13.7	1	26	4
Iverson	18	3	37	4	20	4	36	2
Johnson	5	1	19	0	13	3	24	1
Loxton	4	1	14	0				

FALL OF WICKETS

Wkt	A 1st	E 1st	A 2nd	E 2nd
1st	6	11	43	21
2nd	67	33	99	22
3rd	89	37	100	52
4th	93	54	126	82
5th	177	54	131	92
6th	177	61	151	95
7th	192	126	151	122
8th	193	153	156	124
9th	193	194	181	134
10th	194	197	181	150

Umpires: G. C. Cooper and R. Wright.

☙ 21 ❧

ANIMALS

Hey Diddle Dinketty, Poppetty Pet!

. . . But it is in the old story that all the beasts can talk, in the night between Christmas Eve and Christmas Day in the morning (though there are very few folk that can hear them, or know what it is that they say).

When the Cathedral clock struck twelve there was an answer – like an echo of the chimes – and Simpkin heard it, and came out of the tailor's door, and wandered about in the snow.

From all the roofs and gables and old wooden houses in Gloucester came a thousand merry voices singing the old Christmas rhymes – all the old songs that ever I heard of, and some that I don't know, like Whittington's bells.

First and loudest the cocks cried out: 'Dame, get up, and bake your pies!'

'Oh, dilly, dilly, dilly!' sighed Simpkin.

And now in a garret there were lights and sounds of dancing, and cats came from over the way.

'Hey, diddle, diddle, the cat and the fiddle! All the cats in Gloucester – except me,' said Simpkin.

Under the wooden eaves the starlings and sparrows sang of Christmas pies; the jackdaws woke up in the Cathedral tower; and although it was the middle of the night the throstles and robins sang; the air was quite full of little twittering tunes.

But it was all rather provoking to poor hungry Simpkin!

Particularly he was vexed with some little shrill voices from behind a wooden lattice. I think that they were bats, because they always have very small voices – especially in a black frost, when they talk in their sleep, like the Tailor of Gloucester.

They said something mysterious that sounded like –

> 'Buz, quoth the blue fly; hum, quoth the bee;
> Buz and hum they cry, and so do we!'

and Simpkin went away shaking his ears as if he had a bee in his bonnet.

From the tailor's shop in Westgate came a glow of light; and when Simpkin crept up to peep in at the window it was full of candles. There was a snippeting of scissors, and snappeting of thread; and little mouse voices sang loudly and gaily –

> 'Four-and-twenty tailors
> Went to catch a snail,
> The best man amongst them
> Durst not touch her tail;
> She put out her horns
> Like a little kyloe cow,
> Run, tailors, run! or she'll have you all e'en now!'

Then without a pause the little mouse voices went on again –

> 'Sieve my lady's oatmeal,
> Grind my lady's flour,
> Put it in a chestnut,
> Let it stand an hour – '

'Mew! Mew!' interrupted Simpkin, and he scratched at the door. But the key was under the tailor's pillow, he could not get in.

The little mice only laughed, and tried another tune –

> 'Three little mice sat down to spin,
> Pussy passed by and she peeped in.
> What are you at, my fine little men?
> Making coats for gentlemen.
> Shall I come in and cut off your threads?
> Oh, no, Miss Pussy, you'd bite off our heads!'

'Mew! Mew!' cried Simpkin. 'Hey diddle dinketty?' answered the little mice –

> 'Hey diddle dinketty, poppetty pet!
> The merchants of London they wear scarlet;
> Silk in the collar, and gold in the hem,
> So merrily march the merchantmen!'

They clicked their thimbles to mark the time, but none of the songs pleased Simpkin; he sniffed and mewed at the door of the shop.

> 'And then I bought
> A pipkin and a popkin,

A slipkin and a slopkin,
All for one farthing –

and upon the kitchen dresser!' added the rude little mice.

'Mew! scratch! scratch!' scuffled Simpkin on the window-sill; while the little mice inside sprang to their feet, and all began to shout at once in little twittering voices: 'No more twist! No more twist!' And they barred up the window shutters and shut out Simpkin.

But still through the nicks in the shutters he could hear the click of thimbles, and little mouse voices singing –

'No more twist! No more twist!'

Simpkin came away from the shop and went home, considering in his mind. He found the poor tailor without fever, sleeping peacefully . . .

Beatrix Potter, *The Tailor of Gloucester*

The Animals' Carol

Christus natus est! the cock   Christ is born
Carols on the morning dark.

Quando? croaks the raven stiff   When?
Freezing on the broken cliff.

Hoc nocte, replies the crow   This night
Beating high above the snow.

Ubi? Ubi? booms the ox   Where?
From its cavern in the rocks.

Bethlehem, then bleats the sheep   Bethlehem
Huddled on the winter steep.

Quomodo? the brown hare clicks,   How?
Chattering among the sticks.

Humiliter, the careful wren   Humbly
Thrills upon the cold hedge-stone.

Cur? Cur? sounds the coot   Why?
By the iron river-root.

Propter homines, the thrush   For the sake of man
Sings on the sharp holly-bush.

Cui? Cui? rings the chough   To whom?
On the strong, sea-haunted bluff.

Mary! Mary! calls the lamb   Mary
From the quiet of the womb.

Praeterea ex quo? cries   Who else?
The woodpecker to pallid skies.

Joseph, breathes the heavy shire   Joseph
Warming in its own blood-fire.

Ultime ex quo? the owl   Who above all?
Solemnly begins to call.

De Deo, the little stare   Of God
Whistles on the hardening air.

Pridem? Pridem? the jack snipe   Long ago?
From the harsh grass starts to pipe.

Sic et non, answers the fox   Yes and no
Tiptoeing the bitter lough.

Quomodo hoc scire potest?   How do I know this?
Boldly flutes the robin redbreast.

Illo in eandem, squeaks   By going there
The mouse within the barley-sack.

Quae sarcinae? asks the daw   What luggage?
Swaggering from head to claw.

Nulla res, replies the ass,   None
Bearing on its back the Cross.

Quantum pecuniae? shrills   How much money?
The wandering gull about the hills.

Ne nummum quidem, the rook   Not a penny
Caws across the rigid brook.

Nulla resne? barks the dog   Nothing at all?
By the crumbling fire-log.

Nil nisi cor amans, the dove   Only a loving heart
Murmurs from its house of love.

Gloria in Excelsis! Then
Man is God, and God is Man.

                                                  Charles Causley

Eddi's Service

Eddi, priest of St Wilfrid
In the chapel at Manhood End,
Ordered a midnight service
For such as cared to attend.

But the Saxons were keeping Christmas,
And the night was stormy as well.
Nobody came to service,
Though Eddi rang the bell.

'Wicked weather for walking,'
Said Eddi of Manhood End.
'But I must go on with the service
For such as care to attend.'

The altar-lamps were lighted –
An old marsh-donkey came,
Bold as a guest invited,
And stared at the guttering flame.

The storm beat on at the windows,
The water splashed on the floor,
And a wet, yoke-weary bullock
Pushed in through the open door.

'How do I know what is greatest,
How do I know what is least?
That is my Father's business,'
Said Eddi, Wilfrid's priest.

'But – three are gathered together –
Listen to me and attend.
I bring good news, my brethren!'
Said Eddi, of Manhood End.

And he told the Ox of a manger,
And a stall in Bethlehem.
And he spoke to the Ass of a Rider
That rode to Jerusalem.

They steamed and dripped in the chancel,
They listened and never stirred,
While, just as though they were Bishops,
Eddi preached them The Word.

Till the gale blew off on the marshes
And the windows showed the day,
And the Ox and the Ass together
Wheeled and clattered away.

And when the Saxons mocked him,
Said Eddi of Manhood End,
'I dare not shut His chapel
On such as care to attend.'

Rudyard Kipling

Mole and Ratty Entertain

At last the Rat succeeded in decoying him to the table, and had just got seriously to work with the sardine-opener when sounds were heard from the forecourt without – sounds like the scuffling of small feet in the gravel and a confused murmur of tiny voices, while broken sentences reached them – 'Now, all in a line – hold the lantern up a bit, Tommy – clear your throats first – no coughing after I say one, two, three. – Where's young Bill? – Here, come on, do, we're all a-waiting – '

'What's up?' inquired the Rat, pausing in his labours.

'I think it must be the field-mice,' replied the Mole, with a touch of pride in his manner. 'They go round carol-singing regularly at this time of the year. They're quite an institution in these parts. And they never pass me over –

they come to Mole End last of all; and I used to give them hot drinks, and supper too sometimes, when I could afford it. It will be like old times to hear them again.'

'Let's have a look at them!' cried the Rat, jumping up and running to the door.

It was a pretty sight, and a seasonable one, that met their eyes when they flung the door open. In the forecourt, lit by the dim rays of a horn lantern, some eight or ten little field-mice stood in a semicircle, red worsted comforters round their throats, their fore-paws thrust deep into their pockets, their feet jigging for warmth. With bright beady eyes they glanced shyly at each other, sniggering a little, sniffing and applying coat-sleeves a good deal. As the door opened, one of the elder ones that carried the lantern was just saying, 'Now then, one, two, three!' and forthwith their shrill little voices uprose on the air, singing one of the old-time carols that their forefathers composed in the fields that were fallow and held by frost, or when snow-bound in chimney corners, and handed down to be sung in the miry street to lamp-lit windows at Yule-time.

CAROL

Villagers, all, this frosty tide,
Let your doors swing open wide,
Though wind may follow, and snow beside,
Yet draw us in by your fire to bide;
    Joy shall be yours in the morning!

Here we stand in the cold and the sleet,
Blowing fingers and stamping feet,
Come from far away you to greet –
You by the fire and we in the street –
    Bidding you joy in the morning!

For ere one half of the night was gone,
Sudden a star has led us on,
Raining bliss and benison –
Bliss tomorrow and more anon,
    Joy for every morning!

Goodman Joseph toiled through the snow –
Saw the star o'er a stable low;

Mary she might not further go –
Welcome thatch, and litter below!
   Joy was hers in the morning!

And then they heard the angels tell
'Who were the first to cry Nowell?
Animals all, as it befell,
In the stable where they did dwell!
   Joy shall be theirs in the morning!'

The voices ceased, the singers, bashful but smiling, exchanged sidelong glances, and silence succeeded – but for a moment only. Then, from up above and far away, down the tunnel they had so lately travelled was borne to their ears in a faint musical hum the sound of distant bells ringing a joyful and clangorous peal.

'Very well sung, boys!' cried the Rat heartily. 'And now come along in, all of you, and warm yourselves by the fire, and have something hot!'

'Yes, come along, field-mice,' cried the Mole eagerly. 'This is quite like old times! Shut the door after you. Pull up that settle to the fire. Now, you just wait a minute, while we – O, Ratty!' he cried in despair, plumping down on a seat, with tears impending. 'Whatever are we doing? We've nothing to give them!'

'You leave all that to me,' said the masterful Rat. 'Here you, with the lantern! Come over this way. I want to talk to you. Now, tell me, are there any shops open at this hour of the night?'

'Why, certainly, sir,' replied the field-mouse respectfully. 'At this time of the year our shops keep open to all sorts of hours.'

'Then look here!' said the Rat. 'You go off at once, you and your lantern, and you get me –'

Here much muttered conversation ensued, and the Mole only heard bits of it, such as – 'Fresh, mind! – no, a pound of that will do – see you get Buggins's, for I won't have any other – no, only the best – if you can't get it there, try somewhere else – yes, of course, home-made, no tinned stuff – well then, do the best you can!' Finally, there was a chink of coin passing from paw to paw, the field-mouse was provided with an ample basket for his purchases, and off he hurried, he and his lantern.

The rest of the field-mice, perched in a row on the settle, their small legs swinging, gave themselves up to enjoyment of the fire, and toasted their chilblains till they tingled; while the Mole, failing to draw them into easy conversation, plunged into family history and made each of them recite the names of his numerous brothers, who were too young, it appeared, to be allowed to go out a-carolling this year, but looked forward very shortly to winning the parental consent.

The Rat, meanwhile, was busy examining the label on one of the beer-bottles. 'I perceive this to be Old Burton,' he remarked approvingly. '*Sensible* Mole! The very thing! Now we shall be able to mull some ale! Get the things ready, Mole, while I draw the corks.'

It did not take long to prepare the brew and thrust the tin heater well into the red heart of the fire; and soon every field-mouse was sipping and cough-ing and choking (for a little mulled ale goes a long way) and wiping his eyes and laughing and forgetting he had ever been cold in all his life.

'They act plays too, these fellows,' the Mole explained to the Rat. 'Make them up all by themselves, and act them afterwards. And very well they do it, too! They gave us a capital one last year, about a field-mouse who was captured at sea by a Barbary corsair, and made to row in a galley; and when he escaped and got home again, his lady-love had gone into a convent. Here, *you*! You were in it, I remember. Get up and recite a bit.'

The field-mouse addressed got up on his legs, giggled shyly, looked round the room, and remained absolutely tongue-tied. His comrades cheered him on, Mole coaxed and encouraged him, and the Rat went so far as to take him by the shoulders and shake him; but nothing could overcome his stage-fright. They were all busily engaged on him like watermen applying the Royal Humane Society's regulations to a case of long submersion, when the latch clicked, the door opened, and the field-mouse with the lantern reappeared, staggering under the weight of his basket.

There was no more talk of play-acting once the very real and solid con-tents of the basket had been tumbled out on the table. Under the generalship of Rat, everybody was set to do something or to fetch something. In a very few minutes supper was ready, and Mole, as he took the head of the table in a sort of dream, saw a lately barren board set thick with savoury comforts; saw his little friends' faces brighten and beam as they fell to without delay; and then let himself loose – for he was famished indeed – on the provender so magically provided, thinking what a happy home-coming this had turned out, after all. As they ate, they talked of old times, and the field-mice gave him the local gossip up to date, and answered as well as they could the hundred questions he had to ask them. The Rat said little or nothing, only taking care that each guest had what he wanted, and plenty of it, and that Mole had no trouble or anxiety about anything.

They clattered off at last, very grateful and showering wishes of the season, with their jacket pockets stuffed with remembrances for the small brothers and sisters at home. When the door had closed on the last of them and the chink of the lanterns had died away, Mole and Rat kicked the fire up, drew their chairs in, brewed themselves a last nightcap of mulled ale, and discussed the events of the long day. At last the Rat, with a tremendous yawn, said, 'Mole, old chap, I'm ready to drop. Sleepy is simply not the word. That your own bunk over on that side? Very well, then, I'll take this. What a ripping little house this is! Everything so handy!'

He clambered into his bunk and rolled himself well up in the blankets, and slumber gathered him forthwith, as a swath of barley is folded into the arms of the reaping-machine.

The weary Mole also was glad to turn in without delay, and soon had his head on his pillow, in great joy and contentment.

Kenneth Grahame, *The Wind in the Willows*

The Yule Boar

The idea of the corn-spirit as embodied in pig form is nowhere more clearly expressed than in the Scandinavian custom of the Yule Boar. In Sweden and Denmark at Yule (Christmas) it is the custom to bake a loaf in the form of a boar-pig. This is called the Yule Boar. The corn of the last sheaf is often used to make it. All through Yule the Yule Boar stands on the table. Often it is kept till the sowing-time in spring, when part of it is mixed with the seed-corn and part given to the ploughman and plough-horses or plough-oxen to eat, in the expectation of a good harvest. In this custom the corn-spirit, immanent in the last sheaf, appears at midwinter in the form of a boar made from the corn of the last sheaf; and his quickening influence on the corn is shown by mixing part of the Yule Boar with the seed-corn, and giving part of it to the ploughman and his cattle to eat. Similarly we saw that the Corn-wolf makes his appearance at midwinter, the time when the year begins to verge towards spring. Formerly a real boar was sacrificed at Christmas, and apparently also a man in the character of the Yule Boar. This, at least, may perhaps be inferred from a Christmas custom still observed in Sweden. A man is wrapt up in a skin, and carries a wisp of straw in his mouth, so that the projecting straws look like the bristles of a boar. A knife is brought, and an old woman, with her face blackened, pretends to sacrifice him.

On Christmas Eve in some parts of the Esthonian island of Oesel they bake a long cake with the two ends turned up. It is called the Christmas Boar, and stands on the table till the morning of New Year's Day, when it is distributed among the cattle. In other parts of the island the Christmas Boar is not a cake but a little pig born in March, which the housewife fattens secretly, often without the knowledge of the other members of the family. On Christmas Eve the little pig is secretly killed, then roasted in the oven, and set on the table standing on all fours, where it remains in this posture for several days. In other parts of the island, again, though the Christmas cake has neither the name nor the shape of a boar, it is kept till the New Year, when half of it is divided among all the members and all the quadrupeds of the family. The other half of the cake is kept till sowing-time comes round, when it is similarly distributed in the morning among human beings and beasts. In other parts of Esthonia, again, the Christmas Boar, as it is called, is baked of the first rye cut at harvest; it has a conical shape and a cross is impressed on it with a pig's bone or a key, or three dints are made in it with a buckle or a piece of charcoal. It stands with a light beside it on the table all through the festal season. On New Year's Day and Epiphany, before sunrise, a little of the cake is crumbled with salt and given to the cattle. The rest is kept till the day when the cattle are driven out to pasture for the first time in spring. It is then put in the herdsman's bag, and at evening is divided among the cattle to guard them from magic and harm. In some places the Christmas Boar is partaken of by farm-servants and cattle at the time of the barley sowing, for the purpose of thereby producing a heavier crop.

Sir James George Frazer, *The Golden Bough*

Pig

In the manger of course were cows and the Child Himself
    Was like unto a lamb
Who should come in the fulness of time on an ass's back
    Into Jerusalem

And all things be redeemed – the suckling babe
    Lie safe in the serpent's home
And the lion eat straw like the ox and roar its love
    to Mark and to Jerome

And God's Peaceable Kingdom return among them all
    Save one full of offense

Into which the thousand fiends of a human soul
   Were cast and driven hence

And the one thus cured gone up into the hills
   To worship and to pray:
O Swine that takest away our sins
   That takest away

Anthony Hecht

The Oxen

Christmas Eve, and twelve of the clock.
   'Now they are all on their knees,'
An elder said as we sat in a flock
   By the embers in hearthside ease.

We pictured the meek mild creatures where
   They dwelt in their strawy pen,
Nor did it occur to one of us there
   To doubt they were kneeling then.

So fair a fancy few would weave
   In these years! Yet, I feel,
If someone said on Christmas Eve,
   'Come; see the oxen kneel

'In the lonely barton by yonder coomb
   Our childhood used to know,'
I should go with him in the gloom,
   Hoping it might be so.

Thomas Hardy

Bertie's Christmas Eve

It was Christmas Eve, and the family circle of Luke Steffink, Esq., was aglow with the amiability and random mirth which the occasion demanded. A long and lavish dinner had been partaken of, waits had been round and sung carols, the house-party had regaled itself with more carolling on its own account, and there had been romping which, even in a pulpit reference, could not have been condemned as ragging. In the midst of the general glow, however, there was one black unkindled cinder.

Bertie Steffink, nephew of the aforementioned Luke, had early in life adopted the profession of ne'er-do-weel; his father had been something of the kind before him. At the age of eighteen Bertie had commenced that round of visits to our Colonial possessions, so seemly and desirable in the case of a Prince of the Blood, so suggestive of insincerity in a young man of the middle-class. He had gone to grow tea in Ceylon and fruit in British Columbia, and to help sheep to grow wool in Australia. At the age of twenty he had just returned from some similar errand in Canada, from which it may be gathered that the trial he gave to these various experiments was of the summary drum-head nature. Luke Steffink, who fulfilled the troubled role of guardian and deputy-parent to Bertie, deplored the persistent manifestation of the homing instinct on his nephew's part, and his solemn thanks earlier in the day for the blessing of reporting a united family had no reference to Bertie's return.

Arrangements had been promptly made for packing the youth off to a distant corner of Rhodesia, whence return would be a difficult matter; the journey to this uninviting destination was imminent, in fact a more careful and willing traveller would have already begun to think about his packing. Hence Bertie was in no mood to share in the festive spirit which displayed itself around him, and resentment smouldered within him at the eager, self-absorbed discussion of social plans for the coming months which he heard on all sides. Beyond depressing his uncle and the family circle generally by singing 'Say au revoir, and not goodbye,' he had taken no part in the evening's conviviality.

Eleven o'clock had struck some half-hour ago, and the elder Steffinks began to throw out suggestions leading up to that process which they called retiring for the night.

'Come, Teddie, it's time you were in your little bed, you know,' said Luke Steffink to his thirteen-year-old son.

'That's where we all ought to be,' said Mrs Steffink.

'There wouldn't be room,' said Bertie.

The remark was considered to border on the scandalous; everybody ate raisins and almonds with the nervous industry of sheep feeding during threatening weather.

'In Russia,' said Horace Bordenby, who was staying in the house as a Christmas guest, 'I've read that the peasants believe that if you go into a cow-house or stable at midnight on Christmas Eve you will hear the animals talk. They're supposed to have the gift of speech at that one moment of the year.'

'Oh, *do* let's *all* go down to the cow-house and listen to what they've got to say?' exclaimed Beryl, to whom anything was thrilling and amusing if you did it in a troop.

Mrs Steffink made a laughing protest, but gave a virtual consent by saying, 'We must all wrap up well, then.' The idea seemed a scatterbrained one to her, and almost heathenish, but it afforded an opportunity for 'throwing the young people together', and as such she welcomed it. Mr Horace Bordenby was a young man with quite substantial prospects, and he had danced with Beryl at a local subscription ball a sufficient number of times to warrant the authorized inquiry on the part of the neighbours whether 'there was anything in it'. Though Mrs Steffink would not have put it in so many words, she shared the idea of the Russian peasantry that on this night the beast might speak.

The cow-house stood at the junction of the garden with a small paddock, an isolated survival, in a suburban neighbourhood, of what had once been a small farm. Luke Steffink was complacently proud of his cow-house and his two cows; he felt that they gave him a stamp of solidity which no number of Wyandottes or Orpingtons could impart. They even seemed to link him in a sort of inconsequent way with those patriarchs who derived importance from their floating capital of flocks and herds, he-asses and she-asses. It had been an anxious and momentous occasion when he had had to decide definitely between 'the Byre' and 'the Ranch' for the naming of his villa residence. A December midnight was hardly the moment he would have chosen for showing his farm-building to visitors, but since it was a fine night, and the young people were anxious for an excuse for a mild frolic, Luke consented to chaperon the expedition. The servants had long since gone to bed, so the house was left in charge of Bertie, who scornfully declined to stir out on the pretext of listening to bovine conversation.

'We must go quietly,' said Luke, as he headed the procession of giggling young folk, brought up in the rear by the shawled and hooded figure of

Mrs Steffink; 'I've always laid stress on keeping this a quiet and orderly neighbourhood.'

It was a few minutes to midnight when the party reached the cow-house and made its way in by the light of Luke's stable lantern. For a moment every one stood in silence, almost with a feeling of being in church.

'Daisy – the one lying down – is by a shorthorn bull out of a Guernsey cow,' announced Luke in a hushed voice, which was in keeping with the foregoing impression.

'Is she?' said Bordenby, rather as if he had expected her to be by Rembrandt.

'Myrtle is – '

Myrtle's family history was cut short by a little scream from the women of the party.

The cow-house door had closed noiselessly behind them and the key had turned gratingly in the lock; then they heard Bertie's voice pleasantly wishing them good night and his footsteps retreating along the garden path.

Luke Steffink strode to the window; it was a small square opening of the old-fashioned sort, with iron bars let into the stonework.

'Unlock the door this instant,' he shouted, with as much air of menacing authority as a hen might assume when screaming through the bars of a coop at a marauding hawk. In reply to his summons the hall-door closed with a defiant bang.

A neighbouring clock struck the hour of midnight. If the cows had received the gift of human speech at that moment they would not have been able to make themselves heard. Seven or eight other voices were engaged in describing Bertie's present conduct and his general character at a high pressure of excitement and indignation.

In the course of half an hour or so everything that it was permissible to say about Bertie had been said some dozens of times, and other topics began to come to the front – the extreme mustiness of the cow-house, the possibility of it catching fire, and the probability of it being a Rowton House for the vagrant rats of the neighbourhood. And still no sign of deliverance came to the unwilling vigil-keepers.

Towards one o'clock the sound of rather boisterous and undisciplined carol-singing approached rapidly, and came to a sudden anchorage, apparently just outside the garden-gate. A motor-load of youthful 'bloods', in a high state of conviviality, had made a temporary halt for repairs; the stoppage, however, did not extend to the vocal efforts of the party, and the watchers in the cow-shed were treated to a highly unauthorized rendering of

'Good King Wenceslas', in which the adjective 'good' appeared to be very carelessly applied.

The noise had the effect of bringing Bertie out into the garden, but he utterly ignored the pale, angry faces peering out at the cow-house window, and concentrated his attention on the revellers outside the gate.

'Wassail, you chaps!' he shouted.

'Wassail, old sport!' they shouted back; 'we'd jolly well drink y'r health, only we've nothing to drink it in.'

'Come and wassail inside,' said Bertie hospitably; 'I'm all alone, and there's heaps of "wet".'

They were total strangers, but his touch of kindness made them instantly his kin. In another moment the unauthorized version of King Wenceslas, which, like many other scandals, grew worse on repetition, went echoing up the garden path; two of the revellers gave an impromptu performance on the way by executing the staircase waltz up the terraces of what Luke Steffink, hitherto with some justification, called his rockgarden. The rock part of it was still there when the waltz had been accorded its third encore. Luke, more than ever like a cooped hen behind the cow-house bars, was in a position to realize the feelings of concert-goers unable to countermand the call for an encore which they neither desire nor deserve.

The hall door closed with a bang on Bertie's guests, and the sounds of merriment became faint and muffled to the weary watchers at the other end of the garden. Presently two ominous pops, in quick succession, made themselves distinctly heard.

'They've got at the champagne!' exclaimed Mrs Steffink.

'Perhaps it's the sparkling Moselle,' said Luke hopefully.

Three or four more pops were heard.

'The champagne *and* the sparkling Moselle,' said Mrs Steffink.

Luke uncorked an expletive which, like brandy in a temperance household, was only used on rare emergencies. Mr Horace Bordenby had been making use of similar expressions under his breath for a considerable time past. The experiment of 'throwing the young people together' had been prolonged beyond a point when it was likely to produce any romantic result.

Some forty minutes later the hall door opened and disgorged a crowd that had thrown off any restraint of shyness that might have influenced its earlier actions. Its vocal efforts in the direction of carol-singing were now supplemented by instrumental music; a Christmas tree that had been prepared for the children of the gardener and other household retainers had yielded a rich spoil of tin trumpets, rattles, and drums. The life-story of King Wenceslas had been dropped, Luke was thankful to notice, but it was intensely irritating for the chilled prisoners in the cow-house to be told that it was 'a hot time in the old town tonight', together with some accurate but entirely superfluous information as to the imminence of Christmas morning. Judging by the protests which began to be shouted from the upper windows of neighbouring houses, the sentiments prevailing in the cow-house were heartily echoed in other quarters.

The revellers found their car, and, what was more remarkable, managed to drive off in it, with a parting fanfare of tin trumpets. The lively beat of a drum disclosed the fact that the master of the revels remained on the scene.

'Bertie!' came in an angry, imploring chorus of shouts and screams from the cow-house window.

'Hullo,' cried the owner of the name, turning his rather errant steps in the direction of the summons; 'are you people still there? Must have heard everything the cows got to say by this time. If you haven't, no use waiting. After all, it's a Russian legend, and Russian Chrismush Eve not due for 'nother fortnight. Better come out.'

After one or two ineffectual attempts he managed to pitch the key of the cow-house door in through the window. Then, lifting his voice in the strains of 'I'm afraid to go home in the dark', with a lusty drum accompaniment, he led the way back to the house. The hurried procession of the released that followed in his steps came in for a good deal of the adverse comment that his exuberant display had evoked.

It was the happiest Christmas Eve he had ever spent. To quote his own words, he had a rotten Christmas.

'Saki'

❧ 22 ❧

WAR

1249

On Christmas Day I and my knights were dining with Pierre d'Avallon. While we were at table the Saracens came spurring hotly up to our camp and killed several poor fellows who had gone for a stroll in the fields. We all went off to arm ourselves but, quick as we were, we did not return in time to rejoin our host; for he was already outside the camp, and had gone to fight the Saracens. We spurred after him and rescued him from the enemy, who had thrown him to the ground. Then we brought him back to camp with his brother, the Lord du Val. The Templars, who had come upon hearing the alarm, covered our retreat well and valiantly. The Turks came after us, harassing us right up to the camp. In consequence of this the king gave orders for the camp to be enclosed on the Damietta side, from the stream of Damietta to the stream of Rosetta.

Joinville and Villehardouin, Chronicles of the Crusades

The Siege of Paris, 1870

24 December   We had a cruel *trajet* to Versailles, for the wind was piercing, and the thermometer marked 20 degs. All along the route, however, the German soldiers were preparing for the evening festivities, and every quarter was decorated with a Christmas tree. Mr Kingston is busy organizing a banquet for Christmas Day, and is working indefatigably; and from Mr Odo Russell down, all the English far and near will be present. There are signs of annoyance at Head-Quarters. Telegraphing is not much favoured; and the comments in some of the Press correspondence are objected to. The new French General of the Northern Army, Faidherbe, begins to be talked about, and has had a stiff action with Manteuffel near Amiens. I received an admirable letter from Brackenbury, dated 19th. He is delighted with any work, no matter how hard, which enables him to see service, and I think that those officers who expose themselves to the dislike of their superiors, to the jealousy, and in a certain sense contumely, of their brother officers, are nearly always animated by a desire for adventure or professional knowledge, and not by love of lucre. They incidentally gain a certain amount of popularity, and their names become known to the world; but it is to be doubted if their professional prospects be not somewhat darkened in consequence of the ill-will of the authorities, who have not the courage to forbid officers accepting these special posts on any pretext, and yet are not at all indisposed to evince resentment in a very petty manner, by resisting claims of enterprising and meritorious men. Dr Hassel called. He is not at all jubilant over General Manteuffel's victory near Amiens. The municipality of Versailles are to be fined 125,000f. because they do not provide stores which they have been ordered to get from Germany. This is very harsh, because the stores are actually at Saarbruck; but the Germans will not allow them to pass over the only railway.

Christmas Day   A curious incident last night. I awoke from a deep sleep with the impression that O———, who was sleeping in a room some distance off, had come in and stood at the bedside, opening his lips as if speaking. I tried in vain to catch what he said; this made me very uneasy in my sleep. I had left him late at night in deep conversation with M—— by the fire in my sitting-room, earnestly expounding to him the doctrines or inspirations of the phase of Faith of which he is so devoted an adherent. Later still I went in and found them still engaged, one talking, the other listening. Yesterday, in driving from St-Germain, we had exchanged some curious confidences respecting our own experiences, and I suppose my imagination dwelt much upon the subject; but when I woke up there I saw O———, as I have said, addressing me. 'For goodness' sake, what do you want?' I exclaimed; 'do speak a little louder. Are you ill?' And as I spoke the figure seemed to turn away, leaving a kind of light space by the side of the bed. The fire was burning. I lighted a candle, walked along the passage, looked into O———'s room, and saw he was fast asleep in bed. In the morning I mentioned what had occurred, and added, 'I could have sworn you were in my room.' 'And so most likely I was,' replied O———, very gravely. 'How could that be, when I saw you asleep in bed?' 'Oh! there is the mystery,' he answered quietly; 'I know that I wanted to speak to you last night; and so, perhaps I did.' I thought it better, on the whole, to go on eating breakfast. This Christmas Day is worthy of England – hard frost, snow, trees covered with icicles. The dinner was a very great success. A large hall, handsomely decorated with evergreens and garlands, was prepared in the succursal of the Reservoirs; and the tables, at which some thirty English, with some German officers invited for the occasion, sat, were decorated with exquisite taste. I was requested to preside, as the *doyen* of those who mainly got up the banquet, and Mr Odo Russell, and all the English whom the fortune of war have assembled near Versailles, were present, with one or two exceptions. A plum-pudding *à la Française* was not forgotten; and after a pleasant evening we trudged home, through snow knee-deep, to our quarters. There was a furious cannonade, and the shells came booming up close to Versailles. After dinner the German officers were hurried off by an alarm, and a surgeon who went with them had to perform some amputations before he returned, as a shell had burst in a post full of soldiers outside the town.

26 December How many of the thousands now round Paris would have credited any seer who had told them three months ago they would spend their Christmas outside it? Not one. And of those inside who yelled '*À Berlin!*' how bitterly they would have mocked the prophet who predicted such a *Noël* for them! The cold is Siberian – 'never such a winter known'. And the poor who were once rich are suffering awful privations in Versailles. At 8 a.m., thermometer 18 degs. There was a large attendance of Roman Catholic soldiers at church, and a larger funeral than usual, four officers and eleven soldiers buried. Day by day the procession passes at 3 o'clock, and attracts the same crowd of French, neither more nor less.

William Howard Russell, *The Last Great War*

25 December A merry Christmas! I had to break the ice in my bath, and thaw my toothbrush and sponge by the fire . . .

A merry Christmas! When there is nothing to make merry with, and nobody with whom to make merry. Hospitals crowded with the dying; heaps of dead on our surrounding heights; hardly a family which is not in mourning, and even in grief, which is quite another thing; starvation staring us in the face; fuel burnt out; meat a recollection, and vegetables a pleasing dream. Oh yes! by all manner of means a merry Christmas.

Felix Whitehurst, *My Private Diary during the Seige of Paris*

Saturday, 31 December In the streets of Paris, death passes death, the undertaker's wagon drives past the hearse. Outside the Madeleine today I saw three coffins, each covered with a soldier's greatcoat with a wreath of immortelles on top.

Out of curiosity I went into Roos's, the English butcher's shop on the Boulevard Haussmann, where I saw all sorts of weird remains. On the wall, hung in a place of honour, was the skinned trunk of young Pollux, the elephant at the Zoo; and in the midst of nameless meats and unusual horns, a boy was offering some camel's kidneys for sale.

Edmond and Jules de Goncourt, *The Goncourt Journal*

Old Sam's Christmas Pudding

It was Christmas Day in the trenches
In Spain in Peninsula War,
And Sam Small were cleaning his musket
A thing as he ne'er done before.

They'd had 'em inspected that morning,
And Sam had got into disgrace
For when Sergeant had looked down the barrel
A sparrow flew out in his face.

The Sergeant reported the matter
To Lieutenant Bird then and there.
Said Lieutenant 'How very disgusting
The Duke must be told of this 'ere.'

The Duke were upset when he heard,
He said 'I'm astonished, I am.
I must make a most drastic example –
There'll be no Christmas pudding for Sam.'

When Sam were informed of his sentence
Surprise rooted him to the spot –
'Twere much worse than he had expected,
He thought as he'd only be shot.

And so he sat cleaning his musket,
And polishing barrel and butt,
Whilst the pudding his mother had sent him
Lay there in the mud at his foot.

Now the centre that Sam's lot were holding
Ran around a place called Badajoz
Where the Spaniards had put up a bastion
And ooh what a bastion it was!

They pounded away all the morning
With canister, grape shot and ball,
But the face of the bastion defied them
They made no impression at all.

They started again after dinner
Bombarding as hard as they could;
And the Duke brought his own private cannon
But that weren't a ha'pence o' good.

The Duke said 'Sam, put down thy musket
And help me to lay this gun true.'
Sam answered 'You'd best ask your favours
From them as you give pudding to.'

The Duke looked at Sam so reproachful
'And don't take it that way,' said he,
'Us Generals have got to be ruthless,
It hurts me more than it did thee.'

Sam sniffed at these words kind of sceptic,
Then looked down the Duke's private gun
And said 'We'd best put in two charges,
We'll never bust bastion with one.'

He tipped cannon ball out of muzzle,
He took out the wadding and all,
He filled barrel chock full of powder,
Then picked up and replaced the ball.

He took a good aim at the bastion,
Then said, 'Right-o, Duke, let her fly.'
The cannon nigh jumped off her trunnions
And up went the bastion, sky high.

The Duke he weren't 'alf elated,
He danced round the trench full of glee,
And said 'Sam, for this gallant action
You can hot up your pudding for tea.'

Sam looked round to pick up his pudding,
But it wasn't there, nowhere about.
In the place where he thought he had left it
Lay the cannon ball he'd just tipped out.

Sam saw in a flash what 'ad happened:
By an unprecedented mishap
The pudding his mother had sent him
Had blown Badajoz off the map.

That's why Fusilliers wear to this moment
A badge which they think's a grenade,
But they're wrong – it's a brass reproduction
Of the pudding Sam's mother once made.

Marriott Edgar

The Crimea

So Christmas came, and with it pleasant memories of home and of home comforts. With it came also news of home – some not of the most pleasant description – and kind wishes from absent friends. 'A merry Christmas to you,' writes one, 'and many of them. Although you will not write to us, we see your name frequently in the newspapers, from which we judge that you are strong and hearty. All your old Jamaica friends are delighted to hear of you, and say that you are an honour to the Isle of Springs.'

I wonder if the people of other countries are as fond of carrying with them everywhere their home habits as the English. I think not. I think there was something purely and essentially English in the determination of the camp to spend the Christmas Day of 1855 after the good old 'home' fashion. It showed itself weeks before the eventful day. In the dinner parties which were got up – in the orders sent to England – in the supplies which came out, and in the many applications made to the hostess of the British Hotel for plum-puddings and mince-pies. The demand for them, and the material necessary to manufacture them, was marvellous. I can fancy that if returns could be got at of the flour, plums, currants, and eggs consumed on Christmas Day in the out-of-the-way Crimean peninsula, they would astonish us. One determination appeared to have taken possession of every mind – to spend the festive day with the mirth and jollity which the changed prospect of affairs warranted; and the recollection of a year ago, when death and misery were the camp's chief guests, only served to heighten this resolve.

For three weeks previous to Christmas Day, my time was fully occupied in making preparations for it. Pages of my books are filled with orders for plum-puddings and mince-pies, besides which I sold an immense quantity of raw material to those who were too far off to send down for the manufactured article on Christmas Day, and to such purchasers I gave a plain recipe for their guidance. Will the reader take any interest in my Crimean Christmas-pudding? It was plain, but decidedly good. However, you shall judge for yourself: 'One pound of flour, three-quarters of a pound of raisins, three-quarters of a pound of pork fat, chopped fine, two tablespoonfuls of sugar, a little cinnamon or chopped lemon, half-pint of milk or water; mix these well together, and boil four hours.'

From an early hour in the morning until long after the night had set in, were I and my cooks busy endeavouring to supply the great demand for Christmas fare. We had considerable difficulty in keeping our engagements, but by substituting mince-pies for plum-puddings, in a few cases, we succeeded. The scene in the crowded store, and even in the little overheated kitchen, with the officers' servants, who came in for their masters' dinners, cannot well be described. Some were impatient themselves, others dreaded their masters' impatience as the appointed dinner hour passed by – all combined by entreaties, threats, cajolery, and fun to drive me distracted. Angry cries for the major's plum-pudding, which was to have been ready an hour ago, alternated with an entreaty that I should cook the captain's mince-pies to a turn – 'Sure, he likes them well done, ma'am. Bake 'em as brown as your own purty face, darlint.'

I did not get my dinner until eight o'clock, and then I dined in peace off a fine wild turkey or bustard, shot for me on the marshes by the Tchernaya. It weighed twenty-two pounds, and, although somewhat coarse in colour, had a capital flavour.

Mary Seacole, *Wonderful Adventures of Mrs Seacole in Many Lands*

Ypres

The ruins of Ypres were conspicuous enough a short way along the Canal, but no occasion arose as yet to go nearer. Walking along the greasy black duckboards beside the water was not specially pleasant. The sluggish weather and the general silence and warlessness encouraged us to take life easy; but it was at this time that some poor fellow was charged with a self-inflicted wound, the first instance in the battalion. Perhaps he divined the devilish truth beyond this peaceful veil. It was easier to be deceived by the newness of the communication trenches and the appearance of quite good farmhouse walls in the area of the foremost trenches. This was, I think, the end of the quietest period ever known in the Salient, and one exploited the recent standards of carelessness and freedom of movement, unthinking that the enemy was looking on and taking notes from the low ridge ahead. The lowness of High Command Redoubt was stultifying, for it did not strike the eye; yet it was all that was needed for overwhelming observation of our flat territory.

Now winter, throwing aside his sleep and drowse, came out fierce and determined: first there was a heavy snow, then the blue sky of hard frost. To our pleasure, we were back in a camp in the woods by Elverdinghe to celebrate Christmas. The snow was crystal-clean, the trees filigreed and golden. It was a place that retained its boorish loneliness, though hundreds were there: its odd buildings had the suggestion of Teniers. Harrison's Christmas was appreciated by his followers perhaps more than by himself. He held a Church Parade and, while officiating, reading a lesson or so, was interrupted by the band, which somehow mistook its cue. The colonel is thought to have said, 'Hold your b—— noise' on this contretemps, which did not damp the ardour of the congregation, especially the back part of the room, as they thundered out 'While Shepherds Watched'. After prayers we had supper for the rest of the day, and the colonel visited all the men at their Christmas dinner. At each hut, he was required by tradition to perfect the joy of his stalwarts by drinking some specially and cunningly provided liquid, varying with each company, and 'in a mug'. He got round, but it was almost as much as intrepidity could accomplish.

Edmund Blunden, Undertones of War

Truce

It begins with one or two soldiers,
And one or two following
With hampers over their shoulders.
They might be off wildfowling

As they would another Christmas Day,
So gingerly they pick their steps.
No one seems sure of what to do.
All stop when one stops.

A fire gets lit. Some spread
Their greatcoats on the frozen ground.
Polish vodka, fruit and bread
Are broken out and passed round.

The air of an old German song,
The rules of Patience, are the secrets
They'll share before long.
They draw on their last cigarettes

As Friday night lovers, when it's over,
Might get up from their mattresses
To congratulate each other
And exchange names and addresses.

Paul Muldoon

Just the Sort of Day for Peace

We left the trenches for our usual days in billets. It was now nearing Christmas Day, and we knew it would fall to our lot to be back in the trenches again on the 23rd of December, and that we would, in consequence, spend our Christmas there. I remember at the time being very down on my luck about this, as anything in the nature of Christmas Day festivities was obviously knocked on the head. Now, however, looking back on it all, I wouldn't have missed that unique and weird Christmas Day for anything.

Well, as I said before, we went 'in' again on the 23rd. The weather had now become very fine and cold. The dawn of the 24th brought a perfectly still, cold, frosty day. The spirit of Christmas began to permeate us all; we tried to plot ways and means of making the next day, Christmas, different in some way to others. Invitations from one dug-out to another for sundry meals were beginning to circulate. Christmas Eve was, in the way of weather, everything that Christmas Eve should be.

I was billed to appear at a dug-out about a quarter of a mile to the left that evening to have rather a special thing in trench dinners – not quite so much bully and Maconochie about as usual. A bottle of red wine and a medley of tinned things from home deputized in their absence. The day had been entirely free from shelling, and somehow we all felt that the Boches, too, wanted to be quiet. There was a kind of an invisible, intangible feeling extending across the frozen swamp between the two lines, which said 'This is Christmas Eve for both of us – *something* in common.'

About 10 p.m. I made my exit from the convivial dug-out on the left of our line and walked back to my own lair. On arriving at my own bit of trench I found several of the men standing about, and all very cheerful. There was a good bit of singing and talking going on, jokes and jibes on our curious Christmas Eve, as contrasted with any former one, were thick in the air. One of my men turned to me and said:

'You can 'ear 'em quite plain, sir!'

'Hear what?' I inquired.

'The Germans over there, sir; you can 'ear 'em singin' and playin' on a band or somethin'.'

I listened; – away out across the field, among the dark shadows beyond, I could hear the murmur of voices, and an occasional burst of some unintelligible song would come floating out on the frosty air. The singing seemed to be loudest and most distinct a bit to our right. I popped into my dug-out and found the platoon commander.

'Do you hear the Boches kicking up that racket over there?' I said.

'Yes,' he replied; 'they've been at it some time!'

'Come on,' said I, 'let's go along the trench to the hedge there on the right – that's the nearest point to them, over there.'

So we stumbled along our now hard, frosted ditch, and scrambling up on to the bank above, strode across the field to our next bit of trench on the right. Everyone was listening. An improvised Boche band was playing a precarious version of 'Deutschland, Deutschland, über Alles', at the conclusion of which, some of our mouth-organ experts retaliated with snatches of ragtime songs and imitations of the German tune. Suddenly we heard a confused shouting from the other side. We all stopped to listen. The shout came again. A voice in the darkness shouted in English, with a strong German accent, 'Come over here!' A ripple of mirth swept along our trench, followed by a rude outburst of mouth organs and laughter. Presently, in a lull, one of our sergeants repeated the request, 'Come over here!'

'You come half-way – I come half-way,' floated out of the darkness.

'Come on, then!' shouted the sergeant. 'I'm coming along the hedge!'

'Ah! but there are two of you,' came back the voice from the other side.

Well, anyway, after much suspicious shouting and jocular derision from both sides, our sergeant went along the hedge which ran at right-angles to the two lines of trenches. He was quickly out of sight; but, as we all listened in breathless silence, we soon heard a spasmodic conversation taking place out there in the darkness.

Presently, the sergeant returned. He had with him a few German cigars and cigarettes which he had exchanged for a couple of Maconochie's and a tin of Capstan, which he had taken with him. The séance was over, but it had given just the requisite touch to our Christmas Eve – something a little human and out of the ordinary routine.

After months of vindictive sniping and shelling, this little episode came as an invigorating tonic, and a welcome relief to the daily monotony of anta-gonism. It did not lessen our ardour or determination; but just put a little human punctuation mark in our lives of cold and humid hate. Just on the right day, too – Christmas Eve! But, as a curious episode, this was nothing in comparison to our experience on the following day.

On Christmas morning I awoke very early, and emerged from my dug-out into the trench. It was a perfect day. A beautiful, cloudless blue sky. The ground hard and white, fading off towards the wood in a thin low-lying mist. It was such a day as is invariably depicted by artists on Christmas cards – the ideal Christmas Day of fiction.

'Fancy all this hate, war, and discomfort on a day like this!' I thought to myself. The whole spirit of Christmas seemed to be there, so much so that I remember thinking, 'This indescribable something in the air, this Peace and Goodwill feeling, surely will have some effect on the situation here today!' And I wasn't far wrong; it did around us, anyway, and I have always been so glad to think of my luck in, firstly, being actually in the trenches on Christ-mas Day, and, secondly, being on the spot where quite a unique little episode took place.

Everything looked merry and bright that morning – the discomforts seemed to be less, somehow; they seemed to have epitomized themselves in intense, frosty cold. It was just the sort of day for Peace to be declared. It would have made such a good finale. I should like to have suddenly heard an immense siren blowing. Everybody to stop and say, 'What was that?' Siren blowing again: appearance of a small figure running across the frozen mud waving something. He gets closer – a telegraph boy with a wire! He hands it to me. With trembling fingers I open it: 'War off, return home. George, RI.' Cheers! But no, it was a nice, fine day, that was all.

Walking about the trench a little later, discussing the curious affair of the night before, we suddenly became aware of the fact that we were seeing a lot of evidences of Germans. Heads were bobbing about and showing over their parapet in a most reckless way, and, as we looked, this phenomenon became more and more pronounced.

A complete Boche figure suddenly appeared on the parapet, and looked about itself. This complaint became infectious. It didn't take 'Our Bert' long to be up on the skyline (it is one long grind to ever keep him off it). This was the signal for more Boche anatomy to be disclosed, and this was replied to by all our Alfs and Bills, until, in less time than it takes to tell, half a dozen or so of each of the belligerents were outside their trenches and were advancing towards each other in no-man's land.

A strange sight, truly!

I clambered up and over our parapet, and moved out across the field to look. Clad in a muddy suit of khaki and wearing a sheepskin coat and Balaclava helmet, I joined the throng about half-way across to the German trenches.

It all felt most curious: here were these sausage-eating wretches, who had elected to start this infernal European fracas, and in so doing had brought us all into the same muddy pickle as themselves.

This was my first real sight of them at close quarters. Here they were – the actual, practical soldiers of the German army. There was not an atom of hate on either side that day; and yet, on our side, not for a moment was the will to war and the will to beat them relaxed. It was just like the interval between the rounds in a friendly boxing match. The difference in type between our men and theirs was very marked. There was no contrasting the spirit of the two parties. Our men, in their scratch costumes of dirty, muddy khaki, with their various assorted head-dresses of woollen helmets, mufflers and battered hats, were a light-hearted, open, humorous collection as opposed to the sombre demeanour and stolid appearance of the Huns in their grey-green faded uniforms, top boots, and pork-pie hats.

The shortest effect I can give of the impression I had was that our men, superior, broadminded, more frank, and lovable beings, were regarding these faded, unimaginative products of perverted kulture as a set of objectionable but amusing lunatics whose heads had *got* to be eventually smacked.

'Look at that one over there, Bill,' our Bert would say, as he pointed out some particularly curious member of the party.

I strolled about amongst them all, and sucked in as many impressions as I could. Two or three of the Boches seemed to be particularly interested in me, and after they had walked round me once or twice with sullen curiosity stamped on their faces, one came up and said 'Offizier?' I nodded my head, which means 'Yes' in most languages, and, besides, I can't talk German.

These devils, I could see, all wanted to be friendly; but none of them possessed the open, frank geniality of our men. However, everyone was talking and laughing, and souvenir hunting.

I spotted a German officer, some sort of lieutenant I should think, and being a bit of a collector, I intimated to him that I had taken a fancy to some of his buttons.

We both then said things to each other which neither understood, and agreed to do a swap. I brought out my wire clippers and, with a few deft snips, removed a couple of his buttons and put them in my pocket. I then gave him two of mine in exchange.

Whilst this was going on a babbling of guttural ejaculations emanating from one of the laager-schifters, told me that some idea had occurred to someone.

Suddenly, one of the Boches ran back to his trench and presently reappeared with a large camera. I posed in a mixed group for several photographs, and have ever since wished I had fixed up some arrangement for getting a copy. No doubt framed editions of this photograph are reposing on some Hun mantelpieces, showing clearly and unmistakably to admiring strafers how a group of perfidious English surrendered unconditionally on Christmas Day to the brave Deutschers.

Slowly the meeting began to disperse; a sort of feeling that the authorities on both sides were not very enthusiastic about this fraternizing seemed to creep across the gathering. We parted, but there was a distinct and friendly understanding that Christmas Day would be left to finish in tranquillity. The last I saw of this little affair was a vision of one of my machine gunners, who was a bit of an amateur hairdresser in civil life, cutting the unnaturally long hair of a docile Boche, who was patiently kneeling on the ground whilst the automatic clippers crept up the back of his neck.

Bruce Bairnsfather, *Bullets and Billets*

Joint Burial

One joint burial service which made a lasting impression on the participants took place to the south-west of Fleurbaix, in a waterlogged cabbage patch near the Sailly-Fromelles road – at the scene of the attack by the 2/Scots Guards and 2/Border of 20th Brigade on the night of 18/19 December.

Early on Christmas Day, Revd J. Esslemont Adams, Chaplain of the Gordon Highlanders in the same Brigade and Minister of the West United Free Church, Aberdeen, carried out a burial service behind the lines for one of the 6/Gordons who had been killed by sniper fire the previous day. Subsequently, he accompanied the commanding officer, Lieutenant-Colonel McLean, on his daily tour of inspection. As they made their way through the trenches, they saw some of their men clambering out and talking with the enemy. Colonel McLean rang along the front line and ordered the men to come down, but they ignored his instructions, pointing out that others further along were standing on the top and that 'a number of the enemy were out on their side and gazing peacefully across'. Swiftly taking in the situation, Esslemont Adams realized that this was an ideal opportunity to arrange for the burial of the dead who had been lying beyond the wire since the previous week's attack: the Gordons had not been involved but they were now in trenches occupied at that time by the Scots Guards. He told the CO his intention, then climbed on to the fire-step and strode out into no-man's land. On reaching a small ditch, which ran along the middle of the field between the lines, he held up his hands and called out to a group of Germans, 'I want to speak to your Commanding Officer. Does anyone speak English?' Several German officers were standing together, and one of them said, 'Yes! Come over the ditch.' The Chaplain hurried forward, saluted the senior German present and began to put his proposal to him and his staff.

Almost at the same moment a hare, disturbed by the unaccustomed activity in the field, burst into view and raced along between the lines. Germans and Scots, the latter with kilts flying, gave furious chase and it was finally captured by the Germans.

Adams and the German commander then resumed their 'parley' and the latter agreed to the burial of the dead and that subsequently Adams should conduct a short religious service: the 23rd Psalm would be read and a prayer offered in both English and German.

Throughout the morning the task of collecting the dead went on. The bodies were intermingled and lay dotted over the sixty yards separating the lines. They were carefully sorted out; the British were carried to the British side of the half-way line, the Germans to the German side. Spades were brought and each side set to work to dig the graves.

The Adjutant of the 2/Scots Guards, Captain Giles Loder, had led his battalion's attack on 18 December. On Christmas morning he was in the front-line trenches away to the right, and observed the activity going on opposite the Gordon Highlanders as the bodies were collected and the graves dug. So he climbed over the parapet and walked over the half-mile of open farmland to talk to the Germans and arrange burial for the Scots Guards killed in the same attack. He spoke with 'an extremely pleasant and superior brand of German officer, who arranged to bring all our dead to the half-way line'. There were twenty-nine in all, most of them lying close to the enemy wire. Loder sorted through the bodies, collecting the personal effects, pay-books and identity discs. 'It was heartrending,' he wrote later that day in the battalion War Diary, 'to see some of the chaps one knew so well, and who had started out in such good spirits on December 18th, lying there dead, some with horrible wounds due to the explosive action of the high-velocity bullet at short range.' He detailed some men to bring in the rifles of his comrades but the Germans demurred at this; indeed, all rifles lying on their side of the half-way line they kept as spoils of war.

From his conversations with the Germans, he was also able to find out what had happened to his fellow officers who had been found missing after the attack. Very severely wounded, they had been among those seen by Lieutenant Hulse being dragged into the German trenches. One, Lieutenant The Hon. F. Hanbury-Tracy, had died after two days in the local hospital and had been buried in the German cemetery at Fromelles. Another officer whom the Germans had been unable to name had also died and been buried: from his description the Scotsmen were able to identify him as Lieutenant Nugent. Most of this information came from a French-speaking officer, who kept on pointing to the British dead and saying, '*Les Braves, c'est bien domm-age.*' Loder gained the impression that they were treating their British prisoners well and had done all they could for the wounded.

Twenty years later to the day an article published in a German magazine under the title 'Christmas Peace 1914 at the Flanders Front' gave the view on these events as seen from the trenches opposite. The author was a Major Thomas, Instructor at the Infantry School, Dresden, and the article was written because Thomas had seen Hulse's account of the truce and had felt moved to reply, claiming he had taken a leading part in the negotiations with the Scots Guards. Presumably he was also the 'extremely pleasant and superior brand of officer' referred to by Loder:

The incident, looked at from the German side, was as follows:

The 2nd Battalion of the Westphalian Infantry Regiment 15, whose Adjutant I was at the time, occupied at Christmas 1914 a position in French Flanders beyond Le Meisnil and Fromelles, about 10 miles to the West of Lille. On the 18th December 1914 the British had suffered heavy losses during an attack made in the evening towards our trenches. Their dead had to remain unburied before our Front. As regards the Christmas Armistice mentioned in the letter of the English Officer (the initiative was not taken by us, but by the Englishman), it was a question of burying the German and English heroes who were lying between the trenches on each side. On Christmas Day, at about 11 o'clock, there was a continuous waving of a white flag from the English trench which was about 150 yards from our trench. Soon afterwards a number of Englishmen climbed out of the trench and came towards our front, making signs all the time. My Commander, Baron von Blomberg (a cousin of the Reich Defence Minister), to whom this had been reported, ordered me to find out what the Englishmen wanted. Accompanied by an English-speaking war volunteer, I also went out of the trench to meet the Englishmen. The preliminary greetings exchanged under the gaze of surprise of the men in the trenches on both sides were of a rather embarrassing nature. We heard that it was the wish of the Englishmen to bury on the occasion of the Christmas holiday their dead who were lying before the Front, and they asked us to cease enemy action for an adequate period.

What were we to do? Time was short. We could not very well conclude peace there, and there was no time for making enquiries of the superior department, seeing that neither the regiment nor the general command could assume responsibility for a local armistice, but would probably have to consult first the Chief Command. Major von B. therefore decided without anything further that there should be a local armistice until 1 o'clock in the afternoon, telling the Englishman that their dead must be buried by that time.

Altogether about a hundred bodies were gathered for burial, and there then took place what must surely have been one of the most moving and memorable services of the war. Nineteen-year-old Second Lieutenant Arthur Pelham-Burn, of the 6/Gordon Highlanders, who intended to train for the Anglican ministry, was among the participants. He described the event in a letter to an old Lancing schoolfriend. Burying the dead was 'awful, too awful to describe so I won't attempt it', but the ceremony that followed was different:

We then had a most wonderful joint burial service. Our Padre . . . arranged the prayers and psalm etc. and an interpreter wrote them out in German. They were read first in English by our Padre and then in German by a boy who was studying for the ministry. It was an extraordinary and most wonderful sight. The Germans formed up on one side, the English on the other, the officers standing in front, every head bared. Yes, I think it was a sight one will never see again.

Standing between the ranks of British and German officers, Chaplain Esslemont Adams spoke the familiar words of the 23rd Psalm, and in the cold, clear air they were echoed by the young Saxon divinity student by his side:

> The Lord is my shepherd: I shall not want.
> He maketh me to lie down in green pastures:
> He leadeth me beside the still waters.

> Der Herr is mein Hirt: mir wird nichts mangeln.
> Er weidet mich auf einer grünen Aue:
> und führt mich zum frischen Wasser.

As the service came to an end there was a moment of silence, then the Chaplain stepped forward and saluted the German commander, who shook hands with him and bade him farewell. 'It was an impressive sight,' the Regimental History of the 6/Gordons recorded, 'officers and men, bitter enemies as they were, uncovered, reverent, and for the moment united in offering for their dead the last offices of homage and honour.'

Reporting all this in his letter to his mother, Hulse commented: 'This episode was the sadder side of Xmas Day, but it was a great thing being able to collect [the dead], as their relations, to whom of course they had been reported missing, will be put out of suspense and hoping they are prisoners.' Hulse also remarked that the Germans they had been dealing with were mostly 158th Regiment and Jägers: 'the men we had attacked on the night of the 18th. Hence the feeling of temporary friendship, I suppose.' Summing up the episode in the battalion War Diary, Captain Loder wrote: 'Both sides have played the game and I know this Regiment anyhow has learned to trust an Englishman's word.'

But not all the participants took Loder's charitable view. Private Alexander Runcie of the 6/Gordon Highlanders, who had witnessed the joint burial and subsequently exchanged souvenirs with the Germans, recalled that 'one of our men on the way back from fraternizing showed me a dagger he had hidden and added "I don't trust these bastards." '

Malcolm Brown and Shirley Seaton, *Christmas Truce: The Western Front*

The Official View

24–27 December   Christmas has come and gone, but it has brought no modification of the situation. There has, however, been a change in the weather, which is, perhaps, a matter of greater importance to the hundreds of thousands of men living in the open than is at first realized. It has become much colder.

On Christmas Eve a hard frost set in, and the 25th December was very cold, though it was not bright, for a mist hung over the countryside. On our right, which has been the scene of the most recent action, we captured a short length of German trench. It was also discovered that a group of buildings behind the German front line was being used as headquarters of some sort. The fire of a certain number of batteries was therefore concentrated on the spot, the buildings being first shelled with lyddite, and then the ground all round being searched with shrapnel. It is believed that this bombardment was effective. Fifty dead Germans were picked up in one of the trenches recently retaken by us. It is estimated that in the attack on the village captured by them on the 21st their loss in killed alone must have amounted to 400. In our centre the only incident was the capture of two of the enemy, who came across to our trenches uninvited, ostensibly to wish us the compliments of the season.

The Times Documentary History of the War

Although I have never heard it actually confirmed, I believe a suggestion was made by the Pope to all the belligerent Powers that an armistice should be arranged for Christmas Day. It was further reported that the Central Powers had signified their assent, but that the Allied Governments refused to entertain the proposal. The suggestion was certainly never referred either to Joffre or to me.

Whether this statement was true or not, it is certain that, soon after daylight on Christmas morning, the Germans took a very bold initiative at several points along our front, in trying to establish some form of fraternization. It began by individual unarmed men running from the German trenches across to ours, holding Christmas trees above their heads. These overtures were in some places favourably received and fraternization of a limited kind took place during the day. It appeared that a little feasting went on, and junior officers, noncommissioned officers and men on either side conversed together in no-man's land.

When this was reported to me I issued immediate orders to prevent any recurrence of such conduct, and called the local commanders to strict account, which resulted in a good deal of trouble.

I have since often thought deeply over the principle involved in the manifestation of such sentiments between hostile armies in the field. I am not sure that, had the question of the agreement upon an armistice for the day been submitted to me, I should have dissented from it. I have always attached the utmost importance to the maintenance of that chivalry in war which has almost invariably characterized every campaign of modern times in which this country has been engaged. The Germans glaringly and wantonly set all such sentiments at defiance by their ruthless conduct of the present war; even from its very commencement.

Judging from my own experience, we never had a more chivalrous or generous foe than the Boers of South Africa, and I can recall numerous proofs of it.

For instance, I was in charge of the operations against General Beyers in the Western Transvaal during the latter part of December 1900. On the afternoon of Christmas Eve a flag of truce – that symbol of civilization and chivalry in war which has been practically unknown during this war with Germany – appeared at our outposts, and a young Dutch officer was brought to my Headquarters carrying a request from Beyers regarding the burial of his dead.

Some important movements were then in progress, and I told him we must of necessity detain him there till the next day, but I hoped we would be able to make him as comfortable as possible. When he started back to his General on Christmas morning, I gave him a small box of cigars and a bottle of whisky, asking him to present them to Beyers as a Christmas offering from me.

I had forgotten the incident when, a few days later, two cavalry soldiers who had been taken prisoners by the enemy marched back into camp with horses, arms and equipment complete. They brought me a note from Beyers, thanking me for my gift on Christmas Day and telling me that, although he had no whisky or cigars to offer in return, he hoped I would regard his liberation of these men in the light of a Christmas gift.

When I told this story at the end of the war to my old friend and redoubtable opponent, General Christian Smuts, he expressed himself as very displeased with Beyer's improper use of what was not his own but his country's property. I pointed out to Smuts that it was the spirit which Beyers displayed which mattered – that spirit which was never more conspicuously displayed throughout the war than in the conduct of this same great soldier and statesman, General Smuts himself.

Field-Marshal Viscount French, *1914*

Christmas Bells

I heard the bells on Christmas Day
Their old, familiar carols play,
    And wild and sweet
    The words repeat
Of peace on earth, good-will to men!

And thought how, as the day had come,
The belfries of all Christendom
    Had rolled along
    The unbroken song
Of peace on earth, good-will to men!

Till, ringing, singing on its way,
The world revolved from night to day,
    A voice, a chime,
    A chant sublime
Of peace on earth, good-will to men!

Then from each black, accursed mouth
The cannon thundered in the South,
    And with the sound
    The carols drowned
Of peace on earth, good-will to men!

And in despair I bowed my head;
'There is no peace on earth,' I said;
    'For hate is strong,
    And mocks the song
Of peace on earth, good-will to men!'

Then pealed the bells more loud and deep:
'God is not dead; nor doth he sleep!
    The Wrong shall fail,
    The Right prevail,
With peace on earth, good-will to men!'

                            Henry Wadsworth Longfellow

The Truce of Christmas

Passionate peace is in the sky –
And in the snow in silver sealed.
The beasts are perfect in the field,
And men seem men so suddenly –
  (But take ten swords and ten times ten
  And blow the bugle in praising men;
  For we are for all men under the sun;
  And they are against us every one;
  And misers haggle and madmen clutch,
  And there is peril in praising much,
  And we have the terrible tongues uncurled
  That praise the world to the sons of the world.)

The idle humble hill and wood
Are bowed upon the sacred birth,
And for one little hour the earth
Is lazy with the love of good –
  (But ready are you, and ready am I,
  If the battle blow and the guns go by;
  For we are for all men under the sun,
  And they are against us every one;
  And the men that hate all herd together,
  To pride and gold, and the great white feather,
  And the thing is graven in star and stone
  That the men who love are all alone.)

Hunger is hard and time is tough,
But bless the beggars and kiss the kings;
For hope has broken the heart of things,
And nothing was ever praised enough.
  (But hold the shield for a sudden swing,
  And point the sword when you praise a thing,
  For we are for all men under the sun,
  And they are against us every one;
  And mime and merchant, thane and thrall
  Hate us because we love them all;

Only till Christmastide go by
Passionate peace is in the sky.)

G. K. Chesterton

Christmas: 1924

'Peace upon earth!' was said. We sing it,
And pay a million priests to bring it.
After two thousand years of mass
We've got as far as poison gas.

Thomas Hardy

The Onslaught Resumes

From Fred Emery
Washington, 26 Dec.   The full resumption of the bombing of North Viet-
nam, after a thirty-six-hour Christmas suspension, was confirmed by the
Pentagon today.

What little the spokesman had to say dashed hopes that the suspension
might be extended to secure a resumption of the negotiations. Instead, there
was a clear hint that the onslaught might continue for several weeks.

If the bombing were sustained for so long, the spokesman said, emphasiz-
ing the hypothesis, 'it could very well destroy the military targets round
Hanoi'. He declined to be more specific, although he disclosed that targets
throughout North Vietnam 'including the Hanoi-Haiphong area' were again
being bombed and that 'all our aircraft' were taking part.

This was indirect confirmation that the B52 heavy bombers were again in
action, even though it is admitted that at least eleven of them have been shot
down. At least fifty-seven American aircrew are reported missing in the
week's raids. For this reason alone – that the loss of aircrew is 'excessive' –
Senator George McGovern, the defeated Democratic presidential candidate,
today pleaded for an end to the bombing.

President Nixon, who returned to Washington today after spending
Christmas at the Florida White House, maintained total silence on his bombing policy. There was not even formal acknowledgement that the bombing
had been suspended because of the Christmas season. White House spokes-

[391]

men stolidly continued to decline comment on all matters relating to the bombing and the negotiations.

Some officials privately promoted hopes that there was something afoot in secret diplomatic contacts and, as a guide to the President's attitude, they drew attention to his tribute to President Truman in which Mr Nixon said Mr Truman was 'at his best when the going was toughest'.

However there was little to encourage any hopes of a lessening of the violence, unless it was the North Vietnamese demand for a return to the situation prevailing during the December negotiations. This was clearly short of a demand for an end to the bombing – merely for a suspension of that part resumed with such force a week ago. In the circumstances it would seem conciliatory, but officials maintain there will be no lessening of the assault until the North Vietnamese demonstrate that they are 'serious'.

In the only reported peace demonstration, some 200 persons gathered yesterday outside the White House for an inter-faith church service.

Saigon Though the air war paused for Christmas, there was no real truce on the ground. The South Vietnamese military command said that the Christmas ceasefire was the bloodiest since ceasefires were first agreed on in 1966.

In some eighty breaches of the ceasefire, including three major battles, an estimated 137 North Vietnamese and Vietcong and forty-seven South Vietnamese Government troops were killed.

Radio Hanoi reported today that an American Phantom fighter-bomber was shot down north-east of Hanoi today – the first warplane to be brought down since the bombing resumed.

In Paris the North Vietnamese delegation to the peace talks accused the Americans of trying to flatten Hanoi, Haiphong and numerous other cities – Reuter.

Paris The North Vietnamese delegation said that eight B52s were shot down today – Agence France-Presse.

The Times, 27 December 1972

❦ 23 ❦

IN EXTREMIS

The Berlin–Bucharest Express

In Slotwina Brzesko, Bronia lived near the train station and the Wehrmacht headquarters. It was an advantageous location. Every night at exactly 1.20 a.m. the express train stopped for one and a half minutes, long enough for Bronia to step on or get off the train. Bronia served as a courier, delivering Aryan papers and foreign passports to Jews in various parts of Poland. She had two wonderful connections, Benjamin Sander Landau in Bochnia, who had in his possession seals from all the desirable consulates in the free world, and the ticket seller at the train station, a kind Gentile who arranged for Bronia the correct tickets needed for each occasion.

One day Bronia was traveling to Lvov to bring Aryan papers and make travel arrangements for Reb Hirsch Landau and his wife, formerly from Litvatz and now living in Lvov. It is difficult to describe the despondent condition of Reb Hirsch and his wife. When Bronia entered the cold, dark little room, their faces lit up with such gratitude as she never had seen before. They were overjoyed that they were not forgotten and that their distant relative had come to their rescue. Reb Hirsch was praising the Lord that He had not forgotten His humble servant, and Mrs Landau kept telling Bronia that if an angel had come down from heaven it would have been less of a miracle than Bronia's coming in this difficult time to rescue them. Bronia placed them on a truck and two days later they safely arrived in Tarnow.

Bronia boarded the Bucharest-Berlin Express. It was December 1941. A gentle snow was falling. The train was packed with soldiers from the eastern front going home for Christmas. Next to Bronia sat a woman, a German secretary who worked at a German company in the occupied territories. Now she too was traveling home for Christmas.

At Gorodenko the train came to a sudden halt for passport control. The woman next to Bronia became very frightened. She turned to Bronia and said, 'We are all dark in my family. In the past it was considered an asset. We used to be referred to as the Spanish beauties, but now my dark complexion is a curse. Each time I travel they suspect me, you know, that I am one of them. My family is one of the oldest German families. We never even intermarried with the Austrians!'

'Passports please!' Bronia was searching for her passport. 'No need, comrade,' the officer who checked passports said to blond, blue-eyed Bronia. 'Follow me!' he ordered the German secretary. She left the compartment, never to return. Bronia finally found her passport. It was issued in Berlin, where she had lived since childhood, in her real name, Bronia Koczicki née Melchior, born in Sosnowiec. It even stated her correct date of birth. Slowly, Bronia placed the passport back into her pocketbook.

A German officer took the secretary's place and sat next to Bronia. He looked as if he were in his mid-thirties, with a very handsome face that expressed much suffering and pain. The train proceeded once more on its way. Snow was still falling and the compartment was lit by a dim light from the narrow corridor. Tears began to stream from the officer's closed eyes. He seemed to be having a nightmare. His face twitched and his lips mumbled soundless words. He opened his eyes and turned to Bronia. The tears were still falling on his hollow cheeks. He told Bronia that he was on his way home because he could not take it any longer. 'In Zhitomir it was especially horrible.' He was responsible for it, too; he was in command and he gave the orders to shoot. 'They assembled them all, men, women, and children. We murdered them all, all of them,' he said as he wept. He showed Bronia pictures and documents to support his horrible tale. Bronia looked at them in the dim light. She felt her head spinning; she was afraid she was about to faint. How was this possible? How was it possible to murder innocent people, unsuspecting Jews dressed in their Sabbath finery? Bronia's blood was screaming, Why, why, why? She controlled her emotions, but the officer sensed her great pain, which he interpreted as sympathy for his troubled state of mind. Bronia asked for a picture for evidence. But he told her that as much as he would like to give it to her, he could not do so.

The officer asked Bronia to continue traveling with him. Her understanding and sensitivity would be of great assistance to him, he said, to ease the terrible burden he could not carry alone. Bronia replied that she would like to accompany him, but her duty did not allow her this great pleasure. At Tarnow she quickly parted from the officer and stepped down off the train into the cold, sorrowful December night.

Bronia brought back the news of Zhitomir to the town's leaders. They listened to her gruesome tale and then said, 'Here it will not happen. They kill Jews only in the formerly held Russian territories because they cannot distinguish between Communists and Jews. But here they know we are not Communists. We were never under Russian rule.'

Bronia saw before her eyes a picture of the dead children. She questioned the spokesman of the group: 'How does one mistake infants, small children, babies at their mothers' breasts for Communists?' she demanded.

'Here it will not happen,' she was told over and over. 'Just don't scare the people with unnecessary tales of horror.'

Every night when Bronia was at home, when the Berlin-Bucharest Express rolled by, she would hear in the clickety-clack of its wheels new tales of terror, new names of other Jewish communities. Long after the train had disappeared into the frosty winter night, Bronia would clearly hear the voice of a German officer telling the gruesome tale of Zhitomir.

Based on a conversation of Rebbetzin Bronia Spira with her daughter-in-law, Dina Spira, 10 May 1976.

Yaffa Eliach, *Hasidic Tales of the Holocaust*

Monday 25 December   Christmas – Lunch. Bar. 21·14. Rise 240 feet. The wind was strong last night and this morning; a light snowfall in the night; a good deal of drift, subsiding when we started, but still about a foot high. I thought it might have spoilt the surface, but for the first hour and a half we went along in fine style. Then we started up a rise, and to our annoyance found ourselves amongst crevasses once more – very hard, smooth névé between high ridges at the edge of crevasses, and therefore very difficult to get foothold to pull the sledges. Got our ski sticks out, which improved matters, but we had to tack a good deal and several of us went half down. After half an hour of this I looked round and found the second sledge halted some way in rear – evidently someone had gone into a crevasse. We saw the rescue work going on, but had to wait half an hour for the party to come up, and got mighty cold. It appears that Lashly went down very suddenly, nearly dragging the crew with him. The sledge ran on and jammed the span so that the Alpine rope had to be got out and used to pull Lashly to the surface again. Lashly says the crevasse was 50 feet deep and 8 feet across, in form U, showing that the word 'unfathomable' can rarely be applied. Lashly is forty-four today and as hard as nails. His fall has not even disturbed his equanimity.

After topping the crevasse ridge we got on a better surface and came along fairly well, completing over 7 miles (geo.) just before 1 o'clock. We have risen nearly 250 feet this morning; the wind was strong and therefore trying, mainly because it held the sledge; it is a little lighter now.

Night camp No. 47. Bar. 21·18. T. −7°. I am so replete that I can scarcely write. After sundry luxuries, such as chocolate and raisins at lunch, we started off well, but soon got amongst crevasses, huge snow-filled roadways running almost in our direction, and across hidden cracks into which we frequently fell. Passing for two miles or so along between two roadways, we came on a huge pit with raised sides. Is this a submerged mountain peak or a swirl in the stream? Getting clear of crevasses and on a slightly down grade, we came along at a swinging pace – splendid. I marched on till nearly 7.30, when we had covered 15 miles (geo.) (17¼ stat.). I knew that supper was to be a 'tightener,' and indeed it has been – so much that I must leave description till the morning.

Dead reckoning, Lat. 85° 50′ S.; Long. 159° 8′ 2″ E. Bar. 21·22.

Towards the end of the march we seemed to get into better condition; about us the surface rises and falls on the long slopes of vast mounds or undulations – no very definite system in their disposition. We camped half-way up a long slope.

In the middle of the afternoon we got another fine view of the land. The Dominion Range ends abruptly as observed, then come two straits and two other masses of land. Similarly north of the wild mountains is another strait and another mass of land. The various straits are undoubtedly overflows, and the masses of land mark the inner fringe of the exposed coastal mountains, the general direction of which seems about SSE, from which it appears that one could be much closer to the Pole on the Barrier by continuing on it to the SSE. We ought to know more of this when Evans' observations are plotted.

I must write a word of our supper last night. We had four courses. The first, pemmican, full whack, with slices of horse meat flavoured with onion and curry powder and thickened with biscuit; then an arrowroot, cocoa and biscuit hoosh sweetened; then a plum-pudding; then cocoa with raisins, and finally a dessert of caramels and ginger. After the feast it was difficult to move. Wilson and I couldn't finish our share of plum-pudding. We have all slept splendidly and feel thoroughly warm – such is the effect of full feeding.

Captain Robert F. Scott, *Scott's Last Expedition*

Journey of a Party of California Emigrants in 1846 from Fort Bridger to the Sinks of Ogden's River

19 December   Although the wind was from the northwest, yet the snow which had fallen on the previous night, thawed a little. Mr Stanton again fell behind, in consequence of blindness. He came up about an hour after they were encamped. The wind on the 20th was from the northeast. In the morning they resumed their journey, and guided by the sun, as they had hitherto been, they traveled until night. Mr Stanton again fell behind. The wind next day changed to the southwest, and the snow fell all day. They encamped at sunset, and about dark Mr Stanton came up. They resumed their journey on the 22d, Mr Stanton came into camp in about an hour, as usual. That night they consumed the last of their little stock of provisions.

23 December   During this day Mr Eddy examined a little bag for the purpose of throwing out something, with a view to getting along with more ease. In doing this, he found about half a pound of bear's meat, to which was attached a paper upon which his wife had written in pencil, a note signed 'Your own dear Eleanor', in which she requested him to save it for the last extremity, and expressed the opinion that it would be the means of saving his life. This was really the case, for without it, he must subsequently have perished. On the morning of this day Mr Stanton remained at the camp-fire, smoking his pipe. He requested them to go on, saying that he would overtake them. The snow was about fifteen feet deep. Mr Stanton did not come up with them. On the morning of the 24th, they resumed their melancholy journey, and after traveling about a mile, they encamped to wait for their companion. They had nothing to eat during the day. Mr Stanton did not come up. The snow fell all night, and increased one foot in depth. They now gave up on poor Stanton for dead. A party that subsequently returned from the settlement, headed by Mr Fallen, found his remains at the place where they had left him. His pistols, pipe, and some other articles, were found by him; but his body was in a great measure consumed by beasts of prey.

On Christmas Day the painful journey was again continued, and after traveling two or three miles, the wind changed to the south-west. The snow beginning to fall, they all sat down to hold a council for the purpose of determining whether to proceed. All the men but Mr Eddy refused to go forward. The women and Mr Eddy declared they would go through or perish. Many reasons were urged for returning, and among others the fact that they had not tasted food for two days, and this after having been on an allowance of one ounce per meal. It was said that they must all perish for want of food. At length, Patrick Dolan proposed that they should cast lots to see who should die, to furnish food for those who survived. Mr Eddy seconded the motion. William Foster opposed the measure. Mr Eddy then proposed that two persons should take each a six-shooter, and fight until one or both were slain. This, too, was objected to. Mr Eddy at length proposed that they should resume their journey, and travel on till someone died. This was finally agreed to, and they staggered on for about three miles, when they encamped. They had a small hatchet with them, and after a great deal of difficulty they succeeded in making a large fire. About 10 o'clock on Christmas night, a most dreadful storm of wind, snow, and hail, began to pour down upon their defenseless heads. While procuring wood for the fire, the hatchet, as if to add another drop of bitterness to a cup already overflowing, flew from the handle, and was lost in unfathomable snows. About 11 o'clock that memorable night, the storm increased to a perfect tornado, and in an instant blew away every spark of fire. Antoine perished a little before this from fatigue, frost, and hunger. The company, except Mr Eddy and one or two of the others, were now engaged in alternatingly imploring God for mercy and relief. That night's bitter cries, anguish, and despair, never can be forgotten. Mr Eddy besought his companions to get down upon blankets, and he would cover them up with other blankets; urging that the falling snow would soon cover them, and they could thus keep warm. In about two hours this was done. Before this, however, Mr Graves was relieved by death from the horrors of the night. Mr Eddy told him that he was dying. He replied that he did not care, and soon expired. They remained under the blankets all that night, until about 10 o'clock a.m. of the 26th, when Patrick Dolan, becoming deranged, broke away from them, and getting out into the snow, it was with great difficulty that Mr Eddy again got him under. They held him there by force until about 4 o'clock p.m., when he quietly and silently sunk into the arms of death. He was from Dublin, Ireland. Lemuel Murphy became deranged on the night of the 26th, and talked much about food. On the morning of the 27th, Mr Eddy blew up a powder-horn, in an effort to strike fire under the blankets. His face and hands were much burned. Mrs McCutcheon and Mrs Foster were also burned, but not seriously. About 4 o'clock p.m. the storm died away, and the angry clouds passed off. Mr Eddy immediately got out from under the blankets, and in a short time succeeded in getting fire into a large pine tree. His unhappy companions then got out; and having broken off boughs, they put them down, and lay upon them before the fire. The flame ascended to the top of the tree, and burned off great numbers of dead limbs, some of them as large as a man's body; but such was their weakness and indifference, that they did not seek to avoid them at all. Although the limbs fell thick, they did not strike.

On the morning of December 28th, they found themselves too weak to walk. The sensation of hunger was not so urgent, but it was evident to all that some substantial nourishment was necessary to recruit their bodies. The horrible expedient of eating human flesh was now again proposed. This Mr Eddy declined doing, but his miserable companions cut the flesh from the arms and legs of Patrick Dolan, and roasted and ate it, averting their faces from each other, and weeping.

J. Quinn Thornton, *'Camp of Death'*

The Little Match-Girl

It was dreadfully cold; it snowed, and was beginning to grow dark, and it was the last night of the year, too – New Year's Eve. In this cold and darkness a poor, little girl was wandering about the streets with bare head and bare feet. She had slippers on when she left home, but what was the good of that! They were very large, old slippers of her mother's, so large that they slipped off the little girl's feet as she hurried across the street to escape two carriages, which came galloping along at an immense rate. The one slipper was not to be found, and a boy ran off with the other, saying that it would do for a cradle when he had children of his own.

So the little girl wandered along barefoot, with a quantity of matches in an old apron, whilst she held a bundle of them in her hand. No one had bought a single match from her during the whole day, nor given her a single farthing. Hungry, and pinched with cold, the poor little girl crept along, the large flakes of snow covering her yellow hair, which curled so beautifully round her face, but her appearance was certainly the last thing she thought of.

In a corner between two houses, one projecting beyond the other, she sought shelter, and huddling herself up she drew her poor feet, which were red and blue with cold, under her as well as she could, but she was colder than ever and dared not go home, for, as she had sold no matches, her father would beat her. Besides, it was cold at home, for they lived immediately under the roof and the wind blew in, though straw and rags had been stuffed in the large cracks. Her little hands were quite benumbed with cold. Oh, how much good one match would do, if she dared but take it out of the bundle, draw it across the wall, and warm her fingers in the flame! She drew one out— 'Ritsh!' how it sputtered and burned! It burned with a warm, bright flame like a candle, and she bent her hand round it; it was a wonderful light! It appeared to the little girl as if she were sitting before a large iron-stove, in which the fire burned brightly and gave forth such comforting warmth. She stretched out her feet to warm them, too – but the flame went out; the stove disappeared, and there she sat with a little bit of the burnt-out match in her hand.

Another was lighted; it burned, and where the light fell upon the wall, that became transparent, so that she could see into the room. There the table was covered with a dazzlingly white cloth and fine china, and a roasting goose was smoking most invitingly upon it. But, what was still more delightful, the goose sprang down from the table, and with a knife and fork sticking in its breast, waddled towards the little girl. Then the match went out, and she saw nothing but the thick, cold wall.

She lighted another; and now she was sitting under the most splendid Christmas tree. It was larger and more beautifully decorated than the one she had seen at Christmas through the window at the rich merchant's. Thousands of tapers were burning amongst the green branches, and painted pictures, such as she had seen in the shop-windows, looked down upon her. She stretched out both her hands, when the match was burnt out. The innumerable lights rose higher and higher, and she now saw that they were the stars, one of which fell, leaving a long line in the sky.

'Some one is dying now,' the little girl said, for her old grandmother, who alone had loved her, but who was now dead, had said that when a star falls a soul takes its flight up to Heaven.

She drew another match across the wall, and in the light it threw around stood her old grandmother, so bright, so mild, and so loving.

'Grandmother,' the little girl cried; 'oh, take me with you! I know that you will disappear as soon as the match is burnt out, the same as the warm stove, the delicious roasted goose, and the Christmas tree!' and hastily she lighted the rest of the matches that remained in the bundle, for she wished to keep her grandmother with her as long as possible, and the matches burned so brightly that it was lighter than day. Never before had her grandmother appeared so beautiful and so tall, and taking the little girl in her arms, in radiance and joy they flew high, high up into the heavens, where she felt neither cold, hunger, nor fear, for they were with God!

But in the corner between the two houses, in the cold morning air, sat the little girl with red cheeks and a smiling mouth. She was frozen to death during the last night of the Old Year. The first light of the New Year shone upon the dead body of the little girl who sat there with the matches, one bundle of which was nearly consumed. She has been trying to warm herself, people said, but no one knew what visions she had had, or with what splendour she had entered with her grandmother into the joys of a New Year.

Hans Christian Andersen

Christmas Phantoms

My Christmas story was concluded. I flung down my pen, rose from the desk; and began to pace up and down the room.

It was night, and outside the snow-storm whirled through the air. Strange sounds reached my ears as of soft whispers, or of sighs, that penetrated from the street through the walls of my little chamber, three-fourths of which were engulfed in dark shadows. It was the snow driven by the wind that came crunching against the walls and lashed the window-pane. A light, white, indefinite object scurried past my window and disappeared, leaving a cold shiver within my soul.

I approached the window, looked out upon the street, and leaned my head, heated with the strained effort of imagination, upon the cold frame. The street lay in deserted silence. Now and then the wind ripped up little transparent clouds of snow from the pavement and sent them flying through the air like shreds of a delicate white fabric. A lamp burned opposite my window. Its flame trembled and quivered in fierce struggle with the wind. The flaring streak of light projected like a broadsword into the air, and the snow that was drifted from the roof of the house into this streak of light became aglow for a moment like a scintillating robe of sparks. My heart grew sad and chill as I watched this play of the wind. I quickly undressed myself, put out the lamp and lay down to sleep.

When the light was extinguished and darkness filled my room the sounds grew more audible and the window stared at me like a great white spot. The ceaseless ticking of the clock marked the passing of the seconds. At times their swift onward rush was drowned in the wheezing and crunching of the snow, but soon I heard again the low beat of the seconds as they dropped into eternity. Occasionally their sound was as distinct and precise as if the clock stood in my own skull.

I lay in my bed and thought of the story that I had just completed, wondering whether it had come out a success.

In this story I told of two beggars, a blind old man and his wife, who in silent, timid retirement trod the path of life that offered them nothing but fear and humiliation. They had left their village on the morning before Christmas to collect alms in the neighbourhood settlements that they might on the day thereafter celebrate the birth of Christ in holiday fashion.

They expected to visit the nearest village and to be back home for the early morning service, with their bags filled with all kinds of crumbs doled out to them for the sake of Christ.

Their hopes (thus I proceeded in my narration) were naturally disappointed. The gifts they received were scanty, and it was very late when the pair, worn out with the day's tramp, finally decided to return to their cold, desolate clay hut. With light burdens on their shoulders and with heavy grief in their hearts, they slowly trudged along over the snow-covered plain, the old woman walking in front and the old man holding fast to her belt and following behind. The night was dark, clouds covered the sky, and for two old people the way to the village was still very long. Their feet sank into the snow and the wind whirled it up and drove it into their faces. Silently and trembling with cold they plodded on and on. Weary and blinded by the snow, the old woman had strayed from the path, and they were now wandering aimlessly across the valley out on the open field.

'Are we going to be home soon? Take care that we do not miss the early mass!' mumbled the blind man behind his wife's shoulders.

She said that they would soon be home, and a new shiver of cold passed through her body. She knew that she had lost the way, but she dared not tell her husband. At times it seemed to her as if the wind carried the sound of the barking dogs to her ears, and she turned in the direction whence those sounds came; but soon she heard the barking from the other side.

At length her powers gave way and she said to the old man:

'Forgive me, Father, forgive me for the sake of Christ. I have strayed from the road and I cannot go farther. I must sit down.'

'You will freeze to death,' he answered.

'Let me rest only for a little while. And even if we do freeze to death, what matters it? Surely our life on this earth is not sweet.'

The old man heaved a heavy sigh and consented.

They sat down on the snow with their backs against each other and looked like two bundles of rags – the sport of the wind. It drifted clouds of snow against them, covered them up with sharp, pointed crystals, and the old woman, who was more lightly dressed than her husband, soon felt herself in the embrace of a rare, delicious warmth.

'Mother,' called the blind man, who shivered with violent cold, 'stand up, we must be going!'

But she had dozed off and muttered but half-intelligible words through her sleep. He endeavoured to raise her, but he could not for want of adequate strength.

'You will freeze!' he shouted, and then he called aloud for help into the wide open field.

But she felt so warm, so comfortable! After some vain endeavour the blind man sat down again on the snow in dumb desperation. He was now firmly convinced that all that happened to him was by the express will of God and that there was no escape for him and his aged wife. The wind whirled and danced around them in wanton frolic, playfully bestrewed them with snow and had a merry, roguish sport with the tattered garments that covered their old limbs, weary with a long life of pinching destitution. The old man also was now overcome with a feeling of delicious comfort and warmth.

Suddenly the wind wafted the sweet, solemn, melodious sounds of a bell to his ears.

'Mother!' he cried, starting back, 'they are ringing for matins. Quick, let us go!'

But she had already gone whence there is no return.

'Do you hear? They are ringing, I say. Get up! Oh, we will be too late!'

He tried to rise, but he found that he could not move. Then he understood that his end was near and he began to pray silently:

'Lord, be gracious unto the souls of your servants! We were sinners, both. Forgive us, oh, Lord! Have mercy upon us!'

Then it seemed to him that from across the field, enveloped in a bright, sparkling snow-cloud, a radiant temple of God was floating towards him – a rare, wondrous temple. It was all made of flaming hearts of men and itself had the likeness of a heart, and in the midst of it, upon an elevated pedestal, stood Christ in his own person. At this vision the old man arose and fell upon his knees on the threshold of the temple. He regained his sight again and he looked at the Saviour and Redeemer. And from his elevated position Christ spoke in a sweet, melodious voice:

'Hearts aglow with pity are the foundation of my people. Enter thou into my temple, thou who in thy life hast thirsted for pity, thou who hast suffered misfortune and humiliation, go to thy Eternal Peace!'

'O, Lord!' spoke the old man, restored to sight, weeping with rapturous joy, 'is it Thou in truth, O Lord!'

And Christ smiled benignly upon the old man and his life companion, who was awakened to life again by the smile of the Saviour.

And thus both the beggars froze to death out in the open, snow-covered field.

*

I brought back to my mind the various incidents of the story, and wondered whether it had come out smooth and touching enough to arouse the reader's pity. It seemed to me that I could answer the question in the affirmative, that it could not possibly fail to produce the effect at which I had aimed.

With this thought I fell asleep, well satisfied with myself. The clock continued to tick, and I heard in my sleep the chasing and roaring of the snowstorm, that grew more and more violent. The lantern was blown out. The storm outside produced ever new sounds. The window shutters clattered. The branches of the trees near the door knocked against the metal plate of the roof. There was a sighing, groaning, howling, roaring and whistling, and all this was now united into a woeful melody that filled the heart with sadness, now into a soft, low strain like a cradle song. It had the effect of a fantastic tale that held the soul as if under a spell.

But suddenly – what was this? The faint spot of the window flamed up into a bluish, phosphorescent light, and the window grew larger and larger until it finally assumed the proportions of the wall. In the blue light which filled the room there appeared of a sudden a thick, white cloud in which bright sparks glowed as with countless eyes. As if whirled about by the wind, the cloud turned and twisted, began to dissolve, became more and more transparent, broke into tiny pieces, and breathed a frosty chill into my body that filled me with anxiety. Something like a dissatisfied, angry mumble proceeded from the shreds of cloud, that gained more and more definite shape and assumed forms familiar to my eye. Yonder in the corner were a swarm of children, or rather the shades of children, and behind them emerged a grey-bearded old man by the side of several female forms.

'Whence do these shades come? What do they wish?' were the questions that passed through my mind as I gazed affrighted at this strange apparition.

'Whence come we and whence are we?' was the solemn retort of a serious, stern voice. 'Do you not know us? Think a little!'

I shook my head in silence. I did not know them. They kept floating through the air in rhythmic motion as if they led a solemn dance to the tune of the storm. Half transparent, scarcely discernible in their outlines, they wavered lightly and noiselessly around me, and suddenly I distinguished in their midst the blind old man who held on fast to the belt of his old wife. Deeply bent they limped past me, their eyes fixed upon me with a reproachful look.

'Do you recognize them now?' asked the same solemn voice. I did not know whether it was the voice of the storm or the voice of my conscience, but there was in it a tone of command that brooked no contradiction.

'Yes, this is who they are,' continued the Voice, 'the sad heroes of your successful story. And all the others are also heroes of your Christmas stories – children, men and women whom you made to freeze to death in order to amuse the public. See how many there are and how pitiful they look, the offspring of your fancy!'

A movement passed through the wavering forms and two children, a boy and a girl, appeared in the foreground. They looked like two flowers of snow or of the sheen of the moon.

'These children,' spoke the Voice, 'you have caused to freeze under the window of that rich house in which beamed the brilliant Christmas tree. They were looking at the tree – do you recollect? – and they froze.'

Noiselessly my poor little heroes floated past me and disappeared. They seemed to dissolve in the blue, nebulous glare of light. In their place appeared a woman with a sorrowful, emaciated countenance.

'This is that poor woman who was hurrying to her village home on Christmas Eve to bring her children some cheap Christmas gifts. You have let her freeze to death also.'

I gazed full of shame and fear at the shade of the woman. She also vanished, and new forms appeared in their turn. They were all sad, silent phantoms with an expression of unspeakable woe in their sombre gaze.

And again I heard the solemn Voice speak in sustained, impassive accents:

'Why have you written these stories? Is there not enough of real, tangible and visible misery in the world that you must needs invent more misery and sorrow, and strain your imagination in order to paint pictures of thrilling, realistic effects? Why do you do this? What is your object? Do you wish to deprive man of all joy in life, do you wish to take from him the last drop of faith in the good, by painting for him only the evil? Why is it that in your Christmas stories year after year you cause to freeze to death now children, now grown-up people? Why? What is your aim?'

I was staggered by this strange indictment. Everybody writes Christmas stories according to the same formula. You take a poor boy or a poor girl, or something of that sort, and let them freeze somewhere under a window, behind which there is usually a Christmas tree that throws its radiant splendour upon them. This has become the fashion, and I was following the fashion.

I answered accordingly.

'If I let these people freeze,' I said, 'I do it with the best object in the world. By painting their death struggle I stir up humane feelings in the public for these unfortunates. I want to move the heart of my reader, that is all.'

A strange agitation passed through the throng of phantoms, as if they wished to raise a mocking protest against my words.

'Do you see how they are laughing?' said the mysterious Voice.

'Why are they laughing?' I asked in a scarcely audible tone.

'Because you speak so foolishly. You wish to arouse noble feelings in the hearts of men by your pictures of imagined misery, when real misery and suffering are nothing to them but a daily spectacle. Consider for how long a time people have endeavoured to stir up noble feelings in the hearts of men, think of how many men before you have applied their genius to that end, and then cast a look into real life! Fool that you are! If the reality does not move them, and if their feelings are not offended by its cruel, ruthless misery, and by the fathomless abyss of actual wretchedness, then how can you hope that the fictions of your imagination will make them better? Do you really think that you can move the heart of a human being by telling him about a frozen child? The sea of misery breaks against the dam of heartlessness, it rages and surges against it, and you want to appease it by throwing a few peas into it!'

The phantoms accompanied these words with their silent laughter, and the storm laughed a shrill, cynical laugh; but the Voice continued to speak unceasingly. Each word that it spoke was like a nail driven into my brain. It became intolerable, and I could no longer hold out.

'It is all a lie, a lie!' I cried in a paroxysm of rage, and jumping from my bed I fell headlong into the dark, and sank more and more quickly, more and more deeply, into the gaping abyss that suddenly opened before me. The whistling, howling, roaring and laughing followed me downward and the phantoms chased me through the dark, grinned in my face and mocked at me.

I awoke in the morning with a violent headache and in a very bad humour. The first thing I did was to read over my story of the blind beggar and his wife once more, and then I tore the manuscript into pieces.

Maxim Gorki

So That Is That

Adrian Henri's Talking After Christmas Blues

Well I woke up this mornin' it was Christmas Day
And the birds were singing the night away
I saw my stocking lying on the chair
Looked right to the bottom but you weren't there
there was
   apples
      oranges
         chocolates
            . . . aftershave
- but no you.

So I went downstairs and the dinner was fine
There was pudding and turkey and lots of wine
And I pulled those crackers with a laughing face
Till I saw there was no one in your place
there was
   mincepies
      brandy
         nuts and raisins
           . . . mashed potato
- but no you.

Now it's New Year and it's Auld Lang Syne
And it's 12 o'clock and I'm feeling fine
Should Auld Acquaintance be Forgot?
I don't know girl, but it hurts a lot
there was
   whisky
      vodka

> dry Martini (stirred
> but not shaken)
> . . . and 12 New Year resolutions
> - all of them about you.

> So it's all the best for the year ahead
> As I stagger upstairs and into bed
> Then I looked at the pillow by my side
> . . . I tell you baby I almost cried
> there'll be
> Autumn
> Summer
> Spring
> . . . and Winter
> - all of them without you.

Adrian Henri

December 30th

It is the year's end, the winds are blasting, and I
Write to keep madness and black torture away
A little – it is a hurt to my head not to complain.
In the world's places that honour earth, all men are thinking
Of centuries: all men of the ages of living and drinking;
Singing and company of all time till now –
(When the hate of Hell has this England's state plain).
By the places I know this night all the woods are battering
With the great blast, clouds fly low, and the moon
(If there is any) clamorous, dramatic, outspoken.
In such nights as this Lassington has been broken,
Severn flooded too high and banks overflown –
And the great words of 'Lear' first tonight been spoken.
The boys of the villages growing up will say, 'I
Shall leave school, or have high wages, before another January –
Be grown up or free before again December's dark reign
Brightens to Christmas, dies for the old year's memory.'
May to them the gods make not all prayers vain.

Cotswold edge, Severn Valley that watches two
Magnificences: noble at right times or affectionate.
What power of these gods ever now call to you
For the folks in you of right noble; and of delight
In all nature's things brought round in the year's circle?
Pray God in blastings, supplicate now in terrifical
Tempestuous movings about the high-sided night.

Men I have known fine, are dead in France, in exile,
One my friend is dumb, other friends dead also,
And I that loved you, past the soul am in torture's spite
Cursing the hour that bore me, pain that bred all
My greater longings; Love only to you, this last-year date.

Ivor Gurney

New Year's Eve

There are only two things now,
The great black night scooped out
And this fireglow.

This fireglow, the core,
And we the two ripe pips
That are held in store.

Listen, the darkness rings
As it circulates round our fire.
Take off your things.

Your shoulders, your bruised throat!
Your breasts, your nakedness!
This fiery coat!

As the darkness flickers and dips,
As the firelight falls and leaps
From your feet to your lips!

D. H. Lawrence

Auld Lang Syne

Should auld acquaintance be forgot
 And never brought to mind?
Should auld acquaintance be forgot,
 And auld lang syne!

 For auld lang syne, my jo,
  For auld lang syne,
 We'll tak a cup o' kindness yet
  For auld lang syne.

And surely ye'll be your pint stowp!
 And surely I'll be mine!
And we'll tak a cup o' kindness yet,
 For auld lang syne.

We twa hae run about the braes,
 And pou'd the gowans fine;
But we've wander'd mony a weary fitt,
 Sin auld lang syne.

We twa hae paidl'd in the burn,
 Frae morning sun till dine;
But seas between us braid hae roar'd,
 Sin auld lang syne.

And there's a hand, my trusty fiere!
 And gie's a hand o' thine!
And we'll tak a right gude-willie-waught,
 For auld lang syne.

Robert Burns

New Year's Eve

'I have finished another year,' said God,
   'In grey, green, white, and brown;
I have strewn the leaf upon the sod,
Sealed up the worm within the clod,
   And let the last sun down.'

'And what's the good of it?' I said,
   'What reasons made you call
From formless void this earth we tread,
When nine-and-ninety can be read
   Why nought should be at all?

'Yea, Sire; why shaped you us, "who in
   This tabernacle groan" –
If ever a joy be found herein,
Such joy no man had wished to win
   If he had never known!'

Then he: 'My labours – logicless –
   You may explain; not I:
Sense-sealed I have wrought, without a guess
That I evolved a Consciousness
   To ask for reasons why.

'Strange that ephemeral creatures who
   By my own ordering are,
Should see the shortness of my view,
Use ethic tests I never knew,
   Or made provision for!'

He sank to raptness as of yore,
   And opening New Year's Day
Wove it by rote as theretofore,
And went on working evermore
   In his unweeting way.

Thomas Hardy

[411]

Sketch. New Year's Day. To Mrs Dunlop

This day, Time winds th' exhausted chain,
To run the twelvemonth's length again: –
I see the old, bald-pated fellow,
With ardent eyes, complexion sallow,
Adjust the unimpair'd machine,
To wheel the equal, dull routine.

The absent lover, minor heir,
In vain assail him with their prayer,
Deaf as my friend, he sees them press,
Nor makes the hour one moment less.
Will you (the Major's with the hounds,
The happy tenants share his rounds;
Coila's fair Rachel's care to day,
And blooming Keith's engaged with Gray);
From housewife cares a minute borrow –
– That grandchild's cap will do tomorrow –
And join with me a moralizing,
This day's propitious to be wise in.

First, what did yesternight deliver?
'Another year is gone for ever.'
And what is this day's strong suggestion?
'The passing moment's all we rest on!'
Rest on – for what? what do we here?
Or why regard the passing year?

Will time, amus'd with proverb'd lore,
Add to our date one minute more?
A few days may – a few years must –
Repose us in the silent dust.
Then is it wise to damp our bliss?
Yes – all such reasonings are amiss!
The voice of nature loudly cries,
And many a message from the skies,
That something in us never dies:

[412]

That on this frail, uncertain state,
Hang matters of eternal weight:
That future life in worlds unknown
Must take its hue from this alone;
Whether as heavenly glory bright,
Or dark as misery's woeful night –
Since then, my honor'd, first of friends,
On this poor being all depends;
Let us th' important *now* employ,
And live as those who never die.
Tho' you, with days and honors crown'd,
Witness that filial circle round,
(A sight life's sorrows to repulse,
A sight pale envy to convulse)
Others now claim your chief regard;
Yourself, you wait your bright reward.

Robert Burns

A New Year's Gift, Sent to Sir Simeon Steward

No news of navies burnt at seas;
No noise of late spawn'd tittyries;
No closet plot or open vent,
That frights men with a Parliament:
No new device or late-found trick,
To read by th' stars the kingdom's sick;
No gin to catch the State, or wring
The free-born nostril of the King,
We send to you; but here a jolly
Verse crown'd with ivy and with holly;
That tells of winter's tales and mirth
That milk-maids make about the hearth;
Of Christmas sports, the wassail-bowl,
That toss'd up, after Fox-i'-th'-hole;
Of Blind-man-buff, and of the care
That young men have to shoe the Mare;
Of twelf-tide cakes, of pease and beans,

Wherewith ye make those merry scenes,
Whenas ye chuse your king and queen,
And cry out, 'Hey for our town green!' –
Of ash-heaps, in the which ye use
Husbands and wives by streaks to chuse;
Of crackling laurel, which fore-sounds
A plenteous harvest to your grounds;
Of these, and such like things, for shift,
We send instead of New Year's gift.
- Read then, and when your faces shine
With buxom meat and cap'ring wine,
Remember us in cups full crown'd,
And let our city-health go round,
Quite through the young maids and the men,
To the ninth number, if not ten;
Until the firéd chestnuts leap
For joy to see the fruits ye reap,
From the plump chalice and the cup
That tempts till it be tosséd up. –
Then as ye sit about your embers,
Call not to mind those fled Decembers;
But think on these, that are t' appear,
As daughters to the instant year;
Sit crown'd with rose-buds, and carouse,
Till *Liber Pater* twirls the house
About your ears, and lay upon
The year, your cares, that's fled and gone:
And let the russet swains the plough
And harrow hang up resting now;
And to the bag-pipe all address,
Till sleep takes place of weariness.
And thus throughout, with Christmas plays,
Frolic the full twelve holy-days.

Robert Herrick

[414]

Witching Time

Another witching time is the period of twelve days between Christmas and Epiphany. Hence in some parts of Silesia the people burn pine-resin all night long between Christmas and the New Year in order that the pungent smoke may drive witches and evil spirits far away from house and homestead; and on Christmas Eve and New Year's Eve they fire shots over fields and meadows, into shrubs and trees, and wrap straw round the fruit-trees, to prevent the spirits from doing them harm. On New Year's Eve, which is Saint Sylvester's Day, Bohemian lads, armed with guns, form themselves into circles and fire thrice into the air. This is called 'Shooting the Witches' and is supposed to frighten the witches away. The last of the mystic twelve days is Epiphany or Twelfth Night, and it has been selected as a proper season for the expulsion of the powers of evil in various parts of Europe. Thus at Brunnen, on the Lake of Lucerne, boys go about in procession on Twelfth Night carrying torches and making a great noise with horns, bells, whips, and so forth to frighten away two female spirits of the wood, Strudeli and Strätteli. The people think that if they do not make enough noise there will be little fruit that year. Again, in Labruguière, a canton of southern France, on the eve of Twelfth Night the people run through the streets, jangling bells, clattering kettles, and doing everything to make a discordant noise. Then by the light of torches and blazing faggots they set up a prodigious hue and cry, an ear-splitting uproar, hoping thereby to chase all the wandering ghosts and devils from the town.

Sir James George Frazer, *The Golden Bough*

Ceremony upon Candlemas Eve

Down with the rosemary, and so
Down with the bays and misletoe;
Down with the holly, ivy, all
Wherewith ye dress'd the Christmas hall;
That so the superstitious find
No one least branch there left behind;
For look, how many leaves there be
Neglected there, maids, trust to me,
So many goblins you shall see.

Robert Herrick

[415]

1663

6 January (Twelfth Day)   Up and Mr Creed brought a pot of chocolate ready made for our morning draft, and then he and I to the Duke's, but I was not very willing to be seen at this end of the town, and so returned to our lodgings, and took my wife by coach to my brother's, where I set her down, and Creed and I to St Paul's Church-yard, to my bookseller's, and looked over several books with good discourse, and then into St Paul's Church, and there finding Elborough, my old schoolfellow at Paul's, now a parson, whom I know to be a silly fellow. I took him out and walked with him, making Creed and myself sport with talking with him, and so sent him away, and we to my office and house to see all well, and thence to the Exchange, where we met with Major Thomson, formerly of our office, who do talk very highly of liberty of conscience, which now he hopes for by the King's declaration, and that he doubts not that if he will give it, he will find more and better friends than the Bishop can be to him, and that if he do not, there will many thousands in a little time go out of England, where they may have it. But he says that they are well contented that if the King thinks it good, the Papists may have the same liberty with them. He tells me, and so do others, that Dr Calamy is this day sent to Newgate for preaching, Sunday was sennight, without leave, though he did it only to supply the place; when otherwise the people must have gone away without ever a sermon, they being disappointed of a minister: but the Bishop of London will not take that as an excuse. Thence into Wood Street, and there bought a fine table for my dining-room, cost me 50s.; and while we were buying it, there was a scare-fire in an ally over against us, but they quenched it. So to my brother's, where Creed and I and my wife dined with Tom, and after dinner to the Duke's house, and there saw *Twelfth Night* acted well, though it be but a silly play, and not related at all to the name or day. Thence Mr Battersby the apothecary, his wife, and I and mine by coach together, and setting him down at his house, he paying his share, my wife and I home, and found all well, only myself somewhat vexed at my wife's neglect in leaving of her scarf, waistcoat, and night-dressings in the coach today that brought us from Westminster, though, I confess, she did give them to me to look after, yet it was her fault not to see that I did take them out of the coach. I believe it might be as good as 25s. loss or there-abouts. So to my office, however, to set down my last three days' journall, and writing to my Lord Sandwich to give him an account of Sir J. Lawson's being come home, and to my father about my sending him some wine and things this week, for his making an entertainment of some friends in the country, and so home. This night making an end wholly of Christmas, with a mind fully satisfied with the great pleasures we have had by being abroad from home, and I do find my mind so apt to run to its old want of pleasures, that it is high time to betake myself to my late vows, which I will tomorrow, God willing, perfect and bind myself to, that so I may, for a great while, do my duty, as I have well begun, and increase my good name and esteem in the world, and get money, which sweetens all things, and whereof I have much need. So home to supper and to bed, blessing God for his mercy to bring me home, after much pleasure, to my house and business with health and resolution to fall hard to work again.

Samuel Pepys

Balloons

Since Christmas they have lived with us,
Guileless and clear,
Oval soul-animals,
Taking up half the space,
Moving and rubbing on the silk

Invisible air drifts,
Giving a shriek and pop
When attacked, then scooting to rest, barely trembling.
Yellow cathead, blue fish –
Such queer moons we live with

Instead of dead furniture!
Straw mats, white walls
And these traveling
Globes of thin air, red, green,
Delighting

The heart like wishes or free
Peacocks blessing
Old ground with a feather
Beaten in starry metals.
Your small

Brother is making
His balloon squeak like a cat.
Seeming to see
A funny pink world he might eat on the other side of it.
He bites,

Then sits
Back, fat jug
Contemplating a world clear as water.
A red
Shred in his little fist.

Sylvia Plath

Twelfth Night

At home poor Scarlett is slowly ploughing through a vast mountain of ironing, because the children all go back to school next week. She has put the Christmas decorations back in their box, and the tree outside the back door (it seemed such a shame to burn it when it had given them such pleasure) and swept up the pine needles.

She dreads taking down the Christmas cards, because it makes the sitting-room look so drab and colourless. If only she hadn't spent so much on Christmas they could afford to brighten it up with new curtains or at least new cushions. Later she's got to pack up and post back to Petersfield the gloves, boots and quilted hot-water bottle that Granny left behind, omitting to point out that Difficult Patch had punctured the hot-water bottle.

Upstairs, above the pounding surf beat of Robin's record player, she can hear Nicholas and little Carol screaming at each other. Nor can she expect any help in packing the trunks from Holly, who is locked in her room, reduced to the depths of misanthropy by mugging up St Luke for mock O-levels.

Scarlett feels depressed. Sadly she no longer has the excuse that it's still Christmas to justify the midday nip (a treble vodka and tonic) to keep her going; all the parties are over, and she's already broken her New Year's resolution to lose weight. Christmas, with all its faults, was a break in the monotony of life. But at least she's her own boss, unlike poor Noël, who today went back to the relentless treadmill of the office; and who now, unknown to Scarlett, is roughing it at the Ritz over a three-hour lunch with Ms Stress, trying to piece together who it was that he mauled or insulted at the office party before Christmas.

If only, muses Scarlett, one could have Christmas every five years, then it would really be something to look forward to, like a royal wedding, and she and Noël wouldn't be almost bankrupted every January. If they could give up both drink *and* Christmas they'd be quite well off.

Her reverie is interrupted by little Carol howling down the stairs that Nicholas has decapitated her new Christmas doll, because she'd managed to wipe all his computer games.

'Never mind,' says Scarlett comfortingly, 'it's only 353 days until next Christmas.'

Jilly Cooper, *How to Survive Christmas*

Fading Memory

Well, so that is that. Now we must dismantle the tree,
Putting the decorations back into their cardboard boxes –
Some have got broken – and carrying them up to the attic.
The holly and the mistletoe must be taken down and burnt,
And the children got ready for school. There are enough
Leftovers to do, warmed-up, for the rest of the week –
Not that we have much appetite, having drunk such a lot,
Stayed up so late, attempted – quite unsuccessfully –
To love all of our relatives, and in general
Grossly overestimated our powers. Once again
As in previous years we have seen the actual Vision and failed
To do more than entertain it as an agreeable
Possibility, once again we have sent Him away,
Begging though to remain His disobedient servant,
The promising child who cannot keep His word for long.
The Christmas Feast is already a fading memory,
And already the mind begins to be vaguely aware
Of an unpleasant whiff of apprehension at the thought
Of Lent and Good Friday which cannot, after all, now
Be very far off. But, for the time being, here we all are,
Back in the moderate Aristotelian city
Of darning and the Eight-Fifteen, where Euclid's geometry
And Newton's mechanics would account for our experience,

And the kitchen table exists because I scrub it.
It seems to have shrunk during the holidays. The streets
Are much narrower than we remembered; we had forgotten
The office was as depressing as this. To those who have seen
The Child, however dimly, however incredulously
The Time Being is, in a sense, the most trying time of all.
For the innocent children who whispered so excitedly
Outside the locked door where they knew the presents to be
Grew up when it opened. Now, recollecting that moment
We can repress the joy, but the guilt remains conscious;
Remembering the stable where for once in our lives
Everything became a You and nothing was an It.
And craving the sensation but ignoring the cause,
We look round for something, no matter what, to inhibit
Our self-reflection, and the obvious thing for that purpose
Would be some great suffering. So, once we have met the Son,
We are tempted ever after to pray to the Father:
'Lead us into temptation and evil for our sake'.
They will come, all right, don't worry; probably in a form
That we do not expect, and certainly with a force
More dreadful than we can imagine. In the meantime
There are bills to be paid, machines to keep in repair,
Irregular verbs to learn, the Time Being to redeem
From insignificance. The happy morning is over,
The night of agony still to come; the time is noon:
When the Spirit must practise his scales of rejoicing
Without even a hostile audience, and the Soul endure
A silence that is neither for nor against her faith
That God's Will will be done, that, in spite of her prayers,
God will cheat no one, not even the world of its triumph.

W. H. Auden, *For the Time Being*

On the Thirteenth Day of Christmas

On the thirteenth day of Christmas
    I saw King Jesus go
About the plain beyond my pane
    Wearing his cap of snow.

[420]

Sad was his brow as the snow-sky
   While all the world made merry,
In the black air his wounds burned bare
   As the fire in the holly berry.

At all the weeping windows
   The greedy children gather
And laugh at the clown in his white nightgown
   In the wicked winter weather.

I dragged the desperate city,
   I swagged the combing light,
I stood alone at the empty throne
   At the ninth hour of night.

On the thirteenth day of Christmas
   When the greasy guns bellow
His eye is dry as the splitting sky
   And his face is yellow.

                                    Charles Causley

ACKNOWLEDGEMENTS

For permission to reprint extracts from copyright material, the publishers gratefully acknowledge the following:

HANS CHRISTIAN ANDERSON: 'Little Match Girl' from *Hans Andersen's Fairy Tales*, reprinted by permission of Oxford University Press. SIMON ARMITAGE: 'White Christmas' from *The Dead Sea Poems*, © Simon Armitage, 1995, reprinted by permission of Faber and Faber Ltd. W. H. AUDEN: from *Collected Poems*, reprinted by permission of Faber and Faber Ltd. ROY BARRATT: 'The Bampton Mummers Play', © Roy Barratt. ARNOLD BENNETT: 'Scruts' by Arnold Bennett, taken from *A Christmas Garland* by Max Beerbohm, reprinted by permission of A. P. Watt Ltd on behalf of Mme V. M. Eldin. JOHN BETJEMAN from *John Betjeman's Collected Poems* compiled by Earl of Birkenhead, © John Betjeman 1958, reprinted by permission of John Murray (Publishers) Ltd. EDMUND BLUNDEN: 'An Ypres Christmas' from *Undertones of War* © Edmund Blunden 1928, reprinted by permission of the Peters Fraser & Dunlop Ltd. PAUL BOWLES from *Without Stopping*, © Paul Bowles 1972, reprinted by permission of Peter Owen Publishers, London. MALCOLM BROWN and SHIRLEY SEATON: extract from *Christmas Truce*, © Malcolm Brown and Shirley Seaton, reprinted by permission of Papermac. PETER CAREY: extract from *Oscar and Lucinda* © Peter Carey 1988, reprinted by permission of Faber and Faber Ltd. CHARLES CAUSLEY: 'Innocent's Song' from *Collected Poems*, reprinted by permission of J. M. Dent; 'The Animal's Carol' and 'On The Thirteenth Day of Christmas' from *Collected Poems*, © Charles Causley 1951, reprinted by permission of Macmillan. MARY CLIVE: from *Christmas with the Savages*, © Mary Clive 1955. WENDY COPE: 'A Christmas Poem' from *Serious Concerns*, © Wendy Cope, reprinted by permission of Faber and Faber Ltd; 'The Christmas Life' © Wendy Cope; 'Christmas Triolet' from *Poetry Introduction 5*, © Wendy Cope, reprinted by permission of Faber and Faber Ltd. JILLY COOPER: extracts from *How to Survive Christmas* © Jilly Cooper 1986, reprinted by permission of Methuen. RICHMAL CROMPTON: from *Just William at Christmas* © Richmal C. Ashbee 1955, reprinted by permission of Macmillan Children's Books. From *The Diary of Anne Frank*, translated by B. M. Mooyaart-Doubleday, reprinted by permission of Liepman Literary Agency, Zurich. E. E. DUNLOP: from *The War Diaries of Weary Dunlop* © E. E. Dunlop 1986, reprinted by permission of Penguin Books Australia Ltd. T. S. ELIOT: 'Journey of the Magi' from *The Complete Poems and Plays of T. S. Eliot*, © Valerie Eliot 1969, reprinted by permission of the Book Club Associates by arrangement with Faber and Faber Ltd. YAFFA ELIACH: extract from *Hasidic Tales of the Holocaust* © 1982 Yaffa Eliach, reprinted by permission of Oxford University Press, Inc. FRED EMERY: 'Bombers resume onslaught on N. Vietnam after Christmas Lull', from *The Times* 27 December 1972, © Times Newspapers Limited, 1972. GAVIN EWART: 'England at Christmas, 1982' from *The Complete Little Ones*, © Gavin Ewart 1986, reprinted by permission of Mrs. G. B. Ewart and Random House UK Ltd. E. M. FORSTER: from *Howard's End* © E. M. Forster 1916, reprinted by permission of King's College, Cambridge, and the Society of Authors as the literary representatives of the E. M. Forster Estate. SIR JAMES GEORGE FRAZER: extracts from *The Golden Bough*, reprinted by permission of A. P. Watt Ltd on behalf of Trinity College, Cambridge (Council). ROBERT FROST: 'To a Young Wretch' from *The Poetry of Robert Frost*, edited by Edward Connery Lathem, © 1969, Holt, Rinehart and Winston Inc. ANTON GILL: from *Journey back from Hell*, © Anton Gill 1988, reprinted by permission of HarperCollins Publishers Limited. ROBERT GITTINGS: from *John Keats*, © Robert Gittings 1968, reprinted by permission of Heinemann Educational Books. KENNETH GRAHAME: extract from *The Wind in the Willows*, reprinted by permission of Curtis Brown, London. JOHN HALE: 'John Sheddon Dobie' From *Settlers*, edited by John Hale, reprinted by permission of Faber and Faber Ltd. RODNEY HALL: 'Captivity Captive' from *The Yandilli Trilogy*, © Rodney Hall 1994, reprinted by permission of Faber and Faber Ltd. THOMAS HARDY: 'The Oxen', 'New Year's Eve' and 'Christmas 1924' from *The Complete Poems*, © Macmillan London Ltd 1976, reprinted by permission of Papermac. ADRIAN HENRI: 'Adrian Henri's Talking after Christmas Blues' from *Collected Poems*, © Adrian Henri 1986, reproduced by permission of the author c/o Rogers, Coleridge & White Ltd., 20 Powis Mews, London WI I IJN. ANTHONY HECHT: 'Pig' from *Collected Earlier Poems*, © 1990 Anthony E. Hecht, reprinted by permission of Alfred A. Knopf Inc. MICHAEL HOFMANN: 'Hausfrauenchor' from *Nights in the Iron Hotel*, © Michael Hofmann 1983, reprinted by permission of Faber and Faber Ltd. PETER HOWARD: 'Shepherd' © Peter Howard. TED HUGHES: 'Christmas Carol' from *Season Songs*, © Ted Hughes, reprinted by permission of Faber and Faber Ltd. VIOLET JACOB: from *Diaries and Letters from India*, edited by Carol Anderson, reprinted by permission of Canongate Books Limited. JOHN JOLLIFFE: from *Neglected Genius: The Diaries of Robert Haydon*, © John Jolliffe, 1990, reprinted with permission of Peters Fraser & Dunlop. RUDYARD KIPLING: 'Christmas in India' from *Kipling: Selected Poetry* © Craig Raine 1992, reprinted by permission of A. P. Watt Ltd on behalf of The National Trust for Places of Historic Interest or Natural Beauty; 'Eddi's Service' from *Rudyard Kipling's Verse: Definitive Edition*, reprinted by permission of A. P. Watt Ltd on behalf of The National Trust for Places of Historic Interest or Natural Beauty. PHILIP LARKIN: from *Selected Letters of Philip Larkin*, edited by Anthony Thwaite, reprinted by permission of Faber & Faber Ltd. D. H. LAWRENCE: 'New Year's Eve' from *The Complete Poems of D. H. Lawrence*, © Angelo Ravagli and C. M. Weekley, Executors of the Estate of Frieda Lawrence Ravagli, 1964, 1971, reprinted by permission of Laurence Pollinger Ltd and the Estate of Frieda Lawrence Ravagli; extract 'The Blue Ball' from *Aaron's Rod*, © 1922 Thomas Seltzer, Inc., renewed 1950 Frieda Lawrence, reprinted by permission of Laurence Pollinger Ltd. and

the Estate of Frieda Lawrence Ravagli. LAURIE LEE: from *Cider With Rosie*, ©
Laurie Lee, 1959, reprinted by permission of Chatto & Windus. A. G. MACDONELL:
from *England, Their England* © Macmillan & Company Ltd and the Estate of A . G.
Macdonell, reprinted by permission of Picador. NORMAN MACCAIG: 'Real Life
Christmas Card' from *Collected Poems* (1985), reprinted by permission of the Estate
of Norman McCaig and Chatto & Windus. JOHN MASEFIELD, 'Christmas Eve at
Sea' and 'Christmas 1903' from *Collected Poems*, reprinted by permission of The
Society of Authors as the literary representative of the Estate of John Masefield.
DEBORAH MCKINLAY: from the *Guardian*, 15 December 1995, reprinted by
permission of The Guardian. A. A. MILNE: 'King John's Christmas' from *Now We
Are Six*, reprinted by permission of Methuen Children's Books. JAMES MORGAN:
'All Lit Up', originally printed in *The New Yorker*, 9 December 1994, © James
Morgan, reprinted by permission of The New Yorker. EDWIN MORGAN: 'The
Computer's First Christmas Card' from *Selected Poems*, © Edwin Morgan,
reprinted by permission of Carcanet Press Limited. DESMOND MORRIS: extracts
from *Christmas Watching*, © Desmond Morris, 1992, reprinted by permission.
PAUL MULDOON, 'Trance' from *Quoof*, 'Truce' from *Why Brownlee Left* and 'The
Wishbone' from *Meeting the British*, reprinted by permission of Faber and Faber
Ltd. VLADIMIR NABOKOV: extract from *Speak Memory* (originally published under
the title *Conclusive Evidence*), © 1947 Vladimir Nabokov, reprinted by permission
of Weidenfeld and Nicolson. From *News from the Past 1805–1887: The
Autobiography of the Nineteenth Century*, edited and compiled by Yvonne Ffrench,
'Christmas Day in Prison' (first published in *Lady's Magazine*), reprinted by
permission of Victor Gollancz. From 'Ottoline at Garsington', volume two of *The
Memoirs of Lady Ottoline Morrell*, edited by Robert Gathorne-Hardy, reprinted by
permission of Messrs Goodman and Faber and Faber Ltd. BORIS PARKIN:
'Monstrous Ingratitude', © Boris Parkin. HAROLD PINTER: 'Christmas', from
Collected Poems and Prose, © 1978 H. Pinter Ltd, reprinted by permission of
Faber and Faber Ltd. SYLVIA PLATH: 'Balloons' from *Collected Poems*, © The Estate
of Sylvia Plath 1960, reprinted by permission of Faber and Faber Ltd. BEATRIX
POTTER: from *The Tailor of Gloucester* © Frederick Warne & Co. 1903, reprinted by
permission of Penguin Books Ltd. E. ANNIE PROULX: from *The Shipping News*, ©
E. Annie Proulx 1993, reprinted by permission of Fourth Estate Ltd. JONATHAN
RABAN: 'Christmas in Bournemouth', extract from *Love and Money*, first
published by Collins Harvill in 1987, © Jonathan Raban 1976, reproduced by
permission of The Harvill Press. DAMON RUNYON: extract from 'Furthermore'
from *Runyon On Broadway* © Damon Runyon, reprinted by permission of Curtis
Brown Group Ltd, London. NTOZAKE SHANGE: from *Sassafrass, Cypress and
Indigo*, © Ntozake Shange 1982, reprinted by permission of A. M. Heath &
Company Ltd. BERNARD SHAW: extract from *Shaw's Music 1890–94* © Bernard
Shaw, and Letter of 24 December 1917 to Graham Wallas from *Collected Letters
1926–1950*, reprinted by permission of The Society of Authors on behalf of the
Bernard Shaw Estate. SIEGFRIED SASSOON: extract from *The Complete Memoirs of
George Sherston*, reprinted by permission of Faber and Faber Ltd. SAKI:
'Reginald's Christmas Revel' from *The Short Stories of Saki* and from *Reginald and
Reginald in Russia*, reprinted by permission of the Estate of Saki and The Bodley
Head. DAVID SCOTT: 'Botticelli Nativity', © David Scott. 'Silent Night' (Harm. A.

❧ ACKNOWLEDGEMENTS ❧

J. B. Hutchings, 1906–89) from *The English Hymnal Service Book*, reprinted by permission of Oxford University Press. FREYA STARK: from *A Winter in Arabia*, reprinted by permission of John Murray (Publishers) Ltd. MATTHEW SWEENEY: 'The Silent Knight' from *Fatso in the Red Suit*, © Matthew Sweeney 1995, reprinted by permission of Faber and Faber Ltd. DYLAN THOMAS: extracts from *Memoirs of Christmas* and from *A Child's Christmas in Wales*, reprinted by permission of J. M. Dent. R. S. THOMAS: 'Hill Christmas' from *Later Poems*, © R. S. Thomas 1972, reprinted by permission of Papermac. J. C. TREWIN (editor): from *The Journal of William Charles Macready* © J. C. Trewin 1967, reprinted by permission of Addison Wesley Longman. MARTIN TURNER: 'Panto' from *Trespasses*, © Martin Turner 1992, reprinted by permission of Faber and Faber Ltd. EDMUND WILSON: 'Christmas '33' from *The Thirties*, edited by Leon Edel, © 1980 by Helen Miranda Wilson, reprinted by permission of Farrar, Strauss & Giroux, Inc. EVELYN WAUGH: from *A Handful of Dust*, reprinted by permission of Peters Fraser & Dunlop Group Ltd. W. B. YEATS: 'The Magi' from *The Collected Poems of W. B. Yeats* and extract from *The Vision*, reprinted by permission of A. P. Watt on behalf of Michael Yeats.

Faber and Faber apologize for any errors or omissions in the above list and would be grateful to be notified of any corrections that should be incorporated in the next edition of this book.

INDEX